Ecologies of Grace

Ecologies of Grace

Environmental Ethics and
Christian Theology

WILLIS JENKINS

OXFORD
UNIVERSITY PRESS

2008

OXFORD
UNIVERSITY PRESS

Oxford University Press, Inc., publishes works that further
Oxford University's objective of excellence
in research, scholarship, and education.

Oxford   New York
Auckland   Cape Town   Dar es Salaam   Hong Kong   Karachi
Kuala Lumpur   Madrid   Melbourne   Mexico City   Nairobi
New Delhi   Shanghai   Taipei   Toronto

With offices in
Argentina   Austria   Brazil   Chile   Czech Republic   France   Greece
Guatemala   Hungary   Italy   Japan   Poland   Portugal   Singapore
South Korea   Switzerland   Thailand   Turkey   Ukraine   Vietnam

Copyright © 2008 by Oxford University Press, Inc.

Published by Oxford University Press, Inc.
198 Madison Avenue, New York, New York 10016

www.oup.com

Oxford is a registered trademark of Oxford University Press

Library of Congress Cataloging-in-Publication Data
Jenkins, Willis.
Ecologies of grace : environmental ethics and Christian
theology / Willis Jenkins.
    p. cm.
Includes bibliographical references and index.
ISBN 978-0-19-532851-6
1. Human ecology—Religious aspects—Christianity.
2. Environmental ethics. I. Title.
BT695.5.J464 2007
261.8'8—dc22   2007018720

9 8 7 6 5 4 3 2 1

Printed in the United States of America
on acid-free, recycled paper

for two wonderful naturalists:

my father, physician and farmer
my mother, nurse and nature photographer

Preface

Ecologies of Grace interprets environmental issues through the practical responses of Christian communities and the central resources of Christian theology. It shows how environmental problems trouble the heart of Christian experience and identity, and how theologies of grace can engage, reframe, and maybe transform responses to them.

This project developed over years of international work with Christian communities, study in theological ethics, and teaching environmental thought. More precisely, it developed from the difficulty of integrating those three things: the challenge of environmental problems, the resources of moral theology, and the social practices of faith communities. This book makes an attempt at modeling that integration, bringing together two worlds of professional practice and several literatures in a search for practical environmental theologies.

Living in those worlds and reading in those literatures I have been guided by some wonderful teachers, students, colleagues, and friends. As this book began to take form, it was particularly supported and mentored by Jim Childress and Gene Rogers. Their respective habits of thought shape the project throughout, if only in its aspirations toward Jim's clear ethical framing and Gene's elegant theological argument.

At the beginning of my work overseas I was welcomed into a household that knew the ways of grace in the midst of difficulty and helped lead me to the approach of this inquiry; thanks to Robbinah and Amos Turyahabwe, and Tayebwa, Taremwa, and Tashobya. Later, David Fox took a chance on a young community development worker and encouraged me into successive arenas of cross-cultural partnership. I thank all those who invited me to see their environmental mission initiatives, including Father Pablo Buyagan, J. B. Hoover, Takao Okemoto, Mark and Karen McReynolds, Ben and Vanessa Henneke, Scott and Carol Kellerman, Geoffrey Abaho Tumwine, and Bishop William Magambo.

I have come to see many environments anew from the students who have journeyed with me to Uganda, and with the Young Adult Service Corps volunteers who let me accompany their cross-cultural journeys in other parts of the world. Rob Mark has kept up a running conversation on faith, justice, and environment that has animated project journeys through Uganda, Kenya, Ethiopia, the Crow Reservation in Montana, Nova Scotia, and Honduras. Rebekah Menning has been a sustaining companion throughout, quick to ask the practical question and generous with careful readings of many draft chapters.

I came to appreciate the complexity of teaching environmental problems while a fellow at the Institute for Practical Ethics and Public Policy at the University of Virginia. Especially formative was participation in the Institute's faculty workshops, which brought together specialists from across the university to develop interdisciplinary environmental courses. An early attempt to represent and reorder environmental ethics, as appears in chapter 2, was given as a talk there in 2003 and subsequently much revised as a result of my colleagues' responses.

Some of my reflections on lived theologies I first put to words for training sessions on mission and environment for cross-cultural personnel of the Episcopal Church. Their practical and theological feedback from year to year has been most useful. Further reflection on the ecological dimensions of Christian experience and mission commitments grew out of a 2003 presentation to the Costas Consultation on Mission, and six years of deliberation with the Standing Commission on World Mission. I am especially grateful to the Commission for sending me to participate in the 2002 United Nations World Summit on Sustainable Development and the accompanying meeting of the Anglican Communion Environmental Network.

Early work on Thomas Aquinas was presented to the Lilly "Ecology and Theology" conference at Notre Dame in April 2002, and then published in the *Journal of Religion* in 2003. An early exploration of Sergei Bulgakov was presented to the "Illuminations" conference at Oxford University in June 2002. A portion of chapter 3 on ecojustice was developed for the 2005 Spring Institute on Lived Theology at the University of Virginia, as a presentation with Jürgen Moltmann, whose generous consideration I especially appreciate.

Writing began in earnest while I was a Sara Shallenberger Brown Fellow in Environmental Literature at Brown College in the University of Virginia. The fellowship offered two idyllic years living in Monroe Cottage, the opportunity to teach seminars in the departments of Religious Studies and Environmental Thought and Practice, and conversation with visiting nature writers.

Teaching courses in interdisciplinary environmental thought, I have been continually pushed by the enthusiasm of many students. I have especially learned from the environment and humanities double-majors at UVA, and count myself peculiarly fortunate now to work with students in a joint graduate program of Yale Divinity School and the Yale School of Forestry and Environmental Studies.

I took my first course in environmental ethics with Jon Cannon, and later came back to teach with him at the UVA School of Law in Fall 2005. This EPA veteran's pragmatic tests for theory chastened my interpretation of environmental ethics, if not the theological ventures that followed. For those Chuck Mathewes has provided unrivalled bibliographic enthusiasm and steadfast encouragement.

I am grateful to many others who took time to read and improve draft chapters. Mary Evelyn Tucker, John Grim, and Christiana Peppard helped me clarify the introductory remarks on cosmology and ethics. Holmes Rolston commented extensively on an early draft of chapter 2. Margaret Mohrmann helped clear up ambiguities in the chapters on Aquinas. At various stages I received gifts of reading from Tony Baker, Tim Gorringe, Laura Hartman, Rose Jenkins, Chris Morck, Aaron Riches, and Michael J. Smith. Joshua Hill, Khalial Withen, and Anne Jenkins helped bring the manuscript to final form, and Matthew Riley did the index. The care and erudition of copy editor Mary Bellino saved it from many sins. Mistakes remaining despite so many wonderful teachers and friends are my own, by error or obstinacy.

This book was published with the assistance of the Frederick W. Hilles Publication Fund of Yale University, for which I am grateful to the Council of Fellows at the Whitney Humanities Center.

Contents

Ecologies of Grace

I

Saving Nature, Saving Grace

Christian communities struggle to talk about life on earth and life with God. That is not a new problem; the tensions of worldly life and Christian life generate enduring discussions for Christian ethics. But environmental issues challenge theological traditions in ways unprecedented by debates over Christian attitudes toward war or sexuality or poverty. For environmental issues present moral problems that escape the received frameworks of theological ethics. Species loss and degraded biodiversity obviously arrest our moral attention, but how do they matter for Christian life? New technological capacities seem to exercise transgressive control over organisms, but what part of the Christian story offers approval or critique? Globalizing capitalism changes everything from agriculture to local economies, but how is it measured by theological wisdom? In an urbanizing world, the need for sustainable planning, housing, and energy use calls for imaginative new political forms, but how are they intelligible to Christian communities? Climate change places new dimensions of society in moral jeopardy, but how is that preachable on Sunday mornings?

Some Christian ethicists think those questions outstrip the competency of traditional theological approaches, forcing novel revisions. Others think they can find new capacities in traditional resources. Either way, Christian environmental ethics attends the challenge these troubling social problems present to theological traditions and moral practices. It works to make environmental issues intelligible for Christian communities, significant for Christian experience. This book first investigates how ethicists, activists, and Christian leaders draw on their respective traditions in order to meet that challenge, and then contributes to the project by posing to representative theologians the difficulties their strategies encounter. In the first part I trace strategies of ethical response; in the second I explore theological resources that can help their cause.

One could map those strategies by a number of methods and topics. In order to show how closely environmental issues come to the heart of Christian experience and identity, this book charts the relation of salvation stories to environmental ethics. It shows how the metaphors, logics, and narratives of grace shape major patterns of Christian response to environmental problems. The map thus depicts Christianity's environmental strategies following the contour lines of traditions of salvation as they pursue the practical goals of environmental ethics. This book follows three major contour lines, showing how several distinct strategies make environmental issues matter for Christian experience by situating them within one of three ecologies of grace: redemption, sanctification, or deification.

At first glance, soteriology appears an unlikely starting place, for it seems to focus on the human, the spiritual, the interior, the otherwordly—quite the opposite of environmental concerns. Indeed, some compelling critiques blame the human-centered, spiritualized ambitions of salvation stories for generating the bad worldviews that underlie environmental problems. For better worldviews, therefore, Christian environmental ethics often begins from the doctrine of creation, reconsidering the moral dimensions of religious cosmology. Yet, as we will see, ethicists still rely on the tropes and concepts of grace to make those cosmological reformulations come to life within Christian experience. Even while talking about other things, Christian environmental ethics tends to draw on background stories of salvation at the moments it wants to make environmental issues matter for Christian life.

They draw on soteriological narratives, I think, for reasons of pragmatic resonance. Species loss and threats to biodiversity require urgent and wholehearted responses; relationship with God animates Christian responses. Changes in agriculture and land use alter basic patterns of human experience; views of salvation shape the patterns of basic Christian experience. Technologies grow ominous with gargantuan and transgressive power; Christian conversion envisions powers overthrown and transformed. Unsustainable economies and climate change jeopardize contemporary forms of community; Christian communities form within economies of grace.

Revival and Reforestation

I came to this inquiry while working with several Ugandan community development organizations. I had previously taught in a Church of Uganda (Anglican) seminary, in a small regional school for village priests. As I moved from seminary to village organizing, I learned how Ugandan churches theologically mobilize community responses to new social problems. Core parish committees, sometimes centered around revivalist prayer groups, have adapted community responses to HIV transmission and developed AIDS outreaches; they help feed and school orphans; they start and manage local clinics and schools; they protect water sources, organize microdevelopment loans, and plan community land use. And, as priests give voice and authority to their organic theological innovations, all of those practical responses somehow inflect the community's preaching, prayer, and worship.

For each new social problem, church communities were finding ways to redeploy their traditions (both theological and cultural). New forms of Christian practice were striving to keep unprecedented socioeconomic changes from fracturing the centers of common life. Each mode of response, I began to see, invented some new capacity from their traditions.

Many of these church groups, especially in the deforested hill country of western Ankole and Kigezi, include tree-planting initiatives in their activities. Despite familiarity with their expansive register of social ministries, I was surprised to see very poor church communities, possessed of revivalist evangelical faith, working to replant native trees. To my mind, reforestation was an "environmentalist" issue somewhat removed from more immediate concerns, like treating malaria, and traditionally evangelical concerns, like caring for orphans. Yet here were Christian groups who had started a nursery for seedlings and were planting trees all around the village. Priests regularly approved the practice from the pulpit, and when the local bishop made the rounds his exhortations always included tree-planting (along with marriage, sexual fidelity, and good schools).

Why should the revivalist faith of poor community groups express itself in reforestation? How should we understand this practice? If we were to ask the usual diagnostic questions, we would query their background worldview by tests for nature's moral value and for the relative degree of anthropocentrism. Does the community recognize intrinsic value in the integrity of creation? Does it remove humanity from the center of its worldview? My inquiry in this book began in the apparent unhelpfulness of those standard questions. Results for nature's intrinsic value (low) and anthropocentrism (high) seemed to do a poor job of explaining why revival groups would care about reforestation. Why would tree-planting make it into a sermon headed for an altar call and an outburst of ecstatic dancing? I suspected that I needed to ask theological questions closer to the heart of the community's identity, which meant, for these communities, asking soteriological questions.

That seems true beyond revivalist faith communities. During my time in Uganda I came across Scott and Carol Kellerman, American medical mission-aries with the Church of Uganda, who were discovering the environmental dimensions to salvation in another way. The Kellermans had gone to southwest Uganda to serve the Batwa, an indigenous people recently displaced from their home in what is now Bwindi Impenetrable Forest National Park. The forest-dwelling Batwa found themselves adrift in open cultivated landscapes and, marginalized from even subsistence agriculture, their culture and living condi-tions deteriorated. The Kellermans went to Uganda anticipating medical ser-vice and gospel friendship with an outcast people, but found that caring for the Batwa meant caring for the forest they still know as their only home. They have since been working to reconnect the Batwa to the forest by lobbying the govern-ment to allow regulated access and by soliciting international grants to create inhabitable buffer areas along the edges of the forest.

The Kellermans came to understand the significance of forest protection and access when they heard Batwa leaders locate their dignity within the forest. It pro-vided not just their foods and medicines, but their stories, skills, and virtues. When encouraged to remember that God still loved them outside of the forest, several Batwa leaders replied that their children were losing the names for God because they no longer knew the names of the forest. What could God's love mean apart from its known habitat, the forest of Batwa culture, language, and divine names? The Kellermans realized that God's special friendship with the Batwa inextricably involved their special connection to that forest. Where, they asked me, do environmental theologians offer ways of understanding that involvement?

A few years later, on the other side of the world, I visited the Asian Rural Institute (ARI) in Nasushiobara, Japan. ARI is at once an experimental farm for sustainable agriculture, a training institute for non-governmental organization (NGO) leaders from the two-thirds world, and a remarkable interfaith community.[1] Working among its organic chickens, high-yield rice patties, bio-gas generators, and onsite cannery, college volunteers, staff leaders, and NGO participants from around the world form a life together. The community requirements: everyone works and everyone attends chapel. They decide together how to run the farm and why, and they take turns holding chapel, each in the tradition of her or his own faith.

ARI believes that spiritual, economic, and ecological alienations must be healed together, and that the path to restored communion with each other and with God comes through learning the earth's lessons. Roommates Father Jovy, a Filipino Anglican priest, and Markuse, an Indian Hindu, exemplify ARI's lived theology. Both had graduated from the ARI program and started successful ecumenical environmental initiatives in their home countries, and had now come back as staff. Now they share a simple dorm room and a vision for reconciliation through sustainability. Jovy and Markuse believe that interfaith peace comes through collaborative work to restore human communities to ecological harmony. The daily work of understanding and tending fields is for them also the theological work of understanding one another and creatively entering communion with the divine.

This book began from reflection on those innovative theological responses and keeps them close to mind in its way of proceeding.[2] As I reflected on the implicit theologies of ARI, the Batwa, and the revivalist tree-planters, I began to suspect that the usual ways of writing and teaching Christian environmental ethics do not help us understand them as fully as we might. Those lived environmental theologies no doubt enact worldviews as they embody attitudes toward nature's value and humanity's place among it. But they seem to narrate those worldviews according to distinctive grammars of grace. The patterns of their environmental responses seem contoured by their notions of relationship with God. This book follows that suggestion by showing how Christian environmental theologies reshape ways of living on earth within patterns of living with God—how they reinhabit distinct ecologies of grace.[3]

Religious Environmentalism

Maps have their dangers and distortions, of course. Their depictions must simplify landscapes, which can mislead wayfarers or, worse, insulate the observer by lending her a surveyor's sense of control. The best maps not only show a navigable way through; they overlay terrain with references that express the lay of the land. They help readers rediscover and reorient themselves to a place they perhaps already know. Serene Jones, for example, maps together Christian theology and feminist theory "not so much to reconstruct the terrain of faith as to provide markers for traveling through the terrain in new ways."[4] The first part of this book develops markers by describing practical strategies in environmental ethics. I call these "ecologies of grace" to keep the cartographic metaphors close to earth, for these contour lines shape actual patterns of inhabitation. The second part of the book puts the map to a field test, using it to travel through familiar theological terrain in new ways.

My map of Christian environmental ethics charts a known landscape, but its outlines will appear different from most other maps. The contours of grace in Christian environmental ethics have not often been rendered visible, in part because of charged relations between religion and environmental thought. Especially on the contemporary American landscape, religion and nature sometimes appear antagonistic, sometimes symbiotic, sometimes conceptually fused. Those charged relations sometimes produce organic similarities between descriptions of environmental experience and descriptions of religious experience, yet they also have led to the excision of grace from mappings of Christian environmental ethics. Let me illustrate.

Consider how commonly nature writers reach for a salvific metaphor to communicate the power of an environmental experience. Of course, the rapturous John Muir, who saw cathedrals in the forest and choirs in the storms, and who put the words of Jesus into the mouths of trees, often did. His register was blatantly soteriological ("I pressed Yosemite upon him like a missionary offering the gospel").[5] I have in mind the more subtle reaches of down-to-earth environmental writers, like the scientist Rachel Carson: "There is something infinitely healing in the repeated refrains of nature."[6] Or the usually plainspoken forester Aldo Leopold; when explaining what he learned from "the fierce green fire" in a wolf's eyes and from trying to "think like a mountain," Leopold misquotes Thoreau's dictum, "In wildness is the preservation of the world," to say "In wildness is the *salvation* of the world."[7] He immediately goes on to say that "this is the hidden meaning of the wolf, long known to mountains."[8]

Contemporary environmental writers do this too. Scott Russell Sanders writes that encountering nature involves a kind of faith "in the healing energy of wildness, in the holiness of creation. One of the reasons many of us keep going back to Thoreau and Muir and Leopold and Carson is because they kept that faith."[9] Environmental writing seems to dwell within the literatures of faith, as is attested by the fact that an editor would ask the nature writer Barry Lopez to introduce an anthology of spiritual writing. Lopez does so by focusing on the cultivation of reverence, which allows a landscape to enter and elevate a person.[10] Humans are "creatures in search of . . . a pattern of grace," writes Lopez elsewhere.[11] When "the land gets inside of us," says Lopez, those patterns of grace are crucial for deciding what we will do about it.[12]

These writers seem to sense that they hold a sacred trust, remembering forms of holiness and salves of healing nearly forgotten by an alienated world. Terry Tempest Williams: "There is a holy place in the salt desert, where egrets hover like angels . . . I am hidden and saved from the outside world."[13] Even David Gessner, who professes to be sick of pious writing about nature, cannot help saying in the concluding words of one book, "If we look for it, we will find that a whole world is waiting for us. And it is in that world that we, not seeking it, will find a sort of salvation."[14] Some of our best environmental writers exhibit an organic reach toward grace.

Other cultural observers have noticed this spiritual creep in environmental thought and trace religious valences in American environmentalism, sometimes with dismay. The veneration of nature, the feelings of prophetic alienation, the raptures and epiphanies, the sense of apocalyptic doom, the missional project of personal and cultural transformation—all this makes the environmental movement look religious.[15]

Meanwhile, the religious are beginning to look environmental. Religious leaders from many traditions have committed their respective faiths to addressing environmental problems. Religious communities in many nations have begun to lift their voices for greener policies, and faith-based grassroots organizations around the world work to reclaim, restore, and replant. Religious thinkers regularly propose ecological retrievals, critiques, and revisions of their traditions.[16]

The charged relations amidst religious and environmental thought produce an ambivalence in what we might mean by "religious environmentalism." It could mean the environmental responses and practices of established religious communities. These include a range of phenomena from religious redefinitions of environmental goals to the participation of religious adherents in broader social reform movements. Or religious environmentalism could mean the religious themes of environmental thought. These include a range from the missionary postures of the environmental movement to the spiritual dimensions of environmental experience. And there are hybrid uses of the term, used to describe the reemergence of nature religions, or to communicate the perception that global environmental problems are so complex, terrifying, and significant that they require a religious register for understanding and responding to them.[17]

The diverse, charged, and urgent conceptions of religious environmentalism challenge the organization of mutually intelligible conversations—let alone practical coordination and research collaborations. Participants may arrive to vindicate or vilify religions, and vindicate or vilify modern science; to mine religion's conceptual resources or politically mobilize its constituents; they may represent dominant or minority views from a tradition, and conservative or revisionary approaches to interpreting them; they may have particularist or universalist regard of other traditions, and eagerness or wariness to engage them. They may found their primary hope (or despair) in a view of politics, a particular faith, or a sense of nature.

The pluriform, ambivalent relationship between religious and environmental thought has indirectly led to some confusing maps of Christian environmental ethics. For not only do its cartographers work with one or another sense of that relationship and organize their terrain accordingly. In recent years one particular sense of "religious environmentalism"—a sense formed by suspicion of salvation stories—has informed work within specifically Christian environmental ethics and shaped its representation to wider arenas of religious and environmental thought. The curious result: Christian environmental ethics often avoids making visible the soteriological concepts used natively by revivalist reforesters and instinctively by environmental writers.

After Lynn White: Cosmology and Christianity

For the purposes of enabling useful conversation in so ambiguous an arena, with such diverse participants addressing urgent questions, the interdisciplinary arena of "religion and ecology" has constructed a framework of proven worth: look to how religions shape worldviews, for better or worse, regarding nature's value and humanity's place amidst it. By focusing discussion of religious environmentalism on ecological cosmology, collaborative exchanges can not only accommodate great religious, political, and methodological diversity, but also refer to shared criteria of interest.

Cosmology thus makes a capacious forum, inviting mutually intelligible and practically useful conversation. It entertains analyses of religious narratives or religiously inflected worldviews that shape environmental values or interpret forms of human inhabitation. Mary Evelyn Tucker and John Grim, convenors of the Forum on Religion and Ecology and editors of the Harvard book series Religions of the World and Ecology, thus begin the invitation in their series foreword by connecting religious cosmology and environmental ethics:

> Religions provide basic interpretive stories of who we are, what
> nature is, where we have come from, and where we are going. This
> comprises a worldview of a society. Religions also suggest how we
> should treat other humans and how we should relate to nature. . . .
> Religions thus generate worldviews and ethics which underlie
> fundamental attitudes and values of different cultures and societies.[18]

No matter one's sense of religious environmentalism, then, participants can share the practical task of examining how environmental values are shaped by basic interpretive stories.[19] By focusing on worldviews, the Forum on Religion and Ecology brings together academics, activists, and religious leaders to illuminate the "role that religious traditions play in constructing moral frameworks and orienting narratives regarding human interactions with the environment."[20]

Evaluating that role, participants can work in their various capacities to celebrate, criticize, redirect, strengthen, or revise it.

Within Christian environmental theology, however, the cosmological arena for religious environmentalism has indirectly led to some unhelpful ways of understanding and organizing its own internal pluralism. Cosmological mappings can obscure the native terrain here because, by historical accident, a particular sense of "worldview" already shapes recent theological responses. That is to say, Christian environmental theology has so oriented its contributions to the worldviews discussions that it can misrepresent or obscure significant contours of its own "moral frameworks and orientating narratives." Consequently, it often enters discussions of religious environmentalism with its most powerful and most useful theological resources concealed beneath cosmological overlays.

In 1967, Lynn White published a now famous article, "The Historical Roots of Our Ecologic Crisis," which indicted a Christian worldview for environmental problems.[21] Accepted or disputed, his remarkably generative thesis set the agenda for Christian environmental theologies in the following decades: if problems arise from a religiously anthropocentric worldview with little intrinsic value for nature, then Christian thinkers needs to vindicate their cosmology on those terms, recuperate minority resources from forgotten cosmologies, or propose a new cosmology. Obviously that agenda makes room for great diversity, and quite alternative proposals have proliferated. However, in the success of White's article in sustaining debate, the diverse literatures of late-twentieth-century Christian environmental thought concentrated their development in reference to White's peculiar notion of environmental worldviews.[22]

White's critique of Christianity operated with three assumptions about religious worldviews: that they generate social practices, that they should be measured by the criteria of intrinsic value and anthropocentrism, and that salvation stories threaten environmentally benign worldviews.[23] The legacy of those assumptions can simultaneously overemphasize and overdetermine the significance of cosmology for Christian ethics.

The first assumption permits scholars to focus on how worldviews generate ethics without asking where worldviews come from. What logics of production shape the making of worldviews? Directly after calling attention to the way "religions ... generate worldviews," Tucker and Grim quote White: "What people do about their ecology depends on what they think about themselves in relation to things around them." The editors want to point out the environmental consequence measured by White's worldview diagnostics: "Have issues of personal salvation superseded all others? ... Have anthropocentric ethics been all consuming? Has the material world of nature been devalued by religion?"[24]

Those questions underscore the practical significance of paying attention to cosmologies. In an age of environmental distress, such questions indicate that, as Larry Rasmussen says, "ethics and cosmology are inextricable, indissoluble," because we know that our stories about the world involve a terrible alienation of humanity and ecology.[25]

Within Christian theology, however, accepting the moral significance of cosmology should not distract attention from the patterns by which religions tell their stories, or the practices by which worldviews are generated. What are the grammars of narration? Within Christianity, I am suggesting they may be grammars of grace.[26] How do cosmologies take shape within patterns of religious experience? I am proposing that, within Christian environmental theology, patterns of salvation can help us understand the way cosmologies come alive in Christian experience. To understand how Christian attitudes to the world may be revised and reformed, we need to explore their theological roots, finding their resources for revision and practical logics of reform. Perhaps worldviews give rise to ethics, but suppose that religious communities generate and regenerate worldviews through innovative social practices. Following a clue from the revivalist reforesters, I wonder whether soteriology might illuminate logics of practical adaptation. Following the hunch of the nature writers, I wonder whether vocabularies of grace might name resources for restoring cosmologies broken by alienation.

White's second and third assumptions about worldviews, however, tend to turn attention away from such proposals. By casting suspicion on salvation and organizing debate around criteria of anthropocentrism and nature's value, White's assumptions keep the focus away from soteriological roots while at the same time determining the acceptable content of decent worldviews. Yet both assumptions seem less than certain. In the next chapter we will find a number of scholars in secular environmental ethics questioning the usefulness of anthropocentrism and nature's value for organizing environmental ethics. Should they remain authoritative in the religious field? Then, in subsequent chapters, we will see how Christian environmental thinkers regularly draw on salvific metaphors to restore our lost senses to earth. What theological roots generate that organic reach toward grace?

Ever alive to White's critique, the response from Christian environmental theologies has been garbled. They tend to downplay talk about salvation even when they follow patterns of grace or reach for symbols of redemption. Thus White's notion of cosmology still shapes responses even when a theologian overturns the White hypothesis and blames environmental problems on the demise of a Christian worldview. George Rupp, for example, argues that it "is only when the transcendent God of biblical religion is no longer thought to intervene in the world as either creator or as redeemer that the full force of claims for human dominion over nature becomes evident."[27] His point is that a worldview with transcendence better meets White's criteria for non-anthropocentrism and nature's value. But Rupp still implicitly accepts White's underlying supposition, that a background worldview drives environmental attitudes, and orients his theological response to White's criteria. So do other defenses of Christianity against White: perhaps our worldview was disenchanted by the loss of divine transcendence, the demise of medieval orders, or even the attenuation of personal religious experiences.[28] No matter Christianity's culpability, whether novel threat or paradise lost, some deformed worldview explains the problem and a reconstructed or reclaimed cosmology remains the hinge to an adequate ethic.

Tucker and Grim constructively harness this lasting power of White's thesis in order to shape an arena of practical response:

> While the particulars of [White's] argument have been vehemently debated, it is increasingly clear that the environmental crisis . . . present[s] a serious challenge to the world's religions. This is especially true because many of these religions have been concerned with the path of personal salvation, which frequently emphasized otherworldly goals and rejected this world as corrupting. Thus how to adapt religious teaching to this task of revaluing nature so as to prevent its destruction marks a significant new phase in religious thought.[29]

Christian ethicists therefore know that no matter their position on White, whether they agree or not with his indictment of Christianity, they share in a common task: challenging bad legacies of salvation and revaluing nature. Why not do that by engaging soteriology? That seems to be where the problem lies. Why should Christian theologians talk about nature and worldviews when Christianity centers around talk of nature and grace? Tucker and Grim ask forum participants to focus on practical tasks: to identify resources with "transforming energies" for everyday practice, to renovate senses of "a desirable human presence with the earth," and to look for religious patterns "that differ from those that have captured the imagination of contemporary industrialized societies which regard nature primarily as a commodity to be utilized."[30] Where shall Christian ethicists find resources for transformation, desire, presence, and imagination?

William Schweiker suggests that, in an environmental era threatened by overreaching human power, the theological key for reimagining our myths and transforming our desires lies in reconnecting depictions of creation with concepts of grace. Contemporary ethicists must reunite them, he says, perhaps by reexamining how Thomas Aquinas and Karl Barth integrate creation within redemption. From them, ethicists might relearn how "the story of grace, the new creation, articulates the core meaning of creation." For Schweiker, Christianity's cosmogenic logics of production, the powerful patterns by which Christianity generates new worldviews, source from God's giving and forgiving responses to the world.[31]

Yet environmental theologies often appear chary of salvation talk, especially as it appears in the likes of Thomas and Barth. It seems too individualist, too dualist, too anthropocentric, too otherworldly, too hierarchical, or too gnostic to relate to ecological matters.[32] But just those critiques should elicit reassessments and reinvestigations of the role salvation stories play vis-à-vis Christian environmental ethics. Rosemary Radford Ruether's splendid association of western views of salvation with a technocratic cultural project driven by demons of egoist immortality, misogyny, and a general flight from the earthly entreats further investigations into the charged relations between patterns of grace, forms of social life, and environmental problems. The power of Reuther's critique implies that ways to a "new earth" must include soteriological reconstruction, dismantling poor or violent salvation stories, and naming patterns of earthly grace.[33]

But environmental theologians tend to remain aloof from soteriology, even while their cosmologies appropriate metaphors of salvation and their normative appeals follow major forms of grace. In the next chapter we will hear the complaint of environmental pragmatists that secular environmental ethics has accepted devices of debate far removed from the concerns of lived environmental experience.[34] They want the field to become more "practical" by organizing its pluralism according to the way it makes a difference for moral decision-making. Suppose we ask the pragmatist question of environmental theologies: how do they make environmental issues part of Christian moral experience? Say they describe nature's value in a Christian worldview; what does that value mean for Christian life? What parts of the Christian story guide the way churches should think about species loss or sustainability or community gardens? What role do environments play in God's invitation to participate in the divine life? To become disciples of Jesus Christ?

There are a number of good ways Christian ethicists can answer those questions, but rarely do they organize their answers in reference to grammars of grace. Surveys explaining the options for environmental theology usually organize the field along cosmological axes, using one or another of the criteria that emerged from White's article. So Michael Northcott's *Christianity and Environmental Ethics*, even though critical of White's analysis, organizes environmental theologies according to whether their view of theological reality is anthropocentric, theocentric, or ecocentric.[35] Max Oelschlaeger's *Caring for Creation*, also critical of the White debate, divides environmental theologies by the degree to which their cosmology is open to scientific engagement.[36] Stephen Scharper in *Redeeming the Time* and Paul Santmire in *Nature Reborn* figure the options in environmental theology have to do with the critical mode (e.g., revisionist, reconstructionist, apologist) by which one meets White's challenge to include nature in theological cosmology.[37] *The Greening of Theology*, by Steven Bouma-Prediger, comes closest to soteriology; after arguing against White, it examines proposals in environmental theology by how they reconceive doctrines of anthropology, creation, and God—but stops just short of asking how they reconceive what binds together that cosmological nexus.[38]

Each scholar professes, however, that not cosmology itself but a search for a practical theology of environmental practices animates their work. Bouma-Prediger's fundamental question is how we can "engage in discipleship which envisions care of creation as essential to the practices of Christian faith."[39] Oelschlaeger concentrates on creation stories because he thinks they shape our ethical direction, contextualizing moral attitudes.[40] Northcott recuperates Hebrew cosmology in order to illuminate an ordered relationality between humanity and nature, where ecology shapes moral personhood.[41] Santmire's exploration into Christian cosmological metaphors wants to inform Christian participation in public policy.[42] In other words, each wants to somehow connect environmental issues with Christian identity. They explore cosmology in pursuit of a pragmatic strategy that aims to make nature matter for Christian moral experience. They want something near to what Peter Scott calls a "political theology of nature": an account of how relationship with God shapes relations among humanity and nature.[43] So why call that a cosmological task?

Pastoral Strategies and Environmental Theologies

All of these field guides want to identify and deploy theological resources adequate for making environmental issues intelligible and urgent for human experience.[44] They want what I call a practical strategy. As we might expect, some of the activist participants in the Forum on Religion and Ecology want something similar, and they focus more directly on practical theologies by coming nearer the language of grace. Walter Grazer, who works on environmental issues within the U.S. Catholic Church, chafed a bit at the cosmological reformulations of the academic theologians and said his faith community needs a "pastoral strategy" embedded "within the spiritual and sacramental context of Catholic theology." Grazer wants ethicists to make environmental concerns intelligible within ongoing Catholic practices of prayer, liturgy, and scripture reading. Responses from representatives of the National Council of Churches and the Evangelical Environmental Network exhibited similar strategic focus.[45] The activist participants in the forum seem to want theological resources that bring environmental issues into contact with the lived faith of their communities, and they seem disappointed by what academic theologians tend to offer.

Those activists look for the sort of practical strategy Bouma-Prediger has in mind when he says he wants Christians to answer the question, "So why care for the earth?" with many variations on "Because, in sum, care for the earth is integral to what it means to be a Christian—it is an important part of our piety, our spirituality, our collective way of being authentically Christian."[46] Being Christian undoubtedly involves worldviews, but adherents would unlikely first turn to cosmology if asked, "why be Christian?" They would likely talk about experiences of grace or spiritual vocation or biblical narrative or the way of Jesus.

Susan Power Bratton agrees that environmental theologies sometimes linger in preoccupation with worldviews. "In terms of relationship to the environment, the most important issue," she claims, "is the concept that contact with creation . . . is spiritually beneficial, and that work in, with or for creation forwards holiness or righteousness." Not worldviews but spiritual experience links environmental care to Christian identity. "The key in actual Christian practice appears to be not whether one considers God transcendent, but whether one expects God's day to day activity to be evident in creation." Not so much an aspect of cosmology but an anticipation of experiencing the divine moves Christian practice. Therefore, "contemporary Christian ecotheology is spending too much time arguing with its critics and fretting over cosmology. . . . An emphasis on Christian lifestyles and spiritual practices has historically been a more productive approach." For Bratton, environmental theologies should focus on the role of nature in the dynamics of spiritual experience.[47]

By interpreting the way spiritual practices incorporate nature into Christian experience, soteriological investigations can illuminate productive sites of practical reason and human reform. The White-shaped concentration on worldviews cannot do that as effectively, for its criteria for religious reform can snarl internal debates into exchanges less immediate to the practical issues at hand.[48] Perhaps some religious traditions would rethink themselves more usefully, even more thoroughly, outside the terms of worldviews. Christian communities might find revisiting their christology or their mission commitments more transformative and more helpful for adapting their faith to meet environmental problems. Why insist that they develop new worldviews? Christian ethicists want to redeploy theological traditions "in a way that influences not only the development of doctrine, but also the life of faith." Why not let heart-stretching narratives of God's love decenter our arguments over creation's center?[49]

George Kehm argues that a practical environmental theology must "demonstrate the indispensability to the Christian story of an idea or theological claim: that this idea or claim must be in the story or else the story would not be that story."[50] It must show precisely how, as Luke Johnson writes, environmental problems are "a crisis in Christian identity."[51] Insofar as Christianity revolves around a story of persons healed, covenant restored, sinfulness redeemed, experience made holy, or the world reconciled, so far should environmental theologies seek soteriological roots.[52] A practical Christian ethic, in other words, should show how the environmental crisis amounts to a crisis in the intimacies of God's salvation.

Joseph Sittler, who began writing theology for the environmental crisis years before Lynn White and his respondents, insists that "nothing short of a radical relocation and reconceptualization of the reality and doctrine of grace is an adequate answer to that problem."[53] For Sittler, the church rediscovers its relation to the natural world by reconsidering its teachings on the presence of God for humanity. For in God's saving acts we find a doctrine "large enough and ready enough and interiorly most capable of articulating a theological relationship between theology and ecology."[54] The paradoxes of grace and nature orient human persons to both humble soil and heavenly glories, shaping them for friendship with God and love of the world.

Sittler thus suggests that environmental theologies should focus on showing how life with God and life on earth are shared ventures. But it is no easy task, for as Oliver Davies (among a number of recent theologians) laments, modern theology somewhere lost the facility to hold together divine and natural aspects of createdness. Davies diagnoses that failure in the displacement of theological reasoning from contextually embodied orientations to God. If "our intimacy with God is set outside our intimacy with the world," says Davies, then theology will fail to make sense of creation. In order for intimacy with God to illuminate the way of the world into Christian experience, theology must assume some "intrinsic relatedness of self and world on the grounds of a common relation to the Creator God."[55]

Davies argues that when Christianity fails to maintain triadic relations among humanity, creation, and God's presence, Christian experience loses its sense of the world. Failing to hold together God's invitation to human persons and the human enfleshment within creation, says Davies, Christianity impoverishes both its christology and its soteriology—and so begins to lose the very center of its faith. So Davies raises the practical stakes: if Christians inadequately understand the ecology of God's desire for humanity then they stutter

before the fullness of their gospel. So too the converse: if they inadequately connect God's saving work to inhabiting creation, environmental theologies will sit
awkwardly with Christian identities.[56]

Sittler and Davies thus connect environmental issues to pastoral strategies
from both sides. Without the fullness of grace, a Christian environmental ethic
will falter. Without its environmental dimensions, the Christian story of salvation will falter. That not only issues a challenge but presents an organizing clue:
if Sittler and Davies are right, then we would expect the practical strategies of
Christian environmental ethics to organically reach for soteriological concepts
as they try to communicate the significance of nature for Christian experience.

Three Practical Strategies, Three Ecologies of Grace

Sociologist Laurel Kearns has conducted one of the few survey examinations of
the way public theologies develop their own practical rationalities for environmental issues.[57] Her observation finds "three broadly defined 'ethics' or 'models' emerging among organizational proponents of Christian eco-theology in
the United States," which she identifies as ecojustice, Christian stewardship,
and creation spirituality.[58] The positions tend to align with denominational
identities, Kearns observes, but differ in ways more significant than institu-
tional reference: the three environmentalisms "clearly appeal to different theological frameworks." Expositing those frameworks lies outside the scope of her
project, but Kearns argues that each funds a separate strategy for faith-based
environmentalists, "people who are attempting to make eco-theology 'come
alive in people's minds and hearts,'" so that it "make[s] sense emotionally and
practically to those it intends to reach."[59] Strategies of environmental theology
are practical, Kearns implies, insofar as they animate environmental issues
within Christian experience.

Kearns's research outlines three distinct ways of animation, or three methods for communicating nature's significance for Christian experience. So there
are multiple practical strategies and, as we will see with secular environmental
ethics in the next chapter, each exhibits its own notion of the "practical"—of
what an ethic must do both to engage environmental problems and to make a
claim on moral experience. Uncovering those various notions, and showing
how each one relates to a secular precedent, we will excavate competing and
sometimes complementary notions of what an ethic must accomplish in order
to make both environmental and theological sense.

My map of the field takes Kearns's sociological research as initial evidence
of three pastoral strategies for making life on earth and life with God shared

ventures. Listening to Sittler and Davies, I sort Christian environmental ethics by the ways they draw on concepts of grace in order to bind those ventures together. Following lessons learned from innovative African environmental-isms, I look to how metaphors of salvation guide the formation of practical Christian strategies. Reading secular environmental ethics, I sketch the rela-tion of Christian strategies to their nontheological counterparts. If these carto-graphic cues hold together, traditions of grace function as markers of practical strategies within Christian environmental ethics. Each strategy follows the broad contour line of a theology of grace in order to at once engage environ-mental issues and animate Christian moral experience.

The first part of this book develops that map, showing how three broad strategies within Christian environmental ethics correspond to three broad the-ologies of grace. Ecojustice theologies tend to rely on a view of sanctification in which grace illuminates creation's integrity. Stewardship theologies rely on tropes of redemption, where encounter with God creates vocational responsi-bilities to care for creation. What I call "ecological spiritualities" appropriate themes of deification, by which personal creativity brings all creation into the gift of union with God. Each strategy brings environmental issues within Christian moral experience according to a background pattern of grace. Each strategy thus tries to meet the practical goals of environmental ethics with the attendant promise and limitations of those background views.[60]

My consequent reorganization of the field helps explain why we find cer-tain patterns of normative appeal corresponding to certain theological commu-nities. Evangelicals respond to ethical arguments that would fall flat on Eastern Orthodox ears—and not because of the cosmological criteria. By the test of anthropocentrism, Evangelicals and Orthodox might align fairly closely. Their pictures of grace, however, are exotic to each other, and they generate markedly different forms of environmental ethics. On the other hand, shared patterns of grace indicate that Christian environmentalisms widely divergent in socio-graphic context or methodological commitment may share a normative strat-egy. In chapter 5 we will see how creation spirituality advocates and Orthodox ethicists, though they likely could not share a sanctuary, worry about similar problems and draw from the same theological well to address them. In turn they are liable to similar critiques and face similar normative challenges.

The reader may observe that these three soteriological strategies seem to represent the three major ecclesial traditions: Roman Catholicism, Protestantism, and Eastern Orthodoxy, for ecojustice (sanctification), stewardship (redemp-tion), and ecological spirituality (deification), respectively. As we will see, there is some correspondence between the theological communities that characteris-tically make certain kinds of environmental arguments and the notions of grace standing behind those arguments. Mainline Protestant and Roman Catholic communities tend to make ecojustice arguments; evangelical Protestants tend to make stewardship arguments; Eastern Orthodox communities tend to make what I call ecological spirituality arguments. But these are only tendencies, I suspect, because those communities tend to understand grace and salvation in distinct ways. If a Roman Catholic finds herself drawn to the ethics of ecological spirituality, I would wager that she also finds in the narrative of deifying union a compelling understanding of grace.

Up to now I have multiplied usages of "grace" without specifically defining the term. Beyond admitting that it generally refers to a divinely initiated relationship of God and creation, I will go on doing so. Using grace as a device for sorting diversity relies on supposing that it functions differently within different traditions. What it means for Roman Catholics differs from what it means for Protestants—and famously. What grace means within Protestantism differs in manifold nuance. One might argue that Christian diversity is characterized by distinct expressions of grace and ongoing contests for its definition. So much the better for my map and its usefulness.

Scholars who see the plurality of Christian environmental theologies often struggle to identify shared theological forms within the pluralism or to diagnose the practical implications to their differences. This map tries to illuminate the pluralism, outline its forms of organization, and indicate its practical significance. One of its benefits is that it admits more pluralism, even as it gives the field more coherent form. This map should then be useful to readers from a wide range of interests in "religious environmentalism," from Christian activists to scholars, nonreligious NGO leaders to pastors.

Moreover, insofar as my soteriological interpretation holds, the internal questions and problems of each strategy of environmental ethics can be investigated through those background views of grace. In order to test the usefulness of my map, therefore, the second part of this book works over the practical questions and theological problems arising from each strategy of the first part, putting those questions and problems to a theologian representative of its respective soteriology. For insofar as Christian environmental ethics follows a background pattern of grace, these theologians of grace can help illuminate their full promise, and address (or exacerbate) their most vulnerable liabilities.

This reintroduction to Christian environmental ethics thus proceeds pragmatically, by several measures. First, it sorts the proliferating texts of environmental ethics and theologies by their implicit normative goals, organizing an intelligible plurality of practical strategies. Second, as the Christian strategies transform secular strategies with theological resources, it highlights the consequences for policy and practice. Third, it shows how environmental problems press theological traditions to revise and renew themselves by adapting, intensifying, and redeploying the earthly senses of Christian life. And finally, perhaps most importantly, this book moves toward making better sense of lived Christian environmentalisms by showing how theological resources make complex social problems intelligible within enduring Christian narratives.

Reader's Guide

At this point a guide to the book's layout may help the reader find chapters especially useful to her interests, and to understand how they relate to the other chapters. The book is divided into two parts. The first part surveys the field of Christian environmental ethics; the second offers constructive theological investigations that test the field's background patterns of grace. Part I outlines major ethical strategies of secular and Christian environmental ethics. Part II takes up the questions and problems those strategies face with a theologian representative of each ecology of grace.

We begin with the nonreligious field. Chapter 2 identifies general capacities that environmental problems require from ethics (religious or otherwise). What makes for an adequate environmental ethic? I trace the outlines of an answer by describing criteria proposed in the various strategies of environmental ethics. If we know what secular environmental ethics tries to accomplish, perhaps we can judge how well or differently Christian environmental ethics meets those goals. In other words, the practical requirements for adequately addressing environmental problems offer some initial evaluative devices for reading Christian environmental ethics.

Unfortunately, that is no straightforward initial step, for the field of environmental ethics is a contest unto itself. It still debates its normative tasks, still searches for even a shared notion of what it would mean for an ethic to be "practical." One symptom of that muddled contest will be found in this chapter's thinner conceptual language: describing the field's breadth and goals eludes clear descriptive prose. That complicates the task for Christian environmental ethics, for rather than receiving well-framed problems it must internally decide what makes for an environmental issue and articulate what it would mean to adequately address it.

There are then two reasons for starting with a long chapter on nonreligious theorists in order to introduce specifically Christian environmental ethics.[61] First, I want to show the plurality of normative strategies in nonreligious environmental ethics. That will help us better understand the plurality in Christian environmental ethics by loosing it from the organizing device of anthropocentrism.

By mapping the several broad ways that nonreligious ethics frames environmental problems, we will be able to see how the Christian strategies adopt
similar frames, but by deploying theological concepts transform them, recon-
stituting environmental problems in new ways. The descriptions of the secular
strategies thus allow for heuristic comparison with the corresponding Christian
strategies; in their respective differences lies the Christian contribution to the
public effort to understand environmental problems.

The second reason for beginning within the muddle of environmental theory is to develop a method of dealing with its normative pluralism that in turn
we can use to interpret the theological pluralism in Christian environmental
ethics. By reading environmental ethics for its practical strategies, we can isolate a few minimum practical criteria that in turn can help organize the muddle
of Christian environmental ethics into identifiable strategies. Beginning with
the philosophers, therefore, we can distill the problem-frames with which the
theologians seem to be working and, with their religious resources, transforming. And we can test the theological strategies by the practical criteria generated
from the secular field.

Chapters 3, 4, and 5 then map the Christian strategies. They suggest that
the Christian renditions select one of the secular strategies according as it fits
with a background pattern of grace, and then use soteriological concepts to
expand and intensify that strategy's practical facility. Even when ethicists criticize salvation stories, we will see, they tend to draw on salvific metaphors,
appropriating both their promise and their liabilities. In other words, the theological accounts reach for concepts of grace to help accomplish practical ethical
functions. I read the result as "ecologies of grace"—theological habitats that
shape the significance of nature for Christian experience.

These three chapters therefore describe three strategies organically related to
major traditions of grace and to the practical strategies of environmental ethics.
Chapter 3 shows how *ecojustice* theologies tend to rely on the way sanctification
forms persons by God's presence in creation. Chapter 4 describes *stewardship*
theologies, which tend to follow the obedient discipleship themes in redemption. Chapter 5 uses the rubric of *ecological spiritualities* to gather together proposals united by their appropriation of deification themes, where communion
with creation becomes part of union with God.

These chapters show how various pastoral strategies make environmental
issues significant for Christian moral experience by inscribing them within
notions of salvation. Each chapter illustrates the distinctive theological vocabularies and grammars deployed to orient Christian ethics toward practical engagement with environmental issues. In this section I try to populate the map with
markers of representative texts. Some of the cartographic associations may

surprise; so scanning through the notes here may enrich the reading. Insofar as my map works, it collects general questions and problems for each Christian environmental strategy that can be further tested within those background theologies of salvation.

In part II of the book I try that, putting both the theological problems and lingering environmental questions to major theologians of grace. These chapters are necessarily brief and merely suggestive. Two chapters each on Thomas Aquinas (6 and 7), Karl Barth (8 and 9), and Maximus the Confessor as interpreted through Sergei Bulgakov (10 and 11) allow me to offer three demonstrations of the hypothesis that exploring patterns of grace can illuminate and deepen Christian environmental ethics. Each theologian, in his own way and for his own tradition, made creation a habitat of grace. Reading them through the concerns of environmental ethics I explore those habitats. What hope does Christian salvation offer for earth and the restless desires of its human inhabitants? What forms of healing do the traditions of grace envision for Christian social practices?

I do not mean to propose the authority of these particular theologians for environmental theology. Rather, I want to heuristically illustrate how the problems and promise of Christian environmental ethics can be developed by examining the patterns of grace on which its strategies rely. I might have chosen other theologians (and at times in writing wished I had). In part for their enduring influence on understandings of grace, in part by accidents of education, and in part from a hunch of undiscovered resources, I chose Thomas for ecojustice ethics, Barth for stewardship ethics, and Bulgakov for ecological spiritualities.

Thomas and Barth make convenient figureheads for famously contrasting views of sanctifying grace and redeeming grace. I do not have space to defend or defeat the contrast; I only rely on its fittingness for this environmental exercise. Sergei Bulgakov, a twentieth-century Russian Orthodox priest, is lesser known and much more controversial as a representative of deifying grace. In consequence, those two chapters proceed differently than the ones on Thomas and Barth. I begin with Maximus the Confessor and then develop the fittingness of · Bulgakov for the problems faced by ecological spirituality by showing how he addresses similar challenges by drawing from Maximus.

Each theologian has been followed by scholastic contests of interpretation. Beyond convenient association, I do not claim that these theologians represent the formal difference among Christian traditions, nor that these three traditions comprehend Christian thinking on grace, nor even that these figures must support the environmental strategy I assign them. One could make a good case for using Thomas in relation to each one of the strategies. My chapters try to keep in focus how the environmental questions in part I guide new inquiry into the theologians, and how the theologians may answer those questions. My investigations can at best note the interpretive contests and add to the list of their consequences. These chapters attempt to enter the theological world of each figure as if an ecology of grace, illustrating how it makes nature significant for Christian experience, and how it answers (or fails) the practical questions arising from Christian environmental ethics.

My interpretation of their notions of grace, however provocative, will therefore appear indirectly, as I develop it through peculiarly environmental questions. These chapters begin to limn more ecological renditions of grace, but only insofar as questions from environmental ethics find those capacities in each theologian's account. To find fuller, less novel introductions to each figure, follow the evidence of the notes in part II. To find greener, more novel environmental theologies, look to the notes from the corresponding chapters in part I.

My overall aim is to map the variety of Christian environmental ethics, explaining its patterns, capacities, and challenges, and to invite Christian environmental ethics into more fertile theological ground. I do not then accumulate evidence for a synthetic proposal of my own, but rather work to richly describe three ecologies of grace. The ethical strategies I sketch can and do sit on their own, and I do not intend to privilege any one, nor to argue here that one notion of grace provides more adequate resources than the others for constructing an environmental ethic. I make few comparative remarks, and then for purposes of distinction rather than evaluation.

Some readers may therefore find it useful to read the book in ways other than consecutively. Readers interested in comparing religious and nonreligious environmental ethics could confine themselves to part I. Readers wanting to make sense of the pluralism in environmental ethics could simply read chapter 2. Readers interested in a survey of Christian environmental ethics could read chapters 3, 4, and 5. To fully understand how that survey works, those chapters should be read with chapter 2, but need not engage the theological investigations of the second part. Readers interested in a particular Christian strategy or tradition of grace might choose to read its description in part one and the two corresponding theological chapters in part two (e.g., for ecojustice, read chapters 4, 6 and 7). Those interested in an environmental reading of Thomas, Barth, or Bulgakov could read only the two chapters devoted to each, perhaps looking over the survey chapter describing the Christian strategy in need of theological assistance. So, one might read Bulgakov in concert with chapter 5, which explains why ecological spiritualities should turn to Bulgakov, and what to ask him.

Reinhabiting Theology

In addition to recent work in Africa, I have a second personal reason for mapping a novel path into Christian environmental ethics, and for then spending so much time working with the theologians of part II. We will see in chapter 2 that a number of scholars and activists have begun to criticize the practical scope of secular environmental strategies. They worry that the field's standard frameworks fail to address the full range of environmental problems—not just pollution and species preservation, but sustainable development, regional planning, ecological restoration, building design, agriculture, and environmental injustice. We will see in the following chapters that Christian environmental strategies tend to follow the broad outline of the secular strategies, which in light of the criticisms should give pause. But because they do so by drawing on background patterns of grace (even if obliquely), the Christian strategies transform the secular strategies they follow, sometimes generating uniquely useful ways of incorporating a wider scope of environmental issues into a coherent account of moral experience. Mapping Christian environmental ethics in a new way can therefore illuminate practical theological resources with potential to reorient and reinvigorate public discussion of neglected environmental issues.

My own family background includes a contested history with some of those nonstandard environmental problems. My grandmother witnessed her family's forced eviction from their mountainside farm of several hundred acres in order to make room for the ecological restoration project known as the Shenandoah National Park. Up until a few years ago, my family farmed along the base of Old Rag Mountain, planting apple and peach trees along an uneasy border with the park. On Sundays my grandparents would sometimes walk the hiking trails in order to remember the names of those whose homesteads and gravesites were being overgrown.[62] (Picture my grandfather in his Sunday overalls talking about corn and cabbage fields while hikers in recreational gear pass by.)

In some ways my grandparents lived sustainably, almost self-sufficiently; they had a dairy cow, a few dozen unconfined hogs, some laying hens, a winter's worth of potatoes, and a huge garden—its produce variously canned, frozen, dried, and preserved. They had gravity-fed water, woodstove heat, and their own timber lots. In other ways my grandparents fell victim to unsustainable myths. They faithfully bought the offerings of postwar agrotechnology, from a WWII-surplus bulldozer to market-selected tree varieties to the latest pesticides.[63] Wildlife decreased while cancers burgeoned. In the span of their lives the orchard flourished, faltered, and then failed, as even chemical heroism could not make the land keep pace with the globalizing produce trade. When the Jenkins Apple Orchard finally closed to the public, only three of the county's thirty-two family-run orchards remained.

When my grandparents died, they were buried thirty miles away, in another county, for they feared the park would someday seize more land, and they did not want their bodies to become part of the federal overgrowth! And in a way the park has grown since then. The government has not expanded its borders, nor do hikers yet walk through their abandoned homestead, but the overgrown orchard now welcomes Shenandoah's citizens: bear, coyote, bobcats, beavers, and deer (all once pests) now move across the less adversarial border. Vacation cabins sprout along the park's environs, and exotic property values slowly push out native dwellers. Increasingly the park, rather than farming, shapes the county's rural landscape.

Making sense of living in this part of the Virginian piedmont means making sense of global economics, rural history, American notions of wilderness, sustainability, environmental justice, and ecological restoration. My grandparents made sense of living there by a hearty Baptist faith, which gave thanks for the land's bounty, and bounded greed by gratitude to the Creator and pride by indebtedness to the blood of the Lamb. There were resources in their lived faith for deeper theologies of the land—in Grandma's copious offerings to the great potluck celebrations of local food, in Grandpa's refusal to work on the Sabbath (despite ripe peaches falling from the trees), and in their spiritual satisfaction with a humble life made in a small community on a mountain foothill. But I doubt they ever heard a sermon link thanksgiving and sustainable harvests, or spiritual health and land health, or redemption and ecological integrity. In that absence they were failed by a church that had no ears to hear the scriptures speak to inhabiting this promised place. Insofar as its notion of life with God could not live into the story of the land, the church read its scriptures, preached its sermons, planned its missions, and baptized its members by landless, unsustainable theologies.

Those questions still face the members of our county churches. My family holds on to a portion of farmland adjacent to the park, undecided what do with it. Like others of the many private managers of the Shenandoah Park's buffer zone, we receive advice from conservation organizations, hunting groups, property developers, loggers, and hobby farmers. Meanwhile, the park has begun renovating its relations with those living along its borders, present and past, by asking for citizen help in restoring ecological health and in restoring historical names to seized lands. More than ever, our county managers face decisions about stewarding the land within a changing rural economy. The remaining farm families must decide what it means to farm well, what sufficiency and sustainability look like in a changing landscape and market. So what ethical resources can this community draw on for thinking through these issues?

For many of the participants in these decisions, relevant ethical resources must come in a vocabulary native to their lived faith. Yet most of our local Christian leaders struggle to articulate land use as a matter of faith or to see environmental issues within the Christian story. This book returns environmental ethics to the roots of major Christian traditions to show where they might find practical resources for understanding the way environmental problems matter for Christian identity, community, and experience. And although most of what follows would be unrecognizable to my grandparents' way of putting things religious, I aim to nourish a new shoot from my own roots, hoping to rediscover how to live at home on Old Rag Mountain. Taking a cue from the Christian environmentalisms I have encountered in Africa and Asia, I turn specifically to the traditions of grace.

PART I

Ethical Strategies

2

Three Practical Strategies in Environmental Ethics

As the journal *Environmental Ethics* marked the close of its first decade in 1988, Christopher Stone looked back over an initial generation of discussion and wondered, "What are environmental ethicists trying to achieve, and what are the standards for success?" Surveying the young field's diverse theories, Stone saw various implicit proposals for the goals and standards of adequate environmental reasoning. In order to make sense of its discussions, suggested Stone, to identify itself as a discernible "field" of practical reason, environmental ethics must decide how to organize and evaluate its competing proposals for what makes a decent environmental ethic. Sorting among theories that reflect on a variety of social practices involving a complex panoply of natural and hybrid beings in human and extrahuman systems, imperiled by threats of multiple kinds, requires the field to address some basic prerequisite questions: "What is an ethical system, and what are its minimum requirements? . . . How—by reference to what elements—can one ethic differ from another?" Such questions shape what it means to make an argument in environmental ethics. "Upon their answer," said Stone, "hinges nothing less than the legitimacy of environmental ethics as a distinct enterprise."[1]

Stone used those questions to prosecute his charge that environmental ethics suffered from a blinkering "moral monism." He worried that attempting to assimilate environmental problems into a single ethical framework constrains arguments to the inadequate scope of inherited modes of moral reasoning. In particular, he argued, ethicists need not be forced to choose between anthropocentrism and nonanthropocentrism. The complexity and variety of environmental problems calls instead for a pluralism of ethical approaches. Soon after Stone's article there emerged a debate over the coherence and practicality of pluralism vis-à-vis various monisms.[2] But in that debate, Stone's more important suggestion has often been missed: that making sense of such debates requires some minimum criteria of practical adequacy.

A generation after Stone said that environmental ethics had "not yet made clear, neither to ourselves nor to others, what exactly are the aims and ground rules that govern the composition of an ethical viewpoint," identifying a coherent shape to the field remains an elusive task.[3] While American environmentalism suffers an admitted intellectual crisis, academic endeavors seem only to further fracture discussion, proliferating topics of concern and rehearsing debates over anthropocentrism while the field still lacks a cohesive account of its practical rationality.[4] Without mutually intelligible criteria of adequacy, we still cannot answer what environmental ethics is or does.

Consider the strikingly alternative conceptions of the field implicit in Peter Singer's suffering sentients, Holmes Rolston's natural value, David Harvey's geographic constructivism, Karen Warren's ecofeminist relationality, Herman Daly's ecological economics, and Robert Bullard's environmental racism. Each frames the relevant field so differently that the range frustrates intelligible aggregation. How to understand them in relation to a common concern? Perhaps environmental ethics is, as Aristotle would say, a moral science still in search of its formal object, some rationale by which its inquiries hang together. Maybe it does not know what a successful environmental ethic looks like because it is unsure how to aggregate its phenomena under the aspect of some unifying criteria.

Other fields of practical ethics, such as biomedical ethics and business ethics, have an easier time unifying their inquiries, in part because they reflect upon and for discernible social practices. Biomedical ethics inquires after phenomena known through health care practices, and business ethics after phenomena known through economic practices. But what practices frame the relevant phenomena for environmental ethics? There is no discrete set of environmental practices analogous to caregiving and research for biomedical ethics, no tradition of established normative principles in the way that fairness and trust function for business ethics, not even a bounded terrain of inquiry, if even in the expansive sense of political ethics. The literature of environmental ethics seems to lack even the homeorhetic stability to organize a debate.

Three recent books respond to this critical failure by proposing criteria for moral reasoning less keyed to nonanthropocentrism and more adequate to the complexity of environmental problems. Val Plumwood's *Environmental Culture* describes a practical rationality reshaped by nonhegemonic social and ecological relations; Mick Smith's *Ethics of Place* lets subjective place attachments produce a general form of moral agency responsive to nature, and Christopher Preston's *Grounding Knowledge* develops a new form of practical reason from an ecological epistemology.[5] Though quite different projects, the three share remarkably similar unifying criteria. None pivots around debates over nonanthropocentrism. Instead each champions a form of practical reason reciprocally shaped by extra-human nature, agential practices, and ecological subjectivity. Together they point toward a general form of practical reason for environmental ethics that outlines functional criteria we can use for mapping and understanding the field's various practical strategies.

The rest of this chapter shows how that mapping might go. If instead of trying to reduce the ethical variety to kinds of views on anthropocentrism, we look to how approaches accomplish one or more of those general criteria for a practical rationality, then we can describe distinct yet mutually intelligible normative strategies. Taking chronic disagreement as important evidence, let us assume that various strategies in environmental ethics implicitly answer Stone's initial questions, demonstrating what an environmental ethic is and does. How then do those views satisfy (or dissent from) the functional criteria isolated by Plumwood, Smith, and Preston? Proceeding this way, we can suppose that significant proposals for the success of an environmental practical reason already reside in seemingly incommensurable theoretical frameworks.

The rest of this chapter, then, shows how various environmental theories fall into one of several broad normative strategies, and outlines how those strategies fulfill basic functional aspects of an environmental rationality.[6] Organizing the field by its practical strategies differs from the usual taxonomic device of sorting theories according to their place on an anthropocentric/nonanthropocentric continuum.[7] Parsing the field instead by morphologically distinct uses of practical rationality lets those discrete strategies sketch evaluative markers of adequate moral reasoning, and thus a formal shape to environmental ethics. That in turn will allow us to better understand how the Christian strategies enter the environmental arena, which practical goals they follow, and how they draw on theological resources to accomplish and sometimes transform them. Although a single chapter does not permit exhaustive portrayal of the field nor adequate defense of my interpretation, this initial cartographic exercise need appear just plausible enough to inform questions for subsequent chapters.

Environmental Pragmatism

My suspicion of organizing debates around anthropocentrism, my pluralist description of ethical strategies, and my concentration on practical differences follow major themes in environmental pragmatism. To show how my description of normative strategies resembles yet critiques the pragmatist project, let me begin by showing how environmental pragmatism both accommodates and constricts normative pluralism through its own appeal to the practical.

Environmental pragmatism takes up Stone's challenge to respond to two bedeviling features of debate in environmental ethics: its irreconcilable pluralism and its anxiety to offer relevant help to public policy discussions. One pragmatist anthology thus sets the scene:

> As environmental ethics approaches its third decade it is faced with
> a curious problem. On the one hand, the discipline . . . has produced
> a wide variety of positions and theories in an attempt to derive morally
> justifiable and adequate environmental policies. On the other hand, it
> is difficult to see what practical effect the field of environmental
> ethics has had on the formation of environmental policy.[8]

The pragmatist solution offers to reconcile diverse ethical positions by marshalling collective resources to address shared concerns.

Those shared concerns confront society from multiple sectors of its landscape; not just wilderness areas and wildlife reserves but farmlands, transportation corridors, restored watersheds, urban parks, and suburban backyards. Responsibly engaging the respective kinds of issues that arise from such varied environments requires an adaptive ethical capacity, inclusive of both natural values and human values. It requires some "metaethical framework that understands different environmentalisms as appreciations of different sources of value."[9] We can think of environmental pragmatism, writes Ben Minteer, as a landscape-based civic philosophy, neither anthropocentric nor ecocentric, but "incorporat[ing] critical elements of both sensibilities in a more holistic, balanced, and practical vision of human environmental experience."[10] It thus appeals to synthesized pluralism, to practical civic needs, and to shared environmental experience as a kind of shared moral experience.

Pragmatists defuse pluralism's destabilizing threat by recognizing theoretical diversity as the reasonable outcome of a variety of thinkers addressing diverse and immaturely conceived social problems.[11] In order to appropriate the promise of that diversity, they say, environmental ethics needs to organize itself around practical civic engagement rather than endless debates for and against anthropocentrism. So pragmatists agree that some taxonomic deficiency lies behind the field's inability to organize its literature in relation to a unifying rationale, and they seek to defend a shared version of the "practical" that can bear that rationale. By unhinging their debates from exclusive justifications of value, environmental pragmatists want to enable ethicists to stop defending metatheories and begin converging on policies.

Thus Andrew Light calls for theoreticians to "leave some questions that divide them to private dispute" that they may "publicly communicate a straight-forward position that endorses the trumping ethical and political environmental considerations on which they agree and the practices that expedite their mutually desired goals."[12] That such a consensus indeed exists has been the argument of Bryan Norton's "convergence hypothesis," which tries to refocus ethical attention on particular policy matters by arguing that "if reasonably interpreted and translated into appropriate policies, a nonanthropocentric ethic will advocate the same policies as a suitably broad and long-sighted anthropocentrism."[13] While there may be incommensurable disagreement at background levels of abstraction, say Light and Norton, environmental ethicists tend to agree on the general direction policy should take.[14] So let us reorganize the field by this shared rationale: "if all disputants agree on central management principles, even without agreeing on ultimate values, management can proceed on these principles."[15] In order to rediscover its formal rationale, environmental ethics should return to the issues of the day and the practical political needs of each occasion.[16]

It seems a Rawlsian solution: in the face of political necessity for ethicists to agree on reasonable civic policies, they should strive for an "overlapping consensus," in which persons holding incommensurable background beliefs can yet come to agreement on specific principles, values, or policies by way of different justifications.[17] While the warrant for our background beliefs (e.g., whether, how, and which parts of nature bear moral value) may interest our "private" academic debates, the public priority lies in demonstrating how particular policies support shared political ideals and nurture a pluralist community of hope.[18]

The strategy of environmental pragmatism thus proposes the reason-requiring arena of pluralist public debate as the formal object (or source of intelligibility) of environmental ethics. On this view, the field's debates should organize themselves around and for the practical needs of a participatory, public environmentalist community. Its theories should help ethicists understand environmental problems better, and help them collaborate in describing and advocating the best solutions.[19] Environmental pragmatism, therefore, makes "not simply a claim about how to do philosophy but rather how to do philosophy in relation to a certain set of problems."[20] It is "a new strategy,"[21] reshaping the domain of environmental ethics into "more problem-oriented" practical philosophy, utilizing theories as tools toward collaborative justification.[22]

Notice the multiple kinds of appeal to the "practical." The term "pragmatism" bears polyvalent conceptual associations, sometimes confused or conflated in the discussions of the school of environmental pragmatism. Here we have seen it used four ways: By supposing that (1) civic engagement with practical issues determines norms for meaningful theory, environmental pragmatists (2) use a problem-oriented approach to critique theories that stymie ongoing investigative debate by claiming an objective finality. Pragmatists thus want (3) theories that cleave closely with social experience, in order to satisfy (4) the activist concern for factual consequences.[23]

What Makes an Environmental Ethic Practical?

Two problems complicate environmental pragmatism, and together they challenge its appeal to the "practical." First, the field's pluralism appears to run deeper than the pragmatists assume. While alternative theories for valuing ecosystems may form so many approaches to a similar issue, it is harder to see a shared problem among ethicists describing sustainable planning, those critiquing cultural constructions of nature, and those advocating an ecological form of self-realization. Pragmatists try to contain that pluralism by circumscribing which participatory public community they have in mind.[24] Is environmental ethics for public policy makers, for environmentalist organizations, for natural resource managers, for local citizen boards, for concerned individuals, or for national debate?

Such diverse methods and groups do not simply appreciate diverse sources of value for treating a practical question; they frame entirely different problems.[25] Even if competing theories of nature's value do "converge" in practical recommendations about, for example, how to manage the Shenandoah National Park (SNP), it seems unlikely that bioregionalist, ecofeminist, and deep ecologist accounts would, too.[26] The repeated dismissive references by pragmatists to intrinsic value defenses and (less often) political theory misleadingly suggest that these are the only two arenas of theory production in environmental ethics.[27] But if ethical theory must respond to all the material environments, social practices, and political challenges at stake, then the range of theory environmental ethics must organize threatens to exceed the scope of the pragmatists' notion of "practical."

Pragmatists might respond that, so long as these theories are kept close to the concrete issue at hand (specific management goals for the SNP), the problem's criteria will contain the scope of theoretical pluralism. But that leads to the second problem: if theories are regulated according to their particular relevance, they lose capacity to critique the ways issues are framed, or to isolate new problems.[28] If a theorist questioned whether "management" was really good for the Shenandoah, then the field would start slipping back into the sort of metatheoretical disagreement pragmatism aims to overcome. Yet there are in fact prominent environmental ethicists who "are not so sure that managing . . . is the apt paradigm." "Why not," asks Holmes Rolston, "think of ourselves as authors who are writing the next chapters, or residents who are learning the logic of our home community, or moral overseers who are trying to optimize . . . value on the planet?"[29]

Such questions reopen the pluralist scope of environmental ethics, asking pragmatists just what they intend by appealing to the "practical." Light suggests that "normally our end is to better the environment," or (elsewhere) at least to promote "the long-term health of the environment."[30] But how to know what bettering the SNP would mean? What does a healthy park look like, and how long-term? It seems as ambiguous as the "environment-friendly attitude" Avner de-Shalit proposes as morality's practical goal. Daniel Farber's practicality refers to a prudent balance between "social sustainability" and baseline environmentalist goals, but, like de-Shalit, assumes consensus on those goals.[31] Around the Shenandoah, regional environmental groups do sometimes agree on land management goals, but when they do not the disagreement appears related to different commitments and respectively different views of the practical.

Bryan Norton sometimes appeals to a similar consensus supposedly shared by the "environmentally-sensitive," but has recently attempted to defend its content by proposing "sustainability" as a "keystone term in a new synthetic discourse about how to protect the environment," a "bridge concept" capable of moving the field beyond "ideological environmentalism" by integrating its pluralist approaches to decision making.[32] Using "sustainability" to qualify "practical" would appear an ungainly helper, for as Aidan Davison (among many others) has shown, sustainability is so conceptually absorptive that meaningful use requires unavoidably controversial specification.[33] But Norton makes the controversy itself a resource for specification because he describes sustainability as a social learning process, responsive to the politics of place yet operating over multiple scales of time. Its minimum dictum: maintain conditions for the social experiment to continue. Working visibly within the philosophical tradition of American pragmatism, Norton inscribes sustainability into the democratic project itself, so that pluralist management of its landscape becomes an enduring aspect of authentically democratic society.[34]

Norton thus makes sustainability a form of "adaptive management," assimilating normative pluralism into an engaged cultural experiment and remodeling the field of environmental ethics after its task. The "practical problem" with the field as it stands now, says Norton, is its disjointed conceptual pluralism, which leads to inadequate problem-framing and irrelevant arguments. In response, he proposes that the unifying science for environmental ethics "must be management science," which alone "can teach us to properly frame problems and integrate science in our search for a balanced strategy of development and survival." So reformed, "environmental ethics may someday be seen as an important subfield of adaptive management science, rather than as an abstract, and sometimes abstruse, subdivision of 'the humanities.'"[35]

Norton therefore provides a fulsome pragmatist account of what makes an environmental ethic practical, but returns us to questions about management as a governing metaphor. Rolston will remain dubious about the fate of natural values in a managerial paradigm, and will continue to argue for viewing the environmental task as a matter of respecting nature's objective logic and values. Norton may answer that by "management" he means a set of practices akin to those of Leopold's land ethic, through which "our experience . . . is reconfigured to allow us to think (including to evaluate) like a mountain," yielding a sense of social values conditioned by hierarchical scales of time and community identities tied to place.[36] Or he may point out that his view of sustainability orients management to "a relationship between generations" in which environmental protection creates moral community across time.[37] But then mere practicality seems no less involved in debatable metatheoretical commitments than the theories it would displace.

More importantly, Rolston will refuse to consider his account of intrinsic value as merely one political expression in an ongoing cultural experiment in landscape management. For Rolston, nature's value stands to be lost or protected, regardless of its sustenance for any democratic project; and for Rolston, the task of environmental ethics forms around describing nature's moral standing, not around sustainable political practices. So Rolston does not just defend different background commitments from Norton and the pragmatists; he works with an altogether different conception of the field, and with it a different notion of successful, practical argument.

Pragmatist appeals thus seem to presuppose a theory-laden conception of the "practical," itself often excused from examination; or when defended, then oriented toward one particular strategy of environmental ethics—one focused on the formation of cultural values through political processes. Yet there are other strategies, and with them competing conceptions of what makes for a practical environmental ethic. Accounts of intrinsic value or ecological rationality may engage theoretical debates precisely in order to challenge received moral frameworks and to contest concepts of the "practical" that seem inadequate to the complexity of environmental problems.[38]

In other words, despite their embrace of pluralism, the pragmatists' appeal to the "practical," ostensibly to bring theory back to actual environmental issues, can elide the diversity of environmental problems by smuggling in an unjustified keystone concept that narrowly regulates what counts as an argument in the field. The weakness of environmental pragmatism is therefore not so much its embrace of pluralism as its subtle escape from it. Despite loud rejections of the significance of debating anthropocentrism, pragmatists often still range the field's pluralism along a simplistic non/anthropocentric continuum in order to quickly draw the pluralism down into a practical overlapping consensus in the middle, perhaps called "weak anthropocentrism." The taxonomy by anthropocentrisms makes their middle position appear a reasonable, integrated compromise. But what if the field's practical goals and strategies escape that continuum?[39]

Although environmental pragmatism tends to underestimate the depth of diversity in the field and overestimate the ease of agreement, it does, on the other hand, demonstrate that a first step toward intelligibility in environmental ethics may come through discussion of the practical. The pragmatist proposal, after all, attempts to bring the field into view by proposing practicality as a common object for discussion, a criterion of mutual intelligibility organizing debate among incommensurable theories. The project would succeed if only it better appreciated the way various ethical theories implicitly bear their own conception of the practical.

Suppose we begin from a pragmatist notion that ethical proposals already orient themselves to problems. Suppose we resist reading debate in environmental ethics as the conflict of metaphysical commitments—so resist letting the non/anthropocentric continuum interpret the field—and instead look for the ways in which ethical theories elaborate implicit proposals for practicality.[40] Let us assume that ethicists produce alternative theories not merely to justify a philosophical stance, but to distinguish environmental problems as matters of ethical concern, and that doing so they pursue a notion of what an environmental ethic must do to succeed.[41] What if we initially read Rolston's value theory as a proposal for how to frame environmental issues within human experience?[42] In this ambiguous field, ethical theories are also, and perhaps first, strategies of practical rationality, proposing ways to organize environmental issues within moral experience.[43]

By misreading the theoretical debates in the field as remotely impractical, pragmatists miss diverse indicators for what makes an environmental ethic practical. But if, adopting a pragmatist method, we read environmental ethics for the normative functions they secure, we can outline several distinct modes of practical reason already at work. These practical strategies represent alternative conceptions of the field, but considered together they trace out a pluralist form of the environmental ethics field. Each strategy follows some minimal criteria of adequacy called for by Stone; taken together they might adumbrate the shape of conceptual success. We need only map the strategies to generate criteria for both testing ethical adequacy and conducting intelligible pluralist debate.

Environment and Experience

The pragmatists offer a second clue for developing the mapping exercise. By consistently associating the "practical" with political experience, pragmatists draw attention to the way ethical concepts make environmental issues morally significant within patterns of personal and social experience. Environmental arguments rely on accounts of human experience as they attempt to explain why and how the natural world matters for ethics When, for example, Norton argues that the naturalism of Thoreau and the biocentric imagination of Aldo Leopold lead to an ethic of adaptive management ("thinking like a mountain" is "Leopold's seminal managerial metaphor"), he means to say that we can only make sense of accounts of nature, even from such authorities as Thoreau and Leopold, from within our own ways of interpreting and deciding the human place in nature.[44] Norton prefers management models of sustainability, in part because he thinks that they keep environmental ethics open and adaptive to the changing place of nature within ongoing interpretations of our experience of environments.[45] We should then promote social practices that secure nature's endurance in such condition that it continually supports rich possibilities for interpreting the human experience.[46] That may be too circular to support a robust ethic, but it does point to a general requirement—that an environmental ethic must be able to show how nature matters for human experience.

Anthony Weston's pragmatism pursues a similar tack, arguing that the wealth of ethical pluralism correlates to the various kinds of environmental experience made possible by a wealth of ecological contexts and human practices.[47] Various arguments make sense within certain experiential contexts, the loss of which would in turn impoverish the possibilities of moral discourse. Only when they are rooted in a phenomenology of experiencing nature, says Weston, do values carry normative weight.[48] Pragmatism makes for an environmental ethic, say Sandra Rosenthal and Rogene Bucholz, because "only education of the whole person … can provide the breadth and depth, the sensitivity and imagination needed to harmonize conceptual recognition of the valuable and the immediacy of valuing experiences."[49] Weston, Rosenthal, Bucholz, and Weston thus propose an initial indicator for mapping the strategies of environmental ethics: look to how an environmental ethic makes environmental experience morally significant.

Left at that, we seem to have an impossibly general suggestion, and the ground for ethics tilted toward the anthropocentrism of culturally conditioned experience. But it may be question enough to open a reading and begin sketching a map.[50] How do various ethical strategies make environmental issues significant for human experience? An appeal to the moral experience of environments need not suggest the social determination of nature; it could just as well function to let nature pierce the human soul, critique society, and transform culture. It depends on how the theorist links environmental norms and environmental experience, and asking how at least allows us to suppose that the usual first step in environmental ethics—deciding among anthropocentrism, nonanthropocentrism, or the pragmatist alternative—is not the most helpful. The crucial question is not whether to start from human interests or nature's interests or political interests. The important taxonomic question is rather, how does this theory make environmental problems intelligible to moral experience? For an environmental ethic to be "practical," in other words, its readers must come away with some moral sense to their involvement with extra-human world. How does an environmental ethic do that?

Types of answers to this question vary as much as modes of ethical reasoning, with debates often renewing metaethical skirmishes and rehearsing longstanding philosophical debates. In the rest of this chapter I follow the counsel of the pragmatists, describing alternative proposals with a view toward their mutual intelligibility (if not their convergence), rather than testing the warrants of their respective metaethical justifications.[51] I describe three major strategies, each demonstrating a unique way the environment comes to matter for human experience and practical reason. The first organizes around nature's standing, the second around human agency, the third around ecological subjectivity. In the first strategy practical reason illuminates the claim nature's moral standing exerts on human experience, in the second it shows how human experience variously constructs nature, while in the third strategy practical reason follows the intimate connection of ecological conditions and human subjectivity.

Each of these three general strategies frames a different set of central problems and each describes a different criterion of practicality, often with descriptive reference to rival sciences (roughly: conservation biology, social ecology, and evolutionary ecology). But by mapping them in juxtaposition to one another, we will see how those practical criteria relate to one another. Recall from the beginning of this chapter that Plumwood, Smith, and Preston describe a general form of practical environmental ethics that reciprocally relates nature, human agency, and ecological subjectivity. The following descriptions test whether and how far these practical strategies make up three variations on a general form.

The Strategy of Nature's Standing

The first normative strategy may be the most familiar: the strategy of nature's standing correlates normative obligations with the moral status of the nonhuman world or certain members of it. Ethicists illuminate and defend nature's status in order to make environmental problems visible within our moral experience as harms or trespasses—threats to a moral other. Proposals that organize themselves around nature's moral standing share a common practical logic: nature's "considerability" removes environmental issues from the indifferent efficiencies of resource management, bringing them within the compass of more attentive ethical deliberations.[52] The strategy requires environmental ethics to attend to nature itself.

The strategy of nature's standing often sets itself against the blinkered economic rationalism of many public policy justifications, and perhaps for that reason predominately assumes deontological frameworks.[53] But the broad normative goal of this strategy includes consequentialist forms of practical reason as well, for it includes any form of practical reason that makes environmental decision-making directly responsible to the relative standing of natural entities or environmental systems.[54] On this view, when our deliberations fail to take account of the integrity and complexity of our natural environments, our moral reasoning fails to make adequate sense of our surroundings.

J. Baird Callicott thinks that "the most important philosophical task for environmental ethics is the development of non-anthropocentric value-theory," because he thinks that establishing moral status for the nonhuman world will guarantee inclusion of environmental concerns within basic moral experience. Callicott accomplishes that by appeal to Darwin, Hume, and Leopold, so that as the moral community evolutionarily expands, humans begin to value ecological others for themselves.[55] But presumably Callicott would be open to any normative theory that secures for the environment a moral status adequate to the requirements of contemporary policy questions.[56]

Holmes Rolston, for example, describes for nature a moral status with similar normative functions, but within a value theory nonanthropogenic as well as nonanthropocentric. For Rolston, natural values are objective phenomena available to competent observers of the natural world. They name the individual self-projects every living creature undertakes, its phenotypic expression of a specific form, and attach indirectly but originarily to the evolutionary matrices that produced the individual. Natural beings thus value themselves, he can say, as they pursue the goods of their own kind; humans only recognize and respect this self-valuing, marking their observation with correct attributions of "intrinsic value."[57] While for Rolston the independence of nature's value communicates an important part of its normative implication for moral agents, he and Callicott agree that environmental ethics shapes itself around the moral status of environmental kinds.

The debate between Callicott and Rolston can distract from their remarkable agreement: each proposes a nonanthropocentric value theory in order to inscribe environmental concerns within our practical experience.[58] That strategic agreement extends to the many others working to build an environmental rationality from nature's moral standing. Value pluralism, although rejected by Callicott and Rolston, works out the strategy of moral standing in recognition of multiple sources of value, some natural and some cultural, correlative to diverse kinds of personal and social relationships to an environment.[59] Other ethicists pursue the moral standing of nature while rejecting intrinsic value theories. Eric Katz, for example, roots nature's moral status in its axiological similarity to human subjectivity, eliciting similar norms of noninterference.[60] Tom Regan grounds respect for particular natural entities in the standing they have as subject of a life.[61] Even Peter Singer's sentience-centered utilitarianism, usually considered two spheres away from Callicott's project, pursues a similar practical logic by describing strong moral obligations to those parts of nature capable of suffering. Suffering makes for standing and marks out the members of the nonhuman world morally important for human experience.[62]

One can thus develop the strategy of moral standing by a number of approaches. Sometimes one selects a feature that figures in descriptions of human dignity and points out its presence beyond our species—perhaps some aspect of rational agency (e.g., acting for a good of one's own), but perhaps also sentience, self-organization, or emotional fellowship. Mary Midgley, for example, points to interpersonal sociality in dolphins and asks us to appreciate dolphins for some of the characteristics we appreciate in other persons.[63] In these cases, the reasoning goes that, if we respect other humans in virtue of x (even if x does not fully account for our respect of others), then we owe respect to those parts of nature also possessing x. Other theories, like those of Rolston and Weston, locate the source of value beyond human boundaries, so that nature's moral status may derive from its own natural integrity or its difference from humanity. Here one might argue that nature's activities establish their own intrinsic value (Rolston), or that diverse kinds of environmental experience indirectly testify to a generative human/nonhuman difference worthy of respect (Weston).

Each approach expects some account of nature's moral standing to shape practical reason. The primary task for environmental ethics therefore consists in describing nonhuman entities in such ways as to warrant their moral standing.[64] Ethicists then usually negotiate secondary problems around fact/value, is/ought questions by deploying their description within some philosophical framework that has developed devices for resolving those problems. So establishing intrinsic value may constitute only the first step for such different arguments as a maximizing utilitarianism, a neo-Kantian deontology, or even an Aristotelian virtue ethics.[65] Debates in environmental ethics sometimes confuse objections to nature's moral status with objections to the helping philosophical framework.[66] Disputants often agree on a strategically similar first move, that description and evaluation arise together (as Rolston puts it), with description logically prior, enabling a normative model of conduct by an evaluative picture of reality.[67]

Note the importance of descriptive aptitude for the strategy of nature's standing. Adequately describing nature becomes a central task for environmental ethics, for insofar as the moral order of nature structures practical reason, we must be able to refer to compelling and authoritative accounts of nature.[68] Approaches within the strategy therefore assume the epistemological possibility of producing a credible picture of nature, and attach practical importance to defending a particular science of nature.[69] Rolston, for example, routinely encourages his audience to become competent naturalists because his account of natural value depends on agents knowing the natural world in discriminating detail.[70] For him, value-recognition is simultaneously an exercise in scientific and moral perception. So while (as we will soon see) theorists within the strategy of nature's standing are sometimes accused of perceptual obtuseness to the challenge of describing nature, the strategy can lend itself to championing social practices of attentive engagement and cultivating personal openness.[71]

Two sets of difficult tasks attend the strategy of nature's standing. First, it must show how nature's moral status can bear upon a variety of environmental issues. For certain problems we require the standing of individual creatures (three individual colobus monkeys fated for research), in others that of a species (habitat loss for the red colobus), for others a relation of standing between species (mountain lions and mountain goats, or wild and domesticated creatures), for others the standing of holisms like ecosystems, bioregions, or even a global climate pattern. Other problems involve ambiguous hybrids of human and natural agency (managed landscapes, domesticated species). And for many environmental issues, all of these kinds of standing become relevant at once (as in deciding how to care for the Shenandoah). Solutions might entail hierarchies of complexity, relative value weighting, or the sorting index of evolutionary integrity. Somehow a theory must recognize and sort relevant differences among individual creatures, species, natural processes, and ecological wholes in a way coherent with its original justification for nonhuman moral standing. Complex policy questions require moral standing to bear normative implications across a range of beings, several scales of ecological relationships, and an always ambiguous human/nature distinction.

Second, an adequate ethic must link nature's standing with practical obligations and motivations for human agents.[72] If, for example, an ethic establishes nature's standing by an account of intrinsic value, then that value must at once correlate to features of natural organisms and elicit kinds of moral respect.[73] Without that simultaneous purchase on natural description and moral agency, the ethicist bears the burden of providing and justifying an additional mediating concept (between value and moral agent) to impress the action-shaping force of an intrinsic value attribution.[74]

Conventional interhuman ethics also must show why norms bear motivating obligations, but with regard to nature the task becomes more complex, because the status-bearers differ strikingly from the respecting agent (not least in that they cannot reciprocate moral respect).[75] An ethic might respond by eliding that difference through an ecologically-expanded notion of moral personhood, thus extending intrinsic obligation to others. Or it might maintain a strong distinction, as in the sort of consequentialism in which agents have obligations to optimize or preserve nonhuman value. Some virtue accounts also do this by providing motivation to respect environmental others in the course of pursuing one's own flourishing.[76] These latter two accounts establish ethical concern across species while recognizing interspecial differences, and with some respect for the significance of those differences. In all three cases, the strategy tries to make respecting nature's standing rational for moral agency.

The difficulty of these two internal tasks gestures toward the precise strengths of the next two strategies. Constructivist environmental ethicists investigate the practices that frame nature as a discrete moral object, while those redescribing anthropology focus on intrinsically human obligations to ecological goods. Note that difficulties within the first strategy recommend the strengths of alternative strategies.

The Strategy of Moral Agency

A second general strategy centers on practices of descriptive engagement with the natural world, rather than making them derivative or subsidiary to accounts of nature's standing. This strategy often begins from critiques of the strategy of moral standing, criticizing confident appeals to nature's integrity by pointing out its onerous descriptive requirements and tendentious epistemological claims. If environmental ethics wants to critically modulate deformed environmental practices, then it should attend directly to social practices themselves, rather than attempting to develop their possibility from nature itself. Centering on nature's standing removes from view the practical locus of the problem: bad human practices.[77] Inadequate descriptions of nature are, after all, the cultural consequence of ill-formed social practices. This second strategy therefore works toward criteria of adequate practices by beginning from two objections to the first strategy: (1) the practical reason of nature's standing uncritically repeats a form of reasoning at least partly culpable for environmental problems in the first place, and (2) the descriptive decisions made by the theorists of nature's standing illuminate more about the practices of the descriptor than the essence of the described.

The first objection argues that the strategy of nature's standing, especially in its attempts to establish intrinsic value, fails to escape exploitative forms of reasoning, in which ethics turns on hegemonic, modernist exercises of classification.[78] Since nature's standing often requires stable, isolated descriptions of nature to yield regulations on the human activities arrayed against it, critics suspect that status attributions subtly exercise control over nature.[79] Worse, such "considerability" approaches uncritically assume that "nature" comes under discussion divested of human sociality, and so barren of centuries of symbols and myths born of more intimate human–nature relations.[80] If an ethical theory assumes nature is available only in a scientistic realm of the purely known object before a detached knower, then it concedes all the significant ethical territory from the outset. Implicit in this complaint against the strategy of nature's standing lies a criterion of practical adequacy: environmental ethics cannot remove the human from view, but always already has to do with human practices.

An ethicist in this second strategy often comes to such critiques by appropriating the internal debate within the strategy of nature's standing. Moving from the disagreement among value theorists over the proper unit of moral considerability, one can deconstruct ostensibly objective descriptions that support claims for nature's standing, showing them to rest instead upon subjective decisions or cultural conditioning of the ethical imagination. When value theorists actively debate whether supra-individual entities (such as species, populations, bioregions, watersheds, ecosystems) are valuable or even existent, then it seems value theory flags at just the crucial point: in assessing holistic, interrelational ecological contexts. The debate shows that the exercise of sorting is itself the moral question.[81] It has been decades, after all, since Foucault's *The Order of Things* showed scientific classification to have more to do with social practices than the objects described, thus warranting suspicion that any ethics organized around natural description deals with moral agency only vicariously, as it produces those descriptions.[82] This line of critique particularly vexes ethicists of nature's standing, for it insists that their internal debate can only be understood by moving toward another sort of normative strategy altogether, one that turns away from nature toward the productive significance of human agency.

That fundamental uncertainty about the formal object for environmental ethics (the natural or the social?) relates in part to an unresolved question about the relation of the natural sciences to the domain of practical environmental ethics.[83] Cultural histories of ecological science underscore the contingency of natural description by showing the development of scientific paradigms in concert with social changes, often involving new patterns of normative appeal to nature.[84] The uncertainty leads some critics of this second strategy to suggest that environmental ethicists should not seek descriptions of nature but rather explanatory accounts of the practices of description, and perhaps the reclamation and renewal of more appropriate environmental practices than "description."[85] For this second strategy, the most important social practices for environmental ethics are not naturalist but political.

The strategy's second critical objection intensifies the anthropogenic suspicions to argue that not only the concepts by which we frame the environment, but nature itself, is significantly determined by human activity.[86] Nature's moral standing seems to require a status reasonably independent of human causation, and ethics of the first strategy often award prima facie respect simply for that difference. If the presumptive benchmark of natural things is "wildness," such that some ethicists assign drastically different status to morphologically identical creatures (the difference between a population of wild salmon and one of the same species raised in a hatchery, or between exotic and indigenous swans), then when Donna Haraway celebrates the hybridity of much hitherto considered natural, along with the hybridizing trajectory of human technology, she implicitly points out the disappearing subject matter of the first strategy.[87]

Ethicists such as Roger King and Stephen MacAuley take up that implication, observing that most of our environments are mixed, semidomesticated, marginal areas marked by a constructive human presence.[88] They are suburbs and farmland. That hybridity obtains temporally as well as spatially; one might present the Shenandoah National Park as a monument to an American frontier moment (located just between two mass expulsions).[89] Failing to consider mixed geographies means environmental ethics cannot address such fundamental social practices as agriculture and building.[90] Adequately attending to such geographies requires environmental ethics to shift its focus from nature toward humanity.[91] When ethicists (mischievously or innocently) propose consideration of objects hitherto overlooked by the field—objects like genetically modified organisms, suburban lawns, or urban parks—they reframe the practical task of environmental ethics.[92] The formal object of environmental ethics is no longer nature itself, but human practices.

Debates over ecological restoration have been contested in stark antinomies and otherwise inexplicably heated rhetoric precisely because they concern the formal character of the entire field.[93] They often represent contests between two general strategies. Debates over the status of domesticated animals, restored habitats, and urban environments become crucial tests of the possibility of the strategy of nature's standing, with much made to hang on the discriminatory qualifiers between nature and culture ("wild," "domestic," "artificial"). In the face of troubling questions at the margins, determined ethicists of nature's standing retreat to the safer referential ground of wilderness ecosystems for their primary material object, in turn opening themselves to complaints that they narrow the field to a tenuous and ever-receding arena of relevance.[94] Meanwhile, ethicists of the strategy of moral agency, having learned that they can open space for attention to social practice by casting suspicion on nature's standing, often begin their works with deconstructive sniffs at views of the natural.[95] Consequently, a dispute over normative strategy assumes the outward form of a realist/nominalist controversy, entrenched severely enough to justify pragmatist despair that environmental ethics cannot find a way out of intractable metaphysical disputes.[96]

But because those disputes in fact concern background practical strategies, the debates over "nature" at once intensify and further conceal competition between two distinct conceptions of the field. The ontological contests defend basic notions of practical rationality, one organized around nature's standing, the other around the cultural and political processes of human agency. Moreover, as we have seen, the "practical" complaint of environmental pragmatists against those philosophical contests usually supports the particular strategy of moral agency and its political notion of successful practical reasoning. Insofar as the metaethical disputes continue apart from recognition that they refer to different strategies, the field can easily miss the real practical significance of its differences.[97]

When a critical theory argues that if nature is socially constructed then environmental ethics must address the social forms of productivity, it does so to shape a strategy with a different criterion of practical adequacy.[98] Here practical rationality forms itself around the various way humans relate themselves to their environment: in the mediating concepts, history, metaphors, political configurations (and so on) through which humans are engaged with their environment.[99] Critical delight in counting the ways nature is variously constructed, produced, or projected does more than querulous gadflying.[100] It seeks a turn toward the agential role of the human, which "is being driven not just by intellectual curiosity but also by an increasing sense that existing ways of thinking about nature are *inadequate to practical needs*," that in order to describe the dynamic relations among environment and society, one is "not well served by the noun-dominated languages used for describing both."[101]

The deconstructive critiques therefore not only illuminate the conditioned, contingent, constructed character of our environmental descriptions, but also open space for constructing better sorts of social practices.[102] For example, if a critic can show that the metaphor of nature as resource correlates with the emergence of intensive technological society, or the androcentric exploitation of women, or the growth of a global market economy, then her criticism, however negatively deployed, implicitly imagines counterpractices. Forms of human living only indirectly addressed through the strategy of nature's standing now come to the center. Technological models, political power relations, and forms of economic participation become relevant for environmental ethics.[103] Without that sort of attention, environmental ethics fails to address the engines of environmental distress by excluding human practices from its formal concerns.

Seemingly insouciant, even sacrilegious criticisms of nature may in fact pursue a discrete practical strategy for environmental ethics. Consider William Cronon's (in)famous critique of wilderness: "There is nothing natural about the concept of wilderness. It is entirely a creation of the culture that holds it dear, a product of the very history it seeks to deny. Indeed, one of the most striking proofs of the cultural invention of wilderness is its thoroughgoing erasure of the history from which it sprang."[104] Cronon wants to reveal nature's historical narrative, and especially the symbolic freight born by wilderness areas, in order to daylight the constrictive (and perhaps destructive) character of practices unthinkingly considered environmentalist.[105] While some read Cronon as attacking the last stand of nature's independent integrity, his criticism seeks to open a more promising, more adequate ethical strategy—one that can guide our everyday uses of nature and contribute to a culture of gratitude and wonder.[106] Much of the debate over wilderness wrangles not only over the valences of an American icon, but over divergent practical strategies in environmental ethics.[107]

Constructivist criticism therefore often attends the strategy of moral agency in order to reorganize environmental ethics around the socialization of nature. As Steven Vogel puts it, when the ethicist shows "the extent to which the world we inhabit is always already humanized," she makes us "see the world we inhabit as something for which we are responsible, in both the causal and the moral sense of that word." In turn we realize that "we produce the world through our practices and can change it only by changing those practices."[108] Environmental ethics should "lead one to think differently about those practices, and hence perhaps begin to engage in different, and better ones."[109] For Vogel, "better" environmental practices emerge from better political decision-making processes, and those are better insofar as various representatives of cultural imagination and ethical creativity participate. The goal is to "*make* the world that surrounds us a good one, a beautiful one, one whose structures we can discursively defend."[110] Here the contestability of nature connects practical reason in environmental ethics to social justice, in both distributive and participatory aspects.[111]

The strategy of moral agency makes us see (as Lawrence Buell puts it) how the "environmental crisis involves a crisis of the imagination," and therefore asks environmental ethics to explain "both the pathologies that bedevil society at large and some of the alternative paths that it might consider."[112] Judgment about whether we are indeed making ourselves a good world must then be considered according to "the discussions and aspirations of individuals and communities in conversations with themselves; it is not grounded in the intrinsic value of nature itself."[113] We may still have and protect our Shenandoah National Park, but no longer as something ostensibly justified by the land itself but rather by the character of fabricative human experiences of the land.[114] We might call the park's twentieth-century designation the "ensauvagement" of the Blue Ridge landscape, making explicit how a political decision revises an existing social order in favor of new kinds of environmental practices.[115] The imaginative political decision must sit at the center of our normative debate. For "we cannot answer the practical question about how we are to act except from where we are now . . . [and that] is in a world where the human touch is everywhere and a principled refusal to act is both a practical and a conceptual impossibility."[116]

Cultural imagination, social arrangements, technological enframings, and political power thus become primary domains for environmental ethics. Now Langdon Winner can ask of technological decisions, "Do artifacts have politics?" and Ariel Salleh can directly assess metaphors of environmental practice.[117] By this strategy, environmental ethics requires a politics of nature, "one which expresses the inevitability and creativity of our relationship with nature."[118] Roger Gottlieb calls this change in strategy "breaking free from a bounded environmentalism to become a broader, more socially inclusive movement capable of challenging the very structure and logic of a capitalist social order."[119] Systemic analyses like that of Murray Bookchin demonstrate the capacious scope of cultural critique made available to an ethicist who treats social relations as determinative of environmental problems.[120] Indeed, it may be, as Niklas Luhman suggests, that environmental problems uniquely question the entire communication structure of a society.[121]

Each of these proposals pursues a kind of environmental ethic that begins by evaluating models of environmental practice in their sociopolitical contexts. If the situation motivating proposals for environmental ethics includes disordered exercises of political power, destructive cultural practices, and desiccated environmental imaginations, then it is just those powers, practices, and imaginations that should be subjected to examination, critique, and reconstruction. At the very least, an adequate environmental ethic must indicate the shape of better and worse forms of human agency. It must suggest the multivalent character of richer versus impoverished imaginations, greener versus defoliative power arrangements, just versus unjust politics, peaceful versus violent patterns of cultural habitation. The strategy of moral agency insists that such capacities cannot develop derivatively from nature's standing, but pose practical requirements of their own for an adequate environmental ethic. Otherwise ethics will fail to make sense of the historical, fabricative character of our environmental experience. This second broad normative strategy demonstrates that any adequate environmental ethics must, at minimum, include evaluative markers for shaping the patterns of human responsibility.

The Strategy of Ecological Subjectivity

Two major critiques of constructivist approaches introduce a third normative strategy. The first worries that focusing on fabricative practices may reduce environments to social processes, too easily washing out significant features of our environmental experience (real kinds, living creatures, and actual relations to which we respond). If too single-mindedly attentive to constructive practices, the strategy of moral agency loses its sense of how the natural world impreses our imagination, influences social concepts, and shapes political organization. "The world itself becomes almost silent in the sociological analysis," worries Preston.[122] The constructivists who are sensitive to this problem sometimes describe it in terms of a practical deficiency, failing to make sense of environmental experience:

> For all our sophisticated analysis and conceptual desquamatory moves on nature, the broad left has completely failed to produce a viable alternative to "establishment environmentalism." . . . We are left with a rather antiseptic nature which has little if any political appeal. . . . A new politics of nature will not succeed if it does not rewrite the rich memory banks of experience that are displaced by the critique of ideology.[123]

Without a compelling notion of nature, the strategy of moral agency may imply that an environmental ethic is finally a form of landscape management, assessable only by contemporary social values, and thus, despite its critical stance, unable to challenge dominant rationalities.[124]

Meanwhile, a second critique suspects that productions of nature are no less complicit with modernist technocracy than the classifications of value theorists. Without intrinsic resistance from the nonhuman world, environmental theory relegates itself to the politics of alternative imagination—at best a marginal dissent and perhaps accessory to the defoliative powers underwriting exploitative notions of nature.[125] If environmental ethics would do more than theorize within the cultural logics of late capitalist production, this second critique implies, then it might begin by reimagining humanity, rather than nature, so that ethics can start from some fundamental intimacy between humanity and environment. Perhaps recognizing their jeopardy to such critiques, ethicists working within the strategy of moral agency often conclude by calling for a dialogical relationship with the environment, advocating those forms of moral agency that open persons and societies to engaging, formational environmental relations.[126]

That dialogical element may be one reason why virtue and narrative accounts seem so compelling: attending to the character behind forms of agency and the storied roles humans can play on earth, the environment comes back into the picture as an active agent, though now through constitutive agential relationships. The stories and essays of Wendell Berry, for example, present human characters and communities through their particular geographies, and often evaluate them according to whether and how they let their lives be shaped by the character of the land.[127] Nature's integrity comes to voice through the lives of narrative agents, and simple words, modest gestures disclose a world in which humans and nature cannot be talked about apart from each other.[128] In Berry's *Jayber Crow*, as Mattie Chatham comes to the end of her life in Port William, her simple words, "Oh, he's cutting the woods," do more than name a bad activity. They bear savage geographical loss: the last of an old forest comes to an end and with it the last sort of lives that know how to mourn it.[129] A Kentucky bottomland woods shapes in her a personal wound as deep as a whole life's secret love, and the reader aches for renewal of more respectful ways of living, for love's care realized.

As King points out, such stories help us "to articulate the meaning of moral concepts by embedding them in wider narrative structures and imaginatively embodying them in images of possible life practices."[130] But more than literary paideutic goes on in Berry's stories. Nature reappears with moral status, only now "internally," within personal environmental experience. As in the first strategy, nature again shapes moral response, but now does so as social-ized within human practices.[131]

If we measured the role of narrative and virtue in environmental ethics according to their place on a non/anthropocentric continuum, perhaps as "enlightened anthropocentrism," we would miss this integrative practical func-tion. Narrative and virtue accounts inscribe an arena for natural description within personhood itself. Consider the reflexive reimagination of nature and personhood in Barry Lopez:

> For a relationship with landscape to be lasting, it must be reciprocal. At the level at which the land supplies our food, this is not difficult to comprehend, and the mutuality is often recalled in a grace at meals. At the level at which landscape seems beautiful or frightening to us and leaves us affected, or at the level at which it furnishes us with the metaphors and symbols with which we pry into mystery, the nature of reciprocity is harder to define. In approaching the land with an attitude of obligation . . . one establishes a regard from which dignity can emerge. From that dignified relationship with the land, it is possible to imagine an extension of dignified relationships throughout one's life. Each relationship is formed of the same integrity, which initially makes the mind say: the things in the land fit together perfectly, even though they are always changing. I wish the order of my life to be arranged in the same way I find the light, the slight movement of the wind, the voice of a bird, the heading of a seed pod I see before me. This impeccable and indisputable integrity I want in myself.[132]

Such dialogical accounts anticipate a third general strategy, which restores nature's moral status within an ecologically reimagined humanity.[133] Nature's voice returns to radically reformulate how humans relate to nature from the start. An ecologically revised virtue ethic may do that by extending the paideutic function of the moral polis to extrahuman relations, so humans flourish within mutually constitutive environmental relations.[134] Environmental narratives may do that by assessing moral agency within stories that subvert the abstraction of subject from habitat, recasting humanity in ecological intimacies.[135]

Those reflexive tendencies introduce the strategy of ecological subjectivity, which organizes practical rationality around the intrinsically ecological character of moral personhood. Partly in response to problems that arise from a familiar object/subject seesaw, in which environmental theorists rehearse on another stage long-standing philosophical debates (realism versus nominalism, materialism versus idealism, empiricism versus romanticism), this set of ethical proposals assumes agents and environments are already reflexively related. Inverting the constructivist criticism of the second strategy, and carrying out the moral standing implications of the first strategy, these theorists insist on "recognizing nature as an active participant in the production of self, society, and our ethical values."[136]

This third strategy includes coevolutionary anthropologies, most renderings of deep ecology, most ecofeminisms, environmental psychology, and eco-phenomenology, as well as (perhaps surprisingly) most analyses from environmental economics and environmental justice. While quite diverse in commitment and method, these approaches follow a similar practical strategy: each grounds environmental ethics in the qualification of personhood by its environment.

Deep ecology presents the signature stance of this strategy, although it assumes various representations, sometimes appearing as a political movement, sometimes as a new form of nature spirituality, sometimes as an especially vigorous commitment to nonanthropocentric reasoning.[137] When Arne Naess termed some ethics "deep," he meant to refer to a revisionary way of questioning our received picture of ecology and the human place in it, and, consequently, our way of framing environmental problems.[138] If we face difficulty, he thought, in establishing a normative link between nature's standing and moral responsibility, then, rather than formulate fragile ways to bridge the gap, why not question the assumption of a breach? Are not the theories of the first two strategies trying to deal with problems generated by a disordered fundamental relation, the alienation of humanity from its ecological place? Naess and his collaborators begin from the relation, recentering environmental ethics around "ecological consciousness."[139]

Deep ecology's privileging of ecological consciousness attempts to connect the personal dynamic toward human self-realization with an awakening identification with the wider world, which includes all manner of beings also seeking to realize themselves.[140] Human flourishing is therefore bound up with the goods of nature. Although variously reformulated by many theorists, deep ecology shares that general reunion of nature and personhood. Environmental ethics thus begins from a reorientation of talk about humanity and nature through an ecologically reformed anthropology, preserving nature's integrity with creative human agency.[141]

While deep ecology sometimes attracts rhetorical dismissal as an outlying viewpoint, a number of theories share its its attempt to reframe the fundamental strategy of the field. Associated proposals include those locating humans and nature in a "general economy" of plenitude, those appealing to coevolutionary roles or anthropologies, and those demonstrating the ecological determination of epistemology or valuation.[142] Each insists that a practical, adequate environmental ethic must account for the ecological character of personhood.

However, ethical proposals usually widely separated along the non/anthropocentric continuum also share this general practical strategy. For example, arguments that environmental issues can be adequately addressed by more expansive and efficient markets, if only the real value of ecological services is measured against the full costs of exploitation, may implicitly request public policy to account for a more pervasive relation between society and environment.[143] While sometimes dismissed by ethicists for deploying the same consequentialist framework used to justify pro-growth policies, if the device internalizes economic dependency on ecological conditions and measures objective welfare preferences to preserve nature for its own sake, then its instrumentalism implicitly recognizes some ecological requalifications to being human. Herman Daly and John Cobb seize on that implication by rooting their proposal for ecological economics in a complaint against the individualist anthropology of conventional economic thinking. With all the material relations properly accounted, "we should replace this [individualist view] with an image of *Homo economicus* as person-in-community.[144] Recognizing interdependent relations between individuals, society, and environment, environmental economics takes the measure of those relations in order to make the ecological extent of human interest enter prudential deliberations.

The most interesting similarity between environmental economics and environmental justice accounts, therefore, is not so much their anthropocentrism, but their shared ecological anthropology.[145] By insisting on fair distribution of environmental risks and benefits, environmental justice directs attention to inescapable ecological components of a decent human life.[146] By refusing the "substitutability" of certain natural resources or environmental risks for financial compensation, it resists the individualist anthropology of market preferences and implies some non-negotiable ecological aspects of a human life. Where calls for a human right to a clean, safe environment recognize that protecting human dignity inevitably means protecting its habitat, then they assume some fundamental environmental relations significant for ethical reasoning.[147]

Environmental justice explicitly illuminates those ecological dimensions to personhood when it defends the habitats of indigenous peoples in order to defend their dignity.[148]

Alternatively, if E. O. Wilson and Stephen Kellert are right that humans have evolved natural dispositions toward their environments—"biophilia"— then human flourishing connects with environmental flourishing in a way not unrelated to the way Naess puts it.[149] So too for environmental psychologies that treat subjectivity in terms of its fundamental environmental relations.[150] Assuming those fundamental relations, social proposals might proceed by appeal to an "ecological self."[151] These various ethical approaches share a normative strategy hitherto obscured by organization of arguments around the non/anthropocentric continuum.

One of the chief objections to deep ecology therefore also poses a question to theories sharing its general strategy: will uniting humanity and nature by resolving persons into their ecological relations eventually undermine their meaningful distinction? In face of claims like radical environmental protester David Foreman's—"I'm operating as part of the wilderness defending myself"—one might wonder if an ethic of ecological personhood bends back toward anthropocentrism in its presumption to speak not just for but *as* nature.[152] Without criticism of our conditioning experiences (e.g., androcentric models of subjectivity or consumerist market preferences), nature's voice may be constrained within degenerate forms of personhood. What models of creativity govern the dialogical expressions of ecological subjectivity?[153]

Recognizing environmental economics within this strategy attests to that problem in another way, raising, as it does, worries that a utility model dominates the ecological relation. Again, what if a particular model of ecological subjectivity seems inadequate or distorted—how can we criticize or reconstruct that relationality? In order to address that problem, a number of ecofeminists pursue the strategy of ecological anthropology with closer scrutiny of that fundamental relation. Ecofeminists often follow the third strategy's critique of ethical theories that presuppose alienation of humanity and nature by adjoining to it critical suspicion that the division underwrites a logic of domination. Just as differences between male and female have been constructed to serve androcentric domination, so too differences between humanity and nature have been made to function for anthropocentric domination. The point is not to monadically dissolve the differences, but to deconstruct the politics of separation in order to construct better forms of relationality.[154]

So, for example, Plumwood agrees with the strategic intention of deep ecology—human selfhood thoroughly integrated with nature—but quarrels with its tendency to dissolve the relational intelligibility of that integration. We cannot heal divisions, she says, by monological identification, but need some account of "self-in-relationship" with nature.[155] Karen Warren agrees: rather than dissolving difference, we need a nonviolent notion of difference, of diversity mediated by the metaphors of loving perception.[156] Within dominant subjective models characterized by empathy, care, and compassion, personhood intimately relates to nature without overwhelming it.[157]

Eco-phenomenologies offer a similar way of articulating an ecological self that works good for nature itself.[158] Relying on phenomenological analysis showing how nonhumans "give themselves" to be known within subjective experience, this approach claims that authentic subjectivity discloses the authentically natural—nature itself. In this case, environmental experience might be thoroughly subjective and thoroughly natural.[159] Eco-phenomenologies therefore emphasize the way human agency creatively brings forth the naturalness of the world.[160] David Abram, for example, portrays humans enfolded by perception into an agentially sensuous world, in which experience always includes participation in the experiences of many others. Here we might understand the Shenandoah National Park as a kind of geographical *epoche*, where humans may be reminded that personhood intimately includes and expresses the immediate presence of others.[161]

Each of the approaches in this third strategy pursues a common criterion of practical adequacy: that an environmental ethic account for the ecological dimensions of human personhood. They propose that environmental issues come into moral experience through the experience of subjectivity, and that practical adequacy in environmental ethics therefore means framing environmental problem in relation to ecological personhood.

Minimum Practical Criteria

The preceding brief survey shows that environmental ethics is not an argument over what nature is (even when it is trying to establish that), nor over how nature is produced (even when it does that), nor a new radical anthropology (even when it includes one). Nor is it an intellectual consortium serving someone's environmentalist consensus. Environmental ethics is rather a domain marked out by several distinct strategies, each proposing a kind of practical rationality with its own criterion of adequacy. If Plumwood, Smith, and Preston are right, the three strategies together may adumbrate broadly shared criteria—together describing a complex sense practical rationality. Perhaps taken together the three strategies describe three crucial functions required for adequately understanding environmental issues and making them significant for moral experience.[162] Taken together, perhaps they answer Stone's questions about what environmental ethics is and does.

Consider that one of the most respected environmental ethicists, Holmes Rolston, deploys aspects of all three strategies even as he roundly defends the main outlines of one. While Rolston argues for nature's standing by way of intrinsic value, he carefully attends to objections which accuse that strategy of discounting the role of human practices. Recognizing resources for a more adequate practical rationality, Rolston adopts an aspect of the strategy of moral agency by specifying the kinds of experience and practices required for correctly describing nature's value.[163] And he adopts an aspect of the strategy of ecological subjectivity when he describes valuing as an *ecological* practice that realizes the human role within a coevolutionary narrative. Human identity connects with nature's self-projecting status at the key juncture in his account of nature's standing.[164] There should be questions about how coherently Rolston's assimilations hang with his dominant strategic mode, but the very fact that he attempts to assimilate the strengths of all three strategies points to the functional significance each bears, and perhaps to a broader notion of practical adequacy intelligible across major approaches to the field.[165]

If so, then my mapping of environmental ethics indicates an outline of practical rationality: it must attend to morally significant features of nature, the way human practices shape those features, and the way both social practices and nature come together in ecological aspects of personhood. Plumwood's analysis of the "crisis of reason" faced by environmental theory comports with these findings. Her critique offers a precise negative of the positive criteria I have just isolated. On whether the degeneracy of rationality lies in "inadequate knowledge (ignorance), poor political structures (interest), or badly adapted and human-centered ethical, philosophical or spiritual worldviews (illusion)," Plumwood summarizes: "I have argued that the roots of our current form of ecological irrationality are to be found in all of these things—ignorance, interest, and illusion—and that these different elements work together and reinforce one another to create a larger ecologically irrational response that is embedded in the very framework and structure of our thought systems."[166] The crisis in environmental ethics, in other words, lies in the absence of all three elements of an adequate practical rationality. Her remedy requires clearer perception of nature, better social practices, and a relational cosmology. Plumwood concludes her book with the outline of a "materialist spirituality of place," by which she means to bring out a dialogical, relationally constituted practical reason, responsive to nature's agency and emergent from attentive, communicative environmental practices.[167]

Plumwood's "spirituality" conceptualizes an adequate environmental rationality through a semireligious term, but "place" might do just as well. Consider the agreement of Smith's *Ethics of Place* with Plumwood's environmental rationality:

> Instead of employing modernity's acontextual and disembodied rationality . . . this reconception of ethical being must speak of the constitutive relationship between an embodied ethical experience . . . and specific contexts, that is, environments. . . . I want to argue that radical ecology needs to develop both a "practical sense" and a "theoretical" (or reflexive) language that can do justice to the idea of an ethics of place, that is, of creating new relations to environmental others.[168]

For Smith, "place" describes emergent forms of human agency arising in response to actual encounters with the natural. Modulated by desire and wonder, our reinhabitation of environmental relations opens persons to be formed by nature into some appropriate "habitus."[169] Within a particular account of ecological relations, Smith thus correlates qualified human practices with particular features of the extrahuman world, producing an account of ethically significant environmental experience.[170]

Environmental ethics may find governing concepts other than spirituality or place, but as a field of practical ethics it does require at least a minimal account of how the natural world makes claims on moral agency, how agential practices condition the natural world, and how human personhood is ecologically shaped. A practical reason of the environment requires cultivated perception of one's environment, appropriately qualified responsiveness to it, and a sense of the role of both within personhood. Or we might say that the intelligibility of environmental ethics is illuminated by the light of nature, the light of social practices, and the light of human belonging to the world. Each strategy we have seen focuses one of those lights on the field, but the best theories within those strategies find ways to draw on all three.

In answer to Stone's request for minimal criteria, here then are three functional requirements for a practical environmental ethic: it must (1) describe morally significant environmental features, (2) assess multivalent human practices, and (3) integrate that environment and those practices into some model of human subjectivity. Those are very general and rather modest requirements. Nevertheless, for a field that is still a question unto itself, they suggest a formal shape adequate to the domain of environmental problems. They sketch an outline of the moral science of environmental ethics.

Clearer, more helpful debate might emerge if theorists at least recognized the separate strategies these three criteria generate.[171] If those criteria were accepted as mutually intelligible, relatively shared, and thus minimal standards of evaluation, then a truly useful pragmatism might be possible. We would then have some sense of the "practical" that could organize our arguments, bringing multiple modes of theory into intelligible exchange.

For the purposes of this book, however, I hope to have at least shown that there are in fact several distinct practical strategies, each approaching environmental problems with its own criterion of practical adequacy. In the following chapters I will map the several strategies of Christian environmental ethics, showing how their theological resources allow them to meet one or more of these minimal practical criteria, and to transform the secular strategies. How do environmental problems matter for Christian experience?

3

The Strategy of Ecojustice

The strategy of ecojustice organizes Christian environmental ethics around the theological status of creation. Doing so, it follows the secular strategy of nature's standing: by illuminating the moral standing of nature within Christian experience, ecojustice integrates environmental issues into frameworks of obligatory respect. By recuperating creation itself "as an integral part of the Christian tradition's vision and concern," ecojustice ethicists can extend traditional Christian concepts of respect to address the natural world's vulnerability.[1] For with creation's integrity illuminating a kind of natural value, Christian moral practices must give the earth its due. By naming and theologically describing the "integrity of creation," ecojustice secures modes of Christian respect for nature's standing.

As for the secular strategy, then, some description of nature evokes moral respect and contours right behavior. Here, however, God's relationship to creation grounds and guides that description. By guaranteeing nature's status in virtue of creation's independent relation to the Creator, ecojustice accounts form responsive Christian environmental practices around something sacred, or divinely given, within the world. As it informs Christian moral experience by some givenness of God in creation, ecojustice begins to draw moral respect for nature into a wider theological narrative. A background pattern of sanctification shapes how ecojustice makes environmental problems significant for Christian concern by making God's relation to creation part of God's way into friendship with humanity. A reach for grace helps ecojustice accounts pursue a practical theological strategy that transforms the secular strategy by making respect for nature an integral part of life with God.

Formal Emergence

How and why ecojustice follows a background pattern of sanctification has to do with the ecclesial setting from which it emerged as a pastoral strategy, so a brief historical sketch is in order. Ecojustice permitted a formal approach to environmental concerns within ecclesial commitments to humanitarian problems like poverty, social injustice, and disease.[2] As a pastoral strategy developing in the 1970s and 1980s, ecojustice needed to present the ethical significance of environmental problems while avoiding any debate pitting human interests against nature's interests, anthropocentrism against ecocentrism.[3] In order to make environmental issues part of its churches' enduring pastoral concerns, the strategy redeployed Christian notions of justice to make appropriate response to nature fit with the rationale for existing humanitarian mission commitments.

Throughout the 1960s and 1970s, mainline churches discussed environmental issues within committees concerned for "the responsible society" or "the sustainable society." At first it seemed these churches would approach environmental issues through the ascending U.N. discourse of sustainability. However, by 1990 the relevant World Council of Churches (WCC) group had changed its program name from "Just, Participatory and Sustainable Society" to "Justice, Peace, and Integrity of Creation." The name change connotes both a newfound focus on environmental issues within the church and at the same time, not coincidentally, the emergence of a practical theological strategy.[4] Referring justice to the integrity of creation the WCC churches set their moral compass toward the theological status of creation.[5]

By settling on justice as its overarching moral category, ecojustice accounts could noncompetitively juxtapose human alienations with environmental exploitation, thus meeting the integrative hope of sustainability discourse. More importantly, by incorporating environmental issues within the scope of its justice practices, the church could address them as social problems susceptible to traditional Christian therapy. Ecojustice associated social and environmental problems in a common missiology: as God reconciles the human community, so does God reconcile all of creation. By presenting all creation as an object of God's reconciling attention, the ecojustice missiology drew attention to the vulnerability of creation's integrity within a frame already oriented toward human dignity.

Framing environmental issues under the aspect of justice, a 1989 Presbyterian committee could proclaim that "nature has become co-victim with the poor, that the vulnerable earth and the vulnerable people are oppressed together."[6] Analogously vulnerable, nonhuman creatures qualified as candidates for analogous protections. Christians could call for response to God's loving regard of creation, and do so within the same moral discourse they used to call church and society to remember the human oppressed.

Ecojustice thus became the watchword of an ecclesial movement advocating for the "integration of ecological wholeness with social and economic justice."[7] As Dieter Hessel puts it, a "social agenda of ecojustice extends the emerging ecumenical ethic of just peace to include making peace with the earth." That happens "wherever human beings receive sufficient sustenance and build enough community to live harmoniously with God, each other, and all of nature, while they appreciate the rest of creation for its own sake."[8] The strategy of ecojustice thus developed a way for Christian churches to recognize nature's value and respond to ecological distress from within existing pastoral commitments. Moreover, as it did so, it enabled churches to critically reappropriate and redirect the ascendant "sustainable development" discourse, measuring it by economic justice and ecological wholeness. By broadly appealing to a vision of right relations in creation, ecojustice affirmed nature's own standing within ongoing Christian efforts toward a flourishing human community.

Beginning in the mid 1980s, as North American churches began turning their attention to environmental racism at the same time that South American liberation theologies began winning attention to unfair land tenure, the strategy of ecojustice was compelled to clarify its formal use of justice. Do we understand those right relations within creation in reference to a just human society or to ecological wholeness? Which takes priority in a pastoral strategy: are environmental problems matters of social injustice or ecological injustice? Theologians will answer inclusively, of course, but the questions ask how they achieve that inclusivity.[9] Does creation's moral status posses its own dignity or does it appear under the aspect of human dignity? Does justice render its due to creation indirectly through respect of human persons, or directly through respect of extrahuman creatures?

By the advent of the National Religious Partnership for the Environment (NRPE) in 1993, two distinct public strategies for bringing environmental issues within the purview of justice had emerged. While the ethics of ecojustice evaluated right relations directly in reference to creation's own dignity, advocates of "environmental justice" critiqued environmental degradations with respect to human dignity. Because the two approaches share concern for similar problems, holding together human and environmental degradations under the rubric of justice, they are often discussed together as divergent emphases of a common theological framework. However, even though some environmental justice platforms explicitly affirm the integrity of nature, and most ecojustice accounts insist on solidarity with the human margins, the two strategies deploy justice with respect to separate primary dignities. Ecojustice focuses on creation's integrity; environmental justice on humanity's ecological integrity. (I will further clarify their distinction when we return to environmental justice under the heading of the third major Christian strategy.)

The strategy of ecojustice makes respect for creation a mode of response to God. Right relations with God require right relations with God's creation, which by virtue of its own relationship with God, calls for moral response. As a recent National Council of Churches (NCC) document put it, "God's earth is sacred," and itself a "moral assignment," demanding humans turn toward ways that respect "ecological integrity."[10] That follows the logic of the strategy of nature's standing because the object of our moral attention is creation itself, whose character contours appropriate moral response. However, as we will see, ecojustice theologically intensifies the practical scope of the secular strategy by incorporating its moral response into the distinctive patterns of sanctification. For ecojustice advocates, becoming friends with earth restores humans to friendship with God. And both forms of friendship require solidarity with the human poor and participation in the whole community of God.

To the Earth Its Due

The practical strategy of ecojustice grounds Christian concern for environmental issues in creation's theological status. In a way, this follows the practical strategy of a value theorist like Holmes Rolston, for whom nature's intrinsic value makes environmental problems morally significant and politically urgent. Loss and degradation violate the integrity nature bears. The Christian strategy, however, develops nature's value by its relation to God, calling it sacred, beloved of God and possessed of its own integrity. James Gustafson, in a passage often quoted by ecojustice writers, writes that "we are to relate to all things in a manner appropriate to their relations to God."[11] Now loss and degradation violate a divine relation, diminish the sacred, and offend against the Creator's love. That makes environmental problems not only morally significant, but theologically charged for Christian communities. Devaluing or destroying nature now invites strong biblical words of condemnation: defilement, blasphemy, sacrilege. Ecojustice can thus summon commensurately strong practical responses for the protection of nature and restoration of right relations.

Ecojustice theologians summon and craft those responses by conceiving God's relation to creation in various ways. If God establishes creation's goodness, says Carol Johnston, then the jubilee liberation envisioned by Christian justice extends to all creation.[12] If God's saving, cosuffering presence enlivens creatures, as Jay McDaniel sees it, then we discover that all living things are our neighbors.[13] If God brings creation's goodness into God's plan, then our lives must be shaped by that goodness.[14] If God shows us through our embodied experiences that God values difference, otherness, and integrity, then we must work to protect the vulnerable, diverse body of creation.[15] If God fulfills creation eschatologically, then it already bears intrinsic value and must be preserved.[16] If God's self-revelation comes to us through creation, then humans must attend to nature's voices.[17] Each approach follows Gustafson's guideline: we find ourselves responsibly participating in natural patterns and processes according to their own relation to God.

That ecojustice guideline includes accounts not explicitly bearing the justice moniker yet organized around creation's relationship to God. For example, although James Nash develops Christian love as the most appropriate moral response to nature, he follows the ecojustice strategic rationale by shaping love around the "intrinsic moral significance" of nature.[18] Christians know that moral significance, he says, from the way God's love extends to all creation, and by learning to love nature, we participatively imitate God's love.[19] Nash's love arrives through the framework of justice because God's relation to nature summons and shapes it.

All of these examples follow Gustafson's maxim: right regard for other creatures follows the shape of those creatures' relations to God. Ecojustice illuminates the significance of nature and its distress within Christian experience by the way creation's integrity summons and shapes forms of response. As ecojustice theologians depict the integrity, and the threats arrayed against it, they enumerate responses: love, preservation, inspiration, protection, liberation. Each molds Christian action in right regard of the theological value the earth and its creatures bear by virtue of their independent relation to God. That describes a moral standing stronger than a value nature possesses for its own sake, for creation possesses this theological value as given by God, who loves all creation for its own sake. Its value is both self-possessed and divinely endowed.

In turn, creation's standing exerts exceptionally formative obligations for Christian moral agency. Here we begin to anticipate how ecojustice transforms the secular strategy. For with regard to creation's integrity, agents respect something given by God and beloved of God. The enumerated responses of ecojustice practices thus stand as so many responses to the biodiverse mysteries of God's presence within and for the world. Insofar as ecojustice theologians inscribe those responses within Christian life, they imply that violation or diminishment of creation's integrity darkens nature's importance for Christian life. That would mean that Christian relationships with God suffer distortion and diminishment when creation does—in biodiversity loss, for example, or in exploited creatures. For now that significant aspects of Christian action and experience form around response to God's relation to creation, degradations of nature threaten to obscure that relation, thus impoverishing Christian action and experience. Responding to its deprivation, ecojustice rediscovers how nature makes a formative claim on the Christian experience of life with God.

Transforming the Secular Strategy

We saw in chapter 2 how the strategy of nature's standing assumes a difficult burden of natural description. Critics question both the reliability of the descriptions and their moral consequence. Ecojustice accounts, however, limit their liability to such criticisms by appealing to spiritual practices of theological description. Because the practical responses summoned by ecojustice appeal to descriptions of nature that name how creatures relate to God, the strategy relies on a form of discernment at once naturalist and spiritual. In order to describe creation's integrity it must turn to those practices through which Christians come to understand God's relation to the world. Recognizing nature's standing and specifying the kinds of regard it requires thus entails the capability, disposition, and skills to look at the natural world and affirm its particular relations to God.

What, then, are the practices of discernment? If church communities think that Christians come to know God through love, or prayer, or worship, or charity, or doing social justice, then those practices are also important for discovering and describing God's relations to the natural world. Christians thus discover creation's integrity and its distress through the characteristic modes of becoming better Christians, in the sanctifying ways of friendship with God. Here, by its reach for grace, ecojustice acquires some of the practical capacity of the secular strategy of moral agency, yet without compromising its focus on creation's integrity. For by setting natural perception within ecclesial practices centered around growing into relationship with God, the Christian strategy makes itself accountable to the social productions of nature's description (the criterion of moral agency); yet because for ecojustice the essence of nature lies in its relation to God, ecojustice maintains its moral concentration on nature itself (the criterion of nature's standing). The reach for grace allows ecojustice to integrate the practical functions of both secular strategies, and to do so from within hallmark practices of Christian identity and ecclesial mission.

Consider, for example, Larry Rasmussen's *Earth Community, Earth Ethics*. While he explicitly grounds normative argument in the integrity creation bears by its relation to God, Rasmussen devotes much of the book to evocatively appealing for Christians to "return to their senses."[20] In the course of defending nature's value, Rasmussen recalls Christians into social relations and environmental practices through which they can see that value and respond appropriately. For Rasmussen, these are the practices of the reconciling community of God—especially the various forms of solidarity with the marginalized, presence with suffering, empowerment for the oppressed. Within these practices, thinks Rasmussen, we come to see how all creatures dwell with God; we discover the essence of nature in its relations to God. We recognize God's indwelling presence in creation by living in the world as if it were indeed the house of divine grace.[21] We come to perceive and respond to the integrity of creation, he says, by acting as stewards who know the house rules.[22]

Appeal to *oikos*, "household," the root of both "ecology" and "ecumenical," allows Rasmussen to mutually qualify ecological membership and Pauline practices of Christian community. The practical upshot, he writes, is a Christian version of Aldo Leopold's land ethic; only now creation's integrity determines what ecological citizenship means.[23] Thus Rasmussen shows how Christian discipleship forms humans into land membership; learning to live by grace they learn to "think like a mountain."[24] Christians comprehend creation's integrity, that is to say, by recognizing and respecting ecological principles within wider ecclesial practices of reconciliation. Christians therefore come to understand Leopold's difficult environmental criteria—"integrity, stability, and beauty"—through the difficult practices by which grace conforms humans to God.[25] And in turn, the environmental sciences and natural knowledge inform the heart of those Christian practices, for if "our ways should conform to God's passion for earth and its flourishing," then we must know just how the earth flourishes. In order to conform to God's relation to nature, the center of the ecojustice ethic, Christians must know and affirm the natural sciences of creaturely flourishing and ecological integrity. Ecojustice writers can then find theological endorsement for observing natural limits and adopting sustainable lifestyles.[26] "Fidelity to earth is an imitation of God," says Rasmussen, connecting environmental responsiveness to sanctifying grace.[27]

The ecojustice strategy therefore modifies the secular strategy of nature's standing by involving Christian social practices that can ecologically transform personhood. Respecting nature's integrity requires spiritual exercises that tie Christian virtues to natural laws and ecological relations.[28] The ecojustice respect for God's relation to creation shapes what it means for humans to be in relation to God. Rendering nature its due forms humans in friendship with

God, while primary forms of that divine friendship govern how we come to know nature. Using theological resources drawn from a formative pattern of grace thus lets this Christian strategy strive toward meeting the practical criteria of all thee secular strategies: situated within a pattern of relationship with God, ecojustice develops nature's standing in connection with certain social practices and an ecological anthropology.

One of the most important practices of friendship with God within the strategy of ecojustice, as Rasmussen makes clear, is solidarity with the human marginalized. That distinguishes it from accounts within the strategy of nature's standing that struggle to balance nature's value against the suffering of humans.[29] For ecojustice, morally focusing on creation's integrity means responding to the God of the poor. The church comes to see the ways God indwells creation, says Rasmussen, through solidarity with the poor and oppressed; it knows nature from within "the emotive region of the cross."[30] Practices of social justice hitherto associated with humanitarian mission—practices like charity, simplicity, economic fairness, political solidarity, and compassion—turn out to be indispensable for rightly perceiving the natural world and doing justice to creation. We have to practice loving the weak and suffering with the oppressed, say ecojustice theologians, in order to understand how God loves creation.[31]

That mode of natural description markedly departs from the sort usually found in the secular strategy. Ecojustice recognizes nature's moral status primarily from within the way of following Jesus, not only from scientific pictures of nature.[32] "The focus on Jesus, and not on nature apart from the revelation of a compassionate God," says Rasmussen, "is essential in a very practical way. Without attention to creation crucified, most rich worlders will work to save nonhuman nature but not creation."[33] Apart from solidarity with the poor and friendship with God, they will misconstrue what nature to respect.

As a practical strategy, therefore, ecojustice resists theologically licensing nature's moral status without theological guidance toward appropriate descriptions of nature. By rooting itself in distinctively Christian practices and transformatively engaging notions of personhood, ecojustice shapes environmental ethics around a theological relation running through creation. Says Rasmussen, "the issue for an adequate environmental ethic is not, finally, an upgraded view of nature, even a religiously sensitive one. . . . The issue for earth ethics is the discovery of a power throughout creation that serves justice throughout creation."[34] Seeking out that power, an ecojustice ethic appeals to creation's integrity within humanity's participation in God and God's movement toward all creation. Recalling Oliver Davies (discussed in chapter 1), ecojustice transforms the secular strategy by reclaiming the triadic intimacy of God's ways with the world.

Sanctifying Nature?

The strategy of ecojustice thus generates ways of articulating creation's integrity within a cosmology contoured by grace, or what Paul Santmire calls a "relational ontology." Santmire's own proposal for adding an ontological relation to Martin Buber's two dyads seems unwieldy. But Santmire proposes it because he sees how ecojustice searches for an overarching pattern of grace when it describes how nature's integrity shapes human ethics according to the ways God embraces all creation.[35] For others, biblical concepts of covenant best configure the pattern of that embrace.[36] Since "covenant implies a rightly ordered relationship, whether between people, with God, or with the creation," it refers ecojustice to the Hebraic laws recognizing natural orders while grounding them in God's relational intimacy with God's people.[37] Covenant forms of ecojustice provide for a Hebraic intensification of Leopold's (anti-Abrahamic) land ethic, in which human responses to creation's integrity are formed within an encompassing, relational environment.[38]

Covenant ecojustice accounts use a central biblical trope to link the integrity of creation with both social flourishing and divine order. Following the dual goals outlined for ecojustice by Hessel, covenant portrays "a more relational social order in which the richness of human goods is pursued, and in which the goods of the non-human world are also affirmed and conserved."[39] By doing so within a covenantal frame, however, these approaches intrinsically include the sort of social practices that Rasmussen's ecojustice shows necessary. Moreover, covenantal ecotheologies may comfortably include appeal to stewardship practices without worry about losing creation's integrity to a dominionist anthropology, for here the land mediates God's command and place qualifies human responsibility.[40]

Where ecojustice accounts adopt covenantal frames they further push ecojustice toward admitting and developing its background soteriological patterns. When justice conforms to "a fundamentally interactive account of the relations between the human self, the social order and ecological order, and between all of these and God," then "love of God and the love of life, life in all its diversity, are also intricately connected."[41] Those two statements from Michael Northcott are widely separated in his text, but, they seem to presuppose one another, connecting ecojustice and a life of holiness. George Kehm makes it more explicit: creation's integrity inevitably appears near the saving work of Christ when "the hope for human and nonhuman creation is grounded in the *sola gratia* of God's universal, ecological covenant."[42] We receive grace, these ethicists seem to claim, in some way through God's love for all creation, and respond somehow conformed to that love.[43]

However, ethicists tend to leave underdeveloped those hints of the ecojustice reliance on sanctification. While Rasmussen's ecojustice demonstrates the practical promise of a Christian environmental ethics, and covenantal approaches foreground the biblical trope for uniting God's love and ecological order, both leave us uninformed at a crucial point: how does creation actually conform Christians to the love of God? How can loving nature sanctify human experience? How does living with respect for creation's integrity conduct humans into friendship with God?[44]

Ecojustice transforms the secular strategy by integrating transforming spiritual practices into its account of creation's integrity. Rasmussen shows how loving the earth reintroduces practical reason to intimacy with God through respecting the fullness of God's created community. Northcott unites life within natural orders with life within experience of God's grace. But both remain only suggestive at the point of that intimacy, never quite explaining how conforming ourselves to creation makes us friends with God. Sanctification remains a background note, never explicitly taken up. We are left with only tantalizing clues about the role nature might play to form humanity into intimacy with God.

Natural Evils

Uncertainty over how respect for nature makes a soteriological difference may have to do with a second ambivalence. Ecojustice ethicists disagree over which aspects of nature make up creation's integrity, and whether some aspects are in fact distressing signs of its degeneracy.[45] Rasmussen, for example, declares that nature's indifference to suffering disqualifies it as an ultimate authority in guiding human behavior. Ethicists should rather discern, he says, how things relate to God in recognition that all suffering distresses God, and in faith that ultimate reality bends toward the affirmation of life.[46] Northcott, though appealing to nature's order throughout, argues that some elements of that order are fallen. Theology cannot valorize worldly phenomena like predation, he says, for they menace Christian hopes for a cooperative peace.[47] On the other hand, James Gustafson's unflinching appeal to nature accepts tragedy, affirming that creaturely vulnerability to what Thomas Aquinas calls "natural evil" is part of how God's providence works.[48]

Lisa Sideris points to that ambivalence in Christian environmental ethics and sees (in the case of Rasmussen and Northcott) theological romances of nature that may subtly refuse participative conformity to ecological order (of the sort Gustafson endorses). So it is not just the religious right voicing skepticism of the natural sciences. Whenever a theological ethicist privileges interdependence, balance, and cooperation in nature over evolution, predation, or death, she appears to let theological criteria determine her view of the natural world, in the face of credible scientific reports. If Sideris is right, a number of environmental theologians rewrite descriptions of the natural world even as they call Christians to respect creation on its own principles.[49]

Sideris's critique points toward an unresolved theological question with practical implications for ecojustice: how closely and clearly does nature participate in God? Which parts of nature reflect divine will and providence, and which are distortions of how God would have creation?[50] Forcing the question from the opposite view, Stephen Webb criticizes ecojustice theologies that implicitly legitimate violence or assimilate suffering into "peace" by blithely celebrating God's presence in creation. Should Christians follow Sideris and support a land ethic, with its delight in predators and tolerance for blood? Or should they, as Webb argues, live out biblical peace by adopting pets, supporting zoos, and opposing the reintroduction of predators?[51] Which is the way of God's friendship with creation?[52]

Requiring practices of social justice and solidarity for right discernment of nature, Rasmussen and Northcott recoil from the bloody, decompository parts of nature. For them, the form of God's relation to the world—whether conceived as cruciform solidarity or life-affirming covenant—disqualifies natural evils from creation's integrity. In other words, they implicitly argue that Christian participation in God determines what Christians make of creation's integrity, with dramatic consequences for responding to earth. If Gustafson or Sideris would demur, Northcott and Rasmussen apparently want to hear their reasons in terms of Christian participation in God. We develop a practical sense of the world, they argue, through God's invitation to friendship with the divine life. Here again we see how ecojustice relies on sanctifying grace, for in order to know and respond rightly to creation, God must bring us to our spiritual senses.

The questions posed by Sideris and Webb are not thereby answered. We still do not know exactly how nature's participation in God shapes our own, nor why death and decay might be stripped from what Christian justice may respect in nature. We do not yet know whether Christians should quarantine wolves or reintroduce them. But Rasmussen and Northcott have directed us toward the area of doctrine that must prove creation's integrity: we learn how to respect nature from within sanctification.

From Moltmann to Aquinas: Ecojustice and Sanctification

Jürgen Moltmann, whom Sideris also critiques for misrepresenting nature, develops his view of nature by appealing directly to that descriptive connection

between soteriology and creation. Moltmann's theology, which regularly rede-
velops doctrinal topics and biblical metaphors in light of environmental issues,
consistently exhibits a broad ecojustice strategy, and he points specifically to
sanctification for its basis. Moltmann thinks that Christians should respect
nature in recognition of creation's integrity, while at the same time, he makes
understanding that integrity dependent upon participation in God's ways of
friendship with humans. By explicitly rooting ecojustice in the doctrine of sanctification, Moltmann opens a theological arena for addressing the strategy's
ambivalence about how to practically regard the natural world.

In a trinitarian rendition of ecojustice, Moltmann claims environmental
ethics begins in "recognition of the particular and the common dignity of all
God's creatures . . . [which] is conferred on them by God's love towards them,
Christ giving of himself for them, and the indwelling of the Holy Spirit in
them." For Moltmann this "covenant of creation" is more than romantic
reimagination; he believes it can serve as basis for affirming legal rights for
nature.[53] He wants governments and societies to view nature as "an independent subject with its own rights," protected by international treaty.[54]

However, in order to fully see nature's dignity, says Moltmann, humans
must respond to God's invitation into grace. When animated by the incarnate
Christ and vivifying Spirit, humans discover themselves incorporated within a
world alive with God's presence. In turn, that means that God works personal
holiness in Christian salvation in a way intimately and practically bound to the
work God has already done in creation:

> "Sanctification today" means first of all rediscovering the sanctity of
> life and the divine mystery of creation, and defending them from
> life's manipulation, the secularization of nature, and the destruction
> of the world through human violence . . . Today sanctification means
> integrating ourselves once more into the web of life from which
> modern society has isolated men and women.[55]

For Moltmann, the history of environmental distress must be told alongside
the church's impoverished view of sanctification and modern theology's
simultaneous eclipse of creation and of the Holy Spirit: "For the community
of creation . . . is also the fellowship of the Spirit. Both experiences of the
Spirit bring the church today into solidarity with the cosmos." Experience of
the Spirit leads Christians "to respect for the dignity of all created things, in
which God is present through his Spirit."[56]

In other words, we learn what justice means by experiencing the Spirit in
community, and what creation's integrity means by experiencing the Spirit
in creation. Ecojustice fundamentally "means learning to see life and love it as

God sees it and loves it."[57] Note that because Moltmann holds together Spirit and creation, he talks in terms of spiritual transformation, not cosmological revision.

When Northcott appeals to nature's balance and peace, rather than chaos and predation, he implicitly argues from his view of God's indwelling presence. When Rasmussen calls for solidarity with the oppressed in order to see creation's integrity, he implicitly draws on the paideutic of Christian formation. Moltmann makes their rationale explicit: in sanctification grace animates a person socially, politically, and ecologically. Sanctification names how grace brings a person to her senses (as Rasmussen would say), opening her in personal responsiveness to the integrity, stability, and beauty of the world around her.

Now, whose integrity, what stability, and which beauty? Unlike Rasmussen and Northcott, Moltmann openly defends a theological difference between nature as science sees it and creation as God knows it. For Moltmann that difference runs eschatologically: contemporary nature is a promise of its state in glory, bearing traces of God's love for the new creation.[58] From the perspective of the cross, death and transience signify creation's enslavement. From the place of God's absorption of suffering and Nothingness, evolution actualizes nature's susceptibility to divine wisdom and points to its transfiguration by God's perichoretic life. A theology of creation's integrity therefore celebrates nature's dynamic openness to the future while lamenting its present enslavement to death.[59] In practice, for Moltmann, that means Christians should interpret nature dialogically between natural science and eschatological glory, all the while giving merciful, loving space to the bodies in which God's new creation will dwell.[60]

Moltmann thus binds creation's normative integrity to the sanctifying experience of grace. But he delivers ecojustice into three further problems caused by the discontinuity between nature as it is and nature as God would have it. First, if knowing creation's integrity requires Christian experience, and leads to a view of nature at variance with the going scientific picture, then the practical rationale of the ecojustice strategy seems disingenuous. If ecojustice theologians do not in fact appeal to the standing of nature as it presents itself, but to some power or integrity in creation only perceptible within experience of the Holy Spirit, then their strategy, putatively formed around creation's independent status, seems ready to collapse into subjective experience. Even though Moltmann insists natural science and revealed theology do not compete, his practical response to earth relies much more upon theological experience than natural science.[61]

Second, although ecojustice advocates invariably write against ideological darkenings of creation's integrity, selecting views of nature by theological characteristics may unwittingly evince some restless distaste for our present environment. If ecojustice affirms creation in virtue of its eschatological future, or reads certain natural characteristics as proleptic theological narrative, then it seems to defer nature's due while respecting something different. Ecojustice by *différance* may deaden our senses to earth, attuning us in fact to the nature of some religious cosmology.

These first two problems suggest that an ecojustice strategy must defend a participatory hermeneutic of nature. That is, for ecojustice to mold normative practice by the character of creation, it must show how the sanctifying practices that generate description of creation's integrity are themselves ecologically shaped. At the crucial juncture, Moltmann stops just short of that: he juxtaposes receptive, participative knowledge of nature with receptive, participative knowledge of Christ, but does not explain how they relate.[62] How might gifts of the Spirit be received through participating in creation? How might forms of environmental experience constitute or inform experiences of grace? In order to explain the relation between creation's integrity and Christian social practices, ecojustice needs to prove some sanctifying role for knowing nature.

To test ecojustice possibilities for the role of creation in sanctifying grace, I will later turn to Thomas Aquinas, whose account of sanctification tried to be faithful to both nature's integrity and grace's transformation. Before moving on, however, we must raise a third problem, which prepares our inquiry into Aquinas. Moltmann and others resist identifying the present natural world with God's creation because of theological suspicions about violence, vulnerability, and death. But what sort of land ethic preserves the weak and tells against predation? Sideris claims that no environmental theology downplaying evolutionary processes can guide environmental decision-making. Do Christians want vegetarian zoos or do they want to hear wolves howling again in the Shenandoah? Because of the ecojustice link between creation and sanctification, that policy question forces a theological dilemma, for our own experience of God will be shaped by whether we decide for an ecology of glorious predators or the peaceful "counter-biology of Judaism and Christianity" envisioned by prophets.[63] Which is the world of God's friendship?

A theological middle way might somehow deprioritize death and violence by privileging ecological concepts more likely to function as analogues to the divine life. Moltmann, for example, assimilates death and transience into the temporal dynamism that opens nature to an eschatological future. But that approach may enervate Christian environmental practice from a different angle. If Christian hope for the world cannot appear organically possible from present environmental conditions, then theology makes creation's glory discontinuous with nature's present, divine creation disjunctive with ecology.[64]

Perhaps here the theologian only insistently hopes, pointing out that neither does human resurrection appear organically possible.[65] In that case, failing to preach nature's transfiguration might jeopardize human hopes for a future with God. Perhaps, then, "a theological account of the world can only be an 'imaginative venture, tinged with agnosticism,'" a venture in which "we are bound to re-narrate these stories, in such a way that the violence is denied ultimacy."[66] But how does such overwriting resist the ongoing transformation of the world according to capitalist and technocratic metanarratives? If Christian environmental practices shape the world according to a story not evidently nature's own, why not transgenic species, intensive monoculture, or a strip-mall world? Those are all imaginative ventures, each in some way denying death.

Even if she could divide the Christian stories from the nihilist ones, the theologian would still have dematerialized the process of coming to know creation. The great strength of the ecojustice strategy lies in making environmental experiences a kind of spiritual formation, in which sensing our environments particularly and acutely opens us in new ways to God's ways with the world. But now, if we must turn to imaginative ventures and counterbiological renarrations to finally comprehend creation, then it seems ecojustice finally dislocates spiritual formation from earth. Sanctifying knowledge of creation then comes from theological writing only tangentially related to wolves and rabbits. Suddenly, reading and writing become fundamental environmental practice as theologians try to reimagine fierce green eyes and soft white fur emerging from something more trinitarian than survival strategies harried by death.

Anthony Baker suggests that Aquinas offers the way to keep the sanctifying knowledge of creation close to the earth, for Aquinas describes a noncompetitive, participative relationship between natural knowledge and divine experience.[67] Moltmann's soteriological ensconcement of natural description outlines what that materialism must accomplish for an adequate ecojustice strategy. Ecojustice needs to imagine morality conformed to a habitat shaped by death, finitude, and contingency, yet in concert with hopes conformed to the peaceful world in God. It must affirm that "creation groans for salvation" while loving and being shaped by the graces of its present forms. We need to relate nature's grace and grace's ecology. In order to secure and intensify the ecojustice strategy as practical environmental theology, I turn to Aquinas in chapters 6 and 7, wondering how grace conforming intellects to God might involve justice to wolves.

4

The Strategy of Christian Stewardship

In contrast to the ecojustice focus on creation's integrity, the strategy of Christian stewardship frames environmental issues around faithful response to God's invitation and command. By appropriating the biblical trope of stewardship, this strategy organizes concern for environmental problems around obligatory service to the Creator, who entrusts to humans measured responsibilities for creation. To specify the character of this earthkeeping trust, the strategy looks to biblical accounts of how God invites humans into relationship. Stewardship thus situates the specific call to care for the earth within a general divine call to faithful relationship. By making environmental issues matter for Christian experience in reference to God's actions toward humanity, the stewardship strategy follows a background pattern of redemption. It therefore focuses primarily on faithful practices, describing how to inhabit the providential landscape created by God's special relationship to humans.

Recall from chapter 2 how a strategy of moral agency developed in protest against confident ethical appeals to nature's moral status. The strategy of stewardship harbors a similar worry that ecojustice approaches may appeal to unwarranted views of nature. So instead it configures the moral significance of nature within God's redemptive actions. Grace constructs nature as the environment of God's love for the world, which good stewards inhabit responsibly.

Formal Emergence

Peter Bakken observes that the stewardship strategy simultaneously pursues hortatory, apologetic, and polemical functions. It must make environmental concerns matter for Christian life (hortatory), defend the environmental virtues of that life from skeptical critics (apologetic), and argue against both ecocentric and anthropocentric alternatives (polemical).[1] All three of those functions help explain how the stewardship strategy developed and why it draws on the pattern of redemption to distinguish itself from other Christian and secular environmentalisms. So, as in the previous chapter on ecojustice, a brief historical sketch helps contextualize stewardship as a distinct strategy of Christian environmental thought. Stewardship emerged as a discrete theological discourse in the 1980s, supporting a public Christian environmentalism especially associated with evangelical Protestantism.[2] Of course the steward has long appeared as an ethical persona and has recently enjoyed a nonreligious public career in contemporary social debates about managing public trusts or fulfilling obligations to future generations. A range of environmental theologies across all three strategies refer to it, and church leaders from various backgrounds deploy it. But this one strategy organizes the significance of environmental issues for Christian experience around the normative role of stewardship.[3] Stewardship theologians establish and evaluate environmental responsibilities from God's establishment and formation of human responsibilities for the earth.

While stewardship theologies developed early in Christian environmental thought, it took a decade or so for a distinct pastoral strategy of Christian environmental ethics to cohesively frame environmental problems by Christian obedience. As early as 1961, evangelical Christians expressed concern over environmental problems.[4] By 1970 some theologians had begun developing the biblical trope of stewardship in theological responses to the environmental crisis. Francis Schaeffer and Paul Santmire argued that utilitarian attitudes toward nature were part of a sinful rejection of God's invitation to a caretaking vocation.[5] The first inklings that stewardship could articulate a distinct environmental strategy appeared in John Passmore's 1974 *Man's Responsibility for Nature*, which argued for transforming modern despotism by reclaiming stewardship, rather than the nature romanticisms of early environmentalism.[6]

North American activity toward a discrete strategy began to coalesce in 1977, when Ron Sider published *Rich Christians in an Age of Hunger* and Calvin DeWitt called a stewardship conference held at Calvin College.[7] The next year an anthology of theological essays approached environmental and economic problems under the aspect of stewardship.[8] Meanwhile, DeWitt's conference spurred two important establishments: Evangelicals for Social Action (ESA) in 1978 and the Au Sable Institute in 1980. The ESA would generate the Evangelical Environmental Network (EEN), while Au Sable created and still teaches an environmental and biblical education curriculum oriented toward promoting Christian environmental stewardship. Au Sable also gathered a community of fellows and held ongoing theological forums that helped develop the strategy of stewardship.[9] Au Sable and the EEN subsequently played foundational roles throughout the 1980s and 1990s in framing environmental problems for Christians within the terms of stewardship.

In those decades of headlining environmental problems and growing conservative political resistance to environmentalism, the stewardship movement gathered momentum as a distinctly Christian pastoral strategy. Until two major conferences in 1988, environmental theologies sometimes seemed to provide Christians merely with private reasons to support a leftist social movement.[10] After the North American Conference on Christianity and Ecology, Christian theologies began to frame environmental problems on their own terms, sometimes at variance with mainstream environmentalism, and to describe uniquely Christian forms of response.[11] During that year's second conference, DeWitt said that Christians were just beginning to hear the groans of the earth because until then environmentalism had been only a secular message. Now evangelical Christians were "searching the scriptures" to discover biblical forms of environmental care.[12]

By 1990, when Carl Sagan and a consortium of scientists issued their "Open Letter to the Religious Community," evangelical theologians had framed environmental problems as signs of infidelity to God's plan and as a crisis calling humanity to repent for their sins.[13] In other words, stewardship theology offered a way of understanding environmental issues as challenges to faith and representing them as signs of God's ongoing call to turn toward repentance. Its theological framework therefore allowed evangelical Protestants to respond to the scientists' invitation as part of God's invitation.

In 1993, ESA and WorldVision convened a group of evangelical theologians and church workers to draft "The Evangelical Declaration on the Care of Creation." That document guided the 1994 formation of the EEN and justified its participation in the National Religious Partnership for the Environment (NRPE). The Declaration still serves as a foundational document for contemporary stewardship thinking.[14] The public strategy quickly garnered political resonance as a mode of moral reasoning about environmental problems that could attract new constituents. In 1996 the EEN displayed the strategic power of stewardship environmentalism before a startled Congress and a befuddled but delighted group of secular environmentalists. When the new Congress proposed rolling back the Endangered Species Act, the EEN turned the issue from nature's moral status to faithful earthkeeping practices. Deploying a biblical image of God's promised redemption, their message was "people in their arrogance are destroying God's creation, yet Congress and special interests are trying to sink the Noah's Ark of our day."[15] By turning an environmental issue organized around duties to nature into one about the character of human practices, stewardship theology helped the EEN make species conservation intelligible to evangelical church communities as part of their identity and mission. The legislation was defeated, and an impressed Sierra Club published its thanks to the EEN, along with an apology for its past antagonism to religious communities.[16]

The Sierra Club and others may have welcomed stewardship theologies for their ability to attract religious constituents. But the strategy of stewardship does more than market an alternative environmentalist vocabulary. Stewardship makes environmental issues part of fundamental Christian experience. Doing so by locating environmental problems within the pattern of redemption, it outlines the practical task of environmental ethics in a new way.[17]

Disciples and Deputy Caregivers

The strategy of stewardship appeals to biblical mandates to care for, watch over, cultivate, govern, and/or improve the earth "on behalf of God."[18] For critics that amounts to religious license for anthropocentric domination—and this criticism constitutes the chief challenge a stewardship theology must disprove. The usual first move of disproof finds a way to privilege the pair of action verbs in Genesis 2 over the pair in Genesis 1, so that guarding and tending (*abad* and *samar*) regulate what exploiting and subduing (*radhah* and *habhah*) can mean. One way to privilege the second pair is to situate the Genesis mandates within God's call to conversion, thus emphasizing repentant obedience rather than free license. So while "actively responsible as God's deputy for care of the world," the steward acts as humble servant to a sacred trust.[19] The mandates then resist reckless exploitation, for they set human power in inescapable accountability to God's invitation.

For critics, deputyship, even if humble and accountable, still separates humanity from the rest of creation, making humans inattentive and irresponsible to earth. Moreover, it justifies interventionist, controlling dominion by appealing to a picture of God as distant monarch.[20] To refute these challenges, stewardship must further rehabilitate "dominion," showing how it is shaped by respect for nature and intimacy with God. Stewardship ethicists point out that Genesis immediately specifies dominion with an array of other action verbs oriented toward intrinsic goods of creation, and anticipating the work of Christ. For the EEN, "rulership can only be understood in term of working, tilling, keeping, guarding, enhancing, and protecting the garden of God."[21] The story of Noah, with its ark of ecological salvation, dramatizes this active preservation-ist responsibility given humanity. Moreover, because several of Jesus' parables involve a steward and because "stewardship" translates Paul's use of *oikonomia*, stewardship explicitly connects the creation mandates with New Testament ethics of discipleship.[22] That in turn situates creation care within the Gospels' invitation and Pauline exhortations, further characterizing stewardship by the general shape of a biblically formed life.[23] A theologian can go on to standardize dominion "based on the characterization of *dominium* that is expressed through the biblical witness as a whole and made explicit in the person of Jesus."[24]

The stewardship strategy thus sums up "dominion" in the incarnate way God cares for the world, reshaping it by the ways God's redemptive care claims human response through the Gospel invitations and New Testament discipleship. Keeping and cultivating the earth become fundamental practices of faith, respon-sive to God's fundamental action toward creation in Christ. The practical task for the stewardship strategy then consists in critiquing and reconstructing human freedom in active responsibility for the earth. Approaches often first subvert idolatrous or hegemonic assumptions about human sovereignty by reminding persons that God claims their lives for service and thanksgiving. Toward that end, they might present restorative environmental practices as an altar call for the renewal of faith.[25] They thus reconstruct human freedom through faithful models of environmental practice, specified by the norms of biblical formation.

The normative force for stewardship, therefore, comes not by nature's dignity but from the extrinsic command by which human acts are claimed. Earthkeeping responsibilities derive from God's will, appear as a divine command, and are performed for the sake of loving God. Or put more gently, "we care for God's creatures because it is the appropriate and proper response to God's providential care for us."[26] We care for the earth in grateful response to God's invitation to us. The stewardship strategy thus makes environmental issues significant in light of God's attitude toward human agents, situating environmental practices wholly within the exchange between God and humanity. God's action claims, guides, and measures right human action with regard to other creatures.

Environmental responsibilities therefore matter for Christian moral experience with respect to God's giving and forgiving—the grace of providence and the grace of redemption. "The principle of stewardship is closely linked to the concept of grace: everything comes from God as a gift and is to be adminis-tered faithfully on his behalf."[27] Faithful deputies must remember that, "the earth is the Lord's," received by humanity as a gift within the economy of God's giving. So humans receive creation as gift by receiving stewardship responsibilities for it, and they receive both in virtue of God's way of possessing—by giving, risking, and trusting.[28] Stewardship accounts for the household (the *oikos*) to its master, but in contrast to some secular uses of the term, it is "not a way of managing our possessions; it means rather that we care for what God has entrusted to us."[29] Its practices bear a special representative quality, modeling the character of God's economy.[30] "We image God as we are incorporated through grace and faith into the preservational dominion of God in the world . . . we mirror the sovereignty of the divine love in our stewardship of the earth."[31] As vice-regents or deputies, stewards may care for creation as agents of God's providence and managing participants in the divine economy, but the economy of Christ reveals God's way of ruling and giving. The redemptive action of Jesus Christ illuminates the significance of environmental problems and determines the character of Christian stewardship.[32]

Deputyship may place humans in the role of ancient Israel's sacral kings, but does so through the lens of Jesus. The covenantal role for human governors to mediate shalom (God's fulfilling peace) derives from the way Jesus brings peace to creation.[33] Christ perfects priestly and kingly vocations, fulfilling the covenant, reconciling creation to God, and opening a way for the faithful to participate in God's redemptive work. "Humans participate most fully in God's purposes for creation through personal appropriation of the benefits of Jesus Christ's life."[34] Keeping creation, in this strategy, means participating in Christ's redeeming work. Consequently, claim stewardship theologians, there can be no confession of Christ without care for creation.[35] Environmental stewardship is first and finally Christian discipleship.

Transforming the Secular Strategy

Distinguishing itself as a unique Christian strategy, stewardship at once follows and transforms the secular strategy of moral agency. It adopts key features of agency-focused environmental thought, especially its suspicion of appeals to nature's moral status. In chapter 2 we saw critics like William Cronon argue that we only know the natures our social practices construct, and that nature-focused forms of environmentalism distract us from the real problem: disordered social practices and perverse notions of freedom. Stewardship ethicists effectively argue that we only encounter the nature constructed in our encounter with God. And there God confronts humanity with its disordered practices and calls them into authentic freedom.

In pursuit of that pastoral strategy, stewardship theologians distance themselves from the ecojustice approach by sharpening the distinction between Creator and creation, thus weakening the ground for direct appeals to creation's integrity. As do the environmental constructionists, stewardship theologians worry that ethical appeals to nature's status smuggle in unjustified descriptions of nature. They worry that the ecojustice regard for nature's sacred character may import secular categories into Christian moral experience, thus threatening the ground of ethics in God's self-revelation and weakening the call to stewardship.[36] So develops the apparently odd phenomenon of stewardship ethicists refuting claims for creation's moral status out of concern for creation care. Starting from nature's intrinsic dignity, they worry, may not only introduce a distorting ethical rival to God's prior claim, it can obscure the way creation's moral status is constructed in the particular way God encounters creation. Within God's action toward the world and its claim on humanity, creation certainly has its moral dignity; but for stewardship that dignity is derivative. So this environmental strategy is normatively arrayed *against nature*, precisely in order to show how environmental issues matter within God's call to obedience.

Stewardship ethicists defend that call by maintaining a morally distinct boundary between humanity and other creatures, representing an ontologically distinct boundary between God and creation. "Man is to nature . . . as God is to man," wrote Passmore.[37] For although the ontological difference shows all creatures kin before God's eternal providence, God chooses human creatures to bear the *imago Dei*, living as representative and reminder of God's claim over all creation. Humans live that gift and charge in the exercise of their freedom. God encounters creation in a uniquely elective way, through the human vocation to fellowship with God.

When the 1990 WCC conference "Justice, Peace, and the Integrity of Creation" was led by ecojustice advocates to suggest that nonhuman creatures might also image the divine, some stewardship theologians voiced loud dismay. They feared that the suggestion jeopardized both key distinctions defended by their pastoral strategy—between God and creation and between humanity and nature. They worried it undercut the ground of a vocation to creation care.[38] Conservative Christian critics often charge secular environmentalism with confusing Creator and creation, thereby misplacing the moral authority that properly belongs alone to God.[39] Stewardship theologians protect the normative point of that accusation. Were nature to bear the image of God, then its forms and principles, orders and laws, would carry authority to form human action. Entertaining some divine valence to nature would disrupt the practical reason of stewardship, whose vocation to care is formed in God's redemptive encounter.

Because it preserves the priority of God's action for human freedom, stewardship must introduce environmental issues to Christian concern without dulling human responsiveness to God's command. It locates concern for nature, therefore, within obedience to God's call in order to let God's action determine the moral significance of nature. So while stewardship shares the constructivist suspicion of appeals to nature, it reconstructs nature by God's action in salvation.[40] Grace makes nature, in a sense. Or as Duane Barron puts it, "creation needs the church to show it what it means to be creation."[41] Christian environmental practices therefore testify to what God's saving ways make of creation. They witnesses to the way God has made the world the environment of God's action.

Stewardship therefore appears doubly insulated from any moral claim of nature: obedient stewards conform to God's will, not nature's orders, and Christians discover nature only by participating in God's act. Thoroughly referring stewardship practices to God's will helps overcome the secular strategy's difficulty of offering standards of accountability or evaluation.[42] But if stewardship achieves this by isolating moral deliberation from responsiveness to nature, it has to answer charges that this double insulation makes for a moral practice barren of earth. For not only do stewards conform to God's will rather than ecological science, they discover nature only in the encounter of faith. Does stewardship therefore repeat, if not exacerbate, the secular strategy's weak capacity to offer specific environmental indicators?

That question asks whether the natural world provides merely an arena for faithfulness or whether nature actively shapes obedience. Do stewardship practices enact biblical guidelines or are they shaped by ecological principles?[43] Ethicists try to refuse that dilemma with the rejoinder that they are responsible to both "books" of revelation, Bible and nature (as Dewitt says), so that good stewardship requires a biocentric environmental sensitivity (as Attfield says).[44] Biblical stewardship (say Reichenbach and Anderson) entails preserving the conditions for nature's integrity, stability, and beauty.[45]

But the rejoinder is not as easy as it would seem, for the question forces a strategic dilemma: either stewardship is shaped by nature and so, despite its contrary rhetoric, really develops by the same practical logic as ecojustice, or it is not, and God's call generates environmental practices without regard to environmental feedback.[46] Put practically: to which book do we look first to understand what integrity and beauty mean? Or "individual, community, and biospheric sustainability"?[47] Calls to stewardship often list environmental degradations and recognize natural principles; what makes those appeals ethically coherent as part of God's call? How much normative weight do scientific reports and ecological experience bear for interpreting God's deputyship? Do natural limits and earthly norms form stewardship, and which ones?[48]

Models of Redemption

To answer those questions, stewardship approaches turn to their background theological model. If stewardship theologians think that God's encounter with the world constructs nature, then to show how nature shapes earthcare they must turn to where and how God encounters. And the central moment of God's encounter occurs in the redemptive event of Jesus Christ. Christ reveals the specific form of God's claim on humanity, constructing both the arena of creation and the corresponding pattern of good stewardship.[49] So the pattern of redemption guides interpretation of nature's role within God's command. However, stewardship theologies appropriate the work of Christ in various and sometimes conflicting ways.

One way emphasizes Christ's redemption and vindication of the *imago Dei* in humans. If exploitation represents a refusal of God's gifts and despotism a rebellion against God's rule, then environmental problems are problems of personal sin. Environmental degradation follows from the corruption of God's image in humanity. "It follows that the re-establishment of a proper relationship between humankind and creation depends upon the redemption of that image."[50] By redeeming and restoring humanity, God redeems and restores creation. On this, says Oliver O'Donovan, hangs the project of any fully Christian environmental ethic.[51]

A second way offers a more visible connection to the biblical Jesus by connecting his life and teachings to the stewardship narratives in Genesis.[52] While the New Testament offers few specific ecological guidelines, by connecting human redemption to the Genesis vocation, or Jesus to the Deuteronomic Jubilee years, a stewardship theology can claim that the New Testament's "central message . . . presents a pervasive stewardship calling to all who are redeemed."[53] Stewardship ethicists often lament how frequently discussion of the Genesis narratives takes place without reference to New Testament exegesis—as if Christians could make sense of the Garden directives apart from their fulfillment in Christ.[54]

A third way connects earthkeeping practices to Christ's resurrection victory over forces of chaos and evil in creation. In this case, Christ invites human into obedience in order to participate in God's triumph over anticreation forces.[55] "Because we share in Christ's resurrection righteousness, we are responsible for the care of creation."[56] So earthcare takes up the vocation to witness to and perhaps participate in God's universal reconciliation. A variation on this third way might present Christian earthkeeping as a performative witness to the good news of Jesus. That witness might appropriate and adapt Hebrew land practices in order to show how Christian practices tell the story of Jesus fulfilling the Old Covenant. Or earthkeeping practices might proclaim that "our care for creation is ultimately a witness to Jesus Christ" by enacting humanity's victory in redemption.[57]

In sum, stewardship appropriates the work of Christ in three distinct moments of redeeming grace: (1) Christ calling the Christian to and freeing her for earthly service; (2) responsive discipleship modeled on the pattern of Christ's work; and (3) witnessing participation in Christ's salvific act. The moments become progressively controversial and difficult for answering those questions about the role of environmental sciences for shaping stewardship.

Most stewardship theologies join with DeWitt in proclaiming the "forgiveness that permits joyful service in doing God's work in the world,"[58] or Emmerich in affirming "Christ's power to change the lives of men and women involved in environmental conflict."[59] Environmentally exploitative practices are an outward and visible sign of personal sin; the Word judges that sin, calls humans to repentance, and offers freedom from its bondage.[60] Through the blood of Jesus, the Christian comes back to earth: "restored humanity's proper habitat is earth."[61] In sin, humans live in a shadowy netherworld, the barren landscape of egoism; by grace, they come back home.

David Cassel shows how this first redemptive rationale can legitimate scientific attentiveness. If "stewardship is experiencing and expressing the nurturing aspects of God," then it inevitably moves outward toward others, even nonhuman others. Grounded and shaped by "intimate personal experience of the nurturing aspects of God," the care of stewardship requires loving attentiveness to ecological others, knowing and understanding them in their own integrity.[62] The redemptive experience of God's way of relating to creation on human terms orients stewardship to relate to the rest of creation on its terms.

Difficulties begin to arise in the second moment. Responding to charges that deputyship licenses exploitative dominion, stewardship ethicists respond by modeling the human mandate to govern creation after the pattern of Christ's rule. The lordship of Jesus, after all, characterizes dominion as self-giving service, nothing at all like willful hegemony. Stewards therefore follow in the way of the One who in obedience to the will of God humbled himself into the form of a servant, even unto death.[63] Would-be dominators must become good shepherds and suffering servants—a transformation only possible "because of the sacrament of Christ, which is both a pattern for action and a power enabling us to carry it out."[64]

But patterning stewardship after the form of Jesus radicalizes the figure toward something much more than a responsible trustee of another's concern or mere caretaker of earth's household.[65] Jesus, after all, gives his life for the sake of others, and while knowing and caring for nature may have its sacrificial aspects, most stewardship ethicists do not ask humans to give their lives over for the sake of the earth, but usually call them to prudent self-limitation in view of balanced environmental dwelling.[66] That stewardship ethicists hardly ever mention the growing number of Christian leaders martyred for environmental causes (such as Dorothy Stang in Brazil or Nerelito Satur in the Philippines) suggests they do not quite have in mind Christ's vicarious suffering when they talk of "redeeming nature."[67] Whereas Christ's servant-action moves toward humans, suffering on their behalf, stewardship usually means moving toward God by living with nature in faithful care. Is nature really the one loved and served?

Richard Wright suggests that not Christ's passion but Christ's peacemaking offers the appropriate model for how the steward cleaves closely to earth. Appealing to the kingly mediation of shalom, Wright says God asks the steward neither to dispassionately manage a property trust nor to love nature as a neighbor, but to work in God's cause for a peaceable kingdom. And cultivating the kingdom requires specific local expertise: "God calls us to participate in the redemption of the world. . . . To carry out this task, we need normative information—we must have firm knowledge of the workings of natural ecosystems and the ways that human activities interact with those systems (ecological and environmental science)."[68]

Stewardship in the pattern of Jesus thus brings positive environmental specifications into view, and sets Christians into responsive moral relationships with their natural environment.[69] Because God "sent his Son to redeem his fallen creatures and restore creation's goodness," the stewards of God must attend to that goodness, preserving, sustaining, and nurturing it.[70] As O'Donovan shows, precisely because stewardship theology organizes itself around the form of Christ's agency, it illuminates an ordered moral field for human action. "If the gospel tells of agents rendered free before the reality of a redeemed universe, then the form which their agency assumes will correspond both to the intelligible order which they confront and to the freedom in which they act."[71] The pattern of Christ's act sets Christians into attentive, responsive relationship with earth, as grace "forms and brings to expression the appropriate pattern of free response to objective reality."[72]

But which order and which environmental science does stewardship follow?[73] Perhaps an apt witness to the nurturing responsiveness of stewardship comes from the reflections of careful farmers.[74] Fred and Janet Kirschenmann, who raise organic grains in North Dakota, observe that the Genesis responsibilities "to service and take care" of the earth involve long-term attachments to a small plots. The wisdom to cultivate creation's goodness comes slowly, over generations of working with a place.[75] Richard Thompson, who believed "that

God would teach me how to farm" and turned to the Bible to find out, felt called by the Spirit away from chemicals toward more natural ways of farming. His "biblically based" farming techniques now require understanding his land and animals much better.[76] Wendell Berry, from the Kentucky hills, writes that stewardship as a form of love means knowing how to "use knowledge and tools in a particular place with good long-term results."[77] Larry and Carolyn Olson, small-scale Minnesota farmers, say that faithful land care means learning its soil by "asking a lot of questions and being close to the earth."[78]

In each case, fidelity to Christ's gift of grace entails fidelity to the land, worked out in practical, prudent, appropriately scaled labor.[79] For these farmer-theologians, government policies and economic practices that bring about the end of family farming undo the social conditions that support and empower environmental care. Cleared of "surplus" farmers and their scaled, attentive stewardship, despotic and destructive practices of industrial agriculture take over the land.[80] That supposed surplus watches over the land, embodying grace by maintaining love's knowledge of earth in the skilled, responsive practices of nurturing a particular place.[81]

By conceiving stewardship as a dialogical relationship between steward and land, these farmers move us toward the third moment of redemption, where Christ's salvific work addresses the intrinsic goodness of all creation. Berry suggests God takes an active pleasure in the earth: "Our responsibility, then, as stewards, the responsibility that inescapably goes with our dominion over the other creatures . . . is to safeguard God's pleasure in His work."[82] God's love for all the earth indicates its own dignity and integrity. Susan Bratton thinks that the pattern of Christ's love opens stewardship up to consider how grace engages all creation: "In implementing the stewardship model, we often see ourselves primarily as farmers tending crops or as foresters preventing forest erosion, and thereby avoid the deeper implications," but "agape requires that other creatures and the Earth be free to fulfill their own relationship with God."[83]

Redeeming Nature?

That divine interest in all creation centers in the third redemptive moment. "Redemption in Jesus Christ," in this moment, "extends to the entire household of life with God embracing all creatures."[84] What does the universal scope of Christ's salvific act mean for stewardship? How does earthkeeping participate in the new creation? While most stewardship ethicists appeal to cosmic dimensions of salvation, they do so in strikingly discordant poses.[85] In perhaps the standard position, Ronald Manahan argues that since the effects of sin are cosmic, and the effects of Christ's obedience perfectly extensive, then those "who stand in the obedience of Christ have the most profound reason for practicing caring relationships and stewardship."[86] Inhabiting the reconciliation accomplished by Christ, human relations with all creatures are restored and redeemed. When Christ sets the captives free, he frees them to restorative service in a land damaged by sin. The Christian mission to all the earth means becoming physician and healer to the earth, priests and ministers to all creation.[87]

But what does that mean practically for nature? For some it means "recovering the creative rule that God intended people to exercise toward the natural order."[88] But for others, environmental practices model a new order, the rule of the Kingdom, and thus, at least proleptically, initiate the universal shalom of a new earth. In this case, stewardship redemptively transforms nature, efficaciously realizing Christ's restoration of all things.[89] But how does that redemptive order compare to present ecological principles: does stewardship aim to establish the Kingdom's shalom or to, say, manage for healthy patterns of predation? The question that troubled the ecojustice strategy arises here again: wolves pacified in zoos or wolves chasing rabbits?

Stewardship theologians respond to those questions according to how extensively they think sin has corrupted nature. Is nature redeemed only from human degradations, or is it itself disfigured, in need of redemptive therapy? Holmes Rolston thinks nature mainly needs relief from human pressures.[90] But Calvin Beisner thinks nature suffers degenerately from the curse of sin, and thus requires intensive human control to contain its evil effects, and perhaps thereby redeem it.[91] Ronald Cole-Turner picks up that connection of dominion and redemption, arguing that the healing miracles show how Jesus "intervened redemptively in nature to bring it into greater conformity with God's intentions." Human power should strive to image God in nature ever more intensively. So the "purpose of genetic engineering is to expand our ability to participate in God's work of redemption and creation."[92]

Perhaps leery of technomorphic views of redemption and concerned to maintain creation's goodness, some ethicists prefer to consider earthkeeping merely "token acts" gesturing toward the world's eschatological salvation.[93] Stewardship practices then materially promise a transfiguration barely glimpsed and only imaginatively conceived. But that starts to distance human practices (like farming) from the interest and pleasure God's work seems to take in the earth itself. So others, wishing to retain the salvific character of attentive, particularist environmental practices, argue that ecologically savvy stewardship actively engages and transforms nature for its own sake.[94] "Humans are to become saviours of nature," proclaims Loren Wilkinson, calling for Christian practices to engage the environmental problems. In the work of Christ, God's image-bearers become agents of redemption. For Wilkinson, reaching beyond the usual scope of evangelical theology, good stewards mediate nature's deification.

Remember that the chief criticism of stewardship charges that it provides religious justification for anthropocentric domination. If stewardship finally means redeeming nature, it will be only more vulnerable to that critique. For if the response to the problem of power-sick, arrogant human practices is divinely powerful human practices, the therapy seems a worse poison. Despotic exploitation easily justifies itself as salvific.

To answer that critique, stewardship must explicate the relation of redemption to nature, perhaps restricting itself to the first two moments. But the very fact of several competing models of redemption presents a still more difficult problem. Since stewardship forms around God's saving act, this soteriological diversity troubles the pastoral strategy as a whole, for it suggests such discordant practical models.[95] Do stewards gratefully keep God's pleasure garden, or redeem the fallen world, or guard God's earth from harm, or transform nature into a new earth? Internal uncertainty over how nature participates in Christ's work suggests disagreement over what earthkeeping looks like. In order to resolve that uncertainty the strategy needs to decide how redeeming grace shows what good stewardship works for the earth. For by explaining what grace makes of nature, stewardship will know what to make of natural indicators, and which ones matter for shaping good environmental practices.[96]

Recall how critics complain that the secular strategy of moral agency loses the ability to let the natural world shape moral practices, leaving environmental responses serially vulnerable to cultural caprice. Stewardship is a remarkably malleable concept, claimed by those defending industrial agriculture and those impugning it, those in favor the Endangered Species Act and those against it. A successful stewardship theology has to do better, then, than list environmental problems and invoke biblical curses against earth's destroyers. It must specify the soteriological relation between obeying God's call and God's relationship to the natural world. If earth is the environment of God's action, stewards need to know what God's action means for the earth, so that they can know how the earth should shape their own actions in response.

Both Jürgen Moltmann and Michael Northcott, writing in evaluation of the "Evangelical Declaration," criticize stewardship theologies for disconnecting environmental practices from Christian spirituality by failing to show nature's own significance for God.[97] Oliver O'Donovan fears the management ethos of stewardship may dull the gracious awe by which nature humbles humans before God.[98] Together their complaints imply that without an account of nature's relation to God, earthkeeping remains unaccountable to the manifold flourishing of earth's creatures and vulnerable to bad anthropocentrisms. The challenge for stewardship theology lies in finding resources in its overarching view of grace to detail the moral significance of nature while recognizing the presence of sin and the promise of the world's transformation. How can a redemption-shaped ethic let nature shape human responsibility?

The Environment of Jesus: From Anabaptists to Barth

We have seen that for the strategy of stewardship to secure environmental ethics within the claim of Jesus Christ, it must articulate nature's moral significance from within faithful discipleship. To do so it requires some theological account of how following Jesus involves responding to one's environment, without forgetting creation's travail or its future hope. The peacemaking agricultural traditions of Anabaptist communities may offer suggestions for how to do that. For these communities morally organize themselves around the kingdom orders of Christ, yet have historically worked in close responsiveness to their land.[99] They are, then, particularly well situated to defend a "profound linkage between 'the good news of Jesus Christ' and the questions we now ask about our environment."[100] Because "this heritage has always believed that God has been concerned with the formation of a 'People' who would fulfill God's wishes on earth," its theology already connects God's particular call to humans and creation's destiny.[101] At the same time, "Amish and Mennonite closeness to the land leads to a theology that arises from daily life practices," thus keeping stewardship theology close to the soil of practical questions.[102]

Anabaptist theology, historically formed in persecuted communities, keenly appreciates worldly evil and intensely anticipates a new creation. That sensibility to violence and eschatological disposition might manifest in an otherworldly dualism were it not expressed within Christian communal practices understood as "the process that brings everything under the radical living lordship of Jesus Christ."[103] Testifying to the new kingdom established in the work of Christ, lived theologies from Anabaptist communities give witness to the way Christ's act saves the world from sin, futility, and violence.[104] Historically suspicious of dominant economic and technological orders, working from a social legacy of political peacemaking and holistic development, and within communities still known worldwide for recuperating marginal lands, Anabaptist theologies bear promise for depicting how all creation participates in Christian obedience to Christ.[105]

By showing how living out Christ's call to kingdom illuminates the world as the environment of Jesus, Anabaptist theology suggests how a stewardship strategy might incorporate aspects of covenantal theology without abandoning its primary focus on redemption. The faith relationship between humanity and God remains primary, but as "the context in which faithfulness to God is expressed," nature in turn shapes the faithful living of a particular people in a particular place.[106] For some of these agro-theological communities, planting the seeds of the kingdom of God means cultivating the actual soil of living places. So even though there is almost "no preference to the preservation of the earth in Mennonite theology, Mennonite practice has tended in that direction," working out sustainable, even gentle, environmental practices guided by the lordship of Jesus Christ.[107]

The Anabaptist/Mennonite legacy suggests that redemptionist soteriology, even accompanied by strong senses of worldly evil, need not dislocate humanity from nature. Quite the contrary, it suggests there may be a way to come through faith in Jesus to more sensitive intimacy with the earth. In fact, concern for the way sin denies createdness, along with its commission to extend Christ's peace to all creation, "suggests an Anabaptist environmental theology of salvation, including a green Christology."[108]

In order to explore the promise of those Anabaptist suggestions for the strategy of stewardship, especially the connection of grace and place, I turn to Karl Barth in chapters 8 and 9. Stewardship theologies claim that redemption brings environmental issues under Christ's lordship. Barth's thoroughgoing commitment to the priority of God's act in Jesus Christ provides a doctrinal arena in which to test just how God's action toward humanity in Jesus Christ shapes stewardship practices, and if it in fact orients them to the earth. How might the pattern of redemption restore the earth to human care?

5

The Strategy of Ecological Spirituality

Recall how a strategy of ecological anthropology organizes environmental problems within an expanded view of personhood. A distinct Christian strategy follows suit, framing environmental issues within theological anthropology. Like the secular strategy, it wants to answer the practical questions of the other two strategies by looking to their unity within humanity: "What is the value of 'this world'? How does God will humans to act in relation to the material creation? Underlying these questions is a central concern of theological anthropology: what is the place of humans, as both physical and spiritual creatures, in the created world?"[1]

Theological variety proliferates within what I call the "strategy of ecological spirituality," but its approaches share a common practical rationale: each makes environmental issues matter for Christian experience by appealing to the ecological dimensions of fully Christian personhood. Underlying creation's integrity and faithful stewardship (the other two strategies), say theorists, there is a radical relation of personhood and environment. Environmental lament and redress begin from a primary spiritual communion of humanity and earth, assumed into personal experience with God.[2]

As they describe how grace can heal that communion, restoring ecological dimensions to personhood as humans become closer to God, approaches within this strategy draw on a background pattern of grace as deification. For the strategy illuminates the way of the world into divine participation, as it describes the cosmic significance of personal communion. Used more and less intensively, the deification pattern shapes multiple theologies that deploy cosmology and anthropology to diagnose and practically address environmental issues.

Formal Emergence

Laurel Kearns has shown how "creation spirituality" became a publicly visible Christian environmentalism exhibiting the practical reason of a new cosmic anthropology.[3] This chapter argues that a number of other Christian environmental theologies, some of which would disavow common association, operate according to a similar normative form. Many Eastern Orthodox would chafe at being lumped in common cause with Matthew Fox's creation spirituality, while many in that movement would think immature the unapologetic anthropocentrism of environmental justice advocates. This chapter finds a shared contour and maps the diversity along a shared practical logic: across fundamental theological disagreements we nevertheless find a common strategy for introducing environmental issues to Christian concern.[4]

The diversity of this strategy resists tracing that map historically, but two events in the United States in the 1980's do illustrate how this third form of theological reason distinguishes itself from the other two strategies. During the same period that ecojustice and stewardship developed formally separate frameworks, several Christian environmental groups found that their practical theologies conformed to neither of those two strategies.

Environmental Justice

The Christian environmental justice movement often charts its beginnings from the 1980s involvement of the United Church of Christ's (UCC) Commission on Racial Justice in a predominately black North Carolina county consistently designated for toxic waste disposal. That led to the UCC's 1987 report "Toxic Wastes and Race in the United States," which decried racist distribution of environmental hazards nationwide. The report signaled environmental injustice as a new arena for Christian social witness. As Emilie Townes puts it, the toxic exposures report revealed "contemporary versions of lynching a whole people."[5] Now recognizing ecological dimensions of civil rights and justice, a church coalition publicly reprimanded mainline American environmentalism for racist, elitist agendas, and helped galvanize a National People of Color Environmental Leadership Summit.[6]

Observers often treat environmental justice as a parochial companion to ecojustice, a member of the same ethical strategy, only more anthropocentric in its focus on social justice.[7] However, while the movement was welcomed by many ecojustice advocates, the racial justice events of the 1980s did more than add human dimensions to ongoing reflection on creation's integrity. By tracing racist and sexist logics of domination, environmental justice laid open the way to an entirely distinct practical strategy.[8] Consider the way unjust distribution of toxic hazards led Thomas Hoyt to reflect on Jesus absorbing the suffering of the marginalized: "God thus united with the whole biophysical universe, which is micro-embodied in humans. . . . Humans are of the earth, interdependent parts of nature—and this totality is what God associated with in the incarnation."[9] Showing fundamental human vulnerabilities to creation, environmental justice points to a theological strategy that narrates grace within an embodied human intimacy with creation. By pointing to disembodiments of the self from social community and from the earth, environmental justice summons re-embodiments of self, earth, and God. The response, says Karen Baker-Fletcher, means "to become part of the body of God," redemptively re-embodying an interrelational human self through creative political actions that "participate in God's creation of a new heaven and a new earth."[10]

If we do not move beyond strategies that treat humanity and nature separately, says George Tinker, "we have not yet begun to deal with ecojustice, let alone ethno-ecojustice and racism, as a systemic whole, as a system of oppression rooted in structures of power that touch every part of our lives."[11] The environmental justice movement thus traces ecological disruptions of human dignity to nondualist, nonindividualist, ecologically-relational concepts of human personhood. "The yoking of civil and environmental rights is crucial to ontological wholeness," writes Townes, because they counter serially related lynchings with a spirituality of social and ecological wholeness.[12]

Consider, moreover, how the meager justice of protecting the bare survival of indigenous groups often de facto protects a participative mode of being human within an animate cosmos. Protecting their culture's habitat for the sake of political justice protects a form of ecological culture that makes other environmental strategies look less holistic, even cosmologically impoverished. Environmental justice thus focuses centrally on human personhood in order to show essential relations between environmental quality and human dignity. If they can, gospel imperatives to interpersonal justice and love must then address ecological integrity.[13] Here, nature arrives into moral concern through the environmental dependency of human personhood, and moral norms are shaped according to the mode of that dependency.[14] So while it usually affirms creation's intrinsic goodness, environmental justice keeps that goodness in close association with human dignity.

Environmental justice does not, therefore, produce an anthropocentric version of the ecojustice strategy; rather, its anthropocentrism serves a different pastoral strategy altogether, in which the structure of human personhood illuminates environmental problems and guides Christian response to them. By theologically qualifying that association, environmental justice advocates treat creation's integrity and human dignity as essentially related moral concerns and nonrivalrous moral interests. That practical strategy evinces similarities to creation spirituality, which otherwise might seem socially and ideologically distant.[15]

Creation Spirituality

Around the same time that Christian environmental justice began to distinguish its own theological agenda, "creation spirituality" publicly broke with stewardship and ecojustice environmentalisms. Although its themes had been circulating for at least a decade, a divisive 1987 meeting of the North American Conference on Christianity and Ecology (NACCE) punctuated the coalescence of those themes into a distinct theological strategy. When advocates of creation spirituality complained that conference statements were insufficiently cosmocentric, conference participants were forced to acknowledge significantly different forms of environmental theology under their tent. The broad coalition fractured.[16] Immediately afterward, those of a cosmological bent formed the North American Conference on Religion and Ecology (NACRE).[17] By 1993 the Evangelical Environmental Network had formed itself around stewardship theology, and today the NACCE exhibits predominately ecojustice discourse.[18]

Observers sometimes read the 1987 split as rancor amidst religious conservatives, revisionists, and moderates. But, as Kearns's work implicitly suggests, that reading obscures the way the conference split along strategic fractures, moving away from each other in order to develop distinct practical rationalities.[19] Consider the diagnostic importance of the ambiguous Eastern Orthodox response.[20] Orthodox representatives were reportedly quite upset with the revisionary bent of creation spirituality advocates, yet did not align themselves with either "conservative" stewardship or "moderate" ecojustice factions.[21] That is likely because Orthodox theology often shares the strategic rationale of creation spirituality while maintaining conservative theological methods.[22]

Creation spirituality sometimes presents itself as a "liberation theology for the so-called 'First-World' peoples."[23] Reconceptualizing subjectivity and spirituality within a cosmic story, creation spirituality reclaims nature for alienated human individuals. Humans discover their earthly place by first rediscovering their own inward cosmic orientation, and, with it, the inner mysteries of the cosmos itself. Hence Thomas Berry: "We bear the universe in our beings as the universe bears us in its being. The two have a total presence to each other and to that deeper mystery out of which both the universe and ourselves have emerged."[24] Displaying both anthropocentric and ecocentric indicators, creation spirituality confounds those who would typecast it one way or the other.

As we saw in environmental justice and will soon see in Orthodox theologies, creation spirituality refuses to begin from nature or human practice in prior isolation, and instead addresses their alienation within human personhood as the root of environmental problems. The common creation story and the story of Jesus reveal the same sacred thing: human persons are a living cosmology, active manifestations of the world's communion. "In creation spirituality God has been speaking the truth since the beginning of time. . . . We're just the lucky ones who have come along now in a moment of time to bring it to consciousness, to give a word to it: Jesus."[25] Discovering in the cosmic Christ "the interconnectivity of all things and . . . the power of the human mind and spirit to experience personally this common glue," humans find themselves at once cast in solidarity with all things and uniquely empowered to creatively realize that relationality.[26]

"There can be no anthropology without cosmology," says Matthew Fox; "We are of galactic size."[27] So also the converse: no cosmology apart from the macro-anthropos, the one Berry calls "that being in whom the universe in its evolutionary dimension became conscious of itself."[28] Humanity understands itself and the universe by the mode of their communion. Hence the emphasis of creation spirituality on personal creativity, in which human activity personalizes the cosmic story. Just as the innovative work of Christ gathers into one person the story of the cosmos, so too does human labor bring the cosmos to unified expression. "The living cosmology ushered in by the Cosmic Christ will do more than redeem creativity itself; it will propose creativity . . . as the most important moral virtue of the upcoming civilization."[29]

Creativity lies at the heart of creation spirituality because it names a dynamism shared by creation generally and humanity peculiarly, and, in the movement of creation toward self-realization, the mode of their communion. Personal creativity bears the promise of universal healing, seen in the figure of the cosmic Christ, who binds all things together in his own healing creativity. Living in the way of the cosmic Christ's transfiguration, humans "recover their role as instruments of the New Creation, agents of justice and transformation in a salvific history of renewal and rebirth."[30]

That makes the liberation of human freedom also the liberation for which the earth groans, toward which it already moves. As the cosmic Christ restores human creativity into intimacy with the earth's, God's grace comes by way of the story of creation's grace. Hearing and telling God's story in the universe, in other words, requires knowing nature through freedom, creativity, and celebration—conscious participations in mystery.[31] The new creation of God happens within distinctively human ecstasies: "the wolf and lamb *in us* lie down together," "*in ourselves* [we] find the Cosmic Christ and [we] find a life that binds all things together."[32] Human creativity realizes the meaning of the cosmos, manifests the work of the cosmic Christ; within our own selves we discover "our immense responsibility for the universe."[33]

Transforming the Secular Strategy

Critics complain that creation spirituality elides value differences within creation and a real distinction between humanity and nature. Creation spirituality, they say, steps lightly around nature's suffering and death by setting human creativity in counterpoint to evolution—creativity as cosmodicy. This suggests that creation spirituality's creep toward cosmic monism might really be a creeping hominization, subsuming nature into a triumphant anthropology.[34] In chapter 2 we saw similar critiques leveled at deep ecology and other approaches within the strategy of ecological subjectivity.

However, creation spirituality uses theological resources in a way that significantly transforms the secular strategy. By correlating Christian narrative with the cosmic story, creation spirituality deflects charges of monism and retrenched anthropocentrism by qualifying human creativity with a wider notion of grace. Ecological communion takes after its foundational type: God's communion with creation. Two subtle soteriological differences thus work in harmony to preserve creation spirituality from dissolving ontological distinctions. As human creativity actualizes cosmic union with God by participating in grace, the pattern of grace holds human and cosmic creativity in an elevating tension, itself sustained by the difference of creaturely and divine creativity. In other words, the structure of ecological personhood follows some logic of divine participation. And, despite creation spirituality's revisionary claims, those are ancient Christian logics.

Creation spirituality thus invites theological investigation into the relation of grace and creativity for understanding its broader environmental strategy. Whereas the precise mode of relation between ecology and anthropology seems tenuous in the secular strategy, creation spirituality illuminates a soteriological way to specify the relation: by developing creativity as simultaneous reception of grace and expression of nature. In order to test the promise of the strategy of ecological spirituality, therefore, we need to explore how ecological creativity matters for divine participation.

Sacramental Ecology

Sacramental theologies conduct that investigation by considering worship as paradigm and paideutic for creativity, in several ways.[35] They might appeal to the implicit lessons of ecclesial rites, which guide earthly living by enacting good creativity, and shaping Christian experience and desire accordingly. Kevin Irwin, for example, argues that performed liturgies reclaim our attention to the significance of creation, "to how creation offers motives for praising God, to how creation itself is a demonstration of the divine in human life." For Irwin, the very event of church reminds humans of the cosmic promise of salvation and implicitly resists environmental degradation for the sake of worship's symbolic integrity.[36] Liturgies might dramatize the coordinate role of nature and human labor, admonish all other labor by its example, and thus open Christian spirituality to the voice of creation within God's material presence for humanity.[37]

For others, the shape of the liturgy maps the world of faith and the human place within it. Gordon Lathrop describes what happens in worship as the "ongoing reorientation of the self within the reorientations of biblical and liturgical cosmology." It habituates humans into a practical worldview, "the walking on the ground that goes with this communal reorientation."[38] In a similar way, John Habgood takes notice of how sacraments function as "both a revelation and a transformation," revealing the fundamental character of reality and conforming human perception to it.[39] Sacramental use of creation at once respects its integrity and imaginatively invites the whole world into praise. Inventiveness cooperates with divine love, so that sacramental humans "share a role with God in drawing out the divine potential of the world."[40] For Habgood, liturgical creativity thus redeems the world for Christian perception, that it may reveal the face of God.

Mary Grey seems to have something similar in mind:

> A sacramental poetics is about transformation, the transforming of everyday perception and experience into something that satisfies the deepest longings. . . . By appealing to the basic realities in our lives, bread, water, oil, salt, earth, trees, in word and symbol, prayer and gesture, it wakens a depth dimension and an experience of the sacred. Sacramental poetics has the potential to reenchant a broken-hearted world.[41]

However, if the mysteries of the world rely on human creativity, they assume a certain risk.[42] "Creativity, the essence of sacramental poetic," says Grey, "hovers between the ambiguity of chaos, with all its elements of risk, surprise, excess, threat, and terror, and Divine Mystery in all its beauty and tragedy."[43] Consider the surprising kinds of transfigurations Habgood entertains: "An engineer may see a valley as waiting to be dammed, a chasm as waiting to be bridged, an ugly and unhealthy swamp as potentially a place of beauty and usefulness. Such actions can in their own way become secular sacraments, an enhancement, a liberation of what is already there."[44] How are we to know when those dams liberate a valley's sacred beauty and when they threaten it with human excess?

Without normative specification, appeals to sacramental creativity seem only to open further narrative contests. In response to that problem, Charles Murphy guides sacramental creativity according to respect for nature's integrity. Since Catholic sacramental theology insists grace never threatens nature but only perfects it, so too must human action follow nature's integrity. That requires confidently knowing nature, however, and for Murphy, humans apprehend nature's integrity through a prior moment of creative dominion. Humans come to know earth rightly as they subdue the land.[45]

On that account, creativity can remain dangerously isomorphic with distorted human desires and thus capriciously responsive to the earth's own dynamism.[46] Lathrop's Lutheran sensibilities alert him to the danger of perverse appropriations of grace, and he presents his liturgical cosmology as a subversive proposal for living in a cosmology dominated and distorted by market creativities. He argues that sacramental formation creates a critical dissonance that could open Christian communities to dialogue with indigenous cosmologies, whose practical creativities often better fit Christian parables of cosmic personhood than the modernist discipline of innovation by economy.[47]

Murphy and Lathrop show us that if the strategy of ecological spirituality would fully transform the secular strategy, it needs a theology of creativity that can articulate the communion of earth and humanity within personhood. How do the practical exercises of participating in the divine nature involve participating in earthly natures?

Cosmic Creativity

We can find theological forms of creativity, suggests Jeffrey Pugh, by looking to how the communion of grace is reciprocally shaped by the communion of creaturely becoming.[48] Christian creativity not only discloses the world as sacred but already presumes what John Haught calls a "deep trust in reality itself."[49] Both Haught and Pugh praise process thought for the way it recovers humanity's immersion in a world of dynamic creaturely relations. With nature itself in expressively creative movement and God respondent to that movement, process theology extends Christianity's pilgrimage metaphors to the whole world. Rather than isolated sojourners through an alien world, humans join the pilgrimage of all creation as it overcomes its alienation from the future. On this view, humans may embody creation's history and actively fulfill its future.[50] As persons constituted by the creativity of both God and creation, humans bind all three modes of action into their triadic co-creativity.[51]

So habituated in orientation to the future and responsive to the strivings of all creatures, human creativity opens a central strategic question: "Once the cosmos becomes the mediating context of all theological and spiritual experience, how does this change our understanding of both 'God' and 'humans'?"[52] Practical environmental reason may then require some new theological anthropology, agrees Gordon Kauffman: "If God is understood as the creativity manifest throughout the cosmos, and humans are understood as deeply embedded in and basically sustained by life on planet Earth, we will be strongly encouraged to . . . fit properly into this web of living creativity."[53] By naming God with creativity, Kauffman looks for a way to inflect personhood by a deeper sense of creativity. Specifically, he wants to renovate "reciprocity between consciousness and the world systems in which we live and move and have our being."[54]

These theologians suggest that properly ecological creativity, and with it a holistic personhood, seeks no originary genius of its own, but forms within responsive, dialogical relations with nature. Practical reason, agrees Catherine Keller, "now demands of us planetary practices which find 'face' across the width of the world." If they do not, "our strategies can run shallow. . . . The ethical remains high, dry, and perilously utopic, if not accompanied by a messier therapy: the healing of the systemic repression that I am calling tehomophobia."[55] This fear of earth's personalizing generativity, says Keller, distracts humans in psychotic imaginations of creativity as monadic inventiveness, the voluntarist genius of "ex nihilo." But in earth's embrace we dwell by syncopated accompaniment to a world of creative proposals and contingent occurrences, emergent from divine play amidst earth's own.[56]

Keller's querulously inventive wordplay connotes a creativity more textual than terrestrial; writing seems her overarching model of creation. But Anne Primavesi's similar account ushers earth's creativity more fully into view, while also modeling theory-writing after its logic. Primavesi's fundamental concept for creation is auto-poiesis, by which she means the way all beings participate in creation making itself. Our notions of divine and human acts must "adapt to, take risks with and, ultimately, relate reciprocally to emergent forms within a changing world." Human creativity has therefore a "dual fidelity," to life as it is and as it might be, to the world's present and its future.[57] Creativity moves in "mimetic poiesis," as humans respond to ecological systems by means of dynamic practices that themselves represent the emerging complexity of nature.[58] So creativity conforms to nature's complexifying self-transcendence.

Divinizing Nature?

The strategists of ecological spirituality have at this point naturalized creativity by binding it, etiologically and mimetically, to its evolutionary habitat. Now we ask what feedback effect that human creativity has on the rest of creation. For by making poiesis fundamental to human personhood just as they ecologically habituate it, these theologians associate nature's own agencies with humanity's divine participation, and thus both with God's action in creation. In the strategy of ecological spirituality, the theological figure of human freedom describes three modes of creativity coming together.

That may explain why we find surprisingly strong salvific metaphors from theorists advocating conformity to nature. After calling for responsive, dialogical relations with nature, Ruether says: "Our final mandate is to redeem our sister, the earth, from her bondage to destruction, recognizing her as our partner in the creation of that new world where all things can be 'very good.'"[59] After invoking his "deep trust in reality," Haught lets the earth's "embodiment of promise" require transformative human agency "to reshape the world . . . so that it will come into conformity with what it takes to be God's vision of the future."[60] Philip Hefner, pleading for theological adaptation to ecological place, calls us to enhance nature, "devoting ourselves to its care and redemption . . . pouring our resources into the same effort into which God has poured the divine resources."[61] In her essay rooting personhood in reembodied, ecological epistemology, Ivone Gebara encourages humans toward "becoming creators of ourselves and of the entire living world."[62] Living into this world fully, we "make the presence of God a reality in it," which, Pugh says, amounts to divinization.[63]

Just as they enfold human activity in nature's own agency, these theologians invoke the most dramatic soteriological metaphors—redeeming, reshaping, recreating, perfecting, divinizing. It seems paradoxical: in theologies of the deepest ecological concourse humans assume a typologically divine role vis-à-vis nature. Even as their creativity conforms to nature, humans assume and actualize nature's participation in divinity. Ecologizing creativity somehow elicits closer associations of human agency with the transformative verbs of grace.[64]

These theologians need, then, some account of how those transformative verbs operate nonrivalrously, so that God, humanity, and nature participate benignly in each other's mode of creation. Otherwise their soteriological metaphors seem rather puzzling. If Ruether thinks we are in ecological crisis because "the eschatological god became a historical project . . . identify[ing] essential (male) humanity with a transcendent divine sphere," then why assign her revised humanity a specifically redemptive vocation?[65] If, as Bratton thinks, Ruether's concept of divine agency forms merely an "an analogue of day to day biophysical functions," maybe she uses the salvation metaphors ironically, subversively.[66] But on the other hand, Gebara's proposal for "a more biocentric understanding of salvation" suggests that the endemic appearance of salvation metaphors may drive toward some triadic participation.[67] Maybe they gesture toward grace requalifying personhood from two directions at once: from one side, God embraces all of creation, while from the other creation mediates the divine embrace. Human creativity would then express the communion of nature and grace in a way both ecological and soteriological.

The salvation metaphors, in other words, may reaffirm an intimately natural role for distinctive human agency within a dynamic cosmos.[68] Once a theology makes human creativity etiologically and mimetically dependent on nature, associating creativity with divine action through those metaphors accomplishes two crucial distinctions. First, it resists ecological monism, the threat that humanity might be epiphenomenal to nature. Its unique participation in God animates humanity with a unique ecological role. Living within the divine story lets humans take up and articulate the universe's story, and only thereby tell an authentically human tale.

Second, the soteriological metaphors indicate the ecological size of humanity. Especially in an era of global climate change and genetic engineering, humans live larger than other creatures—so large we threaten even the conventional conceptual functions of "nature."[69] No matter whether by nature, grace, or sin, humans bear adventitious significance for the state of the biosphere and the course of evolution. Suddenly the human creature can denude great swaths of earth, undertake to restore whole ecosystems, and transfer genes across species and even kingdoms. Soteriological metaphors in ecological spirituality can communicate the aegis of human creativity and reform its power according to divine action in nature.

Teilhard's Spiritual Cosmology

Our investigation so far indicates that the strategy of ecological spirituality relies on some nonrivalrous communion of three modes of creativity, which it often symbolizes through the uses of salvation metaphors. The strategy now needs to develop that communion in relation to ecological personhood. Knowing how to do that involves two sets of further questions. What is creation doing? And what is God doing with/in creation?

The first question asks which aspects of nature's creativity humans take up, mimic, and innovate. It shapes what Brian Henning calls an "ethics of creativity."[70] Should we privilege order, balance, and hierarchy, or chaos, change, and networks? How closely and at what scale and speed do humans approximate the dynamism of cosmic development and pluriform emergence? If human creativity occupies the tension between nature's present and its future, what role does it play in constituting either or both?

Consider, for one famous example, the importance of those questions for Teilhard de Chardin—a figure important for a number of theologies in the strategy of ecological spirituality. Teilhard, priest and paleontologist, attempted a theological cosmology through the lens of human evolution. Treating humanity as "the key to the universe," Teilhard read cosmic dynamism through the human, in which, "as a continuation of the very lines of the universe," nature appears in "laborious and industrious concentration" as mind.[71] Reading the long scope of evolutionary history as complexity emerging toward a "noosphere," Teilhard isolated an intensifying dynamism in nature, a vector toward spiritual consciousness. Since that vector presently terminates in humanity, human agency "carries the world's fortune."[72] And since anticipation of its future in Christ sustains the human spirit, the world waits within humanity for its own "Christic" transfiguration. Through science and engineering, now nearly spiritual exercises, humans must, "by laying hands on the spirit of evolution, seize the tiller of the world."[73]

Teilhard's vision worries many who fear the consequences of human power grasping after the tiller of the world. It inspires others who would have human power admit and conform to its unavoidably theological character. However we receive his legacy, note how closely Teilhard ties his ecological spirituality to an interpretation of nature's own acting. Teilhard reads the communion of three modes of creation (natural, human, divine) in earth's evolution, and then concentrates that dynamism into human personhood, which intensively repeats and transforms nature's story.

But why is emergence of mind nature's story, *natura naturans*? Why not interpret the plotline of nature's story as the proliferation of diverse minds? Or perhaps as the development of sensual perception, or the conservation of solar energy, or the maintenance of homeorhetic climate, or the development of symbiotic communities? Or maybe as the nonteleological "goal" of living life for its own sake. Maybe there is no vector, only wild oscillations. Maybe Teilhard valorizes progress and spirit in projection of civilization's vanity, subtly licensing environmental destruction in the name of nature. The strategy of ecological spirituality requires some intelligible form to *natura naturans*, but also must insure itself against conforming to a distorted view of nature. How does Teilhard know what nature is naturing?

Teilhard's answer introduces our second question about what God is doing with/in creation. Although Teilhard appeals to evolutionary history, he interprets that history through God's act in the person of Jesus. His view of the world's way into the divine life drives his interpretation of what nature is doing. Teilhard redescribes geological time under the aspect of the "evolutive" cosmic Christ "mastering the world and imposing his form upon it."[74] So "the real earth is that chosen part of the universe . . . which is gradually taking on body and form in Christ."[75] Behind Teilhard's ecological revision of theology lies a soteriological key, what he calls "a sort of reduction of the universe to the spiritual."[76] Persons therefore intensively repeat an evolutionary story that is shaped by God's story with creation.

So we come to our second question: how does God work with/in creation? For if human agency approximates those verbs of grace, we need to know more precisely what grace does with nature. How exactly does God impose the form of Christ? How does God redeem, reshape, re-create, perfect, or divinize creation? And how does human agency approximate or participate in those works?

For Teilhard, God fashions the cosmos into Christic form by immanently vitalizing creaturely potentialities in view of adopting them into the divine life. But that means that "God's power has not so free a field for its action as we assume: on the contrary, in virtue of the very constitution of the participated being it labours to produce . . . it is always obliged, in the course of its creative effort to pass through a whole series of intermediaries and to overcome a whole succession of inevitable risks."[77] God acts co-creatively, adopting creation by adapting divine cooperation to its expressions and potential.

Theologians working in various revisions of process theology sometimes employ kenotic imagery to describe that co-creative or cooperative mode of divine action. John Polkinghorne, for example, thinks God limits divine agency in order to influence the course of nature in interactive response with natural contingency and order.[78] Arthur Peacocke thinks God makes space for creation to explore its possibilities, letting the generative universe actualize contingent potentialities.[79] God's self-limiting mode of creativity therefore humbles soteriological metaphors, argues Ian Barbour, for divine action establishes and responds to an earthly scale and ecological order.[80] Though less fascinated by the physicists' orders of causation, Catherine Keller's kenotic creativity similarly imagines divine receptivity to ecological becoming. For her, creation's generative chaos, over and around which God's presence invitationally hovers, elicits responsive, anticipatory, other-regarding models of divine creativity.[81]

If, following Teilhard, God's way of acting with/in creation specifies the way human creativity works with/in nature, then humans should make space for nature's generativity and responsively adapt to nature's new shoots. For God lets creation give birth to its own, and then inclusively adopts its innovations into the divine life. Teilhard's way of phrasing the nexus of three modes of creativity in human personhood can make theology vulnerable to technophilic graspings for the "tiller of the world," but he nonetheless shows how the strategy of ecological spirituality can ask humans to make invitational space for the natural world by appealing to God's creative grace. In other words, Teilhard shows how ecological spirituality concentrates environmental issues into a particular mode of creativity lying at the heart of authentic personhood and modeled after God's way of acting.

The Verbs of the Spirit

Our second question therefore begs a supplemental one: what does all this creativity accomplish? If God is transforming nature—or accompanying its emergence, or luring it forward—toward what end? Teilhard suggested the emergence of spiritual consciousness, but as Clare Palmer points out, reading cosmic history as the nativity of personhood might amount to retrenched anthropocentrism on a galactic scale.[82] That view of grace could license manipulations in the name of nature and God, both now perfectly conformed to human machinations.[83] Teilhard's interpretation of nature as evolving subjectivization might in fact "invigorate an aggressive turn against creation."[84]

Teilhard did indeed write of the "hominization" of life on its way to a hyperpersonal Omega Point, but always, says his apologist Henri du Lubac, to meet what he saw as the most important challenge for Christianity in an ecological age: the relation of Christ to an expansive, evolving cosmos. Though his humanizing proposals may have been "hasty and premature," says du Lubac, Teilhard rightly insisted that Christ reconciles the world to God personally and universally.[85] For Teilhard, God invites creation into the divine life through the personal embrace of Christ.

Teilhard's vulnerabilities arise not from the personalizing touch, but because that embrace still implicitly appears rivalrous. Without giving a theological account of how earth's creativity achieves its transformation into the body of Christ, Teilhard cannot exclude violent humanizations. Perhaps because he fails to fully realize the promise of a participatory soteriological model, Teilhard invites fears that humanization, evolution, and divine power conflate into a single cosmic process. In order to describe the role of human personhood in the cosmos, Teilhard needs some noncompetitive notion of grace that explains how divine personhood causes the world to work its own transformation—how the presence of God *increases* creaturely freedom.[86]

In order to find verbs for this divine way of transforming the world, a number of contemporary theologians turn to modes of action associated with the power and presence of the Holy Spirit. For Peter Scott, the Holy Spirit restores creatures into their mutual orientation toward each other, renewing their fellowship, sustaining their lives, and thus eliciting a diversity of creation's own gifts.[87] Denis Edwards dwells on the image of Spirit as midwife, enabling and empowering the world's own generativity, and then making room for new creatures to participate in God's life.[88] Jürgen Moltmann recovers maternal images of the Spirit in order to celebrate God as womb, a living space for creatures to develop, in which they are quickened, and from which they are born to a new life.[89]

For these theologians, the Spirit's active presence does not threaten but actualizes creation's own creativity. In the Spirit, then, we may glimpse how God brings creatures into communion in the divine life, and does through the free agency of creation.[90] In the work of the Spirit we find verbs of grace that usher creation into the divine life by enlivening creation's own verbs. In turn, pneumatological verbs guide how human creativity might mediate creation's participation in God, how creation might anticipate its humanization as glorifying grace.

Moreover, when humans themselves experience the enlivening transformation of the Spirit, they are ushered into God's way of communion. "To be in communion with this Spirit is to be in communion with all God's creatures," says Edwards, because the Spirit who enlivens all things also brings human persons to participate in that indwelling.[91] Human participation in the divine life includes participating in the communion of God with all creation. Ecological personhood finally arrives through participating in divine personhood.

This role for experience of the Spirit seems apropos of ecofeminist concerns to let reflection on empirical, embodied practices critique received pictures of God's relation to creation and revise unhelpful understandings of personhood.[92] For the enlivening Spirit makes environmental experience occasion for personal communion with God and the earth. Sallie McFague's attempt to let environmental experience shape Christian spirituality needs only to find the place of creativity in order to show how grace ushers persons into the cosmic body of God.[93] Transforming grace thus converts humans to earth as it transfigures personhood in the fellowship of God.[94]

With a nonrivalrous view of transforming grace, Teilhard's humanization no longer need threaten creation's freedom. Because that grace orients itself toward participation in Christ, Primavesi's auto-poiesis takes on formed theological significance.[95] By offering soteriological reasons why creativity might be "the most important moral virtue," a transfiguring view of grace can vindicate Fox's fusion of cosmology and anthropology into a "macro-anthropos." By restoring personhood to the communion of creation, participatory grace makes sense of environmental justice claims for the ecological dignity of humans.

In other words, signature work in creation spirituality implicitly relies on a background view of grace that can vindicate an ecological anthropology by appeal to a theological role for human creativity. We turn now to a theological tradition that explicitly begins its moral reflections from the doctrine of *theosis*.

Eastern Orthodoxy and the Bride of the Lamb

In chapter 4 we saw that, when vexed to explain the transformative role of stewardship, Loren Wilkinson turned to the divinizing models available from Orthodox theologians.[96] At the end of his theological reading of nature, Jeffrey Pugh suggests we reconsider the model of Irenaeus, for whom creation was "space for the divinization of the earth creature," "a completion of the world."[97] Teilhard, too, wanted to understand his christogenetic synthesis as "carrying on the speculative effort of the Greek Fathers, in particular St. Irenaeus and St. Gregory of Nyssa."[98] Denis Edwards develops an ecological anthropology in part through revisiting Eastern traditions of the Holy Spirit and its Wisdom christology. When Fox attempts to relate the cosmic Christ to human creativity through the transfiguration, he regularly turns to Russian theologian Nikolai Berdyaev.[99]

There might be more east–west conversation were it not for uncertainty about how to understand an approach with all the trappings of ecological spirituality, yet insistently anthropocentric, even dominionist, and often methodologically conservative. Once again the standard non/anthropocentric taxonomy frustrates development of practical environmental theologies, for the Orthodox tradition offers many well-honed theological resources required by ecological spirituality.[100] When the NACCE split, creation spirituality folks going one way and Orthodox representatives another, a great opportunity was missed for the strategy of ecological spirituality.[101]

After all, Orthodox theology approaches environmental problems with pedigreed theological reflections on cosmic anthropology, transfiguring grace, and spiritual creativity. Its criticisms of western competition between nature and grace, and of atomistic individualism, could support revisionary environmental theologies.[102] It associates very strong soteriological metaphors (deification, humanization, transfiguration) with creative roles for human personhood.[103] Yet it keeps ecological creativity close to environmental justice for the human margins.[104] Orthodoxy guards a repository of textual traditions on the Holy Spirit, and, as the home of iconography, is a lodestone for the aesthetics of spiritual creativity. And to top it off, it is ecclesial home to "the Green Patriarch," Bartholomew I.[105]

Orthodox theologian Philip Sherrard, neatly following the strategy of ecological spirituality, diagnoses the rise of environmental problems in the loss of cosmic anthropology. With nature set outside human personhood, he says, the stage was set for "the rape of man and nature." Healing the violation of both begins in restoring personhood, and for that Sherrard suggests returning to the christological tradition of Maximus. For in Maximus, "the humanization of God and the deification of man" come together in a personal union that embraces the whole cosmos.[106]

Patriarch Ignatius IV of Antioch agrees that therapy for deformed cosmologies should begin by returning to Maximian views of salvation. For Maximus explains the meaning of the world in the cosmic mystery of Christ; that "the Word became flesh . . . to open to us, through the holy flesh of the earth transformed into a eucharist, the path to deification."[107] In eucharistic creativity, says Ignatius, using pneumatological metaphors we have seen before, the church transfigures the cosmos, "giving birth to the universe as the glorious body of a deified humanity." Within the glorified microcosm, the earth becomes the bride of Christ, "whom we must protect from rape and lead to the wedding of the Lamb."[108]

Orthodox theology thus proposes to heal cosmology through divinizing grace, in the figure of the priestly human, whose creativity lifts up and restores all creation to communion with God.[109] Microcosmic humans gather creation into an "ecclesial hypostasis," ushering the cosmos into communion with God.[110] The earth groans not for liberation from humanity, but for liberation into authentic personhood.[111] Once again, worries about manipulative anthropocentrism and degenerate projects arise, and again they must be answered by appeal to participatory grace. But the Orthodox can do that explicitly, within a long tradition of reflection on cosmic transfiguration. When John Zizioulas proposes "ecological asceticism" for chastening human creativity, his sermon rests in a shared understanding of deifying grace.[112] Within that shared understanding, the salvation of the world means its beauty, which humans work to bring forth, that they too may be transfigured by it.[113]

Patriarch Ignatius suggests we explore the ecological promise of Maximian deification by turning to modern Russian theology. In later chapters we will do that, tracing the ecological promise of Maximus through Sergei Bulgakov, testing and developing the strategy of ecological spirituality within the tradition of deification.

Wisdom from the East: To Maximus and Bulgakov

Before we move on however, we must take note of the elusive, typically Eastern figure of Wisdom. Wisdom appears often and yet sparely among Western environmental theologians. She makes brief appearances in the environmental theologies of Ruether, Peacocke, Moltmann, and Fox.[114] Appearing penultimately in their texts, but scarcely personified by Primavesi and Sherrard, she becomes fully thematic in Celia Deane-Drummond, who finds in Wisdom the theological capacity to unite the practical strengths of ecojustice and stewardship strategies, ordering human agency by its situation in a web of natural integrity.[115] Moreover, says Deane-Drummond, Wisdom guarantees that God's action does not threaten but elicits creaturely agencies. Wisdom thus shapes human agency by the web of natural integrity that God's presence sustains and invites.[116]

Edwards agrees, gesturing toward a soteriological nexus: Sophia "can begin to show the inter-relation between the expanding interconnected and self-organizing universe and all its creatures, and the saving work of Jesus Christ."[117] Wisdom, it seems, names the mystery in which God's action in Christ would direct human agency to transformatively engage the world, and thereby participate with creation in the divine life.[118] Deane-Drummond gives a hint of that mystery's ancient logic: "Wisdom holds together the ideas of creation with redemption: Christ as Logos is also Sophia incarnate."[119] Referring back to the way Maximus the Confessor harmonized creation and salvation through Logos christology, Sophia somehow names creatures together with the divine life, and divine creativity together with the heart of the world.[120]

Compare Wisdom's valedictory role in Keller's theology of becoming. As Keller reaches for some conclusive hope to leave her readers, she wonders how she might "designate creation as incarnation," and speculates whether the one

> "in" whom unfolds the universe can be theologized as Tehom, the
> ocean of divinity . . . called by such biblical names as Elohim, Sophia,
> Logos, Christ. The all in the divine, the divine in the all: the rhythm
> of appellations does not name two Gods, or even two Persons. Yet it
> does echo the trinitarian intuition of complex relationality immanent
> to an impersonal Godhead and personalized in the *oikonomia* of the
> creation.[121]

Keller needs a way to name creation's fullness; not God "but the depth of God. Ocean of divinity, womb, and place-holder of beginnings . . . capacity of genesis."[122] Perhaps Sophia, but also Christ, and cosmic womb, and divine ocean—the point is to find a divine name for the generative depth to creation, some inner longing rightly associated with the divine and visible in her economic emergence. In the right sort of embodied cosmic soteriology, says Keller, "Sophia would convey a love spread—excessively—across the material universe."[123]

Wisdom seems to invite the attention of environmental theologians trying to associate creaturely becoming and divine agency. She seems the one toward whom we look when struggling to designate the way creativity transfigures the world. Sophia, says Thomas Merton, names both "the dark nameless *Ousia*" shared by the Trinitarian Persons as well as the living beauty and hidden highest reality of creation. To understand her better, Merton directs the reader to Sergei Bulgakov.[124] Deane-Drummond agrees that "in developing an adequate basis for a theology of creation," Bulgakov's Sophia may best realize the promise of Teilhard's strategy.[125] In chapters 10 and 11, as I investigate how divinizing grace meets the challenges of the strategy of ecological spirituality, I will turn to this Russian theologian who renarrates cosmic deification with Sophia at its heart.

PART II

Theological Investigations

6

Sanctifying Biodiversity

Ecojustice in Thomas Aquinas

In chapter 3 we saw how the strategy of ecojustice relies on some view of sanctification in order to introduce creation's integrity to Christian moral experience. Theologians like Rasmussen, Northcott, and Moltmann ground normative respect for creation in the experience of God's love. Each in his own way suggests that as humans are conformed to God's love for creation, they perceive and can respond to creation's integrity. As it brings them into friendship with God, grace brings humans to their creaturely senses, opening them to a world of normative value. But those theologians left unexplained why conforming ourselves to creation could be part of becoming friends with God, or why life with God might make us more at home on earth. We turn now to Thomas Aquinas to look for an explanation, seeking the soteriological conditions for ecojustice.

Looking to Thomas to reconsider Christian views on nature and justice would seem obvious: he is usually considered an indispensable authority for natural law, which articulates rules of justice from principles of nature, and his theology remains the touchstone for discussions of nature and grace in sanctification. Yet, after forty years of environmental theologies, few works extensively utilize Thomas.[1] That may be because by the lights of the non/anthropocentric continuum, Thomas seems culpable of Lynn White's cosmological sins: anthropocentrism and dominion.[2]

However, as this chapter and the next argue, when read soteriologically for the way creation's integrity matters for sanctification, Thomas offers promising ground for the strategy of ecojustice. Recall that we left the ecojustice strategy with two problems. First, how does human sanctification relate to creation's integrity? And second, how should respecting that integrity regard predation, suffering, and death? In this chapter I let Thomas address the first question by explaining how God perfects humans through human use of other creaturely perfections. In the next chapter I will suggest that Thomas's virtues guide humans toward discriminating creation's goods in the midst of natural evils. While they do not develop a full Thomist ecojustice theology, the two chapters demonstrate that Thomas offers theological resources for satisfying the strategic goal of ecojustice, to conform human behavior to creation's integrity. Moreover, he does so from within his careful system of nature and grace, thus showing how the integrity of a creaturely *oikos* arrives through the divine economy, and how humans come home to earth as they become friends with God.[3]

"Natural Theology": Augustine and Aristotle in Thomas

First a word on which Thomas I have in view, for his textual corpus has generated remarkably diverse theological and ethical figures. An enduring locus of interpretive debate, one of special importance to ecojustice, is his view of the natural knowledge of God. Various Thomisms form themselves in alternate priorities for nature vis-à-vis grace, with consequence for how immediately and intelligibly God may be known by creatures. At one terminus we find an optimistic view of analogy and kataphatic tendencies; at the other, insistence on God's indefeasible otherness and thus apophatic tendencies.[4] Both find explicit textual support from Thomas, for he routinely cites both Aristotelian and Neoplatonist authorities. Two of the most famous: "A mistake about creation leads to a mistake about God" (thinking with Aristotle), but "We are united as to one unknown" (with Pseudo-Dionysius).[5] Clearly Thomas assimilates both apophatic and kataphatic moments, both mystical and naturalist ways. Which side takes priority bears far-reaching ramifications for everything from the significance of the natural sciences to the possibility of mystical experiences.

It well exceeds the competency of this chapter to summarize or evaluate that debate, but I will add to the list of its consequences: our view on how Thomas regulates natural knowledge of God determines how he can assist the strategy of ecojustice. For Thomas develops theological respect for created natures in service to his account of how God brings humans into knowledge of God. That means the central focus of ecojustice theologies, creation's integrity, lies for Aquinas within a soteriological movement toward knowing God—just as we saw with Moltmann and Rasmussen. Thomas integrates sanctification and creation as he combines Aristotelian naturalism and Augustinian mystical ascent, which he does in order to show how nature and grace work together that humans may come to know God. So interpreting how Thomas deals with the question of natural knowledge of God determines what role creation's integrity plays in the movement of sanctification.

Ecojustice needs those figures of Thomas that hold together the theses of Aristotelian empiricism with those of Augustine's divinely moving love. Aristotle's natural realism describes knowing as the conformity of the intellect to thing known. Augustine's emphasis on the spiritual movement of the will describes knowing God as God's love moving the human toward God. Aristotle's scientific taxonomy allows Thomas to specify human nature by the operation of the intellect. Augustine's economy of grace insists that the highest act of human persons, in which they are conformed to God's love, comes as a gift from God. The Thomist synthesis affirms and integrates both sets of propositions, with this result: the embodied intellective act, which discriminates humanity as a distinct species, becomes the site where grace conforms personhood to the knowledge of God through knowledge of creation.

"Thomas fuses Aristotelian naturalism with neoplatonic participation— this non-essential, mere thinking-tool owned by an animal is nonetheless the superadded descending *palladium* which renders us superessentially as we are, more than we are."[6] That apparent paradox is made possible by sacred doctrine as the perfect *scientia*, providing the first principle for all other investigative forms of knowing, and thus constituting the whole world as potentially revelatory.[7] Thomas combines the Aristotelian thesis that human knowing and the natural world structurally belong to each other with the Augustinian proclamation that grace turns persons toward God. For Thomas, theological science "discovers that integrity, that mutual fittingness, that quality of belonging to each other, of human beings and the world," just as it articulates how grace turns and unites human creatures to the divine nature.[8]

In other words, the Thomist synthesis relies on a sanctifying epistemic spiral in which coming to know God requires learning what to make of creation and knowing creation requires coming to know God. By integrating them, Thomas significantly revises Augustine and Aristotle. For Augustine, Christians semiotically "use" natures to refer their desire onward to its infinite rest in God.[9] By setting mystical use to work on Aristotelian natures, Aquinas effectively decelerates the semiotic reference, requiring the intellective work of adequately conforming oneself to the creaturely object one uses to love God.[10] Thomas fills out Augustinian desire with Aristotelian realism, representing a "decisive turn to concreteness" for the mystical ascent.[11] In turn, putting the synthesis from the Aristotelian side, Thomas subjects the theological *scientia* of nature to its proper first principle: in order to know creation in all its diversity and integrity, the knower must be united to the formal cause of both herself and the rest of creation.[12] Adequately knowing creation requires Augustine's mystical ascent.

For Thomas, creation's integrity cannot be separated from the way God becomes friends with humans, because "his view of how our minds are related to the world is interwoven with his doctrine of God."[13] Explains Fergus Kerr: "Our experience of things is not a confrontation with something utterly alien, but a way of absorbing, and being absorbed by, the world to which we naturally belong."[14] At the same time that world naturally belongs to God, and God uses human experience of the things that naturally belong to God to perfect the specific way humans come to belong to God.

So we see that the ecojustice strategist has reason for preferring a certain constellation of Thomist interpretations: those which place an Aristotelian materialism within a participative hermeneutic, such that grace sanctifies persons through their finite, contingent experience. That wide range of interpretations, however, admits nothing like "natural theology," if that means univocal attributions of created effects to the divine essence. Some have licensed such projects from appeal to Thomas's synthesis, and others have condemned him for the same.[15] In order to keep sanctification and creation's integrity closely connected, ecojustice theologies draw on a participative natural theology, in which grace enables humans to come to know God by the excessively significant exercise of their own creaturely capacities. I will defend the rough outlines of that sort of Thomism in the following constructive account of creation's integrity within Thomas's view of sanctification.

Cosmology by Desire: Creation's Integrity as Real Relation

Those who think that Thomas's anthropocentrism offers only problems for environmental theology miss the way he sets humans within a cosmos of creatures bearing their own integrity. Thomas often marks off distinctively human practices from among the great diversity of distinctive creaturely operations precisely in order to explain creation's common ordination to God. Consider his comment on the ravens who call upon God in Psalm 146:9. Thomas says that they "are said to call upon God on account of the natural desire whereby all things, each in its own way, desire to attain the divine goodness."[16] It appears in an article on prayer, which Thomas restricts to rational creatures, apparently excluding nonhumans (*bruta animalia* and lower) from divine communion. Along with many other articles subordinating irrational nature before humans, the passage invites suspicion that Thomas values only intellectual nature.[17] The suspicions seem warranted, considering that subsequent church teaching uses the Thomist privileging of intellectual nature as a "disastrous doctrine" for animal welfare.[18] However, the way Thomas addresses the scriptural ravens contains two hints of a more widely valued cosmos.

First, Thomas wants to preserve the phenomenal world of scripture. No matter how it troubles his schematic convenience, says Bruce Marshall, Thomas will always preserve the *modus loquendi* of scripture. Ravens calling upon God, rivers clapping their hands, stones crying out—such is the biblical world. Thomas proceeds by what Marshall calls "logico-semantic explication," preserving the biblical phenomena by letting the incarnation govern its ontological description.[19] In this case Thomas wants to simultaneously safeguard the distinctively human practice of prayer while preserving the ravens' analogous desire to participate in divine goodness. Both are proper effects of the incarnation, but in different ways according to different natures. Thomas appeals to human rationality in order to affirm the ordination of all creatures to God while preserving their natural differences. Call it a Wittgensteinian distinction between language worlds: the ravens call upon God not as humans do, but as ravens do. Thomas, however, does not let the distinction go all the way down; instead he suggests we know something about what Wittgenstein's lion would mean to say.[20]

The compound, "natural desire" (*naturale desiderium*) contains the second hint of a divinely valued cosmos (and of what lions say in it). The phrase embodies Thomas's synthesis of Aristotle and Augustine by establishing definite, contingent natures oriented to God. A creature is "nothing but a certain relation to the Creator."[21] That relation, characterized by desire, is the most real thing in a creature. Creatureliness also includes a nexus of subsidiary relations—of matter and form, potency and act, essence and existence. These describe the specific way a creature enacts its particular relation to God, the natural form of its desire. Yet all those specific ways actively express a creature's originary orientation to God's goodness.[22] As David Burrell puts it, "the very *esse* (existence, to-be) of a creature is *esse-ad* (existence toward, to be toward) its creator."[23]

One of Thomas's clearest statements of this quotes from both Aristotle and Dionysius, showing how Thomas integrates both sources in order to set creation's integrity within a divinely loved cosmos:

> Now to love God above all things is natural to every nature—rational,
> irrational, and even inanimate—according to the mode of love
> capable for each creature. The reason for this is that it is natural to
> every creature to desire and love something according as it is fit to be
> loved, since "everything acts just as it is naturally apt," as is said in
> *Physics* 2.8. It is manifest that the good of the part is for the good of

the whole; hence each particular thing, by its natural appetite or love, loves its own proper good on account of the common good of the whole universe, which is God. Here Dionysius says, in the book of *Divine Names*, that "God leads everything to love of Godself."[24]

Thomas thus situates the specific natural form of every creature within a cosmology of desire—Augustinian in that creaturely appetites properly seek their goodness in God, Aristotelian in that each creature moves itself in pursuit of its good according to the variety of its proper form.[25] An architectonic *exitus–reditus* movement suspends creatures in a neoplatonic "gyration," whereby God initially wills the existence of creatures and finally wills their "return" to unity with God.[26] "Since all things flow from the Divine will, all things in their own way are inclined by appetite towards good, but in different ways."[27] God moves creatures toward God through each creature's natural operations. Creatures participate in God in the dignity of their own causality.[28] Seeking their own proximate goods, creatures desirously move toward divine goodness according to the manner of their respective natures.[29]

When the lion roars, therefore, it voices its desire for God. But that misleads; rather, the lion's "speech" is in the way it breeds and naps and runs. Perhaps jarringly, lions love God by stalking, pouncing upon, and tearing asunder their prey. Such are their natural operations, their ways of seeking divine goodness. The ravens call upon God by building nests and stealing owl eggs. The rivers clap their hands by falling over cataracts, spreading silt over flood plains, and broadening into fluvial deltas. Wittgenstein's dictum holds: lions and ravens are what they are according to their own life-practices, quite distinct from human practices.

That distinction makes for essential differences among creatures, but alternative life-practices are not strictly equivocal because lion, raven, and human acts are intelligibly gathered under a genus such as "life-practices."[30] So while the term nature refers primarily to a thing's "specific difference" or *quidditas*, or its own life-practice, it also depends on a common notion of begottenness and shared orientation to the Creator's goodness.[31] Thomas's synthetic cosmology thus understands the natural activity of ravens in pursuit of corvine goods as their peculiar pursuit of divine goodness.

Thomas therefore describes a twofold integrity to creation: the fundamental relation of all things to God, and the peculiar natures by which creatures subsist in that relation. That supports the ecojustice appeal to a morally significant relation between Creator and creature, and does so by intrinsically connecting that relation to the specific and diverse characteristics of creatures. Put another way, the immanent and transcendent relations of creation noncompetitively presume one another. The normative use of "creation's integrity" can therefore require respect for autonomous creation in virtue of every creature's fundamental relation to their Creator.

Divine and Creaturely Perfections

When we consider the divine ground of natural desire, creation's integrity acquires even more intense theological character. Thomas thinks that (as John Bowlin summarizes him), "everything is what it is and not some other thing because of the character of its agency—because of the ends it pursues and the manner in which it pursues them."[32] Both those ends and those manners of pursuit derive from God's desire to communicate goodness to creation. For the final end of a creature's proximate goals, the final good of the many natural goods, is the divine nature, to which all those proximate goods conform. "All things desire God as their end when they desire some [proximate] good, whether by intellectual, sensible, or natural desire. . . . because nothing is good and desirable except insofar as it participates in the likeness of God [*nisi secundum quod participat Dei similitudinem*]."[33] Therefore, not only do creaturely goods subsist from God's original desire to communicate the divine goodness; creaturely goods conform creatures to the character of divine goodness.[34] God acts divinely by bringing others into the divine goodness. "God intends only to communicate God's perfection which is God's goodness. And every creature intends to acquire its own perfection, which is a likeness of divine perfection and goodness [*similitudo perfectionis et bonitatis divinae*]."[35]

Divine goodness thus formally shapes creation's integrity, rendering it a similitude of God's goodness. As Anna Williams observes, the etiologically excessive character of God's agency (that God acts for no self-perfecting end, but ecstatically, for the sake of involving creatures in God's act) makes room for creaturely agency to enact some divine likeness, and by likeness to attain toward a kind of union with divine nature.[36] The specific form of that union names, in one way, a specific creaturely nature. Diverse creaturely natures, as so many finite modes of union, together adumbrate the absolute simplicity of God's goodness. Because "all beings apart from God are not their own being, but are beings by participation . . . therefore all things, which are diversified by their various actualizations of existence, some fuller and more complex than others [*omnia quae diversificantur secundum diversam participationem essendi, ut sint perfectius vel minus perfecte*], are caused by one, absolutely perfect, First Being."[37] Each nature represents, as Williams says, a "refraction of God's simplicity in finitude."[38]

The *duplex ordo* of creation's integrity in Thomas thus refers simultaneously to an empirical natural operation and to a similitude of divine goodness.[39] For Thomas, write Milbank and Pickstock, "[a] thing is fulfilling its telos when it is *copying God in its own manner* . . . so a tree copies God by being true to its treeness, rain by being rainy and so on."[40] Ravens on the wing and lions stalking their prey image finite instantiations—in some imperfect, refracted way— of aspects of the divine act.

Later in the *Summa*, Thomas refers back to the article I just quoted (ST 1.44.1) to say that since all things begin from God's goodness "we must conclude that the end of all things is some extrinsic good." That end is God's simplicity, in which creatures participate through their natural desire for natural goods.[41] So humans attribute the creaturely copying of the divine by considering the immediate ends for which ravens and lions act in light of their final end, which humans know from revelation, taught by *sacra doctrina*. The natural goods of creatures, however, remain descriptively regulatory for how humans can understand the final ends of all things in God.

For the ecojustice theologian, that means Thomas ascribes to creation the most intense form of integrity—bearing the self-revelation of God—and does so without offending ordinary natural science descriptions. Ravens do no need to pray in order to live in God's goodness; they copy God in so many corvine ways. Ravens do not secretly perform a human operation, visible only to theologians; in their own operations of cawing and flying and harassing owls they take on the likeness of some divine perfection.[42] Just so they imitate God, according to the intensity of their likeness. Says Thomas:

> All movements and operations of every being are seen to tend to what is perfect. Perfect signifies what is good, since the perfection of anything is its goodness. Hence every movement and action of anything whatever tend toward good. But all good is a certain imitation of the supreme Good, just as all being is an imitation of the first Being. Therefore the movement and action of all things tend toward assimilation with the divine goodness.[43]

Creatures represent divine perfection as they act for their proper ends, realizing the real relation to their Creator that lies at the heart of their existence by realizing the natural perfections that govern the form of their essences. In consequence, creaturely integrity includes not only individual creatures, but the orders by which they are related to one another, and the natural whole they together comprise as the common good of all creation—the ecological contexts that shape natural perfections. Creaturely diversity adumbrates the excessive richness of God's simple goodness, while ecological orders gather so many refractions into an organic harmony. The particular similitudes increase in conformity to God's goodness through their interrelatedness, as they comprise the higher, more complex good of the universe.[44] Simultaneously defending the goodness, order, diversity, and unity of creation by appeal to God's creative will, Thomas repeats this formulation across several works:

> For God brought things into being in order to communicate the divine goodness to creatures and thus be represented by them. And because God's goodness could not be adequately represented by any single creature, God produced many and diverse creatures, that what one lacked in representing divine goodness might be supplied in another. For goodness, which exists in God simply and uniformly, exists in creatures multiply and distributively. Thus the whole universe together participates the divine goodness more perfectly.[45]

God desires that creation's perfection unfold through a plenitude of singular perfections, varying in kind and degree of divine participation, and related to one another through the complex good of the universe. And God desires all this in order to communicate Godself through creation: "God willed to produce creatures for participation in God's goodness, representing divine goodness by resembling it." Yet because "God is represented by creatures as the transcendent is represented by that which is surpassed," God invites a numberless procession of resemblances, each displaying perfections possessed by God simply and supereminently.[46]

Since creation's integrity includes ordered unity and real diversity, articulated in a complex whole, as in a cohesive organism, Thomas suggests we should understand *integritas* in reference to divine wisdom. For wisdom shapes the common ordination of all creatures to their own goods, the universal good, and their final end in God's goodness.[47] "A swallow, for example, is the creature that it is, not an eagle, fish, or slug, precisely because it participates in God's eternal law as only swallows do," explains Bowlin. "And a swallow is a good swallow, a perfect instance of the sort of thing that it is, when it achieves ends that it pursues naturally as a consequence of its swallow-like participation in the eternal law."[48] The integrity of creation names the common dignity of diverse participations in the eternal law of God's wisdom.

Whether "higher" or "lower" participations, whether rational or brute, praying creature or not, all creation shares in that dignity. Because God's perfection exceeds creaturely perfections in a nonrivalrous way, divine wisdom at once diversifies creatureliness while maintaining it in a complex whole. "In a whole the good is the integrity [*integritas*] which results from the order and composition of the parts. Hence it is better for a whole that there be a disparity among its parts ... than that all its parts be equal."[49] Just as individual bodies tend to become richer by the complexity of ordered parts, so too the entire universe.[50] Wisdom does not recuperate creaturely diversity "fallen" into corporeality or irrationality, as Origen's story of original equality among rational creatures would have it. Instead, Wisdom delights in the nonrational and profligately associates with every embodied form.

"The last vestige of Manicheanism in Origen was thus rooted out by Thomas," says Olivia Blanchette, "with the idea of a perfection of the universe that entailed an order of diverse parts intended from the beginning in creation."[51] God wills God's simple goodness by willing creatures who participate in it according to a plenitude of resemblances. God desires ravens to call upon God by acting as ravens, not by learning to sing as angels. So too for rocks:

> Although an angel taken absolutely may be better than a rock, still
> both natures taken together are better than either one alone: and
> hence a universe in which there are angels and other things is better
> than [one] where there would be angels only, because the perfection
> of the universe is seen essentially according to the diversity of
> natures, by which diverse degrees of goodness are filled.[52]

In contrast to a common misunderstanding of the Thomistic "great chain of being," Thomas prohibits reading the variety of creatures along a *moral* continuum. On the contrary, God desires irrational ravens and inanimate rocks, existing for their end in God according to their particular, given capacities. Those capacities together make for "a graduated participation in the perfection of God," with rationality a richer form of participation than lapidarity.[53] But that is not to the demerit of stones: "the diversity of things comes from the principal intention of the first agent, and not from a diversity of merits."[54] God delights in the simple way stones love him.[55]

Thomas thus preserves and intensifies creation's integrity from both sides of his synthesis. On the one hand, Thomas uses Aristotelian stability to discipline neoplatonic participation, specifying the concrete natures God desires, resident in their own networked ecological integrity.[56] On the other hand, "Thomas engulfs Aristotle," as Eugene Rogers says, suspending those natures in the fundamental giftedness of God's creativity. Thomas appropriates natural science for theological science, for all things, on their own immanent terms, "contain within themselves the form of revealability." "They possess an intrinsic under-God-ness, they enjoy natural citizenship in the world that revelation depicts, they already belong to and comprise that world. ... And that under-God-ness is theirs and ours and the whole world's, patient of discovery."[57]

Thomas thus offers the strategy of ecojustice an account of creation's integrity keyed both to ecological science and to the character of God. "Thomas's project stands out as a deeply ecological one in that our relations (and God's relation) to the rest of the natural world are central within it."[58] Thomas helps the environmental theologian secure not only "moral considerability" for creatureliness, but theological reasons to respect individual creatures, biodiversity, and ecological systems. Moreover, by establishing ecological relations and natural habits as similitudes of divine goodness, Thomas makes creation's integrity something that intellectual creatures intrinsically want to know. And by affirming humanity as a natural creature with its own ecological niche, Thomas shows how to integrate humans into an account of creation's integrity. We turn now to the theological desire of humans to know creation's integrity.

How Grace Uses Creation to Perfect Humans

So far, Thomas has provided reasons to respect nonhuman natures that do not rely on an optimistic position on the natural knowledge of God. For the argument about natural theology is not over *whether* things exist by their relation to God, or whether all creaturely goods derive from God's goodness. Theologians debate whether human minds can make reliable attributive statements about God on the basis of those creaturely subsistent relations, but either way they can intelligibly posit divine relationality at the heart of what it means to be a creature.[59] Even that bare attribution at least placemarks creation's integrity as divinely derived and participant in God's economy of goodness. That alone might satisfy the first strategic requirement of ecojustice: the dignity of nonhuman nature.

We saw in chapter 3, however, that ecojustice projects attempting to conform human action to creation's dignity need to show how that dignity relates to Christian experience. Rasmussen, Northcott, and especially Moltmann each suggested that we could make that connection by moving beyond cosmological attributions to soteriological relations, and specifically to sanctification, where grace embraces humans in their earthly habitat. Thomas offers just that, connecting creation's integrity to the specific good of human creatures by involving the nonhuman world in the way grace unites humans with God. Thomas demonstrates that the Augustinian movement of desire, whereby humans "use" the world as visible signs for the sake of enjoying God, is a real creaturely operation, conducted according to the form of human nature working in relation to many other creaturely forms. The result is an intrinsic, reflexive connection between the integrity of creation and the human experience of grace.

Like other creatures, humans naturally desire goods proper to their species. In realizing those goods, they participate also in the holistic good of the universe and some aspect of divine perfection. But in the human case we find a unique difference: as intellectual creatures they attain their specific good through a knowing act that first recognizes and then intellectually internalizes the goods its desires. Since the intellective act seeks to know things in their principle (under the aspect of their end), which includes knowing the principle and end of the intellective act itself, humans desire God in a twofold way. First, the intellect seeks a final cause and first principle of the objects it seeks to know. As creative origin and pure act, God is the end of all knowing and the most intelligible object to be known.[60] In this way human nature is ordered toward seeking the absolute existence in which all creatures subsist. Second, humans desire God as the perfection of their own embodied intellective act, which, as the speciating human operation, is itself a "participated likeness of Him who is the first intellect."[61] In this way humans seek union with God's essence, or the knowledge of God's act in itself. In both cases humans have a "natural desire for a supernatural end"; or a proper creaturely reason to seek a good beyond the competency of human capacity.[62]

Now we might with much difficulty, says Thomas, "after a long time and the admixture of many errors," learn from the initial giftedness of creation some true things about God.[63] We could probably recognize that God exists, even if, absent grace, we cannot discern just how God exists. But those inchoate operations do not fully realize the human good, for they do not bring our highest (most human) operation to the fullness of its object. Only dimly aware of a supernatural end, we are not conformed to it or by it. Human beatitude lies in knowing God essentially, wherein personhood is fully conformed to its highest good by way of union. That sort of knowledge is natural to human creatures in the sense that it authentically perfects the highest good of human nature, as God is both the end of all knowing and the originary act of knowing itself.[64] But it is not within our grasp; we can only receive it from God as a gift. Such is human nature: its mode of self-realization is one especially receptive to God's further giving. The excessive end of their nature opens humans to ongoing friendship with God.[65]

Sanctifying grace takes the gentle, invitational form of friendship because God desires for humans to attain their good in a naturally human way. Since, famously, "grace does not destroy nature but perfects it," God loves humans as part of God's ongoing self-communication to human creatures.[66] The accommodation of grace to human nature is no indication of two autonomous cosmological tiers, but "God carrying out his will for creatures over time and among contingencies, a grace rendered dynamic and courteous to creatures."[67] The

divine economy of grace stays in character with the divine pattern of friendship, and consequently, in character with the capacities of human nature.

That means God assumes two conditions (call them "divine habits") for
friendship with humans. The first respects human finitude: since God exceeds
the capacity of any created intellect, grace finds a way to have finite minds share
in God's own form of knowing.[68] The second condition respects human
embodiment: since humans possess an embodied rationality, grace gives that
share through sensible perception.[69] Together these two conditions imply that
grace brings humans into sharing the form of divine self-knowing through
their own natural engagement with sensible creation. For Thomas, grace unites
human creatures to God in an excessively natural way, sharing Godself through
humanity's epistemic intimacy with the physical world. By virtue of our embodied, discursive, absorptive way of coming to God, "the whole of creation comes
to be for human salvation."[70] God gives Godself to be known in conjunction
with humans coming to understand the truth and goodness in created things.

We can see the way grace actualizes that conjunction by considering the
role of creation's integrity for naming God in questions 12 and 13 of the *Prima
Pars*. Here Thomas explains how grace perfects humans by elevating their natural way of knowing things. Analogical attributions from creation to God, when
guided by revelation, make intelligible some knowledge of God's essence, however partial. Thomas harnesses Aristotelian natural science to at once discipline and intensify the transforming power of the mystical naming described
by Dionysius. God draws us into the divine essence through our naming God
with the names of things we do know—the names of creaturely goods.[71] For
"our knowledge of God is derived from the perfections which flow from God to
creatures, which perfections are in God in a more eminent way than in creatures. Now our intellect apprehends them as they are in creatures, and as it
apprehends them it signifies them by names."[72]

This analogical way of sanctification relies on the strong view of creation's
integrity we have just seen, and orients humans toward it in a new way. For
grace to sanctify in keeping with the character of divine friendship, the relation
between a name and the way it is possessed supereminently by God cannot be
arbitrary. It need not be proportional, but even asymmetrically the created nature
giving rise to a name relates to some aspect of divine nature.[73] Otherwise humans
would not conform themselves to something sanctifiably true; rather grace
would have merely and indifferently transfigured a known object into a divine
sign (the hyper-Augustinian danger). Thomas's account of creation's integrity
guarantees the earthly conditions for God's sanctifying friendship: each creature exists by a real relation to God, expressing through the act of its specific
nature a certain goodness communicated to it by the Creator, comprehensible

by human knowers yet possessed excessively by God. "Because we know and name God from creatures, the names we attribute to God signify what belongs to material creatures, of which the knowledge is natural to us."[74] God communicates divine goodness to humans through our ecological relations to other creatures, relations which in our naming shape us for friendship with God.

Notice that divine naming occurs by invitation to friendship, not as an autonomous competency of the creature. On their own, apart from grace, humans could know God only "as far as creatures represent Him," and that, as we have seen, is refractively, imperfectly, and assymetrically.[75] But Thomas is not as interested in that dubious conceit (the friendless possibilities of naming God by reason alone) as he is in the way grace adopts and intensifies the natural capacity of humans to know created things, so that humans, living in the conditions of revelation and incarnation, can come to know God. Thomas develops Paul's license for reason in Romans 1 ("the invisible understood through the visible") in order to repeat an "invitation to join in the Spirit's glorification of the love between the Father and the Son."[76] Naming God from God's self-communicated creation draws us into a perichoretic movement, in which God's own knowledge begins to circulate through a still-natural human operation. Divine naming catches humans up into a gift already being given, lending human reason a share in the Spirit's economy, so that it knows and loves the Creator by God's own life.

An object is known according to the mode of the knower, says Thomas, so in this case, where creatures want to know a divine "object," God teaches humans a divine mode of knowing. Humans participate in the divine mode by slowly learning a decelerated version of God's own internal act.[77] Within the bonds of that friendship, Thomas will even say (in a reversal of the usual priority) that while revelation teaches barely (that God exists for us), glory-sharing reason learns God essentially: "By the revelation of grace in this life we cannot know God's essence, and thus are united to God as to one unknown; however, we know God more fully inasmuch as many and more excellent of his effects are demonstrated to us."[78] Schooled by revelation and disciplined by spiritual practices, comments David Burrell, grace activates analogical naming to lead us into the knowledge of God.[79] No rival to revelation, analogical activity realizes its promise. As Thomas says at the very beginning of the *Summa Theologiae*, revelation gives to *sacra doctrina* "pre-cognition" (*praecognitum*) of the end of knowing.[80] Already united to God as to one unknown, humans are led to know God by slowly realizing what we already "pre-know" in revelation.[81]

So grace perfects humans through exercise of their natural faculty, and doing so teaches humans how to "use" other creatures. Already Thomas thinks that our highest use of creation is contemplative; now God lends that use a still higher end, giving Godself to be known in creation. Grace conforms the intellect to its divinely excessive object by appropriating its step-by-step conformity with finite objects for the sanctifying exercise of naming, praising, and enjoying God from creation.[82] In those uses of creation for divine friendship, "God by His grace unites Himself to the created intellect," so that "the essence of God itself becomes the intelligible form of the intellect."[83] Given a share of the Spirit's glorifying work, humans know things as if by God's vision, and knowing them truly may anagogically use them to share in the way God knows God.[84] "By this light the rational creature is made deiform [*deiformis*]," as, by naming, the intellect is moved through creatures toward God.[85]

Thomas is pressured toward this rare mention of deiformity by his Aristotelian epistemology.[86] For Thomas, knowing conforms our mind to reality. It is "the adequation of the mind with reality, and this conformity regards the object of knowledge absolutely, as it is in itself. Our minds do not create or fashion reality in speculation: They become what they know, simply and completely, according to their own mode of being."[87] Knowledge signifies that the "the thing known is in the knower," because "the true is in the intellect is so far as it is conformed to the object understood."[88] For Thomas, grace offers God as "the One known in the knower, the One loved in the lover," and yet does so courteously, according to the integrity of human nature.[89]

Notice that at this most intense moment of grace, divinity uniting with human persons, Thomas presupposes persons conformed to their ecological relations. Using creation for naming God requires knowing creatures intimately enough to recognize their distinct perfections. Grace sanctifies humans by adopting their contemplative and practical uses of creation for the purpose of friendship with God. This is then no immediate ecstasy, no easy supply of names. Naming God first requires finding in each creature "the excelling principle of whose form the effects fall short," and understanding how it contributes to the good of the whole.[90] It requires ecological literacy. Sanctifying grace presupposes human creatures already alive to the world around them.

The first step along the way of grace therefore involves learning about such as ravens and elm trees. As Milbank and Pickstock put it, Thomas thinks that "in knowing the treeness of a tree, we are knowing a great deal more besides. Since the tree only transmits treeness—indeed, only exists at all—as imitating the divine, what we receive in truth is a participation in the divine."[91] When considered "under the formality of being divinely revealed"—which is to say, in the company of the Spirit—we may know creatures by their relation to God, "insofar as they are referable to God as their beginning and end."[92] Each arboreal good related to the flourishing of trees displays some divine good, and the order of its relations to its own habitat enacts some aspect of Wisdom. "To put this another way, in knowing a tree we are catching it on its way back to God."[93]

We come to know God, then, by perfecting an environmental aptitude, by letting grace bring us into the excessive promise of our natural intimacy with the world.

Moreover, that natural intimacy must engage and conform human persons in the same way that God's friendship does, for it involves the same relational model: the known in the knower. In that first step of grace, then, humans do not simply collect information about trees as if gathering together resources for an external project; they make themselves vulnerable to the world, reoriented by its wonder, impressed by its sensible truths, and ordered by its organic complexity.[94] Remember Kerr: "not a confrontation with something utterly alien, but a way of absorbing, and being absorbed by, the world to which we naturally belong."[95] Grace teaches us how this ecological membership may become also a share in the divine life. Thomas thus gives Matthew Fox reason to say that in grace we "actually become the beauty and goodness, the awe and wonder, that we take in—and there lies our 'glory.'"[96] We accept God's invitation to join in the Spirit's glorifying work, in one way, by opening ourselves to creation's beauty and goodness, preparing a place for the One who gives himself to be known by letting ourselves be remade beautiful and good.

"The Summa's epistemology is characterized by its maintenance of an Aristotelian starting point in the senses," says Anna Williams, "but equally by the alacrity with which this epistemology becomes explicitly Christian in its emphasis on the mind's union with God."[97] Ecological knowledge becomes sanctifying knowledge because God adopts in the manner that God creates.[98] How fitting that we should be adopted through our created nature. Not automatically, but in the contingency and courtesy of friendship, we are made deiform as God adopts the way our intellects conform themselves to creation. "If the human mind is bound for union with God, the Summa's epistemology seems equally bent on uniting the quotidian with paradisial."[99] It is so bent because Thomas follows the courtesy of grace, uniting humans into the divine life by letting their natural ecological unions bear an excessive goodness. The more Aristotelian his theological scientia, the more christoform in principle, says Rogers. Here a corollary: the more christoform, the more ecological.

When Thomas says that "the consideration of creatures is useful for building up our faith," he intends much more than a begrudging dispensation to something extrarevelational. God uses other creatures to slowly and progressively work in us the gifts of faith and charity. They "inflame" and "intoxicate" us with passion for God's goodness; they tutor that desire by the ongoing display of so many comprehensible goods;[100]and finally they offer themselves to human use—especially the uses of naming, praising, and glorifying, in which God offers Godself to be known, and by which humans, in company with all creation, come into God's friendship.

Ecojustice Intensified

The strategy of ecojustice wants to conform human behavior to the theological status of the natural world. We have now seen that Thomas not only establishes the theological character of nature, but shapes the heart of Christian experience according to creation's integrity. Thomas maintains the fullness of creation in the heart of human salvation, as integral to God's way of befriending humans. Thomas does not see creation as a fungible resource or a mere sign of another reality, but orients it to humans in the promise of Romans 1, that we might know the invisible through the visible. That sort of use requires Christians to attentively engage creation, to know it in love's knowledge, and to let grace teach us how to praise God from it.

With Thomas, the ecojustice theologian can argue for extensive preservation by saying that if we can bless God insofar as we are able to name God, and this we do at least in part by drawing from creation, then it follows that the more creatures we encounter the more names for God we have, and so the greater capacity to offer our praise. There is an availability to God (and in this sense, an embodiment) in God's significability by human names for the natural world. Christians should want biodiversity protected simply in order to be encountered and inflamed by goodness, to know how better to clothe God's name in worship and in prayer. Ecological diversity appears a sort of adumbration of God (God's own phenomenological self-description, given for us), and its preservation promises the continual issue of surprising new descriptions. Christians need not just zoos and gardens for preserving creatures, but whole ecosystems generating an array of life, bound together in a complex unity.

On the other hand, with the extinction of species and the despoiling of places we degrade our aptitude for naming and praising God.[101] If we find ourselves left with only the names derived from things made in our own image, the artifices of our own technology, we have little but our own narrow band of excellences (and those distorted by a host of sins) by which to praise God. The specter of massive species loss threatens a miserable poverty: deprivation of that by which to bless God. And in poverty's blight, vice proliferates, for in a world of our own violent making, one which silences all but human glories, idolatry comes more easily, less noticeably. The iconic traces of God become even more vestigial, while the face of humanity, everywhere reflected off fabricated surfaces, dazzles and fixates our gaze.[102]

Thomas is surely anthropocentric; not only do ravens not pray, they and all the "lower" creatures serve the use of humans. Indeed, he thinks "other creatures are governed as being directed to rational creatures [*quasi ad rationales creaturas ordinatae*]," and seems to require only that humans rule them prudently.[103] However, if we understand Thomas according to contemporary non/anthropocentric criteria, we miss the way his theological vision directs those anthropocentric statements into creation's role in shaping human personhood. When we interpret Thomas's use of creation from his account of grace, we begin to see that ravens materially serve God's way of sanctifying humans, and they do so only by pursuing their own life goods. The more christological, the more ecological. In conditions of grace, the more anthropocentric, the more important creation's integrity becomes.

In other words, Thomas divides humans from other creatures in order to unite them, just as he divides Creator from creation in order to unite them.[104] He orients creation toward the rational faculty of humans because he thinks that God sanctifies humans through the intellectual use of other creatures. David Burrell says Thomas's synthesis "not only linked nature with spirit, the structure of the cosmos with a theory of knowledge, but provided a pattern for action as well, by properly subordinating practical to speculative knowing."[105] Augustine in mind, Thomas rigorously maintains the model of "use" for the human relation to other creatures in order to preserve the highest use: praising God by the names of creatures. So when he says humans may kill animals because "by divine providence they are intended for human use in the natural order," Thomas does not cosmologically license indifferent destruction, but endorses the ecological order underlying a sanctifying dynamic.[106] As we will see in the next chapter, the Romans 1 passage normatively shapes what Thomas means by dominion. Humans naturally use other creatures, and that use is naturally ordained to knowing and praising God from creation.

This doxological perfection of creation in human use leads Thomas to observe that creation's integrity finds two moments of perfection, one in the organic wholeness of the cosmos and one in the beatitude of the saints.[107] Those two ends align conveniently with two desiderata of an ecojustice strategy: nature's own value and the role of that value in Christian experience. Thomas has shown us that the two perfections do not compete, because the sanctifica-tion of Christian experience relies on ecological integrity. The dual perfection suggests also that good use of creation involves not only prudence but also a kind of love. Using creatures for the sake of our own friendship with God means "we should love them for their 'autonomy and consistency,' for what the free love of God has made them."[108] In the next chapter we will investigate what loving creation could mean in the Thomist moral cosmology, and then we will test that love, and with it the notion of ecological sanctification, by posing to Thomas the ecojustice problem with natural evils.

7

Environmental Virtues

Charity, Nature, and Divine Friendship in Thomas

In the previous chapter, Thomas showed us rudiments for an adequate ecojustice strategy: the integrity of creation intimately connected to Christian experience. Now we move toward developing the practical forms of that connection, the habits of graceful inhabitation on earth. In particular, we need to know how ecological habits of friendship with God respond to natural evils. We saw in chapter 3 that ecojustice ethicists sometimes hesitate to locate predation, suffering, or death in their concept of creation's integrity, making for uncertain practical consequences. So now we put the question to Thomas: how do natural evils and sanctification relate to each other within the environmental virtues of God's friendship? How should ecojustice respect an unfriendly natural world?

I turn to Thomas on justice and virtue here not for specific environmental prescriptions but for closer articulation of human membership. I turn to his virtues for that because there we see humanity's natural agency set within creation's orderliness. The virtues report what John Bowlin calls "a kind of human moral ecology . . . a description of our species in its natural environment."[1] They comprise a set of successful responses to our habitat, ways toward flourishing in the midst of opportunity and difficulty.

Of course, Thomist virtues usually concern interpersonal relations, but in their pattern Thomas discloses a background "ecology" of agency: the basic opportunities and difficulties for our species, mediated through the natural and social worlds. The virtues orient, settle, and form humans through so many contextual relations. They discriminate personal and social practices according to the ordered movement of creatures to one another and to God, and according to the principles of God's movement toward us. So what Thomas says on justice and charity outlines a moral ecology in which we find initial guides for Christian environmental ethics.

In service to the strategy of ecojustice, we need to know how Thomas's moral ecology deals with death, predation, and decay. For these negative phenomena not only attend the natural world but seem significant drivers for its forms of life and organization. Raising the question of natural evils with soteriology often takes theologians toward entering the Darwinian contests or trying theodicy; but here I only want to know how Thomas can help ecojustice practices regard natural violence. Does an ethic conformed to the integrity of creation's relation to its Creator affirm a role of natural evils or signify their condemnation? Knowing means the difference between reintroducing wolf populations or constructing more zoos, between locating the sanctifying practices of Christian ecojustice in the Leopoldian management of Lisa Sideris or the pet friendship of Stephen Webb.

Fighting off post-Darwinian hints of nihilism from interpretations of the natural world, Anthony Baker suggested (as we saw in chapter 3) that we turn to Thomas to discover a Christian counterbiology, one in which the story of grace overwrites other sciences. The previous chapter outlined the contours of a Thomist counternarrative, but one that "overwrites" by perfecting, and perfects through courteous friendship.[2] Now by revisiting virtue in light of the sanctifying share given humans in the divine uses of creation (naming, praising, glorifying), Thomas will show us the form of Christian environmental practices within Darwin's unfriendly world.

Habits of the Divine Science

In the previous chapter, we saw how Thomas locates his account of sanctifying grace within humanity's intellectual vulnerability before the world. His theological virtues serve and shape that vulnerability into sanctifying responsiveness. On one hand, this distinguishes Thomas's account from those in which the virtues secure vulnerable humans against an unfriendly world. The exercise of naming God from creaturely similitudes tells against that tendency. On the other, Thomas intensifies the traditional notion that virtues empower agents to make the best of opportunities.[3] For Thomas's virtues help agents make glorifying use of creation, and in the surprising friendship of God, realize divine happiness from those uses.

Thomas devotes no particular section of the *Summa Theologiae* to something called "environmental virtues," but consider the moral ecology presupposed in his explanation of human dominion over the animals in Eden. In that state of innocence, says Thomas, humans did not need or use animals for clothing, meat, or riding—these are all later dispensations to our postlapsarian weakness. However, humans "needed animals in order to have empirical knowledge [*experimentalem cognitionem*] of their natures. This is signified by the fact that God led the animals to [Adam], that he might give them names expressive of their respective natures."[4] Thomas uses this event to explain the meaning of Genesis 1:26, the classic proof-text for Christian dominion, arguing that dominionist use refers first and primarily to the "necessity" of knowing the natures of creation. Thomas repeats that argument elsewhere when expounding the strong dominion of Psalms 8:8, again referring to the Romans 1 passage: we need visible creatures in order to know the invisible things of God.[5] For Thomas, the "natural subjection" (*naturaliter subiecta*) of creatures to human use occurs when God leads creatures to Adam, that he might carefully attend to each one, discern its specific difference in the world, and then, before God, award it a name designating its peculiar participation in creation.[6] Dominion refers to the *naturale desiderium* of humans for a supernatural end; or the moral ecology of sanctification.[7]

This strange event, in which God introduces to human "use" a menagerie of creatures that sin has not yet made subject to exploitative uses, only makes sense in light of creation's sanctifying function. God designs the Garden for two kinds of cultivation: "In the first sense, God placed humans in paradise in order that God might work and keep them [*ut ipse Deus operaretur et custodiret hominem*], and by so working, sanctify them." Fittingly, God cultivates human excellences by setting humans to their own forms of cultivation, that they might thereby learn God's courteous pattern of relationship with creation. Thus sanctifying grace attends the secondary sense, in which humans "dress and keep paradise." Humans do not impersonally steward the possessions of God, but find inherent happiness from working the garden. Caretaking, points out Thomas, was "pleasant on account of human experience of the powers of nature [*propter experientiam virtutis naturae*]."[8]

In the paradigmatic text, therefore, Thomas interprets dominion not as coercive rule but as a sanctifying share in the pleasant labor of enjoying God from creation. In giving them creatures to name, God gives humans the opportunity to glorify the love they themselves experience. In the garden, grace begins to sanctify humans by adapting their natural orientation to creation's goods. In the activity of naming, humans learn each creature, come to understand its place, and, through the attending grace of God, perfect their knowledge by using it to praise God. Humans slowly learn to enjoy God by praising God from their uses of creation.[9]

The liturgical resonances are instructive. Within certain practices, creatures become for humans sacramental, as if they were revelational words, "spiritual things described for us through the similitude of sensible things."[10] In the treatise on justice, appealing once again to the "invisible through the visible" phrase of Romans 1, Thomas affirms that liturgy must be externally performed for the sake of "the human mind, [which] in order to be united to God, needs to be guided by the sensible world. . . . Therefore worship makes use of corporeal things so that the mind may be excited, as by signs, to the spiritual acts by means of which humans are united to God."[11] Worship teaches humans how to use the creatures they are beginning to understand. Adopting Victor Preller, we can hear Thomas saying that humans learn to enjoy God from creation as if the creatures before them were words of a new language. Putting those names into fitting liturgical orders, using them in the ways of loving and praising God, grace leads Christians into a kind of theological fluency. By voicing intelligible praise, that fluency participates in the language of divine friendship.[12] God teaches humans how to master the use of creation for enjoying God, while the grammar of grace ensures that (as Preller puts it) "the formal object of faith is always God himself, as the principle establishing the efficacious order of soteriological causality operative in the empirical referents."[13] In other words, humans attain divine fluency with earth's goodnesses as Thomas's theological virtues shape humanity's "sensuous inhabitation of environment."[14]

Jame Schaefer draws on that connection between happiness (*eudaimonia*) and a humble, cooperative notion of dominion in order to describe Thomist environmental virtues.[15] Yet to many contemporary readers this environmental Thomas seems an innovation, due to the success of rationalist (and sometimes neo-Kantian) modern Thomisms. Jean Porter argues that, by treating personhood autonomously, apart from its connection to other creatures and from its embodiment generally, the modernists sundered nonrational creation from virtue. As the Thomist moral traditions neglected the "moral significance of prerational nature" for human happiness, says Porter, they "left theologians with few resources out of which to bring distinctive perspectives to contemporary debates over bioethics, environmental ethics, or natural rights—precisely the areas in which one might have expected a distinctive Christian voice to be heard."[16] Recovering the utility of Thomas for environmental ethics, therefore, requires recovering prerational and nonhuman nature in his account of the virtues.

However, when contemporary commentators do consider nonrational nature in virtue, they sometimes presuppose an antagonistic confrontation of humans with their habitat, leading them to single-mindedly emphasize the way virtues help humans overcome nettlesome contingencies or secure them from tempests of misfortune. Bowlin's investigation into the "moral ecology" of virtues, for example, begins by arguing that virtues are tools humans use to "work upon the contingencies we confront day to day." Virtues are good "as a consequence of the assistance they provide as we struggle to achieve the good in spite of our human frailties and in the face of the world's resistance."[17] Quite true; but by focusing only on nature's resistance, Bowlin's formulation overlooks the way virtues also help us to respond to the world's invitation into goodness, to be worked upon by daily environmental contingencies of beauty and glory. Bowlin, in other words, does not tell us about the sort of virtues that could respond to God leading animals before us for the sake of our wonder.[18]

We have seen from the exercises of divine naming, exemplified in the Garden menagerie, that virtues must also enable our sensory vulnerability to the world to discover contingent goods and use them for the sake of divine goodness. Seen this way, at the moment of perfecting grace virtues *increase* human vulnerability to the world, opening persons to forms of intimacy with creatures—an intimacy involving fragile connections and transient individuals.[19] Stephen Pope thinks we might even discover in Thomas the virtues of an analogical friendship with nonhuman creatures, suggesting our intimacy with the natural world might include analogical losses and wounds.[20]

Of course human flourishing is indeed physically fragile, at once menaced and sustained by its animate environs. Many virtues do secure life against natural evils (courage, to save life from peril), others accommodate life to limits and finitude (temperance, to moderate consumption), or help overcome the resistance of natural impediments (fortitude to endure putting up hay in the July sun). So much acknowledges creation's integrity, its autonomy from human uses, possessed of its own nonanthropomorphic goods. We live in a world of lions and plate tectonics and a hot summer sun, each with its own proper movements. Those movements may become material causes of natural evils for us or other creatures, but at the same time they partly shape our concepts of flourishing. The specific kind of privation they threaten orders our relations to ourselves and our habitats. The hungry wolf represents for a rabbit a natural evil, but one that partly defines the nature of a flourishing rabbit life (involving excellences of awareness, speed, and fertility). So also the set of natural evils to which we are vulnerable (mediated by such as the bright sun, viruses, and tsunamis) partly contribute to the character of human flourishing.

Remember, however, that Thomas pictures the greatest challenge of creation at the highest moment of human dominion in the Garden menagerie, where the world's membership teaches humanity about goodness. Created, contingent, and chance particularities not only test and threaten virtue, they elicit it. Our habitat invites and attracts human capacities, engaging reason and will with similitudes of truth and goodness. For Thomas, irrational nature cannot appear solely as a looming threat to human integrity, a chronic instability that reasoned action must reactively control. It also "inflames" our souls by way of attracting humans with the taste of goodness.[21] The environmental virtues order the passions inflamed by creation into appropriate practices, and the garden scene reveals two general models of practice: contemplative charity for the sake of communion with God and prudential providence, superintending the good order of earthly communion. Those two virtues shape human dominion (in notion, even if its instance has retreated to primordial myth and eschatological glimpse). They summarize a well-formed internal relation between passion and action formed from an agent's intimacy with her environs.[22]

Against the usual presupposition that grace threatens environmental concern, notice how a theological ("supernatural") virtue, contemplative charity, helps transform the rivalrous valence of the more mundane virtues into ecological friendship. Grace illuminates a moral ecology of friendship with God through friendship with the world. The theological virtues transform not just the content but the entire formality of virtue. Formed in the society of God's self-communicative love and shaped by the fundamental givenness of creation, the highest virtues assume an original and originary peace, undoing any moral ecology of death or politics of scarcity.[23] Thomas thus rejects a heroic concept of virtue, says John Milbank, and with it the thin peace of regulated violences seen in warfare against nature and in economic competition.[24] Thomas still fits virtues in correspondence to the "proper order and proportion wherein consists the idea of justice," but that justice "always presupposes and is founded upon God's original mercy," the overflowing communication of divine goodness.[25]

Charity's Moral Ecology

Since grace works to perfect human action into friendship with God, charity—which is the excellence of interpersonal relationship—forms the order of virtues. As the final end to human action, charity "gives the form to the acts of all the other virtues [dat formam actibus omnium aliarum virtutum]."[26] Friendship with God conforms humans to the self-communicating and self-giving patterns of divine life. Charity makes these virtues epiktatic (as Milbank says), dispossessive (as Hauerwas says), agapeic (as St. Paul says)—rather than self-enclosed or insular.[27] Charity does not simply add Christian content to moral action, new wine in old wineskins, but forms a new modality to agency. For the moral ecology of charity presupposes a world of peaceful differences, wherein agency invites and opens itself to the world's own participations in goodness.[28] Its excellences anticipate the names of creatures, becoming skilled with their glorifying uses.

Charity's attributes therefore must include the fine awareness, receptive appreciation, and rich responsibility that Martha Nussbaum celebrates as "love's knowledge."[29] But, contra Nussbaum's finally tragic Aristotelianism, for Thomas that knowing intimacy comes into harmony with nature's own peace and goodness, for it assumes a cosmos overabundant with divine love. For Thomas, we do not suffer the world's beauty tragically and we do not compete, finally, with the flourishing of others. Charity adapts humans to an abundant, peaceful habitat, as part of the way God adopts them into the abundance of the divine life.

Such extravagant promise for human action can make charity's moral ecology seem the rhetorical metaphor of a supernatural realm. Yet Thomas intends no gnostic imaginations of an alien sphere; he treats charity as the form by which humans materially engage the present world. So we must restrain claims that Thomist charity not only sums up the other virtues, but generates the field for their operation.[30] For Thomas refuses to let the primacy of charity turn this world into an untrustworthy allegory of one more luminous, just as he refuses to make the virtues fearfully secure personhood against the world. Thomas says charity is "mother" and "root" of the other virtues, but those others still remain reliably disclosive of humanity's moral ecology.[31] Indeed, they mark out the subsidiary goods usable by charity. Charity presupposes human facility to discover and identify the proximate goods of creation's integrity.

From Eden, the way of friendship with God was an environmental accomplishment, exercising human faculties for working, keeping, and of course naming. Through charity, grace perfects the nature of a creature whose integrity retains embodied, social, and discursive operations, receptively responsive to earth's own integrities.[32] Charity's gift does not overcome proper creatureliness, says Porter; while the Christian "enjoys a relationship with God of a sort that exceeds all natural aspirations, nonetheless she remains human, an inhabitant of the world and subject to its due claims."[33] Thomas integrates the virtues of enjoying God from creation's goodness with the virtues of successful environmental responses. Indeed these "lower" virtues enable and supply the higher, so that from practical knowledge of cultivating food from gardens we bring gifts for praising God. Thomas's charity does not overshadow those practical gardening virtues, but establishes their sanctifying role.

Consequently, Thomas admits a certain moral significance to natural evils. For virtues are habits fit well for context, and in our ecological habitat many human goods are fragile, scarce, or rivalrous. Humans are vulnerable and finite, by nature susceptible to deprivations, or what Thomas calls "natural evils."[34] Charity does not secure against deprivation; theological virtue promises no earthly talisman against natural evils. Instead, charity represents the use of fragile goods for enjoyment of a friendship of impassible good.[35] God befriends humans in the midst of natural privations. At the edge of our land is a stormy sea; above us a sky of untamable whirlwinds; below the thin skim of green crust, moving plates of molten rock; and living among us, creatures indifferently lethal. Grace perfects a human nature formed by an imperiled, bounded tenure.

For Thomas, God's friendship does not then give rise or rest to discontented fears of creation, nor harbor yearnings for angelic invulnerability, nor underwrite petulant whining about "imbecile" nature and its "murderous" ways.[36] In the gift of charity God does reveal a hidden "true logos of the bios," but humans only receive the gift through practical and liturgical intimacy with creation. Charity turns humans toward the world to truly hear and see our fellow creatures, so that as we glorify God in the names of praise we also discover the place we are given to inhabit and learn how to respond to it in love's knowledge. Grace restores us to membership in this earth community, as God works and keeps the membership that it may yield fruits of divine friendship.

How Charity Uses Humans to Perfect Creation

Love for our human friends gives reason enough to preserve green spaces and support a range of participatory practices with environmental virtues. In our care for other intellectual creatures, we should want both practical and contemplative resources of creation made equitably accessible. With respect to nonhuman creatures, says Thomas, we "wish for their preservation to God's honor and humanity's use; thus too does God love [irrational creatures] out of charity."[37] Thomas's account of sanctification makes access to the wonder and beauty of creation no mere recreational leisure but a primary material good for a flourishing human life.

Thomas thus grounds the typical ecojustice commitment to solidarity with the marginalized, because his theology explains the spiritual poverty of living in unclean, desiccated, or dysfunctional lands. For environments not only mediate socially imposed risks, they offer goods closely associated with friendship, human and divine. A community deprived of participatory access to creation's integrity is deprived of a potential liturgical theater. So many names of God are lost to them. Christians thus have reason to endorse policies that ensure an equitable range of environmental practices and democratic decision-making about land use. Recognizing this connection between creation's integrity and human happiness, some liberation theologians have begun insisting on the relevance of beauty, place, and diversity for social justice.[38] Charity assumes a rich environmental justice.

However, charity also refers to a justice more universal, to active promotion of the goods of creation for itself—and therefore it supports the ecojustice concern for the integrity of nonhuman creation for its own sake. Since charity's abundant relational stance to the world repeats the self-communicating *exitus* of God's goodness and conforms itself to the ordered *reditus* of creation, a general order of divine justice shapes charity's act.[39] Considered by their role within humanity's movement toward God, says Thomas, charity rightly loves all creatures and, especially, the good of the universe.[40]

We have seen how creation's integrity shapes human sanctification. Now Thomas shows how graced humanity in turn helps realize creation's integrity, as the virtues of God's friendship direct humanity's environmental caretaking. Because God offers friendship through the One through whom all things are made, for Thomas, "salvation entails the elevation of the entire natural order in which we live to a new supernatural end."[41] Because God sanctifies through the One through whom God also creates, grace illuminates a second connection between creation's integrity and Christian action.[42] Not only does God perfect humans through their special relation to creation; God perfects creation through its special relation to humanity.

Charity gathers together the "extensive and diffuse" array of creaturely resemblances of God, harmonizing them "intensively and collectively" into a specific human act.[43] Thus "the human being's own perfection is intimately connected with this promotion of the perfection of the universe," for the operation through which God cultivates humanity's friendship involves humanity's cultivation of creation's goods.[44] In the act of their own sanctification humans perform an ecological role unavailable to other creatures: they liturgically gather together every creature's specific desire for divine goodness and lift it toward God in union. So in the very way God cultivates the good of humanity, God uses humanity to cultivate the good of all creation.

Through human charity God perfects both aspects of creation's twofold integrity, as Blanchette explains:

> [Humans] sum up the perfection of the universe intensively in themselves through their knowing, and draw its multiplicity and diversity into a greater unity . . . overcoming in this way the differences that could otherwise keep the parts of the universe from communication within the whole, and bringing them together into what can be most properly called a universe. . . . The reason why intellectual creatures can "intensify" and "collect" the perfection of the universe in this way is precisely that they are themselves capable of the highest Good. . . . They can come to know and love God.[45]

Because Thomas, as we saw in the previous chapter, holds that "all things desire God as their end," then insofar as the human act moves creatures toward

God, he can say that creatures yearn to participate in charity.[46] Particular creatures and the universe as a whole, by seeking their own goods, desire to be included in the human love for God because by the manner of human charity, they too attain their own final end in divine goodness.

The way charity unites that desire, those goods, and that final end in human "use" explains the anthropocentric and hierarchical aspects of Thomas's cosmology. Creation's orientation toward charity's way of lifting creatures to God guides how we should read such passages:

> Every creature exists for its own proper act and perfection, and the less noble for the nobler, as those creatures that are less noble than humanity exist for humanity's sake, while each and every creature exists for the sake of the entire universe. Furthermore, the entire universe, with all its parts, is ordained towards God as its end, inasmuch as it imitates and shows forth the Divine goodness, to the glory of God. Reasonable creatures, however, have in some special and higher manner God as their end, since they can attain to God by their own operations, by knowing and loving God. Thus it is plain that Divine goodness is the end of all corporeal beings.[47]

Humanity's good does not rival the goods of other creatures, true human interests cannot threaten the harmony of creation, for humanity's way to God depends on the goods of other creatures and their ecological harmony. And creation's way to fuller union with God depends on loving, liturgical creatures. So creatures exist "for the sake of humanity," insofar as grace restores humans to their Edenic ecological role, in which, presented with creatures for the sake of knowing God, humans "referred the love of themselves and of all other things to the love of God as to its end."[48] Moving with desire to know God themselves, humans contemplatively range over creation, gathering up earth's pluriform loves into their souls. United and conformed to creatures, says Thomas, the intellectual soul starts to "become all things" as it returns all creation to God in its own divine union.[49] "Therefore, in a certain way the consummation of all corporeal nature depends on human consummation."[50]

Charity thus discloses the "seamless connection of the ordinary and the sublime" that Anna Williams finds in Thomas's unitive epistemology: "Thomas is willing to acknowledge that rightly loving and using creatures is a sort of this-worldly bliss . . . and in so doing, points both to the essential unity of beatitude, and of this life and the next."[51] Rightly loving and using nonhuman creatures incorporates the ordinary into the beatific, inviting our natural relations into a noble friendship with God. "If, for example, one were to know a willow tree overhanging the Cherwell," write Milbank and Pickstock, "our knowing of it would be just as much an event in the life of the form 'tree' as the tree in its wil-lowness and its growing." It would be a perfecting event, and insofar as the tree lives in a world beset by the sins of agonistic violence, it would be a therapeutic event, "a corrective or remedy . . . for the isolation of substantive beings."[52] By "using" things in reference to friendship with God, charity empowers nonhu-man creatures to realize the truth that they display in their treeness, their cloud-ness, their wolfness.

No wonder that misusing creatures might amount to a kind of blas-phemy.[53] In fact, Thomas explains the Fall in one way as a failure to love cre-ation rightly, subjecting creatures to the perversions of an obscene grasping for power.[54] Creatures do serve proximate human needs like food and cloth-ing, but just insofar as ordered toward humanity's need for charity. The anthropocentrism in that only points out our need to love creatures. Subjection cannot license nature's exploitation by distorted desires or tyrannical powers, for the charity of God's friendship seeks the intrinsic goods of created natures. Nature's most important utility for humans turns out to be its very integrity for itself.

Charity thus shapes dominion as its formal arc, ordering all subsidiary uses of creatures to the most noble use of praising and knowing God. And to all subsidiary uses, to all provisioning, art, technology, and recreation, charity refuses any pretense of spiritual finality or moral neutrality. Dominion for Thomas offers no lawless mandate; certainly it would not license the annihila-tive technologies deployed to serve every insane wish of a consumerist market. Quite the contrary, dominion reminds humans that God invites their lives to mean more than their appetites for resources, control, or power.[55]

We see Thomas explicitly reshaping dominion by charity at the beginning of the *Prima Secundae*. At the first of eight articles arguing that no created good can satisfy human happiness, Thomas appeals to the strong dominion of Psalm 8 ("you have made humanity ruler . . . put all things under their feet").[56] As he does in his Psalms commentary, here again Thomas interprets those verses by referring to Romans 1:20, knowing the "invisible things of God through things made," and once again to the Garden story of naming the ani-mals. Linking those three passages makes dominion refer to the role of cre-ation in human beatitude.[57] Dominion reminds humans that God presents them with creation for the sake of inviting them into friendship, that the goods of the world are given to them for the sake of life with God. In the last of those eight articles, Thomas reminds us that the fact that creation is given to human use does not mean that creaturely integrity reduces to human use, even for humanity's ultimate end. The universe is "ordained to God, as to its last end," and only so does it serve humanity's last end.[58]

Natural Evils and Ecological Goods

If grace perfects humans through intimacy with creation's integrity, what are we to make of natural evils—can charity love death and predation? Does sanctification include spiritual conformity to nature's economy of life and death? Is the stalking wolf really an animate representation of the divine mind, or is it a shadowy perversion of true wolfness, and so of God? Thomas's answer attempts a difficult combination: to deny that God wills privation, affirm the formative role of natural evils, acknowledge the environmental effects of human sin, and maintain the epistemic reliability of the world. In other words, Thomas wants to save the phenomena of the world as they appear while maintaining the interpretive priority of biblical narrative. To do so requires showing how charity discerns creation's goodness as it discriminates among moral evil and natural evil. It requires what the ecojustice strategy also needs: a hermeneutics of creation.

For Thomas, natural evils play an ecological role (not to say an evolutionary one), and so function economically for some good; but God does not will them directly as privations for particular creatures.[59] God does will the good of the universe, however, which includes the extension of diverse life even to corruptible creatures and their complex unification in reciprocal, ascending relations. Within that community, creatures are vulnerable to one another's use, according to their unique fit to this corruptible, finite, and temporally extended creation. Each nature sorts itself according to a distinct set of potential privations, negatively correspondent to its unique excellences. Wolves are ravening and lions fierce not by evil or demonic passions (people only say such things from ignorance and fear, says Thomas),[60] but by the habitual character of their actions to avoid starvation and pursue their proper goods.[61] Were the wolf tamed or the lion pacified, it would no longer intelligibly be wolf or lion but something else, perhaps a new species or maybe just a simulacra of something lost.[62] So too for their prey: removed from habitats in which their speed or perceptiveness has its facility, they suffer deterioration. Insofar as they fail to attain the goods proper to their nature, Thomas lets us surmise that bucolic lions "come under the notion of sin."[63] (But he does not let us forget the modality of such language; evil and sin primarily refer to the way rational creatures possess or fail to possess their good, and are assigned to irrational creatures only metaphorically, by way of a shared notion of privation or failure.)[64]

God does not create those privations, says Thomas, but because God communicates divine goodness in diverse intensities, including an array of embodied, corruptible, mortal ones, God exposes creatures to constant risk. Still, that seems odd, and here Thomas's articles struggle at uncharacteristic length, deploying multiple authorities and distinctions to explain why the risk includes inevitable death.[65] God's work must not only give occasion to natural evils, Thomas sees, but permit creation to use death for some higher good, such as metabolically unifying creatures into an intelligible, dynamic, self-moving universe.[66] Apparently, God desires creation to immanently sustain itself, thinks Thomas: "this force intends the good and the preservation of the universe, for which alternate generation and corruption in things are requisite, and in this respect corruption and defect in things are natural."[67] So Thomas settles on this explanation: God intends the sort of self-organizing, complex order that requires the corruption of individual creatures, but that corruption is only accidental to God's will for a rich display of goods immanently harmonized in a universal order.[68] His logic follows the "rule of double effect" Thomas employs elsewhere: God wills a good (diverse creatures in a complex universe) involving an accidental evil (natural privations), justifiable by the proportional worth of the good to the privation.[69]

In the case of natural evils, some commentators find that logic insipidly weak, as if God calculated the options and made a tragic choice—as if God were incapable or, worse, indifferent to a universe of violence and suffering.[70] Against the dilemmas of theodicy, the commentators may be right: suffering, omnipotence, and benevolence do not easily resolve themselves by a logic of intentions. But we should not read Thomas here as trying and vindicating God for the state of the universe. Thomas is not parsing moral evil (as he is when deploying the double-effect rule in the case of deciding murder) but teaching Christians how to embrace a world whose violence and beauty sit ambivalently with biblical hope.[71] In this case the rule functions not to separate an agent from an evil for the sake of the agent's integrity (not to distance God from natural evils for God's sake) but to help practical reason discriminate creation's integrity in the midst of natural evils. It functions to tutor charity in perceiving the lovable.

Thomas is trying to harmonize his connection of creation's goodness and human salvation with the appearances of the world. How can immature intellects discern the real, sanctifying fruits of creation in the midst of an unfriendly world? Thomas answers by discriminating objects from accidents of God's will, in order that we may choose for the objects and disregard the accidents; that we may love the universe and its creatures but not the corruptions to which they are vulnerable. Explicating a difference between primary and subsidiary causalities, the double-effect logic allows Thomas to affirm a natural, even indispensable role for violence and decay in creation without celebrating the privations themselves as goods.

The point is hermeneutic, not juridical. Consider Thomas's association of good and evil in this justification for predation: "A lion would cease to live if there were no slaying of animals; and there would be no patience of martyrs if there were no tyrannical persecution."[72] The good of lions requires some natural evil just as the good of martyrdom arises from some moral evil. The two evils are analogous in occasioning some good, but neither is thereby itself a good. Thomas is not inviting us to debate whether martyrs are worth tyranny or lions worth predation. The point is semiotic: Thomas disqualifies natural and moral evils from the creaturely phenomena by which God may be praised. Because they have no appetible or intelligible form, charity cannot refer suffering, decay, or violence to God's goodness, cannot praise God from death. It instead seeks the goods arising from the midst of those evils—like complex, self-sustaining order.[73] Virtue's perception attends to the lion's excellences, even glorying in the talent of its hunting prowess, but not the pain it causes. Virtue attends all the more to the Serengeti ecosystem that flourishes with lions and antelope and grasses in some dynamic order; but it refuses to regard hunger and pain as goods in themselves.

Although natural evils attend the proliferation of goods, because Thomas sees every creature pursuing some similitude to divine perfection, privation does not finally define or explain any creature. Wolves and deer seek and display certain participated goods, even if contingently they are shaped by each other's threat.[74] However much they reciprocally shape each other as constant threat and contest, lupine cunning and cervine speed derive from some aspect of the divine life, realized in a fundamentally good nature. If flight from natural evils occasions their particular realizations, it is nonetheless active pursuit toward a divine good. That natural goods are vulnerable makes them no less good, no less usable for loving God.

Thomas goes on to preserve that fragile balance of creation's integrity and creaturely corruptibility in discussing the Fall, where he acknowledges that human sin bears ecological consequences without undermining earth's epistemic reliability (and thus its sanctifying facility). Thomas tends to concentrate the Fall's consequences in human experience of the world rather than physical distortion of extrahuman creatures. So thistles and weeds were always there, he says; they only become noxious after Adam and Eve were expelled from the garden.[75] Dangerous animals were always predatory and fierce; they only became threats to humans after humans abdicated their proper dignity.[76] Human sin does introduce a kind of unruliness to the natural order, but not so pervasively as to undermine the integrity of creation or produce a cataclysmic change in the natures of other creatures. "For the nature of animals was not changed by humanity's sin, as if those creatures which naturally devour the flesh of others, like the lion and falcon, would then have lived on herbs."[77] Because sin unleashes no wholesale planetary rebellion (however much it may seem so in the self-made misery of humankind), Thomas forbids us to interpret the natural movements of lions, tsunamis, or parasites as themselves morally evil. He prohibits sin from becoming reason to despise those creatures we find inconvenient, or to excuse us from the labors of learning to lovingly know the earth.

Thomas thus preserves the ecological appearances while denying that either natural or moral evil fundamentally drives the organization of the universe or the formation of specific natures. After sin and in the midst of constant natural evils, creatures still display divine goodness, and so remain available for humans to enjoy the Creator through creation. In the face of natural evils, Thomas carefully upholds the promise of Romans 1:20, the naming of the Garden animals in Genesis 2, and his entire sanctifying structure of contemplative dominion. Natural evils may shape certain instantiations of natural goods, but humans can know those goods as participating in divine perfection without reference to the evil itself. Creation's order may preserve creatures through mutual and mortal dependency, but only because God permits creation its own ordering, as part of the way God communicates goodness to creation.[78]

In answer to our question about natural violence within the ecojustice strategy, then, Thomas acknowledges a morally significant ecological role for natural evils; but by denying them ontological finality, he still locates creation's integrity in God's goodness. The double affirmation relies on a series of careful distinctions, the most important of which is his generic difference between moral and natural evil. That distinction renders natural evils only metaphorically similar to moral evil, which makes privation morally suspect only when under the aegis of some practical rationality. Since nature's processes run by instinct and law, everything not actively ordered by humanity falls under a different mode of judgment altogether, where evils are only notionally related to sin. Let humans manage for the healthy predation of a land ethic, then, as part of their virtuous cultivation of creation's goods.

Humans must still differentiate natural evils and natural goods, that they might identify the true goodness by which creatures are referable to God. Doing so, humans anticipate the absolute flourishing of creation promised by its union with God, the peaceable kingdom known at the beatific end. Creation's future in God does not despise creation's present.

Thomas makes that fragile interpretive balance by relying on his notion of action consummated in the incarnation. Thomas, following Aristotle, views creaturely existence according to an act/potency relation, in which creatures realize the potential of their respective natures through their specific mode of action. Natural perfected acts therefore assume more explanatory burden than the privations that threaten them. Thomas's central ecological mover is creaturely pursuit of perfected act, which assumes stable natures fit into a complex universe. His view of nature therefore privileges natural flourishing and organic cooperation. At the same time, Thomas relies on the interpretive primacy of the incarnation as the form of God's act, the revelation of the fullness of act. Jesus Christ thus reveals the final end of creation, making the invisible manifest in the visible. The One in whom is revealed the peaceable kingdom is the same One through whom all things are made, so the One who establishes a new heaven and a new earth is the same One creatures already come toward in their own flourishing.[79]

True to formula, grace perfects nature, elevating nature by adopting and intensifying its pursuit of proximate goods.[80] Thomas thus preserves a charitable stance of virtue toward the world by refusing to find infamy in creatureliness, disallowing Christian enmity toward creation. Ecojustice may continue to love creation's integrity, including its drama on the Serengeti plains, without surrendering Christian hope for the peaceable kingdom.

Prudence, Providence, and Environmental Policy

Thomas of course wrote for a preevolutionary world, one in which chance, finitude, and death did not appear to play as significant a role as they do now. Nonetheless, by recognizing an ecological place for natural evils while maintaining the sanctifying goodness of creation, Thomas models a ktisiological grammar for ecojustice theologies that preserves together biblical and ecological phenomena. For Thomas, grace renders us vulnerable to creation's originary goodness, practically responsive to such things as predation and chance; yet God's friendship cultivate in us hope of the biblical promise for a new creation flourishing free from privation and violence. We can see that grammar at work in the virtues of prudent stewardship, where agents consider moral and natural evils together insofar as nature comes under the aegis of human practical rationality.[81]

Thomas defines right government as "the preservation of things in their goodness and the moving of things to good."[82] The stewardly virtues of governing some part of the natural world therefore actively and carefully promote creation's own integrity. "For the government of any prudent governor is directed to the flourishing of the things governed, as regards its attainment, increase, or preservation."[83] While Thomist renditions of political dominion have surely been deployed to justify exploitative practices, Thomas's stewardly dominion in fact must operate in attentive respect of creaturely goods and ecological orders. Stewardship is no indifferent regency over a homogeneous resource pool. As Thomas's repeated recourse to the Garden naming scene shows, the ecology of charity modulates dominion by an inclusive sanctifying order: creatures serve humanity in humanity's way to God, which intrinsically includes loving other creatures and promoting their integrity. Any human government over creation therefore serves the end of friendship with God by serving creation's own ends, preserving creatures in goodness.[84]

In other words, Thomas's account of grace refuses any final rivalry between humanity and creation, anthropocentrism and ecocentrism. His synthesis identifies two governing principles in creation, one intensively human and one extensively holistic, corresponding to the twofold perfection of creation in humanity (intensively) and in the universe as a whole (extensively). The created order mediates God's preservative goodness by ordering things into a sustaining whole. Meanwhile, humanity orders particular creatures to its prudential use, taking them into its own order of perfection.[85] These two created principles mediate, as secondary causes, the preserving goodness of God. They are like salt, says Thomas, mediating a kind of preservation.[86] Human stewards are the salt of the earth, preserving it in goodness (unless the salt has lost its savor).

Thomas's notion of environmental management for ecojustice therefore follows his pattern of grace: not coercing nature but perfecting its own intrinsic, natural goods. In its Edenic innocence, says Thomas, human mastery involved no violent coercion, not even practical manipulation. Rather, creatures responded to human leadership as naturally as they do the government of other natural orders—like cranes to their leader, says Thomas.[87] If our technocratic practices make that seem almost unimaginable, it is because sin has corrupted that gentle harmonizing, so that humans must bring forth the goods of creation, for their own use and the common good of the whole, in conditions of conflict. Still, that conflict appears rather limited for Thomas—a few noxious weeds and cavalier predators. Thomas's version of ecological care does not exorcize chaos or overthrow natural evils; it preserves the integrity creation already possesses.

Thomas's theology therefore proves the ecojustice line, "a thriving humanity on a thriving earth." For his excellent, sanctified humans cooperate with creation to bring forth its goods, distributing them for the just benefit of other humans for the good of all creation.[88] Cultivating those goods requires savvy ecology: concern for keystone habitats and healthy ecosystems, for the integrity of nature's own self-regulatory and developmental processes. Here the rule of double effect may helpfully parse the ethics of ecojustice land management: one can reintroduce natural predators in promotion of a flourishing species of deer, while not intending the suffering of particular animals. Or, better: one does not intend the demise of deer for its own sake, but as accidental to a healthier, more diverse and stable Appalachian ecosystem. For the steward "safeguards whatever pertains to flourishing rather than what savours of imperfection and defect," even when flourishing requires mortal threat.[89] Double-effect logic preserves this basic rule of government even when it manages for flourishing by predicted incidence of privation.

Thomas thus shows that the ecojustice strategy can, as Lisa Sideris recommends, adopt a land management ethos instead of romanticizing nature. Yet he accomplishes that precisely through biblical claims for the salvation of humans and the perfection of all creation. That means, as Gustafson says of Thomas that "the basic pattern of ethics is the right ordering of things in relation to each other as each is related to the other for the sake of the purpose of the whole."[90] But, contra Gustafson and Sideris, those relations, purposes, and orders move by the romance of friendship with God. Thomas's theology does ground a prudential land management ethic, but not merely by the immanent "continuities and relationships that persist through laws."[91] Humans exercise prudence for the sake of friendship with God, who befriends humans through their love and practical care for the earth's own flourishing. Thomas therefore grounds practical environmental management within his account of the way grace binds human perfection to creation's integrity.[92]

Conclusion on Thomas

However novel my reading of Thomas, I hope it at least demonstrates that he escapes facile categorization by cosmological centrisms. Instead he harmonizes (or resists the use of) anthropocentrism, theocentrism, and ecocentrism, precisely because he sees that God chooses to move creation to Godself by inviting humans into a friendship shaped by their intimacy with all creation. Attending to the pattern of God's invitation in grace, Thomas understands the perfection of the universe "not as a great chain of being taken abstractly by itself, nor as a structure indifferent to human endeavor, but as an order *whose very internal principle is the rational creature*."[93] The "true logos of the bios," then, is the charitable human, who, inflamed by God's goodness in creation, sums up and returns all things to God.[94] It is, of course, Jesus Christ, the very hypostasis of charity, through whom all things are given, including God's friendship. In Christ, all creation comes to God through God's friendship with humanity.

Ecojustice after Thomas now clearly has a place for nonhuman creatures in the pattern of God's grace. Ecojustice ethicists might wish that Thomas were clearer on how nonrational creation participates in Christ's victory over evil (both moral and natural). For while his Christ models a divine way of being creaturely by turning evils to unexpected goods, an exercise virtuous humans may repeat, Thomas only hints at how nonhuman creaturely flourishing might participate on its own in God's perfecting grace. Does the earth's regenerative, complexifying vitality constitute an intensifying participation in God's goodness?

Finally, notice of a common complaint: Thomas's natures seem static, and that gives rise to two related theological worries, both with practical implications for ecojustice. First, Thomas does not seem to allow nonrational creation to mean something for God's life, except insofar as it is assumed into the way God lets humans mean something for God's life.[95] That means Thomas leaves ecojustice without good theological resources for understanding creation's ongoing creativity. Second, static natures can seem determinative for the shape of grace, discounting the transfigurative effect of grace on creation. If so, Thomas leaves ecojustice ethics without resources for imagining how human sanctification restores and cultivates divine goods from the earth. What beneficent difference does salvation make for the earth itself? Eastern Orthodox and Protestant critics worry, in their respective ways, that Thomas's natures are insufficiently assumed into grace. Both practical critiques may derive from this perennial worry that Thomas lets natures remain autonomously static before divine action, signaling reasons to explore other ecologies of grace. We move now to Karl Barth to explore how an environmental strategy based on redemption constructs nature within the grace of discipleship, and then to Sergei Bulgakov to explore how an environmental strategy based on deification lets grace transfigure creation's dynamism.

8

Stewardship after the End of Nature

Karl Barth's Environment of Jesus Christ

Recall from chapter 4 how the stewardship strategy contours Christian response to environmental issues by the pattern of redemptive grace. Stewardship frames environmental problems within God's call to faithful relationship. In contrast to the ecojustice privileging of creation's integrity, stewardship starts from God's claim on human action. By focusing on response to God's initiative, it follows the pattern of justification. As we saw in chapter 4, stewardship's strategic turn away from nature toward human agency raises questions about the ethical significance of environmental indicators or natural features. How can stewardship conform to the earth as part of following God's call? Does response to God make for practical indifference to the earth? If God turns stewards back to earth in divine stead and redeeming mandate, does stewardship remain a structurally dominant relation?

To answer those questions, stewardship needs to show how God's action makes nature matter for faithful practices. To investigate theological support for an answer, we turn now to Karl Barth, querying this theologian of redemption with the problems of stewardship ethics. Since the strategy of stewardship appeals to the general pattern of grace Barth defended, his theology should display the liabilities and the promise of stewardship. It should also point stewardship theologies toward the most helpful resources within the pattern of redemptive grace. Taking a cue from the farmer-theologians of chapter 4, I will inquire especially after themes of place and reconciliation in Barth.[1]

Why Barth?

The sworn archenemy of natural theology must seem an odd source for any environmental ethic, and indeed Christian environmentalists summon Barth more often as foil than as champion. Among the accusations against Barth: so strongly developing the priority of grace that creation's integrity is annihilated;[2] being so concerned for human response to God's personal command that the ethical arena is narrowly anthropomorphic,[3] so fascinated by God's self-revelation to humanity that he misses the cosmic dimensions of covenant and christology,[4] so fixated on human freedom before God's address that person-hood appears abstracted from ecological place, and nature merely an inert stage for the salvific drama;[5] so rigorously describing reality from redemption that creation appears dully christomonist,[6] so attuned to salvation history that he loses the significance of geographical place in the kingdom,[7] so frightened of nature's generative and disruptive powers that he demonizes ecological fecun-dity,[8] and so beholden to hierarchical relations that human responsibility for creation is inevitably violent.[9]

Moreover, when Barth does make positive observations about nature or environmental experience, they can appear so idiosyncratic and impetuous that the reader is grateful for their earlier absence. For example, Barth finds moral commentary in the antics of captive sea lions, evidence of holiness in good horsemanship, and theological approval of the color blue. Much worse, Barth assumes that female subordination represents a created order, and then lets his theology justify its social forms with simply wicked ethical conse-quences.[10] Barth's use of natural description can look so outrageous one won-ders whether he is ironically demonstrating his point that appeals to nature tend to serve violent human folly. But we are given few places to worry, because in all of his four volumes on creation Barth finds little space to notice particu-lar creatures or natural systems—not even the mountains of his beloved Switzerland.[11]

Even if the silence stems only from Barth's personal opacity to the sensu-ous world, the structure of his dogmatics seems hard ground for environmen-tal restorations. Respondent to the priority of God's act, faithful practices, even earthkeeping ones, seem to bear a formal suspicion of nature. It would seem that any Barthian environmental ethic must recoil from the natural world as from apostasy, for fear it might allow some earthly standard to mediate and govern God's command. Barth's "Nein!" to natural theology keeps the earth silent, making sure Emil Brunner knows their country horseback rambles bear only parenthetic importance for Christian life.[12]

So why go on with Barth? Because stewardship ethics is liable to similar complaints. Barth's protest against natural theology represents stewardship's formal turn away from nature, and likewise must explain the implications for natural life. Those accusations against Barth variously worry that the transcendent otherness of divine grace undermines creation's integrity.[13] And Barth's bizarre environmental observations seem the inevitable consequence of talking about the world after the end of nature. The problems we came across within the stewardship strategy similarly make us worry that focusing on human responsibility before God seems to cut nature out of the moral picture, with uncertain consequences for the moral significance of environmental experience and natural science.

Notice also a certain agreement with the secular strategy of moral standing (seen in chapter 2): rather than unreliable descriptions of nature, ethics begins with the social practices constituting nature. For both Barth and the constructivists, ethics originates within the kinds of freedom shaped in encounter with otherness. Stewardship's transformation of that secular strategy relies on a Barthian insistence that practices are shaped in encounter with God's command. The shape of Barth's moral theology thus both approximates the strategy of moral agency and underlies the way stewardship theologies transform the secular strategy. We can therefore test stewardship's practical promise as a Christian strategy of moral agency through criticism of Barth's wider theological drama. How does the way of Jesus Christ to the world shape practices of responsible inhabitation? How do environmental problems matter within proclamation of redemption? We hope to know after reading Barth how missionary earthkeeping is a practice at once evangelical and earthy.

Christian Ethics after the End of Nature

Reading Barth in pursuit of stewardship, three aspects of his theological method appear especially important.[14] Each presents his "infinite qualitative difference" between God and the world against his ongoing "nevertheless," that God decides for the world. First, Barth insists on the revelational priority of God's act over being; that is, divine aseity determines theological science.[15] Second, a corollary to the first, God's act determines created reality, in both time and space, history and geography. This principle defends the infinite difference from natural theology encroachments while yet affirming creation's immediate dependency on God.[16] A third aspect governs the first two: we know God's act through the particular event of Jesus Christ. God's universal will is elective, revealed in and bound to a particular creature.[17]

In short, Barth thinks theology elaborates reality from within the concrete moment of the Word's self-giving. Since that moment is Jesus Christ, God's declaration about reality occurs with God's saving decision for humanity. The object of the science creates its possibility: Jesus Christ confronts humans with God's claim on their freedom. So humans know God and created reality through their particular response to encountering redemption.

That confrontation leads to three concepts in Barth's ethical method especially important for our inquiry. First, ethics meditates on obediently hearing the Word of God. Its focus therefore is God's will and action, not the relative rightness of human acts. Ethics has to do with faithful witness (*Zeuge*) to God's glory (*Herrlichkeit*), not sanctifying accomplishments.[18] Second, as witness human action may enact a "correspondence" (*Entsprechung*) to God's action. It is permitted and summoned to conformity with the pattern of God's ways. Third, because God calls human freedom into obedient and correspondent witness, human practices may function as a parable (*Gleichniss*) of God's coming kingdom.[19]

Connecting those theological and ethical aspects, we see that Barth determines practical reason by God's act, human freedom by God's decision. Theology begins from the event in which God claims humanity as God's own, and ethics proceeds with theology by demonstrating that claim as God's will.[20] For our inquiry, therefore, we need to know how such as reforestation or sustainable agriculture might conform to the pattern of God's ways and enact parables of God's kingdom.

Already we see two initial departures from the similarly act-centered strategy of moral agency. First, it is God's act, not humanity's, that determines the arena of freedom, and thus God's praxis that grounds normative reflection.[21] Environments come into view, therefore, through the work of God in Jesus Christ, in whom nature is constructed. Second, whereas the strategy of moral agency tends to undermine objectivist appeals in favor of social processes and cultural narratives, Barth insists on the objective ground of Jesus Christ.[22]

There remains, however, an important shared presupposition: both Barth and the constructivist critics suspect that normative arguments deploy natural description in ways susceptible to imperialist programs and narcissist folly. They agree that appeals to nature easily function as subtle ploys to reaffirm human power, which through so many social practices shapes our pictures of nature. Consequently, both Barth and the strategists of moral agency want moral practices justified by the forms of freedom. Insofar as stewardship appeals to free obedience rather than nature's own voice, Barth allows us to examine it as a practical theological strategy of moral freedom.

The shared presupposition, however, produces a shared vulnerability to the charges of antinaturalism levied against both Barth and "postmodern" environmental ethics.[23] If stewardship implicitly dismantles justificatory appeals to nature, it must show whether, and in what way, environmental indicators, like species counts or soil quality, can qualify environmental practices. When and how can the facts of climate change or the charisma of polar bears help shape appropriate practice? For the strategists of moral agency, that question arose in regard to the loss of nature's claim on ethics: after the end of nature, what beyond cultural distaste can critique environmental degradation? Stewardship theologies partially answered that question, but returned it to us in another form: how does the divine call to be good stewards relate to the specific character of the entrusted earth? Their confusion over the pattern of redemptive grace left us without a definite answer, so now we turn to Barth to clarify that pattern, and hence the practical earthiness of environmental stewardship. How is commanded stewardship care for the earth itself?

So we have two basic problems with stewardship for which we hope to find answer in Barth. First, we seek a theologically authoritative model of stewardship, with evaluative criteria for its successful enactment. What are the notes of good stewardship? Are they biblical, ecological, ecclesial, or what? Second, we need to know how stewardship benefits the earth itself, which requires knowing how creation participates in this pattern of grace. In what way does it make sense to say that the "rivers shout for joy and the trees clap their hands" in the election of humanity?

Grace and Place

For Barth, an environmental ethic would have to begin in "the Word of God as it claims humanity."[24] Its measure: that "one's action is good insofar as one is the obedient hearer of the Word and command of God."[25] For any environmental ethic, therefore, "the first task which obviously confronts us is to understand and present the Word of God as the subject which claims us."[26] Then can we proceed to determine how "the hearing and obeying which proceeds from and by the Word of God is one's sanctification."[27]

Those two sets of quotation come from II/2 and III/4, respectively; between them lie three volumes on the doctrine of creation. Barth places creation between the ethics of the doctrine of God and the ethics of the doctrine of creation, the claim of God's Word and the response of creatures. Creation is thus suspended in the moment created by salvific encounter with God's Word, in the crease between God's claim and humanity's response. That Barth elaborates the crease for three full volumes gives initial evidence to its significance. The ethical event "does not happen in empty space [leeren Raum]," as if it were a discontinuous vertical interruption.[28] God claims humans as earthly creatures, and summons their responsive witness in authentic earthling form.[29] So the encounter takes place not in some inert field or blank matrix, but rather "in that special space [bestimmten Raum] made by the concreteness of both these partners and their encounter."[30] Barth wants to talk about creation in the special place made by God's initiative for humanity. In other words, so bound is their environment to grace that humans only discover it within the event of God's encounter.

What stewardship makes of nature often turns on which pair of action verbs from Genesis 1 and 2 it privileges: is the human vocation to exploit and subdue (radhah and habhah), as in the first, or to guard and tend (abad and samar), as in the second? On the difference seems to hang two different world-views. But rather than work to vindicate a model of humanity's attitude toward nature, Barth uses both to describe how grace makes creation the place of encounter with God.

Barth discusses specific stewardship responsibilities in two parts of the Dogmatics: in III/1 as he treats creation in Genesis, and in III/4 in relation to human freedom as God's trust. The first arises from commentary on the Hebrew creation "sagas," while the second appears in his ethics of creation.[31] By beginning with the creation sagas of III/1, which juxtapose the two models of stewardship, and then asking what to do with stewardship under the aspect of command in III/4, which seems to privilege only the dominion side, we uncover a dialectical relationship between grace and place. As we will see, that relation corresponds to a pattern of reconciliation that develops politically while centering christologically. For Barth, God fashions a definite earthly arena of encounter for the Word to issue its invitation; God makes a place for redemption to summon and shape human freedom.

Genesis 1: Theocentric Dominion

In the first creation saga, Barth's exegesis does two important things for environmental ethics: it anticipates the therapeutic pattern of reconciliation and it deconstructs eco-fascist political ecologies. Both rely on anthropocentric assumptions, but, as with Thomas, Barth's soteriological treatment of creation at once affirms and undoes anthropocentrism. Making creation "the external basis of the covenant" directs creation toward servicing humanity, but only because and just insofar as humanity is claimed by God.[32] For Barth, writing the volumes on creation just after World War II, that lets God's claim regulate cultural appeals to nature, and makes any human dominion the provisional sign of God's restorative judgment.

Both of those moments rely on a place-making hermeneutic underlying Barth's exegesis throughout the doctrine of creation. Barth talks about the earthly role of humanity only within the special place made by God's action. God's encounter makes humanity at home on earth, inhabiting creation through relationship with God. The hermeneutic becomes visible from the first creation saga, where Barth reads proleptically what is often read conclusively: humans complete God's six-day work not in fulfillment of the cosmos but in anticipation of God's unique relationship. Right away, dominion represents no general fact about human status or ability, but signifies and awaits God's particularist promise to act for creation.[33] Focus thus shifts from human status to God's gracious invitation.[34] "What is proclaimed in this teleology of creation is not the glory of humanity, but the glory of God."[35] We misread the saga, says Barth, if we see humans at center stage; rather, through humanity's election God claims all creation, making it a definite arena of encounter.[36]

Barth's discursive metaphors unfold by a certain interpretive logic: God fashions creaturely places for the purpose of God's new act in them. Glossing at length the significance of God's Sabbath rest not only keeps the textual gaze on the Creator, but shows how God creates a hospitable space for creatures. During the first six days, "this whole has aimed and moved toward humanity as the inhabitant [Bewohner] of the house [Haus] founded and prepared by God." But humans only inhabit the house "when God in joyful Sabbath rest looks back upon it," and invites humans to respond to the divine joy.[37]

Creation becomes a real living space only within God's covenantal decision for it. But within that decision "the cosmos is a home [Haus] prepared to satisfy the needs of humans and their fellow creatures [Mitgeschöpfe], to nourish them both . . . as precondition for the activity assigned to both."[38] Barth's rhetoric of "home" underscores the hospitable way God's creative acts set creatures into peaceful provisioning relations. (In the first saga, Barth notes, neither humans nor animals eat flesh; creation lives without agonistic struggle.)[39] God spreads a generous table for all creation, fashioning places for creatures to dwell, and doing so in order that, by a further intimation of grace, God may dwell with them.[40]

God's Sabbath rest takes particularist joy in creation's goodness, which God signifies through covenant with humanity. Creation would have been good without it, but God makes the earth good in a further, more intimate way.[41] To that joy and the intimate place of fellowship it makes, dominion stands as witness. Within human inhabitation, the cosmos finds its own home in God by serving God's home-making for humans ("the activity assigned to both").

Note the coordination of Barth's actualism with a notion of cosmic place: creation becomes a special place within and by God's actions toward it. It becomes a covenantal place through the covenantal dwelling practices of God's elect, who receive the earth as gift and promise. Prefiguring his interpretation of the Garden in the second saga, Barth thus reads the Sabbath rest as indepen-dent creative event (*ein selbständige Geschehen*) in which God makes a "special space" (*besonderen Raum*) for more intimate encounter between God and cre-ation.[42] "God was not merely content to create the world," but right away "made it God's own," reserving its sphere for ongoing activity, so that "the sphere of grace is no foreign body" to creation.[43]

Barth's exegetical association of act, place, and home therefore suggests that "dominion" names the responsive practices in which creation becomes a special place of God's indwelling. Biblical dominion does not name a human status, but the elective manner of God's association with creation: "The ascription of this position and function to humanity does not mean that the rest of creation is excluded from this mystery; it describes the manner of its inclusion."[44] Neither then can dominion mean that nature stands inertly available to human machina-tion; rather it names creation's own ways of coming into God's place.[45]

Hence the first of those two things Barth's first saga does for environmen-tal ethics: theocentric dominion provisionally represents God's elective joy for creation, obviously anticipating the election of Jesus Christ. Dominion derives from no natural fact about the world, nor human power, but rests responsively in the pattern of God's action for the world. Dominion names the human response to God's special, place-making turn toward creation on the seventh day. Oriented toward glory, "even after its creation humanity needs the special blessing of God for the exercise of its lordship."[46] Dominion testifies to God's relationship to all creation, standing as a sign ("a very unequal repetition") of the day God turned to creation to joyfully bless it with intimate providence.[47]

Chastening technologically exuberant models of stewardship, Barth notes that God does not offer humans a partnership in the work of creation: "To the tacit annoyance of many readers and expositors, there is no corresponding invi-tation to action as participation in God's creative work."[48] Dominion does not repeat God's sovereignty; it only points to it. In correction to some contempo-rary stewardship approaches, Barth does not envision humans operating on behalf of God in the management of the world. The point of stewardship is the obedient performance itself, testifying to God's blessing. Active companion-ship with God in obedient stewardship becomes the place of God's rest and blessing for creation, not deputized efficient management.

The second point, Barth's resistance of eco-fascism, comes in his insis-tence that other creatures do not share any creative partnership with God either, but respond to divine fiat. Because God possesses all creaturely existence, sum-moning each creature to some distinct manner of service, humans may not religiously fear any natural spirit or cosmic power. If the world is God's, human freedom cannot be held in thrall by any creature. As Walter Lowe points out, God's absolute possession liberates nature's power and diversity, for freed from the transfixed, idolatrous gaze, it appears "various, many-faceted, a festival of innocent difference."[49] The Creator's monological fiat calls forth creation's manifold diversity, so that even those differences riven by phantasms of power (stormy skies) or spectacular size (great whales) need not distract human praise nor threaten their caregiving.

Most importantly, it disallows the tremendous spiritual power of landscapes to terrorize political life. In their own vulnerability and dependency, humans live in the world of God's command, and can thus freely accept their ecological limitation and dependency.[50] Humans need not marshal their powers to clear space for their freedom; freedom need not identify with divine powers in order to make a home by dominating nature; freedom dare not arrogate to itself earth's pliant voice.[51] Because creation already responds to God, "any proud or arrogant usurpation on the part of humanity is rendered impossible at the very root. The plants and trees were there without him and before him," in their own obedience, and so with "their own dignity and justification."[52]

Barth's reading of the saga on this second point, however, runs against the apparent sense of second verse of Genesis, which consequently invites criticism of his entire exegesis. The first biblical image of divine creation does not portray absolute command and response, but a spirit brooding over a formless deep. Barth's inventive, drastic solution: Genesis 1:2 ironically quotes from preexistent pagan myth in order to sublimate it by the command structure of the verses before and after.[53] Throughout his exegesis of the first saga, Barth sustains a polemic against any images or metaphors of co-creativity, especially the aqueous metaphors of creaturely or chaotic agencies.

His especially animated rejection of creaturely agencies permits Catherine Keller's devastating explanation for his bizarre exegetical invention. Keller claims that Barth's rhetoric of creation fearfully abhors the divine feminine, so that Barth intensifies the Creator's logocentric fiat in order to cauterize typologically feminine moments (the spirit brooding over a womb) from the creation story. Barth's polemic demonizes notions of self-generative becoming, immanent mystery, and embodied femininity. Barth's Creator not only commands without need of the feminine, but superfluously, ecstatically rejects all things aqueous, fecund, fluid, material, and chaotic. By demonizing the feminine against a masculine absolute order, says Keller, Barth's "(te)homophobic boundary patrol is guarding at once divine omnipotence and heterosexual potency."[54]

Keller's Barth is frightening enough to freeze a book chapter in its tracks. Not only does Keller portray Barth's doctrine of creation as running by pathological misogyny, but by suggesting that Barth desparately conceals co-creative energies evident in the biblical text, Keller undercuts his account of steward-ship as provisional witness. For if the saga really does contain rivalrous creative forces, God and the primal deep contending together, then affirming the bibli-cal language of dominion would bring humans into the very sort of partnership (humans working with God to contain the chaos) that Barth wants to exclude.

But Keller misreads Barth so willfully it casts suspicion on her entire cri-tique. She reads Barth's exegesis monologically, without reference to Barth's political reading of creation or to what Barth makes of the second saga. But Barth writes dialectically both within and without his text; his reading of the first saga intentionally subverts Nazi political ecologies, and works to set up his reading of the second, where a cumulative theological moment interprets the first. As we will see, Barth's reading of the second saga celebrates creaturely agencies from every side.

Even in the first saga, however, Barth does not flatten earth's agencies; he renders them obediently responsive, "bringing forth plants and trees" as if antiph-onal answers to God's call.[55] Barth had good reason to vigorously resist letting natural voices enter into a theological account of election. His use of the term *Lebensraum* intentionally takes up the vocabulary National Socialism deployed to describe the special "habitat" of the Aryan *Volk*.[56] By ordering the voices of nature to the command of God, Barth's "dwelling-place" (*Wohnsitz*) of human-ity implicitly resists eco-fascist place ethics by subverting the quasi-religious claim of *Lebensraum*.[57] By divesting nature of independent creative powers, Barth strips human dominion from supposing to arrogate them. Barth's exege-sis of Genesis 1:2, written in 1945, speaks in fearful, triumphant rejection not of the divine feminine but of Nazi geopolitics: "God will not allow the cosmos to be definitively bewitched and demonised . . . God will not allow the myth to become a reality"; God has excluded and "passed by this monstrous world."[58]

Then, having excluded the mythic *Blut und Boden* living space, Barth lets the second creation story describe the real human *Lebensraum* in the more inti-mate dwelling place of God's encounter. God's Sabbath act made a general arena of divine command; God's specific garden encounter will make an "actual place" (*wirklicher Ort*) for creaturely response.[59] As his vocabulary shifts from *Raum* to *Ort*, from space to place, Barth can celebrate creation's agencies. In the second saga's definite place of encounter Barth sees co-creative natures and responsive human caretaking, and all in images strikingly similar to those of that second brooding verse of Genesis. Keller somehow misses the aqueous, generative metaphors of this second saga, where humans arrive with the rain and attend a womblike garden overflowing with surprising new life and rivers of water. What should we make of finding such "tehomic" imagery immediately after the text that Keller critiques? We need to know because the imagery of both sagas appears again in Barth's account of Christ's work (involving the vulnerable, opened, watery body of God, attended by a brooding Spirit).

Barth reads the two creation sagas as successive divine encounters making more intimate arenas of fellowship, from Sabbath to Garden, on the way to covenant and the event of Jesus Christ. The real habitats are the places of divine habituation. Obedience in regard of God's two special trees, he says, gives way to obedience in the life of the covenant with Abraham, and then obedience to the cross.[60] Barth's doctrine of creation roots environmental stewardship in the places of God's encounter, ultimately in Christ's redemption.[61]

Genesis 2: Service in Eden

The second saga compels Barth to consider creation and covenant "from the opposite angle": "covenant as the internal basis of creation."[62] From this angle, observes Barth, the earth itself appears most important to God, and humanity is "introduced only as the being who had to be created for the sake of the earth and to serve it." The earth has an "end in itself," for the sake of which humans were created. Arriving on the scene with the rain, humans appear as part of the earth's self-generation, given a particular role in service of "the onward course of creation."[63] They are made from and for the earth, in a specific ecological niche. In this saga, says Barth, we are "dealing with a more intimate connection between earth, beast, and humanity."[64] In the biological community, humanity "has a gap to fill at this point. . . . just as necessary as the watering without which the earth cannot be brought to completion. . . . In spite of all the particular things that God may plan and do with them, in the first instance humans can only serve the earth and will continually have to do so." Belonging to "complete integration into the totality of the created world," humans perform an ecological service: "To make that which has been planted thrive, God needs the farmer or gardener. This will be the role of humanity."[65]

Even though God breathes specially into the human, it is still "the creation of the human who must work and serve under the heaven and on earth, i.e., in relation to fellow creatures."[66] Even as creatures gifted beyond what nature could have expected of a niche animal, humans are "destined, within the framework of the creaturely world, to serve the earth as a grower [*Bauer*] and a gardener."[67] For "the hope of the whole creaturely world . . . [the otherwise] arid, barren, and dead earth is that it will bear the vegetation of God." Human gardening serves that hope, bringing forth fecundity from sparsity; the "human act will be an act of release for the earth, too, and for the whole creaturely world." For the earth's own promise "humans must give themselves to till and keep the earth in order that it may have meaning when God will bring it to perfection."[68] A reader might think it was Wendell Berry summarizing the Hebrew creation story: "And this human is set in the service of the ground from which he was taken, of which he has need and to which he will return."[69]

Notice how these functions mimic Genesis 1:2: whereas there a spirit broods over virtually fecund waters, here a gestative humanity moves over incipient soils. Meanwhile, God provides a "mist . . . rain . . . humidity, without which the service and work of humanity would be in vain."[70] By the time we reach the garden, the chaste mist has become a river of fecundity, producing the "surprise" of trees from shrubs and pleasurable fruits from herbs.[71] Keller's "tehomic fecundity" seems everywhere in Eden. Barth says that

> the most striking statement . . . is that about the river which has its
> origin in the Garden and then divides outside the Garden into four
> branches which encircle other regions. . . . water collected to burst
> forth in Eden, thus bringing to the Garden the fertility it needed if
> God was not to cause the trees to grow in vain . . . All the rivers of the
> earth, and therefore all fertility, all possibility of vegetation, all life on
> earth, have their origin here in Paradise in the one river which
> springs forth in it.[72]

Keller rightly sees Barth at first associate menacing chaos with watery metaphors; however, by the end of the second saga, "it is no longer water averted and restrained but the water summoned forth by God. It is no longer the suppressed enemy of humans, but their most intimate friend. It is no longer their destruction but their salvation."[73] In the Garden God makes a place for creaturely generativity and freedom, for wildness responsive to God's initial act.

Repeating and intensifying the place-making event of God's Sabbath act, Barth treats the Garden of Eden as a new creative event that illuminates the meaning of both creation stories up to that point. Humans are "specially brought there and given rest—an indication that the establishment of Paradise is a distinctive spatial parallel to the institution of the Sabbath as a temporal sanctuary in the first saga."[74] The Sabbath made earth a unique temporal space (*besonderer Raum*) of God's joy; the Garden creates a determinate ecological place (*besonderer Ort*) for God's fellowship.[75] (Notice the change from cavernous *Raum* to specific *Ort*.) Eden becomes the specific locale of God's orientation toward creation, the particular environment of God's favor. "Specially planted by God in a special and limited place [*Ort*]," and uniquely belonging to God, Eden is already a new earth, where the fecund soil and fruitful human labor belong to each other.[76] The Garden "epitomises a good land . . . a place on earth [*ein Ort auf Erden*] where it is clear that the earth which humanity is ordained to serve is also ordained to serve humanity."[77]

Within and for this special place of divine favor, God breathes into humanity a divinely fructifying spirit, that in human work the earth might become verdant. In the Garden, *Lebensraum* gives way to *Lebensodem* (life-breath), the terrifying geopolitical demons to the peacefully fecund spirit of God.[78] God breathes life into humanity, and so sends humans to gestate over the fecund earth. In relationship with humanity, "God creates salvation and life, God wills that the earth should be green, and therefore makes it a watery earth."[79] God's Garden restores water, spirit, fecundity, and vegetation as it gives humans their "dwelling-place and duty."[80]

If we thought we were reading cosmology, says Barth, a certain "higher key" to the text alerts the reader that a historical narrative has proleptically begun: earth's future is at hand in the form of a special covenant.[81] A pleasurable surprise in itself, Eden prepares humans to await new things God will yet do. Notice, says Barth, that where before the good earth had shrubs and mist and satiated humans, now it exultantly produces trees and rivers in which humans find a pleasurable dwelling-place. Eden concentrates and animates the creation sagas in preparation for the coming covenant.[82] The two previous sagas, one in which earth serves humanity and a second in which humans serve the earth, come together in readiness for God's new narrative. Before, "it was not in any way self-evident that humans should be appointed its inhabitants, composers [*Bearbeiter*], and keepers [*Wächter*]"; but now God invites creation into further intimacy by bringing humans into God's special place to live and work. Keeping and composing a local garden, humans fulfill the cosmic vocation of the first saga: in "this part of the earth they fulfill their ordination [*Bestimmung*] for the whole earth and thus actually live."[83]

So Barth appears to marvelously privilege "guard and tend" over "exploit and subdue," as the specific place of Eden determines the actual practices of stewardship. God's rivers and trees shape the patterns of human inhabitation that respond to the earth they find, not one they make. For God placed humanity in a grove with trees already brought forth. "Cultivating," therefore, should be understood as a form of arborism, not silviculture.[84] The steward is a *Baumgärtner*, "ordained to nurture and keep vigil over this orchard [*Baumgarten*]."[85] Analogous to keeping the hallowed temple, stewardship is for Barth a priestly function, "responsible to both God and the creature."[86] In liturgical response to the glory and beauty of God's creative act, stewardship attends to God's will for a flourishing earth.[87] Stewardship keeps faith with the place of God's favor.

Nature Silenced, Freedom Commanded

Stewardship appears startlingly different when Barth returns to it three volumes later in his chapter "The Command of God the Creator" (III/4). If the reader just came from III/1, she might wonder whether she is reading the same author. Whereas earlier the stewardship motif formed around Eden's trees, here divine command relentlessly undoes naturalist preoccupations. From III/1 to III/4 the meaning of stewardship seems to change from ecological to historical, dislodged from Eden's place and resituated in the temporal arena of covenantal responsibility.

In III/4, stewardship appears entirely as obedience to the command of God in Jesus Christ. The labor of the orchard-keeper is now "freedom before God," the natural sociality of male and female now "freedom in fellowship," their duty to cultivation now "freedom for life," and the character of Eden as a bounded place is now "freedom in limitation."[88] Stewardship no longer refers to the particular trees, but to God's claim on human freedom.

Indeed, Barth no longer writes about trees, but shifts the attention of stewardship almost entirely to human life. Whereas in the garden stewardship was an exercise bringing forth earth's greenery, now the object of God's fecund benefit is human life itself. Humans are asked of their own lives questions that previously would have been asked of the orchard: "Will they recognize and appreciate the value of the gift? Will they realize that it is given them in order that they may use, enjoy and make it fruitful?"[89] One might think Barth is only on a different topic now, using the stewardship trope to illuminate a different sort of trust. But this occurs in precisely the place we would expect to find responsibilities to the earth: under the subheading "Respect for Life"—a moniker Barth mischievously borrows from Albert Schweitzer in order to show just how anthropocentrically he means it.[90] Whereas human duties earlier served God's special garden, now "God is obviously not interested in the totality of things and beings created, nor in specific beings within this totality, but in humanity." Barth makes sure our attention does not wander: "Humanity is obviously at issue. . . . Humanity is obviously the object. . . . Humanity is obviously the partner. . . . God stands by humanity."[91]

Not only is the object of stewardship restricted to human life; Barth describes its practice in a new way. Whereas humans nurtured the garden in practical attentiveness, now with regard to human life they stand back in "astonishment, humility, and awe," nearly averting their gaze before a mysterious and holy presence. The skillful care in such as pruning, thinning, and harvesting has given way to a general openness to encounter. For in the environment of God's initiative for humanity, life does not merit respect and its attendant virtues intrinsically, but rather derivatively, insofar as it is the object of God's command.[92]

Only after having disestablished nonhuman life from consideration, only after God's command has thoroughly displaced any natural facts as would-be rivals, nearly as an afterthought, "we may insert what is to be said about the attitude of humans to beasts and plants." And then only after much textual hand-wringing suggesting that we have nothing to say directly about them, for we share no common relationship, only the affinity of an outwardly physical connection.[93] But then Barth does begin to have something to say. Having entirely sidelined nature's standing, silenced its claims before God's command, Barth reintroduces the nonhuman world as a question for the commanded human. He partially rehabilitates Schweitzer, appreciating his insistence that ethics cannot arbitrarily restrict itself to the human sphere, as if some natural facts dictated the boundary. God's command, says Barth, might well have implications past interhuman encounters, and so we should inquire. Schweitzer could be right that plant and animal lives give voice to ethical claims, or at least that they might virtually do so: "If we are really listening in relation to the human life of ourselves and others, we cannot feign deafness with regard to animal and vegetative life outside the human sphere." Thanks to Schweitzer for warning us of this "so warmly and earnestly."[94]

Yet Barth cannot just warmly and earnestly restore ethical responsiveness to the natural world, for having saturated the ethical arena with God's command, fascinating freedom by the summons of God, what could it mean to "listen" to creatures? Their voice represents only humanity's living space, the life that supports our possibility for being claimed: "the world of animals and plants forms the living background [*lebendige Ausstatung*] of the habitat [*Lebensraum*] divinely allotted to humans and provided for them."[95] The natural world is the environment of God's command, and its voices belong to God's initiative for humanity.

What sort of environmental stewardship can that generate? Repeating his description of the human mandate in the first creation saga, Barth says that before God's command humans exercise dominion not *over* the earth, as if it were subject to their command, but "on the earth," as it exists for the sake of humans being commanded.[96] With respect to vegetation that means prudential conservation for the sake of human nourishment. Plants may be freely harvested for food within the limits of sensible use (*sinnvoll Gebrauch*). Senseless waste (*sinnlose Verschwendungen*) or adolescent destructiveness disrespects the supportive role vegetation plays in God's covenant.[97] So wise use witnesses to God's unique call upon humanity—but that seems to stand very far from the careful, joyful arborism of Eden.

Animals fare better. As Barth wrestles with the physical connaturality of animal and human life, he thinks their lives warrant something more than prudent conservation. In fact, Barth sometimes seems ready to temper his command-centered ethics before the mute faces of other sentients. Although he has sundered freedom from its ecological context by force of God's summons to humanity, the biological kinship between human and animals lives seems to press against Barth's categorical treatment.

Barth begins by appealing to the first creation saga, affirming that humans have rights of lordship to use animals. Yet he is drawn toward the "fellow-creature" of humanity, so close a relation and (perhaps romantically now) "so useful and devoted a comrade." Such friends require "careful, considerate, and above all, understanding treatment." Human use of animals requires sympathy, such as a good horseman has, one who "is so completely one with his horse that he always knows . . . what it can not only give but is willing and glad to give." Such a horseman, he even says, "cannot really be without God." Barth further hints toward sympathy with wildness by sneering at those who cage animals for spectacle, and by delighting in the little revolts of captive sea lions.[98]

Then follows Barth's remarkable commentary on the killing of animals for food, in which the dominion of the first creation saga seems to mix with the attentive priestly role of the second. Barth observes that animal-killing is prima facie repulsive in two ways. First, it suggests that the peace of creation, of the human role with their trust, is continually threatened. Second, it too near approximates homicide by annihilating a unique being. In both cases the specter of nothingness menaces the peaceful space of creation. No right of dominion, no human authority or natural law, can justify this, thinks Barth. Killing may, however, be provisionally permitted by the pattern of redemption, as "a representation of that which God in God's grace really is for humanity": a flesh sacrifice, given freely by God on behalf of humanity. Humans may kill animals "only in recollection of the reconciliation of humanity by the Man who intercedes for them and for all creation"—only by participating in the passion of Christ![99]

In relation to care of animals, therefore, stewardship seems to reacquire some of its priestly character as an active and attentive mediation. The good steward may take animals in the course of maintaining the sort of life in which God's word can be heard, but she must remember that only the specific act of the Word permits her doing so. Even as she kills, she must "hear this groaning and travailing of the creature" for reconciliation. Even as she takes, she must care for and befriend animals in expectation that God will satisfy their longing for liberation.[100]

At this point Barth turns to matters of human sickness and health (for remember, all this comes in the context of respecting human life), and we seem left with an ambiguous teaching on environmental stewardship. The main point for environmental ethics from III/4 was that we concern ourselves with nature only by way of God's concern for humanity, and so in material support of the election of humanity. But as we came to its end, Barth was clearly flushed with sympathy for animals, and in support of human responsibility toward animals he invokes Christ's atonement to reinstate the attentive priestly virtues of the sort he earlier described in the Garden. In the course of his rigorous redescription of the ethical domain by the event of God's summoning humanity, Barth seems to pause, arrested by the suffering of nonhuman creatures.

Interpreting Stewardship in Barth

One wonders whether, in the environmental consciousness of the next generation, in the face of species loss and climate change, Barth would have found more occasions to pause. As his record on stewardship stands, however, it appears Barth has only reinstated the mastery of humanity over nature, perhaps slightly qualified by affection for domestic animals. Between the two volumes we have two very different models of stewardship: one a specific creaturely role in concert with earth's integrity, bringing forth its goodness, the other a responsibility to maintain earth enough to preserve the conditional possibility of God's encountering humans. They are what roughly amount to a stewardship of earthkeeping and a stewardship of wise use; one alive with earthly perception, the other drawing our ethical hearing away from nature's voices to the transcendent call of God. Unless we discover another way to understand how the place-bounded earthkeeping role in III/1 relates to the temporally conditioned lordship in III/4, Barth's transition from the idyllic garden to provisional struggle would appear a supercessionist move from paradisiacal stewardship to a postlapsarian environmental realism. And his account of grace would default toward a "wise use" model of stewardship. So how do these two stories of stewardship relate to each other?

The way the dominion language in III/4 repeats themes from the first creation saga (dominion, commandment, *Lebensraum*) offers an initial hint: perhaps as the first saga was transformed by the second's Eden, so too the allotted dominion of III/4 anticipates a surprising new environment. Remember how the Garden became the "actual place" of human responsibility, shaping humanity's living space into God's special place of dwelling. Perhaps the dominion language of III/4 will be transfigured by God's new creative work in Jesus Christ, which makes the special place of humanity's dwelling. Barth already said in III/1 that dominion's honor anticipates and refers to the honor of

Christ's work.[101] We might expect then that the dominion language of III/4 sets the stage for the coming volumes on reconciliation, which narrate God's new work in Jesus. If so, the ethics of creation in III/4 anticipates an ethics of reconciliation in volume IV, where human practices take shape in the environment of Jesus Christ. In the next chapter I will test that hypothesis, for it should finally define how the pattern of redemption specifies the appropriate model of stewardship and the moral role of nature within it.

9

Nature Redeemed

Barth's Garden of Reconciliation

In the previous chapter our search for Barth's model of stewardship pointed us toward God's work in Christ. Even though we began reading Barth for his view of specific practices, the question has delivered us into his renarration of the Gospel. Environmental responsibility now rests in God's initiative for the world in the election of Jesus Christ, wherein human action is habituated to God's reconciliation. So we have been delivered specifically into the doctrine of reconciliation, which is the locus for human responses within Barth's threefold adumbration of God's work. Within justification we can explore, as Barth jarringly puts it, how to understand the Gospel as law.[1] Within sanctification we discover the way obedience is real goodness for the creature. Within vocation we explore how God's act invites earth-attentive obedience. Together we discover how the Gospel commands environmental stewardship, and how Christ's work makes the special place of human obedience.[2]

As the fact and form of God's self-revelation, Christ reveals the pattern of God's ways and works with creation.[3] The first three books of the volume on reconciliation explicate that pattern: the humiliation of the Lord to rescue prideful humanity, the exaltation of the Servant to sanctify slothful humanity, and the glory of Christ to call deceitful humanity to authentic witness. Encounter with Christ shapes human discipleship according to those contours of God's reconciliation.[4] Recalling the place-making function of grace that we saw in chapter 8, we are now poised to see how Barth makes this christological pattern the habitat of human freedom. God's act in Christ establishes an arena (*Bereich*) of human action and a direction (*Fuehrung*) for its response. Christ's act becomes a relational sphere for Christian practices. Choosing *Bereichen* over *Ordnung* (Brunner) or *Mandaten* (Bonhoeffer), Barth makes reconciliation the domain of human obedience, an environment for faithful service.[5]

The spheres of responsibility in III/4 thus anticipate and presuppose Barth's exposition of reconciliation in volume IV.[6] Responsible human action before the Creator is surrounded and elicited by the work of the Reconciler.[7] In other words, Jesus Christ is not simply the exemplary steward, around whom the ethical imagination swirls, wondering what vehicle he would drive. He becomes himself the environment in which faithful stewardship arises, the habitat in which humanity flourishes. Again God's act makes a special place for creatures, only now the grove of Gethsemane is the garden of Christian stewardship.

The Environment of Jesus

Because Christ's work forms the place for God's dwelling with creation, we see its significance for stewardship more clearly if we recall that the Reconciler transfigures the preceding environment of the Creator's providence. Between the volumes on election, by which it is established, and those on reconciliation, by which it is shaped, are the volumes on creation, where the creature exists in its general activity before God. Already suspended in the grace of God's will, creatures live "accompanied and surrounded by God's own activity."[8] Divine providence is their habitat, their living space. In God's providential act creatures have their *Lebensraum*, a space protected from the menace of nothingness.[9] Only later, does Christ's new creative act make this *Raum* into a definite *Ort*, as the Garden did for the Sabbath earth.[10]

First, however, creatures give thanks for the roomy grace of God's allotment. "Gratitude is the precise creaturely counterpart to the grace of God" in the living earth.[11] As the Psalms repeatedly attest, humanity gives thanks alongside all creatures, and so humanity "does no more and no less than all other creatures do with their life. It does no less than the sun and Jupiter, but also no more than the sparrow of the lane or indeed the humblest Mayfly." Stewardship offers thanks amidst a multitude of implicit creaturely thanksgivings. It recognizes that humanity "is not the only creature of God"; but "as God's Word of grace is spoken to humanity in its creaturely sphere, it is also spoken in this greater sphere. . . . They too are threatened and they too are held by the Word of God."[12]

Moreover, insofar as humans uniquely show gratitude through dominion, stewardship mimics God's providence in he sort of actions that do not threaten but create habitat for others.[13] Responsible human agency therefore accompanies (begleitet) other creatures by preserving space for their lives against the menacing threat of nothingness.[14] Barth's insistence that humans cannot know the specific ways other creatures express their gratitude means that we cannot engineer it, improve it, or substitute it for a supposedly equal proxy. We can only make room for creatures to perform their own thanks.[15]

Again, Barth refuses to let dominion mean that humans mediate God's providence.[16] No "natural" or phenomenal characteristics of humanity—not rationality, sociality, or creative dignity—definitively mark off the human from its creaturely fellows.[17] Whatever dominion or service may be allotted to humans refers to the Creator's permission for them to offer unique gratitude.[18] If the human "steps out of [herself] and transcends the limits of the creature," says Barth, it is only as she performs a creaturely duty within an excessive vocation (Berufung).[19] Stewardship thus entails no imperial freedom won in virtue of unique capacity, nor even the just ordering of earth's creaturely judge. It means the humble self-offering of a creature witnessing to the Creator. For Barth, humans are "not the means but only the witness and sign [Zeuge und Zeichen], the liturgical assistants as it were to God."[20] Stewardship is not a form of management, but of invocation (Anrufung).[21]

When we come to the volumes on reconciliation, Barth intensifies the living space of general gratitude into a special place of attentive dwelling practices. Just as the Garden of Eden resituated humanity's dominion, so the work of the Reconciler resituates humanity's vocation. For Jesus at once stands in the place of the cosmos receiving God's sustaining approval and performs the correspondent response of the creature. "Jesus is the one in whose human being and thinking and willing and speaking and acting there takes place the grateful affirmation of the grace of God addressed to the human race and the whole created cosmos."[22] Jesus sums up and perfects the creaturely vocation to gratitude. Humanity becomes the Creator's actual partner only in the definite place of Jesus Christ, the Garden of the real human, from whom God brings forth surprising fruit.[23]

In Christ, God acts redemptively toward humanity, "pitying and receiving this particularly threatened and needy creature within a threatened cosmos of God's creatures," by inviting humans into God's nurturing and guarding act for the whole creation.[24] Humans become members and partners in the covenant not by assuming sovereign privileges, but by encountering God's good favor toward creation and responding to it. As the very creature whose fall permits chaos to menace creation, humans are recuperated into God's fellowship by being given the task of testifying "that the Yes which God as the Creator has spoken to creation should prevail; that all humans and all creatures should be delivered from evil."[25] The Noachic covenant with all flesh is fulfilled in the election of the Reconciler, who comes walking on water; never again shall earth be threatened by the rise of stormy seas.[26]

Against all logical expectation, humans become "guardians" of that act, keepers of creation's goodness after the pattern of their own rescue. They are given a share in defending the Creator's honor, showing God's zeal that earth should remain full of glory.[27] Stewardship thus enacts God's faithful dwelling with the earth by defending the habitat of Christ's reconciling "Yes" to creation.[28] "To embark on that venture," says John Webster, "is not to aspire to become co-regents with God, but rather to enter into and act out an order which, in its specificity and limitation, receives and testifies to the generative action of God in Christ."[29] It is to dwell on earth as in Jesus, where God dwells with humanity.

Christological Subversions: Servant as Lord, Lord as Servant

The work of Christ recapitulates the divine act of creation in a particular creature. Christ "is the concrete reality and actuality of the divine command and the divine promise, the content of the will of God which exists prior to its fulfillment, the basis of the whole project and actualization of creation."[30] The doctrine of reconciliation thus assumes and consummates (*aufhebt*) the theological functions of Sabbath and Garden, at once intensifying, abrogating, and reestablishing them in the kingdom.[31] The work of Jesus Christ gives creation a place in God's act, and that special place shapes the pattern of human service. *Ort* determines *Ordnung*. Christ's work becomes the relational context (*Bereich*) for responsive human action.

Reconciliation makes place for God's surprising vegetation to take root. It is the habitat of the elected community: "We find ourselves in his environment [*Umgebung*]."[32] Christ is both the theater of human action and its specific form. Humans therefore learn how to enact the Creator's "Yes" from within encounter with Christ, "as members of his territory [*als Angehöriger des Gebietes*]."[33] For God's "kingdom and lordship and dominion are concretely the kingdom and lordship and dominion of this man exalted by God to fellowship with God's being and work: the man in whom God became a servant, humbling himself in his Son."[34] Stewardship's dominion follows the pattern of Christ's service.

In chapter 4 we saw that theologians often qualify stewardship within the figure of Christ. They justify environmental responsibility by appealing to the beneficent character of Christ's dominion, so defending stewardship against accusations of coercive control. In Barth, however, the move appears different, for reconciliation does not restore partnership powers; it transfigures the providential order. Christ the servant does not simply establish a new order, but gives himself over in subversion of monstrous orders, letting himself be penetrated by the dark chaos in order that his body, the material Word of God's "Yes," would utter the final "No" against destruction. So appeals to the character of Christ's dominion should generate embodied practices vulnerable to the menace arrayed against all creation, in order to proclaim God's continued "Yes" to creation.[35]

Jesus reigns in submission not to establish a new moral regime, but rather to proclaim and reestablish God's love for creatures, and so regather creation into that love.[36] For Barth, then, stewardship does not mediate or administer Christ's act; it witnesses to what God's body has done for creation. Correspondent human freedom follows Christ's pattern not by managing the world correctly, but by witnessing to God's reconciliation already accomplished in Christ. Stewardship enacts in the world a performance of the way God reconciles all creation.[37]

Ethicists therefore mistake the function of stewardship when they consider it under the aspect of providence, as if it were first a partnership with the Creator later renovated by Christ's reconciliation. That view assumes human ability and claim to rule the world, and then perversely allows the total submission of Christ to in fact reinstate a human prerogative to vizerial dominion. Whatever romantic vision of the servant-king they have in mind, it subtly reifies the static order of a theocratic ecology as it sweeps aside the reconciling function of stewardship. "The existence and work of Jesus Christ do not follow from the gracious act of creation or the gracious act of divine providence. It is for the sake of Jesus Christ that creation takes place."[38] If we read the story of creation and providence from within the special place in which God dwells with us, says Barth, then we must see creation and its keepers in service to each other, for the sake of Christ. That service will include practical acts of ecological care and restoration, insofar as they function as parables of God's kingdom, but it does not plant and manage the new creation.

However, within the pattern of redemption, the witness of stewardship is allotted an active role in God's defense of creation. If we determine stewardship from the place of Christ's work, says Barth, then we see "that within the created order it is the place of humanity to be not only the field and prize of battle, but the contestant in the divine conflict with nothingness which began with creation."[39] For God "the Creator and Lord of heaven and earth and all creatures . . . who preserves and accompanies and controls them all," continues to affirm creation by restoring and moving into unique fellowship with humans.[40] Since Christ stands in the place of humanity, as the field, prize, and contestant, that battle is engaged and that affirmation proclaimed on the cross, "as God's creative Word itself becomes a creature in the cosmos, suffering for the cosmos what it should itself have suffered."[41]

Christ saves all creation from menacing destruction by bringing the blighted creature into the special place of his fellowship. In that grove, the prodigal creatures are granted the creative, caretaking liturgical service of repeating in practical parable Christ's act to guard the cosmos.[42] Though it does not realize Christ's work, it is nonetheless a positive task, like reconstruction after a war, as Timothy Gorringe has pointed out: Barth wanted Christians living in a devastated landscape to know that "human beings are set in the garden to build it up and watch over it."[43] In the reconciling lordship of Christ, humans cultivate the goodness of creation.

Stewards are then those who recognize the cross and in their practical actions testify to the one who rules as servant and serves as lord.[44] God affirms creation in the election of Christ; the "Yes" is pronounced by the One who travels into the place of alienation (*die Fremde*) to illuminate it once again as the land of the promise.[45] Christ's redemptive act for humanity is thus an "epitome of the whole order of creation. . . . As the life of the Saviour, it is also that of the faithful Creator of heaven and earth."[46] Christian witness repeats the Creator's affirmation by following the Lord's servant order, cultivating the true character of creation.

The Menacing Order: Humans as Lords

However, "the human for whom God is God in this way in Jesus Christ is the very opposite—the servant who wants to be lord."[47] Hungry for power and grasping after Christ's claim to royalty, these would-be stewards claim the honor of dominion for themselves without honoring God's will for a peaceful, green earth. Their freedom over earth would be right, but only "to the extent that they did this as real humans, that is, as humans loved by God, created good by God, and ordained by God to this work in the freedom that humanity owes to the grace of the free God . . . the Lord of nature who is at the same time the Servant of God."[48] Claiming the work for themselves, on account of their own transcendent goal, human lordship betrays the promised land into a far place of alienation, a darkened *Fremde*. Apart from the Reconciler's service, humanity not only forfeits lordship, it begins to unleash degenerative, disordered powers, feeding the menace from which Christ delivers creation.

Barth's description of sin here anticipates a common environmentalist diagnosis of the religious roots of ecological problems. Critics like Rosemary Radford Ruether, Carolyn Merchant, and Lynn White explain environmental exploitation by humanity's arrogation of divine prerogatives or transcendent goals.[49] Jürgen Moltmann and Michael Welker extend this critique specifically to Barth, complaining that his conception of the divine act in the subordinating terms of lordship and service serves a modernist paradigm in which humans identify themselves as technocratic lords over the earth.[50] Each of these scholars thinks that the solution involves ecologically refiguring our conception of divine action, that humans might conform themselves to more appropriate relations and goals.

Yet Barth agrees that humans have perversely identified themselves with a destructive image of dominion, and have marshaled religious resources to justify it. In Barth's view, however, the problem does not arise from our notion of divine activity, for it "is not God's fault that we do not feel at home in our creatureliness and in this creaturely world."[51] Humans alienate themselves from earth by refusing to accept God's act, perhaps even by perversely arrogating Christ's sacrifice as royal diadem for human vice-regency, as something running with the grain of foolish powers. Sinful humans do not just shy away from covenant partnership; they attempt to appropriate its honor for themselves, and manage creation as if they set the terms.

Barth therefore agrees that religious justification of human dominion by appeal to God's sovereignty is one of the worst things humans do. Refusing the habitat God's action makes for them, humans will their own geographical glory in the image of false gods.[52] To proud for the faithful service of actual lordship, humans attempt "to pass from the decision of obedience to God to that of their own choice, from service in the garden to rule." They act as if lordship were "that one can penetrate and master and control all things."[53] Arrogating to themselves administrative responsibility for "proper order," while only mutely mouthing the Creator's "No" to chaos and nothingness, humans loose themselves from keeping a mere grove in order to extend homogenizing control over all earth's space. Exploiting resources in the name of stewardship, humans thus reverse the order of grace: they give up their special place (*besonderer Ort*) as they grasp for ever more living space (*Raum*).

"Giving place to nothingness," this disordered management has nihilative consequences.[54] Ostensible dominion becomes slavery to a bewitched earth and a chronic, statutory war against creation.[55] Barth's industrial imagery is dramatic:

> It is humanity who frees and automatizes these spirits to satisfy its
> own wants. . . . It is the human spirit that triumphs in their exploitation.

It is a man who is at the helm, who pulls the levers, who presses the knobs. Nevertheless, they automatically and autonomously rumble and work and roll and roar and clatter outside him, without him, past him, and over him. . . . Still their slaves, they now confront humans as robots which they themselves have to serve.[56]

From this lordless order, "to whose threat humanity is exposing all creation," Christ delivers sinful humans, and so affirms God's "Yes" to creation within the menacing creature itself, repeating in its body God's "No" against nothingness.[57] Then, in the exaltation of Christ, God gives humans the honor of testifying to Christ's redemptive work, illustrating that the enslaving dominion has been cancelled, that humans are liberated from earth and earth from humans. The menace of the prodigal creature has been staved off in God's welcoming her home.[58] The pattern of Christ's work subverts a monstrous order and renews the community of creation. For humans alienated by their own domination, says Bonhoeffer, "there is no way back to earth except the way to God and to our brother. From the beginning the way of humans to earth has only been possible as God's way to humans."[59]

Against Barth's Orderliness

Distinguishing himself from Bonhoeffer's attempt to christologically adjust the teaching on created orders, Barth asks, "In Bonhoeffer's doctrine of the mandates, is there not just a touch of North German patriarchalism?"[60] Yet clearly in Barth's revision of orders into relational spheres there remains more than a touch of his own patriarchalism. Tracing the "anarchic" directionality and soteriological fittingness of the Reconciler's pattern makes the very best of Barth's hierarchical order.[61] In several key areas Barth's orders are less susceptible to therapeutic interpretation. Against the grain of his own theological critiques and politics, Barth can be sexist, heterosexist, hierarchalist, and absolutist. Even though his account of reconciliation bends toward the transgressive as the fitting orientation of the transfigurative, Barth himself often rigidly holds on to fixed positions of hierarchy and subordination. In the way of the Reconciler, Barth develops every resource to subvert and transfigure social orders masquerading as the natural divine, but in his ethics keeps certain hierarchies closeted away.

That troubles stewardship ethics especially, because Barth discusses human dominion in relation to the order between sexes, and when he traces the pattern of Christ's lordship, legitimates male dominion as a sign of Christ's work in a way structurally similar to the symbolic dominion of stewardship.[62] Analogously, male dominion cannot be claimed in virtue of natural male characteristics, but is given as a correspondent sign (permitted and commanded) to God's initiative for humanity them in Jesus Christ.[63] Against his own cautions, Barth appropriates the work of Christ to secure a hierarchical order, and one we know functions violently. That makes it difficult to read stewardship dominion as merely honorary, testimonial, and service-oriented without worrying about de facto violence and exploitation.[64]

Moreover, by linking such dominion to Christ's rejection of nothingness, in just the way we have shown he does for stewardship, Barth implicitly demonizes uppity females as agents of evil. In this case Keller is exactly right to impugn Barth for marshalling an absolutist view of divine sovereignty to suppress and demonize the wild, transgressive feminine.[65] And Barth is simply wicked to counsel oppressed women not to seek liberation, that they might witness to the order of redemption.[66]

Moltmann suggest things are even worse, that both Barth's order and its demonizing trajectories stem from his hierarchical conception of God. If Barth describes inner-trinitarian relations in terms of command and obedience, says Moltmann, then he licenses authoritarian social organization, assigning mastery to disembodied male-typed humans who think they are divinely separated from female-typed nature.[67] Barth's theology, in other words, begs an entire range of ecofeminist critiques. Moltmann therefore suggests scrapping the lord/servant pattern of Christ for relations more reciprocal, mutual, and perichoretic: "Not order above and below, but a shared, communal, cooperative life corresponds to the threefold God—a life which is the enfleshed promise of God's kingdom."[68] Moltmann counsels Barth to relieve his fixation on the obedience of Christ and discover a more perichoretic divine act in the Spirit.

Thus a crucial interpretive question for Barth's potential in Christian environmental ethics: is his stewardship theology inextricably linked to male–female subjugation and violent social orders? That question does not just apply idiosyncratically to Barth. Because of the way Barth's treatment of ethical order follows from the work of Christ, these criticisms against Barth raise questions for the general strategy of stewardship. Can a strategy make its object human responsibility and confidently avoid sanctioning perverse social orders? Or do its hierarchical ethical relations inevitably tend to license exploitation? If stewardship repeats Christ's affirmation of creation, is nature's wildness implicitly demonized (like the uppity woman)?

Answers to those questions depend on how pervasively one prioritizes Barth's pattern of reconciliation, on how far one thinks Barth can be revised by his own christocentric commitments to think theological ethics entirely within the work of Christ. Is Barth's *Ordnung* really developed from the reconciling praxis of Christ, in which the community of grateful creatures also participates; or, is it a static hierarchy imposed by a bad view of nature?[69] How does habitation in Christ's *Ort* generate anew creation's *Ordnung*? Can following the pattern of Christ include response to nature's own generativity and resistance?

Nature Restored

Whatever one concludes about Barth's orders, however, notice how Barth makes the debate revolve around the character of God's act and responsive Christian practice—not around the status of nature itself. By disestablishing nature as initially significant and redescribing material reality within a relational sphere initiated by God for the purposes of fellowship, Barth lets the environment of Christ's act determine the model of environmental responsibilities. The critical questions about Barth's orderliness ask, in part, how earthly nature flourishes within the environment of Christ. We need to know whether and how far nature shapes the practice of stewardship, and therefore we must ask what becomes of nature in Christ's work. Is it fecund and formful, bringing forth a community in which freedom finds its tending place, or is it an inert arena for the exercise of Christ-patterned freedom? Here we can finally ask Barth that question arising from the strategy of stewardship: How relevant are the physical indicators of nature for shaping our service to the Creator's "Yes" to creation?

Barth's answer follows and intensifies the formula of Calvin, who sees creation as the "theater of God's glory," now scandalously darkened after the fall.[70] For Barth, however, not only has sin darkened human eyes to the divine light in creation, that light was originally hidden in mystery. From nature alone, "the knowledge of God as Creator is a hidden one."[71] We cannot know precisely God's relations with other creatures, so we cannot on that basis recognize ethical obligations to them. How creation manifests the glory of God remains a secret, a mystery about which we cannot speculate on our own.[72]

However, in the garden of reconciliation Christ's encounter illuminates the meaning of nature, providing a basis for ethical obligations. Here Barth intensifies Calvin's formula in a second way. Now set within the environment of God's work, the cosmos becomes an *active* theater: "The self-declaration of God does not take place in a dark and empty and indefinite sphere, but in one which has real existence, fullness, form and brightness."[73] Just as nature seemed disqualified from moral attention, Barth restores it in the work of Christ, the real place of creation.[74] In the environment of Christ, creation's witness no longer speaks abstractly and mysteriously, but concretely as the "sphere and place of the reconciliation."[75]

Securely emplaced within the event of grace, Barth can say surprisingly affirmative things about nature. By the coming of the Reconciler, the "self-witness of creation can also speak and tell of what God says, and *therefore speaks as from God.*" Nature's witnesses "are taken, lifted, assumed and integrated into the action of God's self-giving and self-declaring," and thereby "instituted, installed, and ordained to the *ministerium Verbi Divini.*"[76] Removed from the competency of natural science, Barth finds it safe even to say that "nature does objectively offer a proof of God."[77] From within the garden of reconciliation, Paul can tell the Roman gentiles "the greatest news concerning them: that God has in fact . . . since the creation of the world been declaring and revealing Himself to them." No general scientist could say such a thing; "it needs no less than an apostle to tell them this."[78] As Nigel Biggar summarizes, "Only from within the Word of God can one know what is and what is not truly 'natural.' But from that perspective there is nature to be seen."[79]

Dwelling within the Word, natural science comes into its own, bearing even theological import. Now, says Kathryn Tanner, "the simplest facts and the most mundane experiences of life in this world, from the rising of the sun that conquers darkness to the land that keeps back the sea, reflect God's victory in Christ over what threatens us through our own fault."[80] Reoriented to earth as the place God meets them in fellowship, says Barth, humans can see how each creature serves God's will, and "does this in the individuality and particularity given it with its creation by God, in the freedom and activity corresponding to its particular nature."[81] The corresponding recognition that "even the humblest being in the most obscure part of the created world fits in somewhere and has . . . a God-given right of self-actualization" encourages ecological investigations.[82] Since creation is the theater of God's glory in its own specific and definite forms, Barth even suggests that "theater" may not be the most apt metaphor for nature, for it misses how God works in nature through nature's own active agencies.[83]

The point here for stewardship ethics is that from within the special place of God's act in Christ, nature does indeed bear moral significance and even theological voice. For nature's phenomena testify to the work of reconciliation by flourishing within God's special place on earth.[84] When humans are encountered by the Word, they enter that special place with its surprisingly verdant blessings. Theologically received, natural sciences do indeed illuminate the place in which humans encounter and respond to the Word.[85] The regular phenomena of nature, its laws and orders, its rhythms and dynamism, its contrariety and diversity, while they do not emanate from or repeat the divine life, serve the work of God, and so become ethically relevant for stewardship.[86] "What they say can so harmonize with what God says that to hear God is to hear them, and to hear them is to hear God, so that listening to the polyphony of creation . . . is listening to the symphony for which it was elected and determined."[87]

Within the place of Christ's encounter with them, stewards therefore hear in these voices a "summons and invitation to the active ordering and shaping of things."[88] Only now that activity follows the pattern of Christ's work by listening attentively to the self-attestation of creation in all its natural phenomena, and by learning to responsively repeat to it the Creator's affirmation.[89] That requires knowing natural kinds and attending ecological conditions in order to elicit the earth's flourishing. Would-be masters are reformed into loving arborists, performing the environmental service to which they are set by their Redeemer. Stewardship thus resituates humans within their habitat, restoring their authentic creatureliness by awakening them to creation's significance for God's claim on them. In Christ, as anticipated in the Garden, humans find their proper environmental role, tending the earth as witnesses to glory.

Barth restores nature to theological ethics within the human vocation made in Christ's call. Neither "remote or alien" from human freedom, nor present only for our contemplation, it meets us as a "task" to which we are set.[90] "To put it dramatically," says Barth, anticipating Bulgakov, whom we will meet in the next chapter, "it yearns and cries out to be humanised." Nature "awakens and stimulates" human work, calling freedom into reciprocal service, in which—much as God's act elicits symphony from creation—nature serves the creativity of humanity, that humanity may truly exist for creation.[91]

Barth's Anthropocentrism

We have already seen in Thomas Aquinas how a form of anthropocentrism may bend toward respect for nature's integrity. Barth presents an anthropocentrism that bends toward respect in a negative way, by limiting overconfidence and abuses in descriptions of nature's integrity. The provisional anthropocentrism of Aquinas enables human knowers to come into God's friendship by praising God from created natures. Barth's anthropocentrism refuses the supposition that humans can say anything particular about God from other creatures, and so chastens the quasi-religious tendency to appropriate nature in cultural apotheosis.[92] Aquinas presupposes anthropocentrism for creaturely sanctification; for Barth it serves his emphasis on analogical discontinuity.

Barth's anthropocentrism follows from his noetic christoformity. He thinks we can only speak of creation through God's self-revelation in the human

Jesus, so theology's "understanding of God's creation is 'anthropocentric' to the extent that it follows the orientation prescribed for it by the Word of God: the orientation on humanity."[93] God has given humans no specific word concerning other creatures, and so no way, beyond a general attribution of createdness, to understand how their lives participate in God's.[94] Creation can only be received in mystery and approached as gift.[95] Barth's anthropocentrism therefore works to limit human aegis, in both descriptive claim and efficient power.

For both Aquinas and Barth, therefore, a relative anthropocentrism situates humanity in its ecological context with a certain humility, because for both it emerges from a soteriology that places humanity within God's act toward creation. For both we know nature only through a constructive act of interpretation shaped by grace.[96] Because God's act toward creation takes place in Jesus Christ, they are both anthropocentric to the degree they are christocentric.[97] For both (although in different ways), faithful response to Christ reshapes human freedom to its natural habitat insofar as grace informs human action.

That Barth allows himself to be drawn into positive discussion of nonhuman nature and its relation to God, despite his ongoing polemic against natural theology and his aversion to the "antichrist" *analogia entis*, is perhaps the most dramatic evidence of Barth's christocentrism: rigorously following the self-declaration of the Word of God requires theology to glance toward the habitat of those addressed by the Word. "But without this glance it could not fulfill its function to the human who is set in this world . . . [The Word] illuminates the world. It makes it known—heaven and earth—as the sphere in which God's glory dwells and in which God concerns Himself with humanity."[98] Against his own tendencies, Barth makes a special place for nature.

Yet we must ask whether Barth cuts short his sidelong glance at creation, and by doing so fails to fully cultivate the moral significance of nature for stewardship. By insisting that nature remains a mystery to which humans have no revelational access, Barth may fail to follow his christology as far is it might go. When confronted by scripture alluding to a direct relationship with God, as in creation's praise, Barth invariably comments that it intends merely "a reflection of God's lordship over humanity and an echo of human praise."[99] Here again, his anthropocentrism follows from his insistence that we cannot know how God relates to others—though that need not mean "any unbecoming depreciation of our fellow-creatures."[100] The salvific work of Christ has only humans as its object.

Yet Barth may be open to interrogation by the question he famously put to Calvin on the doctrine of election. Barth christologically intensified the doctrine of election by asking whether God's will concerning human salvation was really so obscure and mysterious; had it not been revealed in Jesus Christ?[101] Perhaps there is a parallel question to ask with regard to creation: is God's relationship to nonhuman creation really so hidden and mysterious? Has not something concerning creation's relationship to God's saving love been revealed in Jesus Christ? The biblical witness to the Reconciler as Pantocrator, the one who gathers up all things, seems to testify to a fuller extent of Christ's work. If Barth keeps the soteriological focus on humanity, then part of his anthropocentrism seems unreformed by his christological method.

Beyond a "glance" sideways to the others of the planet, Barth avoids any extended soteriological embrace by interpreting the relevant New Testament passages as christological attributions rather that salvific cosmophanies.[102] For Barth, the consistent association of "all things" with the work of Christ reiterates the priority and authority of God's initiative, but communicates little of its specific content. Where Barth seems ready to recognize the soteriological scope to the Johannine and Pauline prologues, his paragraphs inexplicably drift into talking of humans alone.[103]

Is Barth's reluctance to let reconciliation include all creation christologically and exegetically consistent? Or does he suppress nature's participation because of his polemics against natural theology and his personalist commitments? Asking that question, we approach debates over the form of Barth's analogical reasoning, for its answer entails deciding whether, as von Balthasar thinks, Barth's presentation of God's claim upon creation relies on an implicit form of *analogia entis*, or, as McCormack thinks, Barth's *analogia fidei* is dialectical from start to finish.[104] There is no settling that argument here; suffice it to note that a contested arena of Barthian interpretation has significant implications for the fate of creation in Barth. If we are with von Balthasar, then Barth arbitrarily restricts Christ's act from aspects of creation it ineluctably illuminates; if we are with McCormack, then Barth rightly inscribes creation wholly within the anthropocentric encounter. For stewardship ethics that may mean the difference between earthcare for the sake of earth's own participation in grace and earthcare for the sake of human obedience alone. On this, it appears, reading Barth cannot settle the matter, but only underscores the practical significance of interpreting the pattern of grace.

The Landscape of Salvation History

Throughout this reading of Barth I have traced instances of grace making place—the way God's creative acts make habitats for God's fellowship with creation. Barth's exegesis of the creation sagas show the Garden as proto-place;

the promised land of Israel forms the landscape of the covenant; the advent of the Reconciler makes the environment of Jesus Christ an earthly habitat of faith. Each of these places shapes human freedom in responsive attentiveness to the specific giftedness of their environment.[105]

Timothy Gorringe takes that place-making trajectory in Barth's theology as grounds for a Christian ethics of the built environment. Understanding reconciliation in relation to creation, he says, requires thinking about Christian community in relation to ecological order, and therefore treating the material design of our everyday world as a fundamental relation, a Barthian sphere.[106] For Gorringe, Barth's anti-nature polemic allows Christian ethics to integrate ecological and social environments under the call of Christ.[107] Peter Scott agrees, saying Barthian commitments disclose the way that "in the actions of the triune God, the concretion of the world is given: the theological task is then to explicate the dynamics of this concretion."[108] Reading Bonhoeffer, Scott shows how God's action makes the body of Christ the concrete place of divine fellowship.[109] Gorringe and Scott suggest that Barth may show how stewardship ethics could open Christian deliberation on environmental questions to more comprehensive scope, including such issues as urban planning, agriculture, and sustainable development.

Again, however, there is reason to suspect that Barth fails the promise of his own theological trajectory. Throughout his *Dogmatics*, the convertibility of space and time as measures of God's allotment allows Barth to temporalize space to such extent that places can seem to dissolve into the historical lineaments of *Heilsgeschichte*. For example, in III/4.56, "Freedom in Limitation," he describes only temporal limitations, and uses spatial metaphors to do so—as if creaturely living-space involves only history, not also landscape. In just the spots we would expect it, Barth omits geographical formation to freedom. The latter half of III/2 and all of III/3 are taken up with describing the place of humanity in time, creation as history. No longer bounded by trees and rivers planted by God, humans are known by a given span of time. Or consider the first sentence of IV/1.59: "Reconciliation is history." Thus the geographical resonance of *Fremde* is lost to the temporal stretch of *Geschichte*. The environment of Jesus Christ seems a matter of political history, requiring little mention of promised land or covenanted earth.

As we saw in chapter 8, the dominance of temporal concepts derives at least in part from Barth's resistance to the eco-fascist politics of bioregional identity. Walter Brueggeman has suggested that these political commitments led him to intentionally omit geographical and ecological aspects from the covenant, thereby influencing a generation of biblical exegesis to read old and new covenants in terms of political history.[110] In the wake of Barth's resistance to bad naturalisms, in other words, the covenant was de-placed as its land was dis-placed by time, leaving Protestant theology ill positioned to address ecological problems and vulnerable to awkward recoveries of the environment by theologians convinced that Protestant orthodoxy adores only history.[111]

Conclusion on Barth

Paul Santmire reports his disappointment in a personal encounter with Barth in which the senior theologian was roundly critical of Santmire's proddings to produce a theology of nature.[112] As this chapter has argued, Santmire seems to have missed the place Barth's theology had already made for nature: the way of the Reconciler restores nature to theology and humans to the earth. Yet as we have also seen, there are ambivalences, shortcomings, and inconsistencies in Barth's thought that may explain why Barth himself could not tell Santmire of that place. Barth failed to engage sufficiently and seriously with the natural world, for which he is rightly faulted. Despite his love of country retreats and mountain walks, it was the world of letters and politics that captivated his extratheological attentions.[113] But, as I have labored to show, that bias is not necessary to his theological commitments. Quite the contrary; in only a few cases do substantial dogmatic or interpretive decisions lie behind Barth's evasion of nature, and even here they appear unnecessary from Barth's wider project. Otherwise his theology bends the other direction, as God claims human freedom within the environment of Jesus.

In answer to the problems with stewardship ethics, Barth's account of grace counsels stewardship away from the hubris of partnership models and shows how it might theologically accommodate the use of natural sciences and environmental experience. Barth also lets stewardship theologies imagine how to talk about a place ethics of Christian witness, thus showing how stewardship may be well suited to engage issues like agriculture, built environments, and ecological restoration. Of course Barth also displays lurking problems, especially around gender, the meaning of creation for God, and historicism. Those new problems return us to stewardship theologies with new questions, asking whether and how they can overcome the vulnerabilities evidenced in a pattern of grace they share.

But Barth has at least secured a theological arena for sorting out those questions. After Barth, the strategic logic of environmental stewardship can rely on the way of the Reconciler establishing habitat for humans to witness to God's will for a flourishing, exuberant earth. Barth shows how, as John deGruchy puts it, "this covenantal relationship between God and humanity expressed in faithful stewardship is the first presupposition of the doctrine of reconciliation."[114] In other words, Barth sets stewardship right in the midst of grace, in the heart of Christian identity, where God meets humans for fellowship in the Garden God has specially planted. After Barth, Christian environmentalists may claim that conversion to the way of Jesus entails care for the earth, and that earthcare bears comparable theological significance to practices like feeding the poor and preaching the good news.

Barth shows how redeeming grace leads back to the earth in freedom, responsibility, and gratitude. In Jesus, humans begin to learn how to live at home on earth as in the promised land of God, as in our Father's house:

> If we are told in Him who we are and are not, we are also told in Him where we belong, where we have to be and live . . . Jesus Christ is God's mighty command to open our eyes and to realise this place is all around us, that we are already in this kingdom, that we have no alternative but to adjust ourselves to it. . . . What is this place and kingdom in which God's direction summons the human to awaken and remain and act? . . . It is the place and kingdom which already surround her, in which she is already placed, in which she has only to find herself. . . . It is the house of her Father, and she needs the Father's guidance to act in it and therefore to be free. But she receives and has this. . . . Because it is not in ourselves but in Jesus Christ that we are free, that we are the covenant-partners and children of God.[115]

10

After Maximus

Ecological Spirituality and Cosmic Deification

"The Orthodox Church makes no separation between natural and supernatural revelation." With this sentence Dumitru Staniloae opens his multivolume *Orthodox Dogmatic Theology*. He goes on to show how the deification tradition of Maximus the Confessor preserves creaturely integrity.[1] Vladimir Lossky, in *The Mystical Theology of the Eastern Church*, states, "The eastern tradition knows nothing of 'pure nature' to which grace is added as a supernatural gift." The tradition of Maximus, he says, teaches instead a dynamic, deifying movement of the whole creation into union with God.[2] Alexander Schmemann opens his celebrated book *For the Life of the World*, by lamenting the impoverished secularism caused by alienated realms of nature and grace. In therapeutic contrast, he writes, Orthodox liturgy presents the figure of human priests celebrating the feast of all creation in communion with God.[3]

All three twentieth-century theologians frame the distinct contribution of Orthodox theology by setting it against some western rupture of nature from salvation.[4] All three appeal to the theological tradition of Maximus for reuniting nature and humanity within a cosmic economy of deification. Now recall that in chapter 5 we encountered a series of ethical approaches addressing environmental problems from within a view of ecological personhood, each attempting to overcome modernist alienations of nature from humanity. The strategy of ecological spirituality frames the Christian significance of environmental issues within a fundamental union of humanity and nature, a relationship formed by all creation's intensifying union with God. The strategy thus follows the general pattern of deification by rooting humanity's ecological relations within divine participation. This chapter and the next consider the promise of contemporary renditions of the Maximian tradition for developing that environmental strategy and for working out its most serious problem— correlating divine grace and creaturely creativity.

Recall how meticulously Thomas works to integrate grace and nature, and how arduously achieved was Barth's indirect relation between vocational responsibility and its earthly context. For Thomas, grace uses nature to shape persons; for Barth, grace calls humans into responsibility for nature. But the Orthodox critique of western views of nature refuses any prior separation between grace and nature, personhood and creation, such that grace might connect them for the first time. Instead, Orthodox theology usually assumes that creation's integrity and humanity's relation to God are already irrevocably bound together. Salvation does not use nature to sanctify, nor does it orient human responsibility to care for its environment; assuming cosmic personhood, it unifies all creation with God by unifying humanity with the divine life.

This third soteriological tradition—*theosis*, or the way of deification—rests in the tradition of the Eastern fathers, who continually defend theological conditions for authentic creaturely experience of transfiguring communion with God.[5] Their major conceptual innovations—such as the *epiktasis* of Gregory of Nyssa's participation in the eternal Trinity or the ditheletic christology of Maximus—often counter notions of divine–creaturely relationship that would threaten authentic communion. Hallmarks of Eastern theology, such as the pneumatology of Symeon the New Theologian and the divine energies of Gregory Palamas, secure the possibility of finite creatures experiencing the impassible God.

One of those theological conditions especially apt for our inquiry is microcosmic anthropology, where grace heals and divinizes humans through their active interconnection with all creation. Consider Theodore of Mopsuestia's summary:

> Wanting to make one cosmos of the universe and to epitomize in one
> being the whole creation, which is composed of such diverse
> natures. . . . God constituted humankind as the link of all things.
> This is why [God] has brought everything back for their use, in order
> that the entire creation might be united in them and they might be
> for it a manifest pledge of friendship.[6]

Deification thus appears to generate a cosmic anthropology that liberates human creativity to discover its unity with the earth and befriend creation with the friendship of God. We start our search for the theological conditions of eco-logical spirituality here in the microcosm, testing its facility for answering con-temporary questions about the relation of natural dynamism, human creativity, and divine participation.

"*Logoi* in the Logos": The Cosmic Legacies of Maximus

Maximus receives the title "Confessor" for his persecuted defense of Chalce-donian christology—a defense that permanently established microcosmic anthropology. His vindication of an unconfused union of two natures in Christ therefore relates to the more practical theological concerns of ecological spirituality. For Maximus, the integrity of Christ's personal union lies in cre-ation's prior ordination to divinization, and in the mediating role human per-sonhood plays in actualizing that destiny. Maximus uses *theosis* to set the saving work of Christ within nature's own immanent movement toward God and humanity's active interconnection with the cosmos.[7] Doing so, he explicitly affirms God's desire for union with the whole cosmos, and opens the way for later theological discussions about the ecological importance of human creativity.

Maximus inventively coerced Greek conceptual frameworks to approve the Chalcedonian dyophysite (two natures) formula, against compromising simpli-fications from Antiochene moralism on one side and Alexandrian monophysit-ism on the other.[8] Maximus insists on the unwieldy, paradoxical formula because he sees how christology determines salvation, and how salvation gen-erates cosmology. For Maximus, the incarnation reveals three cosmic myster-ies: *createdness*, how the finite, teeming world could relate to the infinite, simple Creator; *personhood*, how the human willfully possesses its embodiment and realizes its nature; and the *theurgical church*, how liturgy gathers up the world and transfigures it into the body of Christ.[9] Together these three mysteries articulate the way of the world into union with God, and set the agenda for con-temporary Orthodox environmental theology.[10]

The Mystery of Createdness

Maximus sets the ontological stage for a real and unconfused union of two natures in Christ by appeal to a participationist identity of creation in God. God's transcendent difference from the world does not threaten creation, but establishes it for communion with God.[11] The world's nondivinity rests in divine gift as difference received for the sake of meaningful union. God brings forth the cosmos out of nothingness through the Word, in order that creatures may come into divine fullness through the Word. Referring creation's difference to its destined union, and with christology on his mind, Maximus can then say that in diverse, transient creatures "the one *Logos* is many *logoi*" and "the many *logoi* are the one *Logos*."[12] His formula safeguards the integrity of the incarnation by explaining how the Son remains divine while assuming a creaturely nature: since creatures already are finite participations in the Logos, Christ's union of creaturely and divine natures repeats and perfects God's initial creative act. Within human personhood, Christ draws creatures into more perfect union with God, as Christ "recapitulates all things in himself."[13]

The incarnation is, then, for Maximus, a microcosm of creation and glory, a theophany that circumscribes the world within God's saving action. For if "the Logos is the place of all the *logoi*," comments Lars Thunberg, then Christ "is the centre of the universe in the same manner as he is the centre of the economy of salvation."[14] "With us and through us, Christ embraces the whole creation," says Maximus, "bringing together the extremes, uniting them by wrapping them around Himself. . . . Thus he recapitulates all things in himself [*ta panta eis heauton anekhephalaiōsato*], showing that the whole creation is one, as if a human [*khathaper anthropon allon*]."[15]

The cosmic christology Maximus deploys to defend Chalcedon thus brings all creation within its divinizing aegis. By revealing the Logos as the secret heart of the world, Christ's incarnation reveals the world's communion with God, in whom its diverse natures already abide.[16] Christ embraces all creatures, uniting them in his person with their own essence and their divine destiny. The Logos indwells all things, as a soul to a body, says Maximus, calling creation the "garment" and "flesh" of God.[17] By assuming that cosmic body, Christ elevates creation into union with God.[18]

The "*logoi* in the Logos" formula affirms the intelligible goodness of creation in a way reminiscent of Thomas's analogical participation.[19] But there are two important differences in Maximus. First (as Lossky insistently points out), while Thomas correlates creaturely natures with divine nature, Maximus correlates them also with God's will.[20] That opens a theological dimension of freedom in Maximus's ktisiology not explicitly obvious in Thomas. In contrast to relatively static Thomist natures, the Maximian view anticipates natures dynamically transformed by God's will for union. Second, by locating the unity of creation in the microcosmic personhood of Christ, Maximus intensifies the ecological importance of freedom, for personal agency unifies the cosmos within itself and with God. So we are brought to the second and third mysteries, concerning the mediating roles of personhood and creaturely freedom.

The Mystery of Personhood

Maximus affirms a real union of two natures in Christ by opening a tensive distinction between nature (*physis* or *ousia*) and personhood (*hypostasis* or *prosopon*).[21] "The hypostatic union between Christ's divine and human natures," says Maximus, "draws his humanity into union with his divinity, in every way, through the logic of personhood [*kata panta tropon, tō tēs hupostaseōs logō*]. This union realizes one person composite of both natures [*mian amphoterōn apotelousa tēn hypostasin syntheton*], inasmuch as it in no way diminishes the essential difference of those natures [*physin*]."[22] The tension between *hypostasis* and *physis* charges personal activity with a creative responsibility to realize the real nature of things, manifested perfectly in Christ. The "logical" character of the world waits upon some way of acting to bring it forth in practical expression. "Become what you are," exhorts Maximus, in his practical spirituality. Natures become real as they are integrated into hypostatic action (*enupostaton*); the *logoi* exhibit their divine ground through personal expression.[23]

Human engagement with nonhuman natures, therefore, is not merely fitting for humanity (as perhaps in Thomas) but cosmologically central. The created universe comes to its full existence within a *hypostasis* capable of embracing and synthesizing multiplicity. The microcosm realizes a union between humans and nonhumans that enacts the final union of God and the world, itself grounded in the union of two natures in Christ.[24] Human personhood embraces and holds together the alienated world, and so "is the way of fulfillment for what is divided." Through practical and contemplative ascetic struggle, humanity "unites paradise and the inhabited world to make one earth," overcoming all the alienations of the cosmos, until it finally "unites the created nature with the uncreated."[25] Thus human personhood actively seeks and reveals "the whole creation wholly indwelt [*holos holō perichoresas*] by God."[26]

That christological difference between *physis* and *hypostasis* governs an ontological distinction Maximus makes between *logos* and *tropos* (essence and mode of existence, roughly), which in turn opens "nature" to theological determination at both creaturely and divine ends of our discourse.[27] On the one hand, Maximus suggests that *ousia*, the term used to designate the shared divine nature of the Trinity, may be conceptually distinct from its three hypostatic actualizations.[28] Taking advantage of the trinitarian economy developed by the Cappadocians, Maximus asserts that the divine "substance" only exists within modes of divine life, as it is communicated through the personal communion of Father, Son, and Holy Spirit.[29] God indwells but also exceeds whatever we could mean by "God's nature" or *ousia*.[30] (Later we will see how

Bulgakov's sophiology attempts to biblically assume and theologically deter-mine the *ousia* Maximus opens to investigation—and why that may help eco-logical spirituality.)

On the other hand, at the mundane end of theological discourse, created natures also subsist within microcosmic activity, as *logoi* in the person of Christ. That tropological subsistence (or mode of existence) makes for an ontological dynamism that renders nature plastic to hypostatic action. Because created natures exist in and for the person, they are susceptible to the personal com-munion of God, as they are to human social practices. Though the *logoi* them-selves cannot be destroyed (which is why the Fall does not distort nature in itself), they may be variously realized or misused (which is why the Fall remains catastrophic).[31] Because creation exists for God's will to indwell and transfigure it, Maximus uses the tensive distinction of *logos/tropos* to affirm the ontological availability of the world to hypostatization—its aptitude for *theosis*.[32]

This double determination of nature, from divine *ousia* and toward created personhood, may be seen in passages where Maximus describes the Logos at play in creation. Following Proverbs 8:31, Maximus quotes Gregory Nazianzen: "The high Word plays [*paigei logos aipus*] in every kind of form."[33] The flux and flow of the creaturely world moves in pursuit of hypostatization, seeking union with God. We live in the transience of an eddied "middle," "flowing, eternally-moving, divinely contrived . . . [for] the whole divine economy, capable of making wise those who are taught by it to hope always for change, and to believe that the end of this mystery for them is that . . . they might be securely deified by grace."[34] As a parent pedagogically plays with a child, capturing her imagination toward an ascent of understanding, divine Wisdom lures human imagination toward the destiny of creation.[35] Contra Origen, transience results not from an impoverish-ment of divinity, but from God's loving presence within creation.

Natural change and ecological processes therefore provide natural indica-tors of the way creation anticipates divinization and invites fulfilled person-hood.[36] As Jean-Claude Larchet points out, the anthropocentric moments in Maximus do not subdue the cosmic scope of deification; rather they reinforce it, for creation awaits its elevation through personhood.[37] In its movements and changes, creation groans for humanization, that its natural desires for God may be liberated into voices of praise, modes of communion.

The Mystery of the Theurgical Church

Maximus defends Christ's unconfused union of two natures by making their identity the product of a freely creative personal act. At stake in the terminologi-cal controversies, says von Balthasar, is a question about freedom.[38] At stake in

Maximian christology, then, is the possibility of good technology, of ecological creativity. How can personhood embrace others (in the case of the incarnation, that which seems antonymously other) without violating the participant natures or becoming some novel thing itself? Von Balthasar suggests the shape of an answer in the title of his study on Maximus: *Cosmic Liturgy*. The freedom exercised by Christ gathers together creatures as if liturgical characters, who become refulgently true to themselves in their roles performatively constituting the body of Christ.

Maximus therefore must describe the inventive will in order to show which sort of liturgical roles are appropriate for nature. Otherwise the plasticity of nature before hypostatic action makes creation unresistant to perverse dominations and technological manipulations—to stories celebrating human glories, rather than divine.[39] (Recall Habgood in chapter 5: do dams express the glories of creation or do they obstruct it? How would we know?) For Maximus, Christ's way of personhood qualifies hypostatic inventiveness, in the fact that "there is one hypostasis realized from the two natures and the difference between the two natures remains immutable."[40] Christ's creativity does not fabricate some new substance; his synthesis involves no *tertium quid*. Rather it realizes both natures in a noncompetitive, divinizing union of freedoms. Christ's freedom does not act against passively inert natures, but brings to expression nature's inner glory, thus liberating its own "voice," realizing its own mode of existence. Just as grace moves the human will to move itself, so the hypostasis does not arbitrarily master one nature with the other, but noncompetitively expresses both.[41]

The transfigurative dimensions of ecclesial liturgy exemplify Christ's form of communion in difference. In *The Church's Mystagogy*, Maximus depicts the church in creative praise at once imaging the world and drawing near to God.[42] For as the liturgy makes present the body of Christ, it unites creatures, as if a single human, mediating their differences "by transcending them and revealing them," illuminating creatures as garments of the transfigured Christ.[43] In its liturgical embrace, the church constitutes creation as the glorified body of Christ. "The world for St. Maximus," writes Paul Evdokimov, "is a 'cosmic church' in which man exercises his priesthood. As the priest of nature, he 'offers it to God in his soul as on an altar.'"[44] The liturgical action of the church enacts the salvation of Christ, who "holds together [*sunechōn*] all beings in the power of wisdom [*tē dynamei tēs sophias*] and embraces [*periechōn*] them . . . abolishes all war between beings, and unites all in peace and friendship and undivided harmony."[45]

So Maximus anticipates the peaceable kingdom of the ecclesial economy, where Christians reconcile the world as they dwell within it, transfiguring creation through worship, offering the world to God as they enter into the communion of the cosmos. Christian ascesis trains perception to know the world's desire for God and shapes freedom for life in that cosmic communion. That is why "all Christians are called to an 'ascetic' life broadly understood, insofar as every believer must aspire, through disciplined practice (*praxis*) and contemplation (*theoria*), exercising every level of the life of the soul and the body, to participate in the transfiguration of the cosmos . . . and thereby to share actively in Christ's mediation of the new creation."[46]

These three legacies from Maximus shape the way Staniloae and Bulgakov articulate the Orthodox proclamation to a modern world in danger of losing its sense of createdness: creation's integrity (*logikos*) in Christ, the mediatorship of humanity as microcosm, and the promise of creative freedom. Maximus licenses Staniloae and Bulgakov to understand earth's natural economy as a created analogue to perichoretic communion, to bring all creation within Christ's saving purpose, and to concentrate Christian responsibility for the world in christoform creativity.[47]

The World Made Human: Deification in Staniloae

Dumitru Staniloae, a Romanian theologian writing from a westward-looking Orthodox church, takes up the legacies of Maximus to proclaim the cosmic dimensions of salvation for a world to which they seem nearly lost. Maximus explained the cosmic dimensions of Jesus Christ; now Staniloae glosses how receiving the cosmic Christ's gift of salvation entails receiving the gift of the world. Developing a Maximian cosmology of deification, including a "mystical materialism" based on the "*logoi* in the Logos" formula, Staniloae, "more powerfully than any other Orthodox writer of our day . . . presents a convincing theology of the world."[48]

In Staniloae, says Andrew Louth, "themes familiar from Maximus constantly recur, but thought into a context responsive to the problems faced by a faithful Orthodox theologian in the twentieth century. So the cosmic dimension of Maximus's thought is a touchstone in a discussion that is aware . . . of the power humans now have to destroy and poison at least the small part of the created order they inhabit."[49] Staniloae explicitly places environmental problems against an Eastern view of salvation, consciously correcting alienations of humanity and nature by deification and letting environmental problems impugn western distortions of personhood and creation.

"Salvation and deification undoubtedly have humanity as their aim, but not a humanity separated from nature, rather one that is ontologically united with it."[50] This thesis opens the volume on deification in Staniloae's great opus, *Orthodox Dogmatic Theology*. In fact, he opens each of the first two volumes of that work by distinguishing the Orthodox view from western antinomies between nature and salvation.[51] Orthodox soteriology, he says, follows Maximus, who taught the cosmic embrace of the incarnation and the power of resurrection to transfigure all creation. Therefore, in its view, the "economy of God . . . consists in the deification of the created world, something which, as a consequence of sin, implies also its salvation."[52]

"For Staniloae," writes Emil Bartos, "the cosmological vision in which the entire cosmos is called to be deified is present in the very constitution of the human being."[53] Staniloae works from the cosmic anthropology of Maximus, where "humanity is the link of connection among all the diverse parts of reality." Maximus himself inherits this view, says Staniloae, from Athanasius: by healing human personhood, Christ restores humanity to a unifying cosmic role.[54] By implication, salvation is at once personal and cosmic, as it liberates persons to embrace all creation.

Staniloae's anthropology therefore agrees with themes we have seen in the strategy of ecological spirituality, which similarly refuses to consider God's presence for humans apart from intrinsic human connections to creation. Apropos of environmental justice, Staniloae points out that contemporary environmental degradations starkly remind us that "nature is the condition not just of individual human existence, but also of human solidarity," because it is "the medium through which the human being can do good or evil to his fellows."[55] As we saw in chapter 5, ecological mediations of human injustice testify to the interdependence of humanity and nature, and of all creation.

Uniting themes from environmental justice and creation spirituality, Staniloae goes on to say that "each person in a certain way is a hypostasis of the entire cosmic nature, but he is this only in solidarity with others," by "an ontological bond with all creation."[56] This Maximian anthropology allows Staniloae to write things near the ken of Matthew Fox: "As the only being in the cosmos conscious of itself, we are, at the same time, the consciousness of the world."[57]

Staniloae's contemporary adaptation of Maximus focuses on the way human activity elevates creation into divine communion. Relying on the Maximian cosmology in which the *logikos* world naturally anticipates its embrace in personal activity, Staniloae uses strong agential language to describe the hypostatic activity of the ecological human. "The rational spirit as subject penetrates the rationality of matter as object and assimilates it within the rationality of its own body," says Staniloae. Those metaphors would certainly be violent within modernist assumptions that humanity and nature are separate and competitive.[58] But here, he says, personal activity meets and lifts up creation's own essence, that "the whole cosmos . . . may come to have a share in the quality of being subject." Human activity, ennobled and transfigured like the body of Christ on Tabor, communicates the transfiguration of the world.[59]

Staniloae reads such intensive agency in the saving presence of Christ. The incarnate Logos penetrates the world, illuminating the *logoi* with their true glory. Christ the Microcosm spiritualizes creation for its use in personal communion.[60] Moreover, by healing personhood and restoring it to its mediating role, Christ reveals the fundamental orientation of the nonhuman world toward the rationalizing, spiritualizing agency of personal communion.[61] The "enhypostatization" of humanity in the Word for Staniloae forms "the foundation of the doctrine of deification," because in humanity Christ assumes and restores creation to personal communion.[62]

Rather than imagining a cosmic salvation beyond humanity, therefore, Staniloae concentrates cosmic deification within the moment of human salvation.[63] Commenting on *Ambiguum* 41, where Maximus describes the incarnation reconciling created and uncreated, Staniloae says that this means, "humanity is called not only to humanize the creation by transforming it into a cosmos, actualizing all its virtual beauty, but also to intercede for its deification." Recalling the Maximian image of Christ drawing the alienated members of creation into his body as a "macro-anthropos," Staniloae circumscribes creation's destiny within human personhood: "Creation becomes a cosmos in humanity because in humanity it is unified and fully humanized. . . . Human arms are broader than all the dimensions of creation."[64]

Staniloae's doctrine of humanization relies on the tensive interval Maximus established between *logos* and *tropos*, which preserves the integrity of natures through a synthetic, noncompetitive personhood. In his commentary on the *Ambigua*, Staniloae's first article explains Maximus's distinction between *ousia* and *hypostasis*.[65] The first volume of his dogmatics opens by locating itself in the Maximian tension between the "rationality of the world" and its destiny in human personhood.[66] These instances are of more than ordinal importance; Staniloae interprets Maximus to direct cosmology so entirely toward personal communion that "without humanity the cosmos does not have meaning for God."[67]

Staniloae's phrasing recalls the interior conceptualizations found in creation spirituality: "the world *within* [the] life of humans . . . only *in* human subjects does the world discover and fulfill its meaning."[68] But Staniloae seems far from the humble reflexivity creation spirituality advocates would prefer: "It is the world that has been created to be humanized, not man to be assimilated into the world or into nature."[69] Staniloae envisions the world's "macroanthropic" destiny to connote nature's subordination, for it "to bear the entire

stamp of the human, to become pan-human."[70] The point of the transfiguration, it turns out, is "the superior power of the person over nature, and the
dependence of nature on person."[71]

So forcefully does Staniloae claim the Maximian theme of cosmic personhood that his emphasis on the personal theatens to overwhelm the natural:
does the original rationale for Maximian cosmology, two unconfused natures
in Christ, survive in Staniloae's personal communion? Does the personal communion bring forth nature's own immanent projects, as in Maximian christology? Or does deification confuse, suppress, violate its participants? Those
questions press the concern of ecological spiritualities for an appropriate model
of ecological creativity.

For Staniloae, the movement of deification realizes God's will for creation,
as displayed in the spiritualized garments of Christ on Tabor, where material
becomes transparent to divine glory. In light of the transfiguration Staniloae
can say that the "world was created in order that . . . [humanity] might raise the
world to a supreme spiritualization, and this to the end that human beings
might encounter God with a world that had become fully spiritualized."[72] So
perhaps Staniloae's theology comports better with Teilhard de Chardin than
Matthew Fox. Teilhard interpreted evolutionary processes as teleologically converging toward human consciousness, where they at once discover their perfection and anticipate some further transcendence (see chapter 5). Staniloae says
creation's processes become purposeful within the human project, which has
"needs which are always growing and becoming more refined."[73] Elastic, flexi-
ble, malleable, "the rationality of nature serves the progress human reason is
making toward the supreme meaning."[74]

Staniloae's Romania was simpler than today's consumerist societies of
Europe and North America. He means to emphasize human responsibility
before the gift of the world, but read in the powers of globalized capitalism
Staniloae's rhetoric may undermine the natural sense of that gift. He repeatedly describes nature as purposeless, repetitive, bound to the futility of autom-
ata.[75] Staniloae intends to invoke the way a loving community spiritualizes its
environment, but his rhetoric betrays Teilhard's intuition that creation itself
can direct that love—while yet retaining Teilhard's vulnerability to techno-
industrialist exploitation.

At issue is Staniloae's use of the Maximian christological grammar.
He writes, "The supreme spirituality of Christ . . . contains within itself the
power to cover the automatism of nature. The *defeat* of this automatism of
repetition . . . is the result of actualizing the higher power of the Spirit which
overcomes nature without destroying it."[76] If any of Staniloae's metaphors
for hypostatic agency—defeat, overwhelm, utilize, perfect, humanize—allow

suppression, domination, or violation of natures, then he concedes precisely the point Maximus was at pains to defend. The Word does not dominate human nature (as in the monophysite view) but rather liberates it. On that point the whole project of deification rests, but it is a point Staniloae seems to truncate to mere nondestruction. The vocabulary here should be actualist: the hypostasis realizes, vitalizes, makes present the created natures. Nowhere does Staniloae deny this grammar; but his vocabulary struggles to accommodate the christo-morphic dynamism of Maximus's *logoi*, and so to express the world's own salvation.[77]

In consequence, the gift of the natural world appears so fluidly "malleable" that it hardly presents intrinsic qualifications for good and deifying use.[78] Maximus's evasive, resistant, pedagogical play of Wisdom rarely appears in Staniloae.[79] Instead, Staniloae must determine human freedom with other theological resources.[80] For shaping ecological personhood, Staniloae offers two formative specifications: ascesis and eucharistic gift-exchange.

Ascesis preserves the tensive distance between nature and hypostasis from collapse by guarding against the "enslavement" of will to nature. Asceticism, says Staniloae, purifies our senses to see creation rightly and will to use it bless-edly.[81] But ascesis only negatively purifies here; for positive construction of eco-logical creativity Staniloae returns to the liturgical mystagogy of Maximus.

Staniloae repeatedly visits eucharistic gift exchange when specifying the unifying role of the human microcosm. A human works upon the earth "in order to make it in his turn a gift to others," ultimately blessing and returning the gift to God.[82] Again collecting themes from environmental justice and cre-ation spirituality, here human economies take up nature's economy in order to invite personal participation in ecological goods. For Staniloae the eucharistic liturgy contains the highest instance of personal communion, as humans fulfill the theurgic interval between God's offer and their own response with creative, reconciling, elevating uses of the world.[83]

However, where Maximus would say the liturgy brings forth and celebrates the world's own natures, Staniloae stays silent. Because his overwhelming model of hypostatic activity impoverishes his vocabulary for expressing the yearning of creation itself, Staniloae struggles to articulate the way liturgical creativity liberates the world. Eager to celebrate humanity's potential to gather creation into a cosmic liturgy of a divine gift exchange, Staniloae leaves aside the Maximian promise for celebrating the earth's own animate praise.

So despite offering a theology of the world, Staniloae seems to not fully make sense of creation's groaning. But he does recover the cosmic scope of sal-vation resident in Maximus, thus opening theology to the cosmic breadth of Christ's embrace. It is not quite "thinking like a mountain," but Staniloae at least insists that the church cannot think of salvation apart from mountains: "The brilliance of Tabor will display itself through the whole world. The world becomes a single transfigured mountain."[84] Saved by the cosmic Christ, we are saved into the heart of the world, and there transfigured within it.[85] In order to envision that transfiguration in concert with creation's own groaning, we turn to another east/west Orthodox bridge figure.

The World as Bride of the Lamb: Deification in Bulgakov

Sergei Bulgakov also claims the image of the world in the transfigured mountain of Tabor. But more clearly than Staniloae, Bulgakov retains the integrity of the *logoi* in the mountain's own distinctive aptitude to radiate as Tabor. I have suggested that Staniloae's cosmic deification too strongly phrases the subjugation of natures to personhood. Implicitly emphasizing the Cyrillian side of christology, Staniloae's deification threatens to overwhelm created natures by a transmutative assumption into personhood. Bulgakov recovers creation's voice within Maximian christology, offering important resources to contemporary questions about ecological creativity.

Bulgakov's career project for a biblical theology attentive to the life of the created world began in his own conversion experience. He retells his remarkable journey from Marxism to Christianity via German idealism from an epiphany of earth's glory. Journeying across the southern Russian steppes toward the Caucasus slopes, Bulgakov remembers, the sunset gilded spring grasses and from a blue distance, "the mountains spoke to me." Yet he knew he could not understand this voice by his Marxist or philosophical resources. "I listened to the revelation of nature. . . . Yet, contrary to my intellectual convictions, I could not be reconciled to nature without God." Then,

> suddenly and joyfully . . . my soul was stirred. I started to wonder what would happen if the cosmos were not a desert and this beauty not a mask or deception. . . . What if the merciful and loving Father existed, if nature was a vestige of his love and glory . . . what if all this were true?
>
> . . . O mountains of the Caucasus! I saw your ice sparkling from sea to sea, your snows reddening under the morning dawn, the peaks which pierced the sky, and my soul melted in ecstasy. . . . The first day of creation shown before my eyes.
> . . . And that moment of meeting did not die in my soul, that apocalypse, that wedding feast: the first encounter with Sophia. That of which

the mountains spoke to me in their solemn brilliance, I soon recognized again . . . on different shores and under different mountains.[86]

As do a number of writers working within the strategy of ecological spirituality, when Bulgakov cast about for a biblical figure in which to express the voice of nature and its intimate presence with the human spirit, he settled on Sophia, the Wisdom of God.[87] A second epiphany, experienced beneath the dome of St. Sophia in Istanbul, confirms his choice: "I am in the world and the world is in me," he exults, "This is indeed Sophia."[88] Bulgakov's lifelong occupation with dogmatic sophiology, much debated and often misunderstood, develops the aptitude of the Caucasus for Tabor and the way mountains everywhere might communicate the whisper of God to the human soul.[89] As did Maximus, Bulgakov insists that belief in the real humanity and divinity of Christ implies "the real unity of the world in the Logos."[90] Maximus did so in order to preserve the christological conditions of salvation; Bulgakov does so to preserve the soteriological scope of Christ.

Working out the dynamism of cosmic deification, Bulgakov displays obvious influences from the German idealists Schelling and Boehme, as well as the speculative Russian sophiologists Soloviev and Florensky. But at root he is working out a possibility opened by Maximus's crucial distinction between *logoi* and *hypostasis*, and attempting to express its salvific extent through the biblical trope of Wisdom. Bulgakov sees, as Maximus did, that Chalcedon's defense of dyophysite christology affirms the integrity of creation and its hope of real union with God.[91] Furthermore he takes the hint from Maximus's "*logoi* in the Logos" formula that we should understand nature's economy as a created analogue to perichoretic communion, and "draws an all-pervasive analogy between nature and the structure of inner-trinitarian relationships."[92]

Staniloae follows that same hint, but Bulgakov is more keenly aware that too strong an emphasis on the three hypostases can implicitly deny the reality of the divine nature they possess.[93] Staniloae's celebration of personhood nearly silences talk about their shared *ousia*, with the consequence that created natures too are silenced by intense hypostatization. Bulgakov's generative innovation is his kataphatic treatment of *ousia*.[94] We cannot understand the way creation participates in God (and so how human creativity unites with the earth), he thinks, if we do not specify the character of the divine nature shared by the trinitarian persons. "Divine Wisdom (*Khokmah, Sophia tou Theou*) corresponds to that Divine principle . . . in the Holy Trinity which is usually defined as *ousia* or *physis*; but in its self-revelation."[95] Refusing the neo-patristic prohibition against such kataphasis means that "nature, the *ousia*, rather than being thrown out into the outer darkness of mystery, reveals itself as a relational modality."[96]

Bulgakov's exposition of *ousia*'s biblical names, in other words, develops the possibility of his Caucasus epiphany.[97]

We can read Maximus's concern for Christ's created nature in Bulgakov's concern for the world's integrity: "nothing can be divinized which has not the capacity and ontological aptitude to receive such a gift, which does not bear within itself some intimate exigency for such an end."[98] The revelation of that gift through Christ means that "our thought must be governed by the inclusion of creation in God's own life."[99] Bulgakov therefore searches for the theological aptitude of the world for union with God, much as Maximus searched for the aptitude of human nature for adoption by the Logos. That means theology must again produce formulas that substantially unite creation with God while preserving the tensive space for freedom in their distinction. Again, theology seeks a grammar for unconfused union.[100]

Bulgakov opens *The Bride of the Lamb* by presenting the problem of creation in familiar christological terms. Whereas cosmology often seems pushed toward either monism or dualism (toward cosmic Apollinarianism or Nestorianism, one might say), the Christian solution comes in the terms of Chalcedon, expressed in a Maximian distinction: "The world's existence is a special *modality* of being."[101] God unites with the transfigured world in the same way that Christ unites divine and human natures. "This union of the two natures should be understood in the same way as the di-unity of the Divine and the created Wisdom."[102] In the person of Christ we see creation's aptitude for deification through God's manner of deifying.

Interpreting creation through God's incarnation, Bulgakov adopts the Maximian *logos/tropos* distinction, and uses it to defend God's unconfused union of creation. Expanding the use of this incarnational distinction to the whole created world, Bulgakov inverts its focus. Now instead of referring to Christ's divine person, *tropos* refers to personalizing modes through which the world realizes its divine *logos* compositely with the created *logoi*, making one world from both natures without diminishing their essential difference. Bulgakov describes the created world as a trope of divine nature, as *logoi* become ways of assuming and enacting the divine nature. The theological condition for God assuming the world into trinitarian communion thus rests in God's giving the world its own share in hypostatizing the divine *ousia*. Creation itself has a personalizing capacity, for it exists "as a divine life in the process of formation."[103] Wisdom names how the glory of God's inner life is "realized in the life of the world in its general process of *entheosis*."[104]

Bulgakov establishes his own sort of tensive distance within the way God acts for creation between what he distinguishes as divine and created Wisdom. Just as Maximus saw the mystery of the world in the incarnation, so Bulgakov sees that "the world's being must be included in God's own life, must be correlated with this life, must be understood not only in its own being for itself, but also in its being for God."[105] At the same time, theology must resist cosmic monism, preserving the integrity of that mystery from the wash of pantheism. "A way out can be found only by transferring the question to another plane, *metabasis eis allo genos*, from the static to the dynamic plane."[106] Wisdom, shared in the divine life, given to creaturely life, and creatively dynamic in both, presents the biblical figure of this unconfused union.

> Thus, the world simultaneously has both the statics of its fullness
> and the dynamics of its becoming; and, clearly, the two mutually
> condition each other. This dual foundation of the world also corresponds to the dyadic character of God's self-revelation in the Divine
> Sophia, who is the foundation of the creaturely Sophia.[107]

Anticipated by *ousia*, Sophia functions as a narrative guarantee, permitting the church its story of a divinely-loved world, as surely different from God as it is destined for divine union: "One must know how to simultaneously unite, identify, and distinguish creation and God's life, which in fact is possible in the doctrine of Sophia, Divine and creaturely, identical and distinct."[108] Knowing how is a narrative skill, mediating present integrity and future glory through Wisdom.[109] In Wisdom, Bulgakov can unconfusedly unite divine and created natures, which connects this present earth with the new earth of the glorified Jerusalem (the "bride of the Lamb" in Revelation 21:9–11)—thus explaining how the southern Russian mountains nascently radiate with the glory of Tabor.[110] Bulgakov's sophiology exposits this grammar of the mountains' own voice, nature's own economy, derived from the way of the world toward God.[111]

Personal Creativity and Cosmic Salvation

Bulgakov's chief vulnerability (aside from the chafing his adoration of Sophia provokes) lies in his successful recuperation of creation's agency. With the world's natural processes imitating and participating the divine life on their own, Bulgakov can seem to displace personal salvation with a general ontological optimism.[112] Indeed, Lossky criticizes Bulgakov for dissolving salvation into an inevitable cosmic process.[113] We have seen that vulnerability also in Teilhard de Chardin, to whom Bulgakov is sometimes compared; but Bulgakov recognized and refuted it from the beginning—and he did so by theologically specifying his notion of creativity.[114]

In response to worries that he was displacing salvation with cosmological optimism, Bulgakov's "Ipostas' i ipostasnost'," distinguished hypostasis from hypostatizability, and suggested the role personal creativity plays in God's divinizing action.[115] As early as 1907 Bulgakov made clear his commitment to personal freedom, criticizing first Marx and then the Russian intelligentsia for justifying promethean social programs by appeal to mechanically optimistic ontologies.[116] In both critiques Bulgakov reclaims the ascetical freedom of personal salvation. Asceticism, he says, counteracts the humanist tendency to sneak implicit notions of salvation into progressive social processes, thereby undermining the integrity of humanity.[117] Unlike religious faith, "atheistic humanism is unable to maintain simultaneously both personality and the whole."[118] For that, one needs the microcosmic tradition of Maximus, wherein personhood actively embraces all creation. Christianity's personal salvation, says Bulgakov, grounds the possibility of peaceful and comprehensive social action.[119] "Russian asceticism . . . does not deny this world, but embraces it."[120] Bulgakov thinks that his theological account of creativity can secure nature's economy within the personal dimensions of Christ's cosmic work.[121]

Bulgakov sees the role for human creativity in Maximus's image of embrace, and in his own doctrine of Sophia shows how that embrace participates in both divine and cosmic creativity. For humans meet a world in whose creatures and processes God has "released his own nature into the freedom of creativity in nonbeing, called to being." As a contingent, free trope of the divine nature, the cosmos manifests a "relation between the divine principle of the world and creation [which] is defined not according to the mode of repetition but according to the mode of creativity."[122] Bulgakov thus situates personhood within a dynamic wisdom ecology by placing his account of worldly creativity within the Maximian tradition of the microcosm. In words Maximus, Teilhard, and Fox could all approve, Bulgakov writes that "man, as part of nature also carries within himself the self-consciousness of nature as a whole. . . . Each human individual potentially partakes both of *natura naturans*, the creative soul of the natural world, and of *natura naturata*, nature as it exists at present."[123]

Bulgakov's wisdom theology promises to show how the salvation of humanity amounts to the liberation of all nature, and to do so through an ecological anthropology immanently bound to a divine presence in creation.[124] In the next chapter, I explicate that promise by examining Bulgakov's account of creaturely creativity and divine intimacy, looking for the way his view of cosmic salvation attempts to unite the personal and cosmic, the divine and the creaturely, this earth and the new. For now the key to understanding the ecological promise of *theosis* depends on how human creativity can illuminate the link between Caucasus and Tabor.

II

Thinking Like a Transfigured Mountain

Sergei Bulgakov's Wisdom Ecology

In the course of an otherwise celebratory exposition, Hans Urs von Balthasar warns his readers that in regard to creation Maximus comes perilously near gnosticism, and that modern Orthodoxy inherits this vulnerability. When, in contrast to Thomas, Maximus associates death and finitude with sin,

> one cannot deny that here some shadows of Platonism are darkening the Christian view of the world that Aristotelianism had brightened; a feeling about creation is accepted and propagated here that has influenced both the Byzantine Middle Ages and the 'Sophianism' of modern Russian religious philosophy. The 'Sophia' that Bulgakov sees as a remarkable intermediate being . . . flows down . . . through Byzantium, from ancient Platonic and Gnostic springs. A certain ineradicable mistrust for an autonomous, objective nature . . . a mistrust, in fact, for the fundamental analogy between God and the creature—has always characterized Eastern thought.[1]

Von Balthasar points to a theological ambiguity inherited by the strategy of ecological spirituality in its use of deification concepts: within a world still becoming (or reclaiming) its true reality, what does communion with creation mean? Does grace transform humans by an earthy ecology or a mystical ecology? For the ethics of ecological spirituality, those questions ask how nature participates in humanity's spiritual creativity. How do we know when technology, art, and construction express the glories of creation and when they fracture it, alienating us further? How do we know when our cultivation brings forth the saving beauty of the world? Within a world simultaneously imperfect, glorious, and corrupted, what does authentic transfiguration look like?

We see the ambiguity of the East, says von Balthasar, in Dostoevsky's Aloysha, in his "enchanted gesture of kissing the earth and his angelic, other-worldly nature."[2] Aloysha is an especially instructive example with regard to Bulgakov, for he was deeply influenced by Dostoevsky, and experienced three epiphanies similar to those of Aloysha.[3] We have read of his conversion in the Caucasus Mountains, not unlike Aloysha's rapture beneath the starry sky. Another occurred during a visit to a monastery, where he was embraced and forgiven by an elder (a *staretz*), in the pattern of Aloysha's pivotal relationship with the *staretz* Father Zossima.[4]

The most pivotal, however, is the third, which occurs at the funeral of Bulgakov's four-year-old son, Ivashechka. Aloysha's earth-embracing epiphany had come after the scandal of Father Zossima's quickly decaying body. Aloysha had expected that, by virtue of his deifying nearness to the divine presence, the elder's body would have resisted putrefying corruption. Early in his career, Bulgakov, too, was appalled by the odor of death, by the way life and history both seemed parasitic on corruption. He was influenced not only by Dostoevsky's recoil from ugliness and Vladimir Soloviev's neo-gnosticism, but by the views of Nikolai Fyodorov, who thought humans might technologically appropriate the power of the resurrected life and overcome death.[5] How significant, then, that Bulgakov, like Aloysha, experiences in the midst of death's despair an epiphany of glory: "the sky had opened. . . . Everything became clear, all of the suffering and the heat dissipated and disappeared in the heavenly azure of this church."[6] Later he writes to a friend: "I have never experienced such agony in my life. . . . But the hour of death was so wonderful, God's presence so tangible, his eyes raised to the heavens so lit up, that I experienced not the horror of a last parting, but religious excitement. . . . And my entire life was illumined by this life."[7]

Just as Aloysha envisions Father Zossima's invitation to join the heavenly feast, so Bulgakov mystically experiences the funeral liturgy as a personal encounter with the glory of Christ's resurrection.[8] Both Bulgakov and Aloysha find themselves confronted by the face of a new creation in the midst of death, and both leave the experience in ecstatic embrace of the earth.[9] Like Aloysha, Bulgakov arises from his epiphany a sojourning fighter for the love of creation, unmoved by those who find his devotion to Sophia evidence of unorthodox enthusiasm.[10]

One crucial difference, however, distinguishes Bulgakov's devotion to Sophia from the gnostic renaissance in modern Russian culture. For Bulgakov, Sophia opens the cosmic implications of Chalcedonian christology, and thus leads to affirming precisely what von Balthasar thinks Russian sophiology fears: a fundamental analogy between God and creation. Dostoevsky, though famously hoping in beauty, remained haunted by the evil face of the world. Soloviev, his poet-philosopher colleague, metaphysically resolved that hope against its haunts by invoking a primeval fall of creation into dark, futile agonism. Soloviev retells the ancient gnostic myth of fallen Sophia; creaturely wisdom fell away from divine wisdom, and she threw herself into death and suffering. The female figure of Sophia for Dostoevsky and Soloviev therefore appears capricious, as much rebellious whore as icon of divine beauty.[11] Bringing to mind infamous phrases from Francis Bacon, their earth must be pursued and penetrated by a rational logos for its restoration to beauty.[12]

Bulgakov deploys the figure of Sophia with much different valences.[13] "Sophia in her fallen aspect," says Wendy Wiseman, "is muted to the point of erasure, and so . . . Bulgakov has abandoned one face of Sophia to the shadows, marking his departure from both Dostoevsky and Soloviev."[14] Because "his Sophiological project is an attempt to deepen our understanding of the Chalcedonian dogma," Bulgakov understands the feminine face of the earth in its own dignity, as some immanent presence of divine love.[15] So far from gnosticism is Bulgakov, so seriously does he take the creaturely dignity that Maximus defended in christology, that pantheism becomes his nearer problem.[16] Bulgakov wants to affirm that the world has no other foundation than the divine life, so that its life variously manifests God's self-revelation. For him, the figure of Sophia suggests nonagonistic creativity, where the economy of creation actively realizes the beauty of God, illuminating earth's shadows with glory, as the deifying presence of God increases and brings forth the creatureliness of the world.

Createdness and the Problem of Creativity

In chapter 5 we saw how the strategy of ecological spirituality begs a theological account of creativity. Attempting to bind together divine presence and nature's dynamism, its theologians often appeal to humanity's role in a co-creative cosmos. Sometimes they draw on microcosmic themes to express nature's voice within personhood, sometimes they let sacramental forms typologically shape creativity, sometimes they place human and divine agencies in dialogical reference to independent natural processes. By various ways, they consistently assume human creativity somehow functioning at the center of an ecological view of grace. The practical implications of their ethical proposals hinge on specifying that functioning. Bulgakov's meditations on Sophia offer a way to integrate ecological grace, ecological creativity, and ecological science.

Oliver Davies (as we saw in chapter 1) blamed the absence of "createdness" from theology on the separation of personhood from reflexive intimacy with God and the cosmos. In his view, without createdness theological ethics will run into the sort of difficulties we saw in chapter 5: ambiguous use of soteriological metaphors, competition between natural processes and divine providence, totalizing views of personhood—each a problem of alienated relations. Robert Miner traces such ruptures back to modernist distortions, when creativity became the unilateral power of human genius, unqualified by relations either natural or supernatural.[17] Displaced from theological and ecological intimacy, this distorted creativity isolates humanity in direct proportion to the perfection of its exercise—the more intense the action, the more violative and coercive toward others. Bulgakov and his Russian contemporaries often critiqued just that sort of agonistic subjectivity, seeking to restore relationality to creative freedom.[18]

The strategy of ecological spirituality sometimes attempts a similar restoration, but struggles to specify which sort of actions rupture personhood from relations natural and divine, and which restore it to deifying intimacy. That relationship of creativity, ecology, and grace guides how a theologian uses and interprets soteriological metaphors of environmental practice (redeeming, restoring, healing, transfiguring nature). As we saw at the end of chapter 5, references to Sophia proliferate at just the moment theologians arrive at that difficulty. Seeking unitive, noncompetitive ecologies of grace, theologians look toward the biblical figure of Wisdom. At the site of world's encounter with God, Wisdom seems to gesture at once toward the Spirit bringing forth life and toward creation's own yearning for liberation.

Bulgakov embraces Wisdom because it roots cosmic deification in a consubstantiality of creaturely and divine life that yet preserves an illimitable difference between the two. By letting Wisdom determine the creaturely meaning of *ousia*, Bulgakov can maintain the integrity of both nature and personhood, and consequently the union of creaturely and divine. In Bulgakov, sophiology restores that lost theological key: the intimacy of God, humanity, and creation.

The question of creativity uniquely pressed upon Bulgakov for two additional reasons. First, by historical context: while Bulgakov was rediscovering Sophia through the writings of Soloviev, the Russian intelligentsia of the Silver Age were agonizing over the authenticity of personal, ecclesial, and national expression.[19] Bulgakov had trained as an economist, devoting his dissertation research to assimilating peasant agriculture into Marxist projections. His topic troubled the Russian adoption of Marxism because of the rural peasant's iconic symbolism for Russian identity, representing (especially for the intelligentsia) the role of noble earth in the economy of Russian life.[20] Bulgakov departed from Marxism dissatisfied with its promethean attitude toward inert nature, and looking for a way to explain how human labor brings forth the face of the land.[21] If Bulgakov could connect authentic cultural expression with the character of the land, his theory would speak to the central concerns of the Russian *Zeitgeist*.[22]

To develop that kind of theory, Bulgakov turns from economic materialism to continental idealism (Hegel and Schelling especially), but recoils from its celebrations of subjective freedom because they seem totalizing toward the material world. Then, reading Soloviev, "the image of a living nature in constant interaction with man, no longer merely an inert object to be conquered, captured his attention."[23] Bulgakov saw in Soloviev's creaturely and divine Sophia a way opened between materialist and idealist philosophies. Soloviev showed him that it was "possible to have a worldview on whose basis one might be a materialist—that is, conceive oneself as in real unity with nature and humankind—yet at the same time affirm the independence of the human spirit." Soloviev suggested to Bulgakov the possibility of a "religious materialism," in which "the fate of nature, suffering and awaiting its liberation, is henceforth connected with the fate of man."[24] Reading Soloviev, in other words, Bulgakov glimpsed a path toward recovering an animate cosmos by reconnecting the groaning of creation with the salvation of humanity. As Soloviev himself anticipated, the linchpin for that connection must be theurgical; "Bulgakov explicitly and by name adds theurgy to theosis, thereby enabling with this ancient resource, more justice to be done to the modern sense of the importance of human fabrication."[25] By recovering creativity within deification, Bulgakov finds resources to address the practical creativities of everyday life.

The second reason Bulgakov must address the question of creativity follows from his restoration of natural dynamism to cosmology. By accepting the historicity of the cosmos and conceiving its processes as a kind of life participating in God's life, Bulgakov must explain what earth is up to, how nature natures. His answer: "Creation's task is to actualize itself, to find itself by its own creativity." The world discovers itself as the creaturely life of divine Wisdom, "a possibility that is ceaselessly being actualized" by its immanent entelechies, the self-realization of its natural processes. "The life of the world is accomplished on the basis of its 'laws' or energies; its 'evolution' is the dynamic development of its statics."[26] The world discovers itself as a temporal trope of God's eternal life, as "God in eternity translated into process and temporality."[27]

Because he thinks that the world discovers the divine life in its own ways, Bulgakov must develop a theology of earth's creativity.

Teilhard wanted something similar, but absent a theological account of how creaturely dynamism participates in divinity and why towards intellectual communion, Teilhard's system can appear coldly inevitable and tacitly promethean.[28] Where some theologians might save the world's integrity by carefully levying out divine agency, Bulgakov instead extends the rule of noncompetition: God's freedom does not threaten but rather increases creaturely freedom. Analogously, authentic human creativity must not threaten but rather bring forth nature's liberation. To explain how, Bulgakov concentrates the function of Maximus's microcosm into human labor, where creaturely and divine Sophia are united.[29]

In Bulgakov's account of creativity, we find the sense of Aloysha's epiphany (and Bulgakov's own), along with a vision of the good economy and responsible technology. Contemporary Christian theology, observes Rowan Williams, has developed few models that hold together God's act of creation, creatureliness, and creativity. One of the few is Bulgakov's sophiology, Williams goes on to say, and it incorporates those three into a biblical pattern of salvation.[30] Glimpsed in the church's liturgy and generated from Chalcedonian christology, Sophia underlies a model of divine participation that brings forth the fullness of creation through human inhabitation.

Humanizing the World

After Maximus, one could talk about the way of creation into union with God as a kind of "humanization," for through the incarnate human embrace God connects and restores the cosmos. We have seen how Staniloae's version of humanization overwhelms nature, the "anthropocosmos," with humanity's communion with God. Bulgakov turns humanization away from alluding to nature's subjugation, using it instead as "a way of expressing St. Paul's vision of the liberation of the cosmos," by affirming that "every productive act is a foreshadowing and partial consummation of that ultimate liberation."[31] Natural and human powers do not threaten or overwhelm but perfect one another within God's way of union with the world.

Bulgakov developed theological conditions for that harmonizing triple agency in his 1925 essay "Ipostas i ipostasnost'," which defended sophiology as a dogmatic extrapolation of Orthodox christology. There he roots his theology of creation in the character of God's act: God creates in reciprocity and self-giving, communicating Godself to another.[32] Creation responds in analogous pattern, living by the glory of God received in its heart—creaturely Sophia, Bulgakov calls it. In its perfection that life will fully attain the character of the divine life, the love circulating within God—divine Sophia.

Bulgakov's sophiology carefully affirms creation's divine heart not as some semidivine person, but as a sharable love awaiting possession by persons. Wisdom is not a hypostasis, but *ipostasnost'*, "the capacity for being hypostatized."[33] Variously rendered by his translators as hypostaseity, hypostaticity, and hypostatizability, *ipostasnost'* means, says Bulgakov "the capacity to hypostatize oneself [*ipostasirovat'sia*], to belong to a hypostasis, to be its disclosure [*raskrytiem*], to give oneself up [*otdavat'sia*] to it."[34] It means the world's susceptibility to become personal love. Bulgakov interprets the Wisdom character of the Old Testament personally but not as a Person.[35] She is at once "the objective principle of divine self-revelation and life," and the creative mystery at the heart of the world.[36] His terms confound clear causative designations because they bear both passive and active connotations, and Bulgakov seems to intend both.[37] The world creates itself in the glory of God by giving itself over in surrender to another.

Just as Bulgakov adopted the *logos/tropos* function of Maximus in order to explain createdness, here he seems to adopt and invert the Palamite essence/ energy distinction in order to present creaturely subjectivity as simultaneously passive and active. Gregory Palamas protected mystical union from offending divine impassibility by distinguishing divine energies from divinity in itself, or divine essence. Bulgakov places humans in union with God's activity of realizing the divine essence of creation, so that the hypostatic "energies" of humanity bring forth the nascent divine "essence" of creation, as part of their own participation in God's ecstatic relations.[38]

So qualified, human creativity assumes its deifying microcosmic role reshaped by a divine mode of freedom and divested of agonistic presuppositions. That allows Bulgakov to develop the cosmic implications in Maximus and Palamas by making hypostatization of divine glory the salvific ecological function of humanity. Maximus and Palamas had insisted that "deification is an enyhpostatic and direct illumination," thus locating its operation within human personhood.[39] Bulgakov maintains that emphasis on the personal, as well as the rule inherited from both fathers that divine and creaturely action cannot compete, by presenting humanization as God's way of having the cosmos make its own way into God.

That represents a radical departure from modern assumptions about human agency. Reversing its usual valence as a presumptively violative threat to nature, transformative human action brings forth nature's essence, responding to its longing for liberation.[40] In anticipation of the true Adam, "the organizer of the world according to the image of its sophianicity [*sofiinost'iu*]," says Bulgakov, "all creation groans, awaiting its liberation through the sons of men."[41] Reversing the usual flow of nature/culture, here creation flourishes within the sustaining resources of human action. Human cultivation works "to raise the world, by humanizing it, to the perfection implanted in it."[42] The claim seems counterintuitive, but recall how Thomas Berry and Mathew Fox locate much of their ecological liberation theology "within" human personhood, in the cultus of creative expression. Their strategy not only ecologizes person-hood, it implies the possibility of harmonizing forms of human and natural agency. Bulgakov's theme of humanization realizes that possibility in the sophi-anic creativity of a Wisdom ecology: "as the human being is a microcosm and the world is an anthropocosm, so the realm and power of the Church extend to the entire universe. All of nature thirsts for the body and blood of Christ."[43] Creation thirsts for the Son of God, groans for the daughters and sons of humanity. Through its liturgical cultivation, the church slakes and liberates creations, sustaining and vivifying creatures within its glorification of God.[44]

Here Bulgakov appropriates the models of humanity "summing up" and "embracing" the cosmos that we saw in Maximus, only now developed so that they refer at once to the essence of creation and to the glory of the divine life. Sophianic creativity is simultaneously shaped by the immanent wisdom of cre-ation and the shared love of the Trinity. Remember how Maximus refused to accept a monophysite view in which divine freedom overwhelmed created nature. For Maximus, the christological controversy was as much a debate over the character of personal freedom: agonistic, violative, and competitive on one side, realizational, perfective, and liberatory in Chalcedon.[45] Bulgakov's sophi-anic creativity adopts the freedom of Chalcedon. "So far from dominating nature," says Eugene Rogers, in Bulgakov, "the human being participates in Christ's undoing of the fall by *befriending* nature instead of seeking like Adam to rise above it."[46]

So while, as Rogers muses, "some passages about the human consumption of nature sound like a brief for Monsanto," we can read Bulgakov's exultantly humanizing passages without the worries that attend Teilhard's technophilic optimism or Staniloae's overwhelming personalism.[47] For, unlike both Teilhard and Staniloae, Bulgakov qualifies the transforming act of human agency in relation to creation's own reception of divinity. Consider this example:

> Because he is one with nature, man resurrects his own dormant
> forces by simultaneously resurrecting those of nature, transforming
> matter into his own body, tearing it from the calcified skeleton of
> *natura naturata* and warming it with his flame. The shroud

gradually falls from the already putrid body of Lazarus, who awaits
the command, Lazarus, come forth![48]

It reads like progressive triumphalism in religious garb, recalling Fyodorov's
bizarre optimism and vindicating Dostoevsky's recoil from decay.[49] But
Bulgakov's Chalcedonian view of freedom prevents him from interpreting the
world's transfiguration as some promethean accomplishment, the wresting of
form from chaos, a novel achievement against a rivalrous force.[50] Human labor
mediates the new heavens and the new earth, but rather than inscribing the new
over a defeated landscape of the old, Bulgakov's images of mediation are those of
a midwife, attending the birth of new life from within. Human creativity "makes
manifest the sophianic face of creation," summoning forth nature's own immanent glory.[51] "In economy, in the conscious re-creation of nature, we can see a
certain adumbration and anticipation of that liberation of *natura naturans* from
the fetters of the *natura naturata*."[52] At their best, human cultures and economies give expression to earth's inner glory, bringing forth creation's freedom.

As Maximus showed, Christ's power does not coerce because it does not
penetrate matter as if blankly or demonically vacuous. Instead it summons
nature's powers and participates in its forms, unifying creation with its divine
source. For Bulgakov, the death of Pan in the coming of Christ does not desa-
cralize the world, setting Christian axes to primeval forests.[53] It means nature's
true mystery and full glory may be revealed, the sacred character of ancient forests brought forth in sophianic craft. "Nature awaits its humanization," says
Bulgakov, already possessing "its own spirit-bearing character."[54]

Empowering creation's agency becomes the distinct service of human freedom, which through "missions of religious creativity," elevates the world in
anticipation of cosmic union.[55] Those Christian missions do not set out into the
world to defeat nature, but to unleash it, to liberate it into the glory for which it
yearns. Unlike the assumptions of so much western "development," such "creativity is not an arbitrary and willful imposition upon nature, but a participation in the divine creativity manifested in nature, which is its necessary ground
and condition."[56] The church does not erect itself in defiance of a howling jun-
gle nor in redemption of empty space, but with wisdom, care, and skill attends
new births from the womb of creation.

The midwifery metaphors describe one aspect of Bulgakov's sense of freedom, but the microcosmic activity of the divine-humanity invites maternal and
landscape metaphors as well. Human labor receives the earth's incipient life into
its own body, and brings forth the subjective expression of Sophia. Community
development responds to and makes manifest the earth's self-revealing divine
glory—a kind of bioregionalism of Mt. Tabor.[57] Formed in relation to the earth's

own natural energies and within personal communion with God, human work does not create absolutely or imperiously. For "nature too labors and creatively participates in its self-creation," and human work joins and fructifies nature's own dynamic responsiveness to God's generative call: "Let there be!"[58] Drawing on both the active and passive senses of *ipostasirovat'sia*, Bulgakov renders humanization reflexive: it actualizes the creaturely glory by which it is itself animated. Humans "master" such a world by "defending, affirming, and broadening life"; and their divinizing actions are measured in the light of nature's responsive radiance.[59] The ethic of creativity here, says Deane-Drummond, is "active co-operation with the transformation of the world according to Sophia."[60]

The microcosmic creativity of humanity thus cleaves closely to the expressive promise of creation itself, because—for Bulgakov as for Maximus—therein lies the nascent promise of deification, revealed in the person of Christ. The "essential content and life-giving energy proper to creation" could not be undone by sin, and is now restored by Christ to the active personhood of the church. Humanization must "receive the action of natural grace which is manifested in creation by virtue of the initial creative act, just as it is necessary to receive the creative word that resides in creation . . . these are the word from the Word and spirit of God from the Holy Spirit." The microcosm receives and personalizes creation's divine ground, elevating the impersonal natural world to its share in the divine life.[61]

So nature immanently inhabits and shapes the "earthly construction that goes forward to meet the divine construction," just as Christ's creaturely nature fully inhabited and shaped the character of his divinely-human life.[62] At its highest, says Bulgakov, creativity does not escape the world, but discovers the glory and mystery at its heart, and experiences itself as one with "the world soul."[63] Nature epiphanies, like Bulgakov's own, experience that enfolded mystery, when beauty undoes fractured, grasping persons, emptying them of themselves and filling them with the fullness and unity of creation. Then the human "unites with the Sophianic basis of its own being, deepening and affirming itself in it not from without, but from within, by the power of chastity." Like Aloysha's jubilant embrace of the earth, here "creative work is not absolute, for it is not from itself, it is defined by the sophianicity of its nature."[64] It is the earth's own expression of divine glory, embodied in the span of a human embrace.

Divine Creativity: Kenosis and Ascesis

Bulgakov knew the subjectivist perils of granting humanization a central role in cosmic deification, and his simultaneous appeals to sophianicity and chastity signal the ways he limits transformative freedom. Bulgakov was worried by the growing thrall of "economism," subjugating earth's economy to a self-legitimating market of consumerist desires, and he loathed the place of empty novelty in this fool's economy.[65] For Bulgakov, that devilish parody of freedom begs the church to reclaim its christological teachings on creativity and divinization:

> Our epoch is characterized by a broad development of creativity "in its own name," by a deluge of anthropotheism, in the form of a luciferian creative intoxication, and by an immersion in dull sensual paganism. These developments . . . can be overcome only by the unfolding of a positive Christian doctrine of the world and creative activity. . . . This is only a further unfolding of the Chalcedonian and ditheletic dogma, according to which . . . the entire power of the human creative will and energy in Christ are united with the divine nature. . . . In the light of this dogma, the "cosmos" is not the "kingdom of this world" but God's radiant creation, which is raised by [humanity] toward deification.[66]

Against the foolish excesses of the worldly economy Bulgakov narrates a wisdom ecology, itself formed from the deifying economy of grace. Against the formless change of consumerist innovations, Bulgakov qualifies creativity within an ascetic frame. The referent for both is Maximian christology, whose "sophiological foundations" he has already defended.[67] Theology must affirm Christ fully united with creation, and discover in his mode of union the divinizing model for wisdom's practice.

The church knows two primary witnesses to this model: one in the kenotic gift of Christ's earthly life, and another in the ascetic tradition that mirrors it. The life of Christ narratively dramatizes the character of the trinitarian economy, and thus of the initial creative act. The lived theology of the ascetics, actively responding to and participating in Christ's life, narratively dramatizes the responsive creativity of creation.[68]

Even before the cross, writes Bulgakov, creation is a type of the Son's sacrifice. God's creative act repeats the Father's eternal generation of the Son and the Son's self-giving for the sake of the Father's love.[69] Created through the Son, the cosmos is a gratuitous instance of this self-giving: the Word communicated into nothingness, that the shared love of the Trinity (a.k.a. Sophia) might be made manifest anew.[70] In a second moment of trinitarian kenosis, God communicates to the world a glory it cannot yet fully return, thus opening within the perichoretic life an interval of risk, of non-return.[71] This deceleration of perichoresis for the sake of the nondivine opens a tensive space of contingency, an interval from which come the mighty cedars of divine blessing as well as the dead tree of the cross.[72] The form of God's creativity opens the body of God, at once inviting and establishing the response of creation. "The divine kenosis . . . simply *is* the divine essence"; it is, in other words, the exuberant fullness that lies at the heart of the world in Sophia.[73] The sacrifice of the cross dramatizes this kenotic plenum: violated on the dead tree, God incorporates violent, deadening creatures into the transfiguring shoot of Jesse.[74] The cross perfects divine creativity, its "sacrifice of divine love," showing how "in the incarnation of Christ, the world itself becomes the body of Christ," given for the sake of union.[75] The sacrifice of the cross reveals the beauty at the heart of creation.

The presence of the Holy Spirit testifies to the way divine creativity seeks not simply recovered union, but differences multiplied in the way of union— hence Bulgakov's refusal to think of transfiguration as *apocatastasis* (universal restoration to a previous state of innocence). Hovering over that interval of contingency, as over the waters of chaos, the Spirit brings forth an abundance of living responses. Bulgakov attributes to the Spirit "the actualization of the generative power of the earth and water as the maternal womb, the proto-reality which has been seeded with the words of the Word."[76] Rogers puts it more neatly: "The Spirit rests on the Son . . . as the Spirit hovers over the waters of creation to elaborate the intratrinitarian interval with a diversity of creatures destined to fill the earth."[77] The kenosis in divine creation anticipates a joyfully pleromic response, elaborating creation in beauty and glory.[78]

Bulgakov's account shows that environmental theorists need not worry that divine agency threatens to violently overcome earthly creativities, for God's creativity operates kenotically, invitationally, generatively.[79] Neither need we think kenosis conceives a withdrawal of divine freedom; on the contrary, it suggests a relationally intensive form of self-giving creativity.[80] If we understand creativity within Maximian logic of cosmic deification, as Bulgakov does, God's transfiguration of creation actualizes the bursting forth of creation in its own wild glory.[81]

Divine creation does not then suppress the wild nor domesticate difference; it invites both. In Rogers's gloss, "God's husbandry alongside (*para*) nature in grafting the wild olive into the domestic does not overturn nature, but parallels, diversifies, and celebrates it."[82] The advent of Jesus and his transfiguring salvation does not homogenize the world's harvest, as if divine beauty dulled the world and faith ended laughter, joy, and creativity.[83] On the contrary, before the creative acts of God the rivers clap their hands, the stones cry out, and the mountains quake with radiance.

It falls to humanity to express that wild glory in personal communion, to "humanize" the generativity of the cosmos into a shared perichoretic gift. But in order to elevate the sophianic form of creation, to elaborate the interval of divine kenosis, humans must perceive that glory. Bulgakov further chastens creativity, therefore, by appealing to the tradition of the desert fathers and the monastic Russian *staretz* to make asceticism a hermeneutical practice for receiving and interpreting the glory of creation.

Within a Wisdom ecology, deification "represents a dogmatic call both to spiritual ascesis and creativity, to salvation from the world and to a salvation of the world."[84] Here the disciplines of desire connote no hatred or repudiation of earth, but rather embrace creation: "[Asceticism] is not an acosmism (and certainly not an anticosmism), not an absence of love for the world as God's creation. . . . For this world, as God's creation, man must have love, for he is connected with it forever according to creation, and his salvation includes the salvation of the world."[85] Bulgakov follows his friend Pavel Florensky, who argues that "the higher the Christian ascetic ascends on his path to the heavenly land . . . the more clearly will he see the inner, absolutely valuable core of creation," until eventually he realizes all the world joins his prayer: "Trees, grass, birds, earth, air, light . . . all things pray and sing the glory of God." Finally the ascetic confesses his ecological solidarity with this cosmic liturgy: "I saw a way in which I could speak with God's creatures." In true asceticsm, Florensky shows, an ecological expansion of the human person occurs, "leading the ascetic to the absolute root of creation, when washed by the Holy Spirit, separated from his selfhood through self-purification." There he finds "that root of creation which is given to him through coparticipation in the depths of Trinitarian love."[86]

Bulgakov rephrases Florensky in Maximus's vocabulary of transfiguration: "to the illumined eye of the ascetic, the world presents itself as the living garment of the Godhead, as his Word, clothed in the Holy Spirit."[87] Then he extends this vision beyond Florensky's monastic few to qualify the universal task of the church.[88] The contemplative "art of the ascetic" represents the whole church's relation with the world "which consists in struggle with the world out of love for the world."[89] The narrow way of discipline is the church's way into the heart of the world and the world's way into a divinizing economy.[90]

Bulgakov's ascetic emphasis at once vindicates the environmentalist worry that progressive capitalism assumes a self-justifying salvation narrative, while yet insisting that Christian responses cannot dispense with soteriology, but rather must restore its full promise with "the ascetical self-regulation that goes with it."[91] Against subtly promethean social programs of progressive humanism, Bulgakov's ascetic humanization renounces cultural tendencies to apotheosis. Writing presciently in 1909 against atheistic reform plans in Russia, Bulgakov worries over any "heroic" program, confident in its mandate and effectiveness, and so given to "inherent self-worship and . . . substitution of itself for God."[92] Impervious to the claims of history or the findings of natural science (think of contemporary environmental debates here), such political projects can act as if all the world were just resources for a grandly inventive plan. That, says Bulgakov, is the mentality of destruction. In contrast, the asceticism of Christian creativity exorcises itself of savior delusions or sure knowledge of historical process, opening itself to authentically transformative tasks in the humility of acknowledged sin and finitude.[93]

Together, kenosis and ascesis specify a mode of human creativity that opens places for creation's generative diversity and renounces its own glory for the inner beauty of the world.[94] It is simultaneously characterized by the deifying gift of the perichoretic life and by creation's striving to receive it.[95] Rowan Williams summarizes:

> The human calling to share the love and the liberty of God has to be in this perspective a calling to "let be." The paradox of real human creativity is that it is not the flexing of our human, our created will . . . the imposing of order, the dredging up something new out of the depths of our interiority; [rather] our creativity is most fully and freely expressed as humans when we, as artists, stand back and let-be . . . it is the depth of the world occurring where the artist is because the artist has somehow exercised the asceticism of setting aside preferences and purposes and all the rest of it, so that something occurs.[96]

Only so does humanity incorporate the world into a "macro-anthropos," grafting the wild olive into the city of God by embracing and befriending creation, by setting forceful preferences aside to let something occur.

The Economy of Wisdom in the Life of the World

For Bulgakov, the sophic economy is no mere metaphor: he retains the materialist bent of his earlier Marxism by understanding that humanizing production as so many practical extensions of human embodiment.[97] The practical *technai* mediate Bulgakov's vision of glory: in the "integral synthesis of all human works directed at the humanization of the world, . . . the laborer's hammer blow is included along with the chemist's analysis and the engineer's design . . . along with steam power and air travel." If that sounds aggressively technophilic, it is because of our bellicose industrial economy—all the more reason for theology to reclaim creative industry and recast technology. Bulgakov knows that reconciling grace must embrace and transform the center of human activity, so he embraces consumption and production, air travel and chemistry, and refers them to the Genesis mandate "to dress and keep the earth."[98] By resituating economic and technological practices within the Edenic economy of creation with Creator, in Bulgakov's view, Christianity offers healing for the industrial economy's alienation from earth, and in a new economy, the liberation of earth from technological violence.[99]

By making economy a general feature of createdness, Bulgakov helps integrate Christian social practices into deifying grace. For example, because he nests the usual fiscal sense of economy within a general economy of creation, and makes that subsidiary to the trinitarian economy of love, Christian Jubilee campaigns become more than moralist; they creatively and correctively illuminate the ultimate purpose of economy.[100] So too for patterns of consumption: within the sophianic economy, they become a "means of communion with the flesh of the world."[101] In both cases, the creativity of Christ exorcises and transforms the historical, materialist processes that titillate desire into consuming the vacuous surfeit of a destructive economy. Now "production becomes a serious and responsible way of laborious preservation and reconstruction of life."[102] Industry elaborates the interval of God and creation, diversifies the life of the world for the glory of God. Economy is now eschatological craft.[103] Humanity "makes the economic system into a work of art, in which each product glows with its own idea, and the world as a whole turns into a cosmos."[104]

It sounds like a sophianic version of the Jeffersonian tradition, perhaps Wendell Berry gone Orthodox. Consider Catherine Evtuhof's summary:

> Bulgakov's instruction to treat economic activity as a creative process inspired by Sophia amounts to an ethic of joyful and creative labor. The economic process should be seen as analogous to the creation of a work of art, the joyous investment of the products of nature with their own essence. Bulgakov's instruction to the *khoziain* [independent small share-holder farmer] is an ethic of labor infused with joy, for every stone he moves and every furrow he plows partakes of the Divine Sophia and reproduces in microcosm the universal drama of Fall and Resurrection. . . . Just as a person attending the Orthodox liturgy and partaking of the Eucharist experiences the cosmic drama of Christ's resurrection . . . so each man relives the Fall and Resurrection as he works in his field. His labor resurrects the soil, redeems it from the inert, lethargic sleep into which Adam plunged it with his original sin.[105]

Now, offering a solution to the problem that troubled his dissertation on Marx and spurred him toward conversion, Bulgakov incorporates the agricultural economy, and with it the Russian romance of the soil, into the Maximian vision of the church's mystagogy. Discovering through joyful labor the sophianic face of the earth, and liturgically sharing it in the communion of God, Bulgakov's liturgical *khoziain* represents an icon of the divinized cosmos as a diverse household (*khoziaistvo*).[106]

His student Alexander Schmemann stayed clear of sophiology, but he discovered "the life of the world" in Bulgakov's liturgical philosophy of economy (*filosofiia khoziaistva*).[107] Bulgakov's theurgical appropriation of Maximian deification—the microcosm "called also to become a cosmourgos"—allows both theologians to emphasize how daily material practices participate in the divine life by participating in the life of the world.[108] Practical creativity then produces the life of the world by incarnately summoning earth's own reproductions of its beauty, thus reenacting the life of God in creation.

Practicing Transfiguration

We have left undeveloped a theological site important to the strategy of ecological spirituality. Although his sophiological cosmodicy has taken us far from gnosticism, Bulgakov so occupies himself with narrating creation's glory that he never quite tells us how the Fall relates to the shadow side of creation. Consequently, his Wisdom ecology leaves us uncertain what to make of tsunamis, predation, disease, and death—and so how the daily practices of a Wisdom economy respond to such natural phenomena.

Bulgakov will refer to the Fall in significantly different ways. Sometimes he appropriates Soloviev's gnostic terminology to describe the "fall" of creaturely Sophia into nothingness.[109] In this sense the Fall makes, almost benignly, the temporal span of creation's dynamic becoming. In other places Bulgakov refers to the Fall in a demonic sense, in the rebellion of humanity and the angels—those who should have hypostatically brought forth glory from the "fall" of Sophia. In still other places he narrates a shadow immanently haunting all creation; "an anti-form, as it were, a grimace of being, the phantasms of Achamoth."[110]

His textual evidence confounds clear interpretation. But Bulgakov's sophiology asks us to read any deep conflict in the drama of salvation history within the interval of God's giving, in the tensive span between the attraction of Wisdom and a refusal of creatureliness—receiving or refusing God's gift of life.[111] Apparent violence stems from the shudders of the world in refusal, the outcome of Lucifer's paroxysmic anger, exhausting itself in protest against its own root in divine love. But that violence cannot rend the heart of the world, that anger cannot offend creation's essence. Following Maximus, Bulgakov asks us to imagine "not a substantial only a functional corruption of the world."[112] The world falls in a failure of creativity, not in essence, but modally, by a sub-personal trope.

How Bulgakov understands the ecological effects of that parasitic irrationality remains unclear. But his homilies do suggest that however we imagine the Fall, our conclusions must follow from the christology of incarnation. Drawn into the Easter life of Jesus, "the human spirit—as it rises to life—can find no part of nature that is dead and not rising to life with it, and it summons all of nature to the Resurrection of Christ."[113] Because of the incarnation the church affirms that "world has now become the kingdom of Christ, and there is no other principle of being in it."[114]

The mystery of the world's corruption thus resides in the wounds of Christ. Preaching on Easter, Bulgakov indicates his move away from the necrophobia of Fyodorov and Dostoevsky: the resurrection is not a victory over death itself, he says, but "eternal life shining out of death." It is a "transfigured and victorious suffering, just as light is a victory over 'the darkness of the abyss,' and God's world invests the 'empty and formless land' with color and order."[115] The body of Christ remains wounded, yet somehow those wounds transfigure, even joyfully.

Notice how Bulgakov poses Dostoevsky's question about death, as well as his solution in beauty, but answers with a hope no longer agnostic. Bulgakov proclaims that we find world-saving beauty on the cross; the hope of the world on a dead tree transfigured.[116] The Wisdom of creation is revealed in the foolishness of the cross, whose beauty humanity must not only accept, but practically express.[117]

> Does this not speak of a new service of the Church, one that has not yet been fully revealed in the heart of [humanity] and in [its] history: the service of realizing the work of human participation in the transfiguration of the world . . . ? Is it not of this that the words of Dostoevsky speak: "Beauty will save the world and will rebuild its primordial image, of which the Creator saw that 'it was good'"?[118]

What practical ecological stance toward predation that might entail remains difficult to imagine. But it at least implies a model of divine action opening itself in vulnerability to creation, and then bringing forth beauty from the heart of createdness to transform suffering into joy, violence into peace. In the church resides the resurrection power to embrace the creative beauty even in predation, and to bring forth from its destruction the redemptive promise of the wild city of God. Bulgakov invites us to interpolate ecological questions into the biblical images of salvation: the lion and lamb, eternal life, the green city of clear waters, the end of tears. Bulgakov sends us to the holy mountain of Tabor to have glory teach us how to think like a mountain.

Listen to the way he preaches the Day of Transfiguration: "What was it that the mountain, and the air, and the sky, and the earth, and the whole world, and Christ's disciples saw? . . . It was a revelation of the Holy Trinity as a whole—of the Father sending his Spirit upon his beloved Son and in him upon all creation, to which Christ united himself by assuming human nature." Here creatures, drawn by the Spirit into the embrace of Christ's glory, see revealed the mystery of the cosmos in a vision of God's creative act uniting creaturely and divine Wisdom. Creation sees the perichoretic life opened to it, and there proleptically experiences its divine destiny. What the mountain knows, the disciples proclaim, that "the light of the Transfiguration has already penetrated into the world and abides in it":

> But what does "transfiguration" mean? Does it mean that the old
> image is cancelled, or that it is truly revealed in glory, in the all-
> subduing—because it is all-convincing—manifestation of beauty?
> "It is good to be here"—"very good." This is how the world is created
> by the divine Providence, though it is not as yet revealed to human
> contemplation. And yet on Mount Tabor it is revealed already.

In the euphoria of the moment, Peter wants to build something—a creative response to express and house the goodness of the place, to let the microcosmic figures of glory dwell within the summit of creation. But a cloud settles protectively over the mountain, telling the church to listen to Jesus—to hear just how creation is "very good" before presuming to construct something. Connecting the "very good" of the Creator with the disciples' response, "it is good to be here," Bulgakov places the dynamic heart of creation in the creative body of Jesus. From Jesus, the disciples learn the goodness and beauty that the mountain already reveals. "It follows Christ on the way to the cross; in the world beauty is crucified. It is sacrificial beauty. . . . Yet it is beauty. And it is the feast of this sacrificial beauty that we celebrate on the day of the Lord's Transfiguration."[119]

Bulgakov finally refers humanity's constructive creativity to the cross, where God's kenotic creativity transfigures the brokenness and alienation of the world. Christ's body embraces the world's woundedness, anticipating the cosmic body resurrected in glory. Yet even on the cross, Christ's body makes creation beautiful because precisely there, in those wounds, Christ personally receives and reunites creation.

Conclusion on Bulgakov

For the ethical strategy of ecological spirituality, Bulgakov demonstrates the possibility of making a theological place for creativity. Moreover, by making that place directly within his account of deifying grace, he helps contemporary ethicists work out the connection between their patterns of ecological personhood and their practical models of creativity. By uniting transfiguration and economy, Bulgakov lets the Orthodox tradition of *theosis* shape the practical forms of ecological personhood. Technology, construction, art, and especially agriculture participate in the divine life by participating in the natural heart of the world. By disciplining ecological personhood within the ascetic imitations of Christ's self-sacrifice, and setting it in the elaborative interval of the Spirit, Bulgakov figures creativity by the earth's wisdom. Creativity attends, liberates, births, realizes, hypostatizes creation's own goodness, and doing so restores human personhood and social economies to the earth. Then, as human economies take the shape of earth's wisdom, imitating the pattern of God's deifying presence, they overcome their alienation from both nature's economy and the divine economy.

Restoring humanity to the earth, Bulgakov teaches, begins in the everyday works of better designing, building, working, and cultivating. But before setting out to transform a death-haunted world, he preaches, first look up to the hills and see how the mountains reveal God's glory. In a world haunted by alienation, we must think like a mountain: the most practical environmental action we can take is to let beauty save the world.

12

Conclusion

Renovating Grace

In the course of researching and writing this book I have sometimes been asked which ecology of grace works best. Which strategy should environmentalists use? Which rendition of nature and grace should pastors preach? At other times I have been asked how theologies might need revision for an environmental age. Are these ecologies of grace really sustainable? How might we reconstruct a comprehensive environmental theology? I have consistently demurred, for this has remained an exercise in ecumenical understanding rather than a comparative evaluation or a reconstructive proposal. But the exercise does have its implications. By mapping the theological patterns that make environmental problems urgent and intelligible to Christian communities, it points toward ways of using those background sources more openly and usefully. Moreover, insofar as ecologies of grace illuminate how environmental problems matter for Christian life, this book shows why ecology makes a claim on Christian identity, and how environmental crises could pressure change in the way churches tell their salvation stories.

For sustainability workers, civic reform activists, and community leaders, the map bears possibilities for better understanding, more effectively upsetting, and more cooperatively working with Christian groups. For Christian ethicists and theologians, it summons further exploration of their native theological terrains, in order to rediscover new roots of practical engagement and find fertile ground for the seeds of new witness. For clergy, this book invites renewed reflection on the pastoral dimensions of "nature and grace," on the ecological dimensions of the experience and telling of salvation. For observers of "religious environmentalism," the map points out new lines for critical inquiry into the relations of religious and environmental thought.

For example, we now know how ecojustice theologies develop respect for nature in relation to Christian commitments to the marginalized, why those commitments make it difficult for ecojustice to espouse an unmodified land ethic, and how turning that difficulty to a theologian like Thomas Aquinas not only helps resolve a policy stance, but illuminates a relation between biodiversity and spirituality. We know why creation spirituality practitioners, environmental justice advocates, and Eastern Orthodox thinkers, even when perhaps reluctant to collaborate, may address similar environmental problems and frame them by similar theological themes. We have seen why complaining that stewardship theologies devalue nature will carry less argumentative force than, say, critiquing distorted social orders imported into their models of responsibility. Portrayed on broad landscapes of grace, the pluralism of Christian environmental ethics begins to make practical and pastoral sense.

Still, my map has its limitations for in-depth explorations of local terrain. Particular church communities may prove hard to locate on this chart, perhaps because they share characteristics of several ecologies of grace. Moreover, associating Thomas, Barth, and Bulgakov with the three major ecclesial traditions of Christianity, I have let the reader suppose that those traditions neatly map onto respective ecologies of grace. The everyday theological life of church communities is undoubtedly more complex, often telling the stories of grace in compound, hybrid, or innovative ways. This book only suggests that as they do, their capacity for environmental response will likely follow suit. One could further test the hypothesis by using this book's map of strategies to diagnostically test ecclesial statements, tracing how church bodies draw on multiple patterns of grace, or perhaps renegotiate those background logics as the struggle with new issues.

In any case, the survey and the theological explorations do not aim for sociographic description but for heuristic models that can inform social ethics. By correlating patterns of theology with patterns of environmental response, we can better understand why certain Christian communities respond as they do. Understanding those patterns, community organizers might more effectively develop ecumenical collaborations and public initiatives. In turn, Christian ethics can better attend to those theological resources already organically at work, using soteriological resources both for developing better responses and critiquing current ones. By grace, Christian environmental ethics can inscribe environmental problems more urgently and disturbingly within the lived faith of Christian communities.

My approach, therefore, has been at once ecumenical and traditionalist for the sake of being insistently pragmatic. Where there is a "back-to-the-sources" spirit to my account, it is because I think that those sources help articulate the pluralism of Christian environmental ethics and reconnect it to lived expressions of faith. Where I have asked for a charitable look at salvation stories, it has been in order to summon Christian communities to develop more effective responses. Where I have argued against the standard sorting devices of environmental ethics, it has been for the sake of rendering human experience more vulnerable to the haunts of environmental destruction.

That vulnerability points to another pragmatic reason left undeveloped by the cartographic framing of this book. Among the moments of grace elevating and transforming the human heart, there is also a moment of wounding, of knowing and naming the ways that darkness diseases our hearts. Environmental books often begin with catalogs of distressing ecological indicators—rainforest destruction, carcinogenic pollution, wetland loss, species depletion, climate change. I have stepped lightly past what sickens the heart in order to claim the ecological goodness and beauty that transform the heart. But "the transformation of the heart such beauty engenders is not enough . . . to let me shed the heavier memories, a catalog too morbid to write out, too vivid to ignore."[1] The transformed heart must know the destruction and remember the loss. To finally acquit itself of the suspicion that salvation stories spin opiates and license pride, an ecological grace must include expressions of lament and ways of repentance. Insofar as the patterns of grace can do this, they offer something desperately needed by contemporary environmental consciousness: a register of response at once adequate to the slow terror of ecological degradation and hopeful of meaningful response.

Salvation is, after all, for the lost. Reclaiming our ecologies of grace can give us vocabularies of lament to name our sickened witness to prodigal powers defiling beauty, choking life, and wasting habitats. Just as important, salvation narratives retain the memory of lostness in their restorations. There lies a hint for how soteriological explorations can help guide responsible ecological restoration and inform sustainability initiatives, even in the midst of destabilizing environmental crises. For these two ambiguous, contested social responses—restoration and sustainability—name human gestures toward living in a new kind of ecology. They may represent ways of turning that recognize past harms and looming threats, while trying to live in hopeful justice in the present. Or they may represent self-congratulatory covering excuses that mask the violence of the past and defuse judgment from the future in order to reinstate confidence in relentlessly exploitative human powers. Christian ethics cannot remain indifferent or oblivious to whether the official practices of restoration and sustainability will generate a social ecology of life or merely adorn a social ecology of death.

Christianity's own ecologies of grace, this book suggests, offer rich narratives for thinking through social practices of repentance, restoration, and sustenance. But where they cannot, contemporary Christian soteriologies may require adaptation so that grace can challenge and inform discourses of restoration and sustainability. This book has not developed revisionary criteria for theology, but given the close connections we have seen between patterns of grace and patterns of inhabitation—divine experience and earthly experience—adaptation means much more than simply updating the church's rhetoric. For an age of climate change, mass extinctions, and unjust resource use, an adaptive sense of grace is gospel witness. It guides how the church can proclaim: set before you are the ways of life and the ways of death; choose life. Here in these concluding pages I can only sketch a few hints of a sustainable theology of grace. Let me begin from a nascent lived environmental theology.

Ecological Restoration and Theological Lament

My father-in-law, a fly fisherman and Reformed Church minister, laments the "lost" rivers of western Michigan. Consider the Muskegon. For tens of thousands of years it flowed as a river of life, its watershed a conifer forest so thick that even gentle winds turned its needle-whispers into a roar. The scent of millions of white pines would billow with the winds, the fragrance sometimes carrying far out over the freshwater lakes to the east and west. Below the trees—some eight feet in diameter and two hundred feet tall—lay a thick carpet of needles, soft to the feet of lynx and elk. In the river swam the elegant Arctic grayling and the ancient lake sturgeon, along with dozens of other fish species. Spawning in the Muskegon's abundant nutrient flows, fish would churn the waters in tremendous seasonal surges. Wolves knew its riverbanks, wild rice grew in its shallows, and flocks of migratory birds annually returned to its estuary wetlands. For thousands of years this powerful matrix of life shaped its course in conversation with soil and rock.

Then, in a geological instant, the Muskegon was clogged, silted, dammed, warmed, leveed, polluted, and sickened. Enslaved to prodigal powers, it bore thirty billion board feet of clear-cut logs downriver to blade-screaming clusters of mills. And then it bore millions of tons of silt from the resulting erosion. Fires spread across its needle-carpeted watershed, the slash and stumps burning so hot that seeds and rootstocks were scorched lifeless. Still more soil slipped into the Muskegon. Now sluggish and flood-prone, its current was channeled and dammed. As its bloated waters warmed and served as sewer to manufacturing waste, twenty species of fish were extinguished from its waters. Its wolves were shot, trapped, and poisoned; its wetlands drained, filled, and leveed. The lynx and elk disappeared. Even the fisherman who flocked to the Muskegon in the nineteenth century began leaving it in the twentieth, seeking life-giving waters elsewhere. The river seemed lost.[2]

Yet the century or so in which the Muskegon has been so ravaged represent a blink of time in its history and its likely future. The river was here long before the loggers and will likely remain long after the last dam gives way. Some new day will see fish return, if not the Arctic grayling, then something else, perhaps something beautiful like the imported Chinook salmon. Or maybe even, with enough time, some new indigenously adapted piscine form. So long as rain falls on the Michigan peninsula and flows from inland soils seek the lake to the west, its waters bear the promise of new life.

So what sense does lamenting its loss have? The "deep time" question matters for all environmental problems, especially when framed as sustainability issues. Why care about mountaintop removal when plate tectonics makes an ongoing business of removal and replacement? So long as humans can manage the consequences, why care about species extinction when there have been other great extinctions in the past? By describing the ecological dimensions of grace, this book has in a sense offered reasons for lamentation, theologies of loss even in geological time. Diverse species of life, Aquinas taught us, matter for our own experience of life with God. The power of grace to pierce, convert, and bring us near the heart of God, Bulgakov showed us, may come to us through great mountains. For the hundreds of Reformed churches (in a Protestant kaleidoscope of kinds) within its watershed, the Muskegon is an offer of grace, a sign of covenant with God. Its "loss" means that part of their experience of grace is jammed, silted, obscured, polluted, and hauntingly vacant of its original promise. But its destruction not only impoverishes the covenant; for a tradition that treasures the scriptural image of a landed people betrothed to God, the defilement of the Muskegon watershed signifies a ruptured marriage. To live by the lost river means to bear the pain of infidelity. For the covenant's faithful, it wounds the soul.

Many citizens of western Michigan silently ache before such loss, but fumble sheepishly for words to say why. These Reformed churches hold a biblical vocabulary that can give reasons for the reflexive wounding of land and soul, enabling expression of the ache of loss. Their story of grace, therefore, has capacity to enable political voice and civic action. So too for mountain-top removal mining, Amazon deforestation, empty forest syndrome, and the whole morbid catalog. Aldo Leopold wrote that to have an ecological education is to live alone in a world of wounds. Add a theological education and at least we need not live alone or silently with those wounds.

More importantly, the healing of grace might teach citizens what to make of the wounds of memory and the healing efforts of ecological restoration. The waters of the Muskegon have flowed more hopefully in recent decades. Egregious chemical pollution has been halted, and better sewers constructed. One dam has been removed and others have been modified to restore a more natural riverbed with cooler waters. A citizen watershed alliance has formed, and since the year 2000 tens of millions of dollars have been raised for riverine and wetlands restoration. Members of the ecological community have begun to recover and return. No wolves yet, but many bird populations have rebounded. They do not yet roar in fragrant winds, but second growth trees stand tall, sometimes in patches approaching a forest. The Arctic grayling still cannot tolerate its warm waters and the sturgeon seem uncertain what to make of fish ladders. But steelhead trout and Chinook salmon fisheries have made the waters churn with life again, and fishermen return. They are not Odaway fisherpeople, of course, but these new peoples have begun to become native to its waters, and come to it with memory.

Leopold lived out his days on a ravaged Wisconsin farm, working a slow and careful restoration. Geological time sustained his sense of beauty, integrity, and stability, which he waited upon in the ordinary time of seasons, recorded in a monthly almanac of life in Sand County. In western Michigan, developing a native sense of grace means reorienting ourselves to the offer of covenant in a sin-ravaged watershed. It means experiencing life with the forgiving God by experiencing the ecological restoration of the Muskegon watershed as a kind of forgiveness from the land. Its wounds, the scars of sin, we know from the perspective of geological time, or at least riverine time, in whose deep past and long future the Muskegon runs. Yet grace shapes our perspective by "ordinary time," the liturgical seasons that give us the earth in loss and hope, that we may live in hopeful attendance of the slow, almost unnoticed returns of grace to a sin-ravaged landscape. There is in them a kind of forgiveness.

Of course, reading restoration and redemption together could make for dangerously triumphant confidence in our management schemes. Even without a "forgiveness" overlay, some environmental ethicists worry that ecological restorations make facile restitution for a destructive past.[3] Some oppose restoration discourse as a lie and a farce, as if imported salmon and a "naturalized" riverbed could make the Muskegon the river of life it once was. Add a redemption story and society might perversely suppose human works can atone for its morbid catalog of sins. As always, good theology must guard against cheap grace. A covenant ecology of forgiving grace may be able to hold together the lament with the practical actions of restorative hope. Like a marriage broken and renewed, the reconciliation does not erase the past; its forgiveness holds that haunt. A covenant sense of grace might then keep the restorative practices of watershed management from a cheaply engineered forgetting, thus humbling proud sustainability innovations.

Remember from chapter 2 how appeals to "practical management" and "sustainability" function ambiguously, absorbing multiple agendas, visions, and excuses. Environmental pragmatism seems to falter before the uncertain references of its appeal to the "practical." It may be that a covenant notion of forgiveness can hold the infamously plastic term "sustainability" to the memory of beauty lost and the hope of ecological health. For covenant can invoke an ecology of grace that laments a land lost and ruined, calls a people back to the heart of God in the land, and prophetically envisions the barren places blooming again. Its concept of grace thus keeps sustainability from forgetting the ruin of nature's integrity by substituting capital health for land health in its obligations to the future.

More could be said, and much more theological work needs to attend to the ascendant moral discourse of sustainability. The example here merely suggests how logics of grace can usefully engage civic environmental reform efforts, perhaps even chastening the cheaply salvific tendencies of restoration and sustainability. The example also points to a practical criterion for comparing and reforming ecologies of grace: they cannot inure Christians from environmental distress, but must let the morbid catalog pierce hearts and darken souls. Then they can offer the healing salve that brings from those wounds a transforming hope—not a hope that forgets lostness and ruin, but a practical hope that replants in the midst of it.

Meanwhile, in the Reformed churches, the ministers might preach the saving words thus:

> Jesus said, "Put down your nets, and I will make ye fishers of people." Well, after a century of taking nearly every fish and every tree, we have finally put down our tired, frantic nets long enough to be caught by the grace of God. And here we are, gasping at our destruction, accused by the barrenness of our land, and stuttering before our infidelity. Yet Jesus forgives, offering to restore us anew to the covenant of peace. To accept that covenant means we are permitted and commanded to work restitution for the damage done to this land by our sin, by our infidelity to the covenant of life. As we are restored to relationship with God so must we restore this watershed. Indeed, our acts of restoration are the very ways God restores us to

the covenant ecology of abundant life. And as we do—as we restore wetlands and take down dams—the land rejoices and the river claps its hands. We are offered forgiveness as the birds return with an olive branch and the waters stir with life once more. Fish are running on the Muskegon, ye sinners; cast your lines for the heart-skipping tug of grace, for a glimpse of a broken marriage reconciled, a taste of the river of life restored and running through the garden cities of God.[4]

Sustainable Theologies

If particular theologies of grace seem well fitted for civic lament and especially apt for engaging sustainability discourse, then we begin to see how contemporary problems may exert pressure on narratives of grace to adapt. My mapping gave short shrift to covenant environmental ethics because, I confess, it did not easily fit my typology. But it did not precisely because it does conform to my hypothesis. Covenant theologies tend to balance themes of justification and sanctification, conversion and order, and that makes for an environmental ethics that balances the responsibility of stewardship with the created orders of ecojustice. Covenant environmental ethics thus represents a minority tradition of its own—one that by its hybrid character seems to bear a special charism for the kind of lamentation creation's groaning requires.[5] Insofar as the Reformed churches share a covenant conception of grace, they may share in that environmental capacity. Insofar as, say, Pentecostals do not share in covenant patterns of grace, they miss its charism for environmental response, and thus its practical capacity to engage sustainability issues.

Throughout this book I have noted practical difficulties for each ethical strategy in order to suggest that revisiting background theologies of grace could help resolve or reframe those problems. But the converse must be said as well: environmental issues not only press Christian traditions to rearticulate and redeploy, but also perhaps to adapt their understandings of salvation. If, for example, stewardship theologies cannot generate wholehearted lament over the loss of the Muskegon because they isolate the human soul from nature's distress, then environmental problems may suggest something inadequate and unworthy of belief about theologies bounded by a narrow redemption. Indifferent silence before beauty defiled and rivers lost would indicate that this way of telling the story hardens hearts. And the lifted lament from covenant theologies would mark a source for healing those theologies: returning to the "married land" may restore the fullness of redemption. Or, if creation spirituality offers a particularly apt framework for working reconciliation in ecologically alienated communities, then perhaps deification soteriologies commend themselves to the wider church for a desperately needed pastoral facility.

Occasionally we see this pragmatic reconsideration of soteriology already in process in the hybridizing or revisionary tendencies of some environmental strategies. When it comes up against the conceptual limits of its own habitat of grace, a strategy may let its practical problems turn it toward borrowing or adapting new concepts of grace. For example, nearly everyone appeals to stewardship to lay claim to its ability to hold freedom to divine accountability, and insofar as they do, they draw their strategy toward God's encounter with sinful human freedom. They draw, that is, on a pattern of redemption that may be foreign to or minority within their own narrative of grace. But in chapter 4 we saw some stewardship theologies, pressed for an integrated model of human responsibility, appeal to Orthodox formulations of humans as priests of creation. Then in chapter 5 we saw the mediating personhood of theosis modified by process theology in order to inflect spirituality by the emergent creativities of evolutionary ecology. In these cases, response to particular social problems moves creative thinkers to propose alterations to background patterns of grace in order to expand the practical capacity of an environmental theology. The pragmatic efficacy of their adaptations will be proved by its use: if communities use it to understand and facilitate responses to environmental issues, then the adaptation has taken on meaningful life within Christian experience.

But we must take care in our adaptive inventions, for environmentalists find it challenging enough to mobilize Christian communities without the additional burden of convincing them to adopt alternative pictures of salvation. Some have breezily dismissed traditional soteriological concepts for the obstacles presented by their apparent supernaturalism and anthropocentrism. But I suspect summary dismissals and their speculative replacements present their own kind of obstacle. Before such urgent problems requiring wholehearted and innovative responses, why present additional theological challenges to Christian communities? Adequate Christian response to environmental problems may indeed require revisions and adaptations to its stories of salvation, but we ought first to exhaust the practical potential of those stories. And when we do risk revisionary proposals, we best serve our practical initiatives by letting the problems themselves, the wounds of the earth, do the work of agitating communities and challenging their notions of grace.

A pragmatic turn to grace still encourages constructive, even revisionary work in environmental theology. Theology still must strive to imagine greener worlds, interpolating cultural narrative with environmental problems, to integrate those imagined worlds with social justice commitments, and still must propose therapeutic theological adaptations.[6] My work here merely counsels that work to excavate, reinvent, and manufacture sustainably. What specific social problems mobilize adaptations? What sort of communities could hear and adopt those revisions? We otherwise squander our theological imaginations, in effect silencing the earth's groans by lifting them up to unknown audiences or for unclear problems. At least in regard to the earth's distress, we cannot let theological writing turn upon itself, as if constituting its own religious practice in the exercise of reconstructive arguments. For these times, a sustainable theological ethics must interpret the living earth for living Christian communities.

As I mentioned at the beginning of this book, for my own native community that means helping us understand what it means to inhabit a changing rural landscape. Should we embrace, reform, or resist its changes? How can Christian commitments inform county debates over new developments and affordable housing, economic opportunity and local character, agricultural lands and a new economy? For my own family those questions concentrate around an overgrown apple orchard at the edge of a national park. A sustainable theology for my family must be able to remember the harsh wound of forced removal, the fearful wounds of cancers, and the slow-draining wound of failing in the new agricultural economy. It must make sense of a land whose history records two native expulsions, whose food production has fled to other lands, and whose once-lost wildlife now return. And it must open a habitable future for a land in which the promise of possession has changed so drastically.

In order to become a theology of sustainability, some ecology of grace must make the daily practices of cultivation, preservation, husbandry, hunting, and retreat part of the practices of life with God. For it is surely by grace that we could name the goodness of searching for spring merkels, that we would know whether and which trees to log, and that we would work out some peace with the bears who break fruit trees, the coyotes who take young goats, and the beavers whose pond-raising threatens a barn. Shall we manage it for wildness? As a capital investment for future generations? Should we sell it to the Nature Conservancy, rid ourselves of vehicles, and move into green condos in an urban center? Shall we build retreat facilities, perhaps with charitable environmental education programs? Shall we find our way back to farming through goats and organics, maybe this time through community-supported agriculture?

A sustainable theological ethics may not offer specific answers, but it must at least help our community make sense of how the land sustains us and what that sustenance has to do with a belief in God's sustenance. It must at least inflect, if not tutor, our imaginations for how we might be able to sustain possession of the land in a way that delights God's heart. That means learning to walk humbly and love justice in a new economy of land and faith. How can theological ethics teach those lessons?

This book has only mapped the terrain from which those lessons might come, and here in the conclusion offered a few hints. Lament and restoration name crucial capacities for a sustainable environmental theology. They suggest something that a practical environmental ethics must be able to do in the coming decades of its witness and engagement. It must be able to remember an ecological world of wounds, to creatively disturb complacent communities, to reclaim and enrich cheapened traditions of grace, and then set the world's woundedness toward restoration by making sense of the many mundane practices of sustainability. It must see, name, and remember injustices to the land's inhabitants and to the land; it must see, name, and summon life-giving futures for ecological communities. It must know the full range of land membership, integrating the practices of living on earth: preservation and use, loving and eating, serving and taking, guarding and cultivating, letting-be and managing, participating and creating, receiving and giving.

Reconstructing Grace: Gender Trouble and the Eclipse of the Spirit

The need to develop theologies of sustainability hints at changes in the patterns of grace this book has described. But deeper changes may be required as well. For by returning to traditional sources this book has put on display some serial liabilities shared across all three ecologies of grace. By engaging the internal problems of each ethical strategy in reference to one representative theologian, I have assigned Thomas, Barth, and Bulgakov more authority than perhaps warranted—certainly in relation to environmental ethics but also as representatives for specific traditions of grace. In the face of some of the weaknesses shared by these three theologians, further exploration with alternative theologians would be welcome. But those shared weaknesses also helpfully list some enduring challenges to constructing sustainable futures from our ecologies of grace. Two of those problems bear at least brief mention here, for the sake of marking out reconstructive tasks ahead.

I have argued that since Christian environmental ethics tends to follow the normative patterns of background views of grace, we can deal with their practical problems in conversation with representative theologians. Where the theologians raise problems of their own, we should test the ethical strategy for similar vulnerabilities. Aquinas, Barth, and Bulgakov also share a set of serious problems, leaving an uncertain legacy for environmental ethics. Are these problems endemic to soteriology, idiosyncratic to their personalities, or peculiar to this sample of classically orthodox, male, European theologians?

For the most disturbing example, Thomas, Barth, and Bulgakov share hierarchical assumptions about gender. Barth's wider theological narrative might subvert his gender manipulations. Thomas inherits his view of female subordination from Aristotelian science; with better science presumably he would have corrected his view and its moral implications. Bulgakov seems to do better, since he celebrates the divine feminine; but his male and female nonetheless refer to transcendental types of agency, active and receptive. Bulgakov bends both types, so that activity involves a moment of passivity and receptivity involves a moment of creativity—but the dominant assumption remains. The fact that all three theologians I chose to assist environmental theology display troubled understandings of sex and gender raises serious questions about their use for contemporary social ethics. Are their gender views merely personal or contextual bias, or are they symptomatic of an insidious fault line in Christian concepts of grace? Either way, can environmental theologies appropriate the practical patterns of grace without importing associated gender inheritances?

Those questions highlight the significance of embodiment for ecologies of grace. Each strategy I have explored relies on bodily connections to nature and grace, although sometimes I have described the connection only indirectly. The shared gender trouble among the theologians calls for more direct attention, for insofar as the ecologies of grace include inadequacies or subjugations in a significant dimension of embodiment, the connections of nature and grace in human experience will likely turn out inadequate or subjugated. A sustainable environmental theology requires first a sustaining theology of embodiment.

Ecofeminist critiques and contributions may therefore prove crucial to the future of Christian environmental ethics. In the introduction, I explained this book's new map by referring to the feminist cartography of grace conducted by Serene Jones and to Rosemary Radford Reuther's field-opening critique of the modernist soteriology of progress. The next step for understanding and revising concepts of grace might begin by overlaying my map with Jones's, in order to find generative intersections of feminist theory, concepts of grace, and ecologies of Christian experience. That could start theology toward fully embodied, wholly ecological soteriologies, perhaps of the sort Ruether has in mind.

The challenge of embodiment for ecologies of grace could open productive interactions of environmental ethics with biomedical and sexual ethics. The connections could serve those domains of practical ethics with notice of their environmental significance, but more importantly would offer to the environmental field a developed literature of reflection on social practices and human embodiment. Perhaps better understanding how environmental issues matter for Christian community involves better understanding how embodiment, sexuality, and gender do. For a field that often struggles to overcome the perception that it focuses on nature as rival to human interests, these connections could also reclaim the human significance of even the wildest ecological issues. That in turn could reclaim and revitalize the environmental justice movement, which sometimes languishes as a special interest of applied social justice.

Considering the underdeveloped connections between embodiment, social injustice, and ecologies of grace, environmental justice offers a diversely populated site for exploring and reconstructing that nexus. With further theological attention to the lived theologies of its practices and further exploration of its background commitments, it could help shape a sustainable ecology of grace. If it is so that sustainable theologies require the capacity for lament, then womanist theologies in particular might teach Christian ethics how to accept the help of environmental justice. For womanist theologies often connect lament and loss to embodiment and social justice along lines that renovate concepts of grace.[7] Delores Williams, for example, writes of remembering racist oppression through an activist wisdom that opens possibilities for social transformation. Williams goes on to note an ecological trajectory in womanist thought, saying that its environmental-justice "emphasis upon survival and quality of life" supports a "quest for salvation on earth" that directs church mission to "active opposition to all forms of violence against humans (female and male), against nature (including nonhuman animals), against the environment and against the land."[8]

My map describes ecofeminist and environmental justice approaches as particular examples of a general strategy, susceptible of explanation and development by a deification ecology of grace. But the gender trouble across representative soteriologies suggests that they may bear de- and re-constructive significance across the terrains of Christian environmental ethics. At least, ecofeminism and environmental justice, especially as integrated in womanist thought, highlight capacities required for a sustainable ecology of grace.

Reconnecting theology to the land, writes womanist theologian Karen Baker-Fletcher, requires reconnecting it to embodiment and the Spirit.[9] That points to a possible correlation between the gender trouble and the second theological impoverishment common to the three theologians: an eclipse of the Spirit. Barth especially suffers from pneumatological privation, but Aquinas too seems uncharacteristically ambiguous on the role of the Spirit, while Bulgakov assigns typologically pneumatic functions (glorification, transfiguration) to Sophia. If Stephen Bouma-Prediger rightly observes that creation went into eclipse for theology about the time that pneumatology did, then the restoration of ecologies of grace seems linked to a recovery of the Spirit.[10] As contemporary theology wonders where the Spirit went, answers might suggest how to recover creation, as well.[11] Here Pentecostal theology may find its environmental charism, showing theology how to rediscover the Spirit and creation at once.[12] For it seems that making sense of the Christian experience of earth entails making sense of the Christian experience of the Spirit. The recent proliferation of environmental pneumatologies senses the promise of a simultaneous recovery: the spiritual dimensions of living on earth and the ecological dimensions of living in the Spirit.[13] The future of Christian environmental ethics seems to depend on theologies of grace unshadowed by the eclipse, revivified in the Spirit.

The three theologians of this book show why that work may be especially urgent for developing an ethics and theology of sustainability. All three support very active models of humanity's relationship with nature, which nonetheless find ways to make peaceful room for nature's independent integrity, even rendering human experience benignly vulnerable to nature's goodness and beauty. That capacity to integrate activity and passivity may help construct models for addressing agency-intensive environmental issues, such as agriculture, restoration, and energy technologies, while retaining connections to originary environmentalist intuitions to preserve wilderness. The verbs of the Spirit seem especially helpful here, for the Spirit's activity is often associated with making present the activity of another. The Spirit rests on the Son, glorifies the divine love, inflames the apostles' speech, vivifies creation, diversifies the gifts of faith, gives witness to unions creaturely and divine. Rediscovering how creation makes a difference for the human experience of God may involve rediscovering how humans participate in the verbs of the Spirit, putting our developments and economies more at peace with wilderness and wildness. As the international community tries to imagine and integrate the practical harmonies evoked by "sustainable development," Christian theology can help by rediscovering the sustaining Spirit.

Returning to the Spirit and to embodiment means wrestling at once with doctrines of God and doctrines of creation, with the body and the trinity, and their earthly intimacies.[14] Naming the way of Christian experience into intimacy with earth through intimacy with God will require a second look at how Christians describe economies of sin and ecologies of the fall.[15] So sustainable theology may well require reconsidering and reworking the central themes and relations of Christian theology. It might even mean rethinking our axioms, as Lynn White said. But now, by entering that rethinking through the narratives of salvation, we know the union those axioms must serve and precisely why we would rethink them: to restore nature to grace.

In order to start those theological reinvestigations in the most helpful ways, we might return to sites of Christian community practice working out new understandings of life with God through innovative environmental responses. So in conclusion I turn to some of the lived environmental theologies that seem to body forth adaptations of grace. Each offers clues toward a socially embodied, sustainable ecology of grace.[16]

Renovating Grace: Lived Environmental Theologies

In the introduction, I mentioned that this inquiry began from experience with the practical initiatives of faith-based projects in Africa and Asia. I suggested that the usual investigative questions for environment and religion failed to understand the lived theologies of these projects and their communities. Tracing patterns of grace this book has tried to outline more adequate and helpful understandings. Along the way, however, I have not returned to those "organic" Christian environmental theologies, in part for wanting to develop heuristic models rather than anthropological descriptions, and in part because I think those innovative Christian practices have already begun to renegotiate and renovate their background concepts of grace. These emergent lived environmentalisms indicate a shifting terrain that complicates cartography. So in closing, let me suggest that as theology joins the global search for sustainability, it might consider these fresh tellings of good news, of the earthly life united with the divine life.

Consider the revivalist reforesters of southwestern Uganda. While I think that reading stewardship ethics by the background patterns of redeeming grace may shed light on their practices, I think those practices also begin to reshape and renovate the standard revivalist preaching of redemption. The unique place-ethics of these village communities comprehends everything from water protection to orphan care to reforestation within the call of Jesus—and in turn revises what theology usually makes of the phrase "call of Jesus." By confessing failures of tree care or good soil practice as sins susceptible to healing by the blood of Jesus, the blood and the call begin to mean something new. Within a traditionally communitarian society in the throes of change by globalizing individualism, these church communities work out the social dimensions of a revivalist faith that bears far-reaching political and ecclesiological ramifications. Redemption means resistance, place-attachment, social responsibility— and the surprising trees of God are its witness.[17]

This book therefore maps ecologies of grace that are in the midst of change, or at least ripe for change in the ongoing negotiation of Christian theology by the contextual practices of faith. My "strategies of grace" offer no comprehensive, static template for understanding and developing environmental ethics. For in turn, faith-based environmental practices reshape Christian understandings of grace. Faithful ways of living on the earth rehabituate Christianity's understanding of God's life with humanity.

The interfaith community at the Asian Rural Institute in Japan seems a good example of my hypothesis that environmental justice and creation spirituality share a theological strategy, for the ARI seamlessly integrates the insights of both, and does so through a shared sense of earthly creativity. But it would not quite be fair to say that the creative agricultural community of the ARI merely puts in practice a version of Bulgakov's deification economy. By simultaneously pursuing ecumenical fellowship and sustainable agriculture for poor communities, the ARI community also reshapes visions of earth and humanity in union with God. They sense the divine embrace across wider human diversity than Bulgakov imagined, tying the glory of transfiguration to justice for the poor of all faiths.

Or imagine what becomes of the environmental regard won by ecojustice theology in the ecological knowledge of the Batwa. "Respect for creation's integrity" seems only the thinnest approximation of a knowledge so thorough and pervasive that it sustains language, culture, and even the dignity of an entire people. The Batwa remind those of us living at an abstract remove from our habitats of the vagueness in our notions about doing justice to creation. If sanctification names the way doing justice to creation shapes Christian experience, then the forest conformity of Batwa language and culture testifies to a vision of sanctification almost mystical in its earthy knowledge.

I said at the outset that environmental ethics sometimes struggles to address issues in urban planning, participatory community restorations, sustainable development, and agriculture. Taking more seriously the traditions of grace lived, preached and practiced by particular communities, we might better understand the environmental promise of Christian faith. Imagine what witnessing to God's radical claim means to Amish farmers, who cultivate environments of Christ on their own careful terms. Or how Roman Catholic commitments to sacramental reconciliation could mobilize urban restorations, community gardens, and even building design. Mainstream environmentalism fails to meaningfully engage those practical domains of our common life; by addressing them as important dimensions of Christian community, Christian environmental ethics could help reintroduce to public debate these major arenas too often left to the invisible hand and other unquestioned logics of salvation.

The unprecedented complexity and scope of environmental problems put our ethical and religious traditions at jeopardy. These innovative Christian responses put soteriological traditions at jeopardy in a different way: they potentially alter our concepts of life with God. The various churches of the Philippines recognize more than a dozen environmental martyrs: priests and lay faithful who have been killed while resisting exploitative logging or mining. Their struggle continues in the lives of those like Father Pablo Buyagan, who organizes indigenous churches for reforestation. In 2005, Sister Dorothy Stang was murdered for assisting indigenous peoples' resistance to rainforest destruction in the Amazon. The struggle in Latin America continues through those like Father José Andrés Tamayo Cortez, whose nonviolent protests against environmental destruction have earned him threats on his life.[18] By risking their lives, these environmental martyrs testify to the way environmental problems threaten the heart of the Christian faith. By giving their lives, they challenge and revitalize our understanding of nature and grace, of life on earth in the context of life with God. Tertullian famously said that the blood of martyrs is the seed of the church. The blood of these martyrs must be the seeds of a reforesting, resisting, replanting, restoring church.

Notes

CHAPTER I

1. For more about ARI, see http://www.ari-edu.org. John Cobb has recognized ARI as a "fine example" of good sustainable development; Cobb, *Sustaining the Common Good*, 59.

2. For a description of these and others, see Willis Jenkins, "A New Earth Day: Emerging Anglican Environmentalisms," *The Witness*, April 20, 2005 (www.thewitness.org).

3. I borrow the term "lived theology" from Charles Marsh. See Marsh, *God's Long Summer*.

4. In a way analogous to Jones, I hope the maps will help us travel through environmental theory and theology in new ways, and so better understand the contours of lived environmental experience. But in the environmental case I use it conversely to Jones, whose "cartographies of grace" layer feminist theory "over the terrain or landscape of Christian doctrine to see how the lines of theory might map the contours of theology." Here it works the other way, with the patterns of grace remapping environmental theory, but for a similar aim: that theologies may be seen as "lived imaginative landscapes, which persons of faith inhabit." Here that inhabitation is more literal, with patterns of grace shaping how Christian live in the land. Thus "ecologies" rather than "cartographies." See Jones, *Feminist Theory and Christian Theology: Cartographies of Grace*, 19, 50.

5. John Muir, *John Muir*, 238.

6. Rachel Carson, *Sense of Wonder*, 87.

7. From "Walking," in *Henry David Thoreau*, 239.

8. Leopold, *Sand County Almanac*, 137.

9. Sanders, *Hunting for Hope*, 39.

10. Lopez, "Introduction" in *The Best American Spiritual Writing 2005*, xvii–xxiii.

11. Barry Lopez, *Resistance*, 11.

12. Lopez, *Arctic Dreams*, 411.

13. Williams, *Refuge*, 237.

14. Gessner, *The Prophet of Dry Hill*, 181. Cf. Gessner, *Sick of Nature*.

15. See Thomas Dunlap, *Faith in Nature*; Robert Nelson, "Environmental Religion."

16. See an example of this sense of religious environmentalism in Gary Gardner, *Inspiring Progress*.

17. For description of its recent hybrid sense, see Bron Taylor, "Nature Religion." Roger Gottlieb uses the term all three ways, but seems particularly focused on the final sense; Gottlieb, *Greener Faith*. E. O. Wilson draws on all three senses of religious environmentalism to plead for cultural change; Wilson, *The Creation*. The energy and ambivalence has attracted several efforts to give formal shape to the study of religious environmentalism; see note 20 below.

18. Mary Evelyn Tucker and John Grim, "Series Foreword," xvi.

19. I will use "cosmology" and "worldview" similarly, as they are within this field. There may be this distinction: "cosmology" connotes more thickly storied patterns of perceiving; "worldview" might indicate only a few assumptions about the character of reality. See Mary Evelyn Tucker, "Religion and Ecology: The Interaction of Cosmology and Cultivation"; *Worldly Wonder*; and "The Role of Religions in Forming an Environmental Ethics." Cf. Elizabeth Reichel, "Cosmology."

20. For more on the Forum on Religion and Ecology (FORE), see http://environment.harvard.edu/religion/information/about/index.html. Recently the International Society for the Study of Religion, Nature, and Culture has undertaken efforts to develop this arena of interdisciplinary exchange into a formal academic field; see http://www.religionandnature.com and the associated *Journal for the Study of Religion, Nature, and Culture* edited by Bron Taylor. See also Taylor's introduction to the *Encylopedia of Religion and Nature*. Working separately, Roger Gottlieb offers his own definition and survey of a new academic field; see *Greener Faith* and the *Oxford Handbook of Religion and Ecology*. FORE and its associated Harvard book series seem to differ by inviting interdisciplinary conversation around a few questions of mutual intelligibility and common concern, rather than attempting to define a new discipline of inquiry. Appreciating both the pragmatic engagement and the particularist plural-ism afford by FORE's restraint, my critique here focuses on the way Christian participants have often under-represented the disciplines of Christian thought within environmental conversations—thus making those conversations less practical, less particularist, and less pluralist.

21. Lynn White, "The Historical Roots of Our Ecologic Crisis."

22. Cf. Elspeth Whitney, "Lynn White, Ecotheology, and History."

23. Bryan Norton suggests that White's article also shaped the development of secular environmental ethics, feeding its initial preoccupation with intrinsic value; Norton, *Searching for Sustainability*, 79. For further complaints about the article's effect on the secular field, see Ben Minteer and Robert Manning, "An Appraisal of the

Critique of Anthropocentrism and Three Lesser Known Themes in Lynn White's 'The Historical Roots of Our Ecologic Crisis,'" 163–76.

24. Tucker and Grim, xix. See also Mary Evelyn Tucker and John Grim, "Introduction," *Daedalus*, 4.

25. Say Tucker and Grim: "From a worldview there emerges a method for action, from a cosmology there arises an ethics." From the Preface to *Worldviews and Ecology*, 12–13. Larry L. Rasmussen, "Cosmology and Ethics," 178.

26. The metaphor of "grammar" for a tradition's narrative logic is George Lindbeck's, from *The Nature of Doctrine*. Mapping patterns of grace need not, however, assume Lindbeck's approach to theological traditions. Later in the chapter we will see William Schweiker—who disagrees with Lindbeck's "Yale School" approach to tradition—propose that theology attend to patterns of grace in order to respond to environmental problems.

27. George Rupp, "Religion, Modern Secular Culture, and Ecology," 24–25.

28. For example, Alister McGrath, *The Reenchantment of Nature*.

29. Tucker and Grim, "Series Foreword," xxv.

30. Tucker and Grim, "Series Foreword," xxi, xxiii, xxv.

31. Schweiker, *Theological Ethics and Global Dynamics*, 10–39 (quoted at 34; reference to Thomas and Barth at 24 n. 44).

32. See, for example, Sallie McFague's description of a common theological agenda against the problems with salvation: Sallie McFague, "An Earthly Theological Agenda." Although focused on the doctrine of creation, Norman Wirzba takes up these legacies of western salvation in his inquiry into the "ecology of creation," offering neo-agrarian reconstructions to soteriology. See Wirzba, *The Paradise of God*, 18–22, 48–60, 184–89. Wirzba asks: "Can we learn to see in the care of the earth and the care of each other our most profound religious task? Can we come to understand our salvation as inextricably bound up with the glory of the whole creation now understood as the extension of God's hospitality and delight" (22)?

33. Rosemary Radford Ruether, *New Woman, New Earth*, 186–211; *Sexism and God-talk*, 257–8.

34. "Secular" carries a range of connotations and a contest of definitions, sometimes polemical. I use it only to distinguish between "nonreligious" or "philo-sophical" environmental ethics and Christian environmental ethics.

35. Michael Northcott, *The Environment and Christian Ethics*, 41–42, 83–84 (on White), 124–63 (for his typology).

36. Max Oelschlaeger, *Caring for Creation*, 20–25 (on White), 118–83 (for his typology).

37. Stephen Bede Scharper, *Redeeming the Time*, 23–52; H. Paul Santmire, *Nature Reborn*, 10–15. Santmire says White's thesis had an impact analogous to Luther's Ninety-Five Theses (15). Cf. Janet Parker and Roberta Richards, "Christian Ethics and the Environmental Challenge," 114–22; Joseph K. Sheldon, *Rediscovery of Creation*, 1–3.

38. Steven Bouma-Prediger, *The Greening of Theology*, 4–6 (on White), 10–22 (on the tasks for ecological theology).

39. Bouma-Prediger, *Greening of Theology*, 11.

40. Oelschlaeger, *Caring for Creation*, 123–24, 182–83.

41. Northcott, *The Environment and Christian Ethics,*, 122; also 71, 77, 83, 92, 105, 161–66.

42. H. Paul Santmire, *The Travail of Nature*, 7.

43. Scott describes it as one that "directs theological attention not to the natural sciences nor the 'value' of nature but instead to the interaction between un/natural humanity and socialised nature." Peter Scott, *A Political Theology of Nature*, 3.

44. "What writings and themes in this field of theology . . . are especially helpful in fostering understanding of and engagement in the environmental challenge?" Dieter T. Hessel, *Theology for Earth Community*, 14.

45. William Somplatsky-Jarman, E. Walter Grazer, and Stan L. LeQuire, "Partnership for the Environment among U.S. Christians," 573–90 (quoted at 581).

46. Steven Bouma-Prediger, *For the Beauty of the Earth*, 179.

47. Susan Power Bratton, "The New Christian Ecology," 261–65. As she clarifies elsewhere, Bratton thinks that after we investigate cosmological inadequacies we need to know how the traditions are responding on their own terms, not only how they might be revised; "The Undoing of the Environment: Assessing the European Religious Worldview," 231. See her own attempt to argue for wilderness from spiritual experience rather than cosmology: *Christianity, Wilderness, and Wildlife*. Bronislaw Szerszynski makes that point another way, arguing that religious worldviews resist sweeping diagnostic assessments. We understand how religious views matter for environmental issues, he suggests, by first investigating the way religious practices continually socialize nature. Bronislaw Szerszynski, *Nature, Technology, and the Sacred*, 7–10, 31–64.

48. Thomas Sieger Derr, "Religious Models for Environmentalism."

49. Margaret Farley, "Religious Meanings for Nature and Humanity," 110–12.

50. George H. Kehm, "The New Story: Redemption as Fulfillment of Creation," 91.

51. Luke Timothy Johnson, "Caring for the Earth: Why Environmentalism Needs Theology," 18.

52. Ernst Conradie argues that the Christian possibility for hope in the face of environmental degradation "requires a recovery of the soteriological roots of eschatology." Conradie wants theologians to ask: "What metaphors and images should guide, inform, and inspire the Christian hope for salvation from sin, liberation from oppression, victory over evil and healing from environmental degradation?" Conradie, *Hope for the Earth*, 294, 299. Cf. Sally Kenel, "Nature and Grace: An Ecological Metaphor."

53. Joseph Sittler, *Essays on Nature and Grace*, 6.

54. Joseph Sittler, "Ecological Commitment as Theological Responsibility," 180; Cf. Bouma-Prediger, *The Greening of Theology*, 66–75.

55. Davies Oliver, *The Creativity of God*, 6–7.

56. What is "needed is not an ethic of creation but an ethic of createdness," agrees Christoph Schwöbel, going on to say that the source for an ethic of createdness lies in the doctrine of salvation; Schwöbel, "God, Creation and the Christian Community," 150, 67.

57. Another isolates six traditions of Christian environmental theology, organized around attention to basic components of environmental issues: Raymond Grizzle and Christopher Barret, "The One Body of Christian Environmentalism."

58. Laurel Diane Kearns, "Saving the Creation: Religious Environmentalism," 3. See also Kearns, "Saving the Creation" and "The Context of Eco-Theology." Jean-Guy Vaillancourt and Madeleine Cousineau repeat Kearns's typology in Vaillancourt and Cousineau, "Introduction." For different reasons, Daniel Cowdin comes very near to recognizing the same three Christian strategies, organized around practical logics; Cowdin, in "The Moral Status of Otherkind in Christian Ethics," 277–83.

59. Kearns, "Saving the Creation: Religious Environmentalism," 4, 305.

60. Ernst Conradie maps the field of environmental theology with an eschatological typology, arguing that eschatology unites soteriological views with the views of creation; Conradie, *Hope for the Earth*, 2–4, 44–50, 338. Compare with David Bosch, who shows how various notions of salvation bear practical consequences for church mission, from building schools to saving souls to empowering indigenous peoples' associations. Bosch, *Transforming Mission*, 392–400.

61. I thank Holmes Rolston III for asking this question and suggesting possible answers.

62. The closing frame of the park's controversial visitors' video, "Shenandoah: The Gift," showed a gravestone being overgrown as the narrator approved nature's reclamation. The video was reworked in 2001 with more favorable mention of the hollow folk. For more on the contested histories of the park, including my great-grandfather's and great-grandmother's names, along with the compensation they were given for the land (in the appendix), see Darwin Lambert, *The Undying Past of the Shenandoah National Park*.

63. On the relation between war, technology, farming, and environmental problems, see Edmund P. Russell, *War and Nature*.

CHAPTER 2

1. Stone, "Moral Pluralism and the Course of Environmental Ethics," 142.

2. See Callicott, "The Case against Moral Pluralism," and Wenz, "Minimal, Moderate, and Extreme Moral Pluralism."

3. Stone, "Moral Pluralism and the Course of Environmental Ethics," 148.

4. On the crisis of theory within American environmentalism, see Shellenberger and Nordhaus, "The Death of Environmentalism: Global Warming Politics in a Post-Environmental World." Whatever its merits, their essay shows an inadequate and fractured sense of practical reason among those for whom environmental ethics should be most important.

5. Plumwood, *Environmental Culture*; Preston, *Grounding Knowledge*; Smith, *An Ethics of Place*.

6. Erazim Kohak also makes use of "strategies" in order to organize his overview of the field of environmental ethics. However, although he uses "strategies" in a similar sense—to investigate how theories make sense of their implicit requirement

for practicality—he divides the field differently, cleaving more closely to the conventional non/anthropocentric continuum than I do. See Kohak, *The Green Halo*, 105–55. See also Smith, *An Ethics of Place*, 198–99.

7. The centrism continuum seems to hearken back to a seminal article: Routley, "Is There a Need for a New, an Environmental Ethic?" Once "human chauvinism" was identified as the field's problem, anthologies began organizing texts according to the measure of their disdain for it. For example, Robert Elliot introduces his edited volume with an explanation of the axial difference between human-centered and non-human-centered approaches; Elliot, *Environmental Ethics*, 1–12. For a more recent example, see Kristin Shrader-Frechette's introductory essay, which uses centrisms to explain the development and future of the field; Shrader-Frechette, "Environmental Ethics." For a strong defense of the non/anthropocentric taxonomy, see Sylvan and Bennet, *The Greening of Ethics: From Anthropocentrism to Deep Green Theory*. For two other suggestions about why the continuum may confuse ethical discussions, see Kohak, "The Ecological Dilemma: Ethical Categories in a Biocentric World," and Midgley, "The End of Anthropocentrism."

8. The opening page quote goes on: "The intramural debates of environmental philosophers, although interesting, provocative and complex, seem to have no real impact on the deliberations of environmental scientists, activists, and policymakers." Light and Katz, *Environmental Pragmatism*, 1. But "the original grounding intuition of environmental philosophy," says Light in another anthology introduction, "was that philosophers should do it so as to make a contribution to the resolution of environmental problems in philosophical terms. But if those terms produce only arcane discussions by a few theorists of issues such as the intrinsic value of nature, we will have failed in our aspirations to make a contribution to the resolution of environmental problems." Light and de-Shalit, *Moral and Political Reasoning in Environmental Practice*, 9. This anxiety sometimes plays out in the "Comment" section of the journal *Environmental Ethics*; see issues 24, no. 2; 25, no. 1; and 26, no. 1. See also Marietta and Embree (eds.), *Environmental Philosophy and Environmental Activism*.

9. Luke, "Solidarity across Diversity: A Pluralistic Rapprochement of Environmentalism and Animal Liberation," 346. Luke's article responds to Callicott's attempt to place animal welfare outside the formal definition of environmental ethics; see Callicott, "Animal Liberation: A Triangular Affair."

10. Minteer, *The Landscape of Reform*, 4.

11. For example, Weston, "Before Environmental Ethics."

12. Light, "Materialists, Ontologists, and Environmental Pragmatists," 259.

13. Norton, *The Search for Sustainability: Interdisciplinary Essays in the Philosophy of Conservation Biology*, 11. See also Norton, *Toward Unity among Environmentalists*. 14. James Sterba proposes political convergence around environmental justice in order to satisfy "both sides." Sterba, "Reconciling Anthropocentric and Nonanthropocentric Ethics."

15. Norton, *The Search for Sustainability*, 50.

16. Light, "Materialists, Ontologists, and Environmental Pragmatists," 264.

17. John Rawls uses the metaphor of "overlapping consensus" in *Political Liberalism* to describe justifications for politically reasonable agreements made by citizens with different background "comprehensive doctrines." Avner de-Shalit explicitly works out a Rawlsian conceptual vocabulary, deploying "reflective equilibrium" to gesture toward the integration of values that environmental ethics should offer the policy-making public. See de-Shalit, *The Environment between Theory and Practice*.

18. Thompson, "Pragmatism and Policy: The Case of Water," 198–200. Light notes that publishing in "obscure academic journals" probably counts as private; Light, "Materialists, Ontologists, and Environmental Pragmatists," 263.

19. See also de-Shalit, *The Environment between Theory and Practice*, 29: "The best way to achieve this would be to start with the activists and their dilemmas . . . a theory that reflects the actual philosophical needs of the activist seeking to convince by appealing to practical issues." See also Norton, "Applied Philosophy vs. Practical Philosophy: Toward Environmental Policy Integrated According to Scale" and "Integration or Reduction: Two Approaches to Environmental Values."

20. Light, "Callicott and Naess on Pluralism," 134.

21. Katz and Light, *Environmental Pragmatism*, 5.

22. Norton, *The Search for Sustainability*, 50. See also Brennan, "Moral Pluralism and the Environment."

23. These four senses of course derive in various ways from the school of American pragmatic philosophers, including C. S. Peirce, William James, and John Dewey. Environmental pragmatism may sometimes appeal directly to these philosophers. See, for example, Fuller "American Pragmatism Reconsidered: William James' Ecological Ethic"; Crosby, "Experience as Reality: The Ecological Metaphysics of William James"; Rosenthal and Bucholz, "Nature as Culture: John Dewey's Pragmatic Naturalism." This sense may be deployed to claim that the conception of environmental ethics as a dualistic feud between anthropocentrists and nonanthropocentrists results from discounting the historical influence of pragmatist thought on early environmental reformers. See Minteer, *The Landscape of Reform*, and Norton, *Searching for Sustainability*.

24. Light thinks environmental ethics is "tethered practically, if not methodologically, to a larger environmental community," which he specifies as natural resource managers; see Light, "Has Environmental Ethics Rested on a Mistake?" 15–16, 21. Norton sometimes appeals to resource managers, but usually appeals to a participatory group local to the decision at hand; see Norton, "The Re-Birth of Environmentalism as Pragmatic, Adaptive Management," 26.

25. Mark Sagoff describes major differences in conceptions of the "practical" between national advocacy groups sharing a narrow interest and local citizen groups trying to accommodate broad interests, in *Price, Principle, and the Environment*, 205–25.

26. On the practical difference even relatively similar metatheoretical commitments make, see Katz, "A Pragmatic Reconsideration of Anthropocentrism," and Stenmark, "The Relevance of Environmental Ethical Theories for Policy Making."

27. Eric Katz observes this pragmatist scapegoating of value theory, and notes the implicit weakness that follows: if value claims are vindicated, then pragmatism loses its normative purchase. Katz, "Searching for Intrinsic Value: Pragmatism and Despair in Environmental Ethics," 307–18. Light acknowledges a possible preoccupation with value theory but thinks the structural argument holds. Light, "Environmental Pragmatism as Philosophy of Metaphilosophy?" 325–26.

28. See Plumwood, *Environmental Culture*, 125.

29. Rolston, *Conserving Natural Value*. 226. See also Katz, "Understanding Moral Limits in the Duality of Artifacts and Nature," 142–43.

30. Light, "Callicott and Naess on Pluralism," 130; Light, "Compatibilism in Political Ecology," 179.

31. De-Shalit, *The Environment between Theory and Practice*, 5; Farber, *Eco-Pragmatism: Making Sensible Environmental Decisions in an Uncertain World*.

32. Norton, *Sustainability: A Philosophy*, 358, x–xiii, 1–16, 47–59.

33. Davison, *Technology and the Contested Meanings of Sustainability*.

34. Norton, *Sustainability: A Philosophy*.

35. Norton, *Sustainability: A Philosophy*, 149, 75, 120. Norton sometimes compares environmental management to decisions regarding trust funds; Norton, "Environmental Ethics and Weak Anthropocentrism," 188; *Sustainability: A Philosophy*, 305. Thompson uses a sustainability model generally similar to Norton's to make environmental ethics adequate to agricultural issues; see Thompson, *The Spirit of the Soil: Agriculture and Environmental Ethics*, 3–13, 147–49.

36. *Sustainability: A Philosophy*, 225, 336. For an assessment of how Norton's practicality assumes an intrinsic value theory, see Minteer, "Intrinsic Value for Pragmatists?"

37. *Sustainability: A Philosophy*, 331–2.

38. See Varner, *In Nature's Interests? Interests, Animal Rights, and Environmental Ethics*, 28. For a recent reiteration of the pluralist threat to deep criticism, see Lucas, "Environmental Ethics: Between Inconsequential Philosophy and Unphilosophical Consequentialism."

39. See Norton, "Environmental Ethics and Weak Anthropocentrism." David Schlosberg complains that academic accounts of environmentalism and environmental ethics have a chronic tendency to constrain the pluralism and elide the differences. Schlosberg proposes a "critical pluralism" that "offers a way of understanding the construction of diverse understandings of and reactions to the reality of environmental degradation," claiming that "attention to the differences inherent in the response to the environmental crisis can illuminate the reality and origins of that diversity." Schlosberg finds in the environmental justice movement the embodied forms of this "critical pluralist practice." Schlosberg, *Environmental Justice and the New Pluralism*, 4–39 (quoted at 10, 15).

40. Light often hinges his pragmatist proposals on an indictment of value-committed ethics: since they have been too unrealistically nonanthropocentric, the field must claim the pragmatic potential of anthropocentric positions. See Light, "Has Environmental Ethics Rested on a Mistake?" Norton deploys a similar schema in "The

Re-Birth of Environmentalism as Pragmatic, Adaptive Management" and in *Sustainability: A Philosophy*, 180–91. See also Minteer, *Landscape of Reform*, 1–7, 153–5.

41. Mark Michael makes a similar point, noting that "essentialists" and pragmatists constitute the field in contrary frames; see Michael, "What's In A Name? Pragmatism, Essentialism, and Environmental Ethics."

42. Eric Katz confesses as much, defending his own axiological nonanthropocentrism on strategic grounds, that it at least disqualifies instrumental rationalities from ethics of the wild. His metaethical position, in other words, defends the moral status of nature in order to maintain a rationality responsive to the peculiar character of nonhuman nature, which Katz implicitly holds as a functional requirement for any adequate environmental ethics. Katz, "Searching for Intrinsic Value," 308–9, 314.

43. See Jenkins, "Assessing Metaphors of Agency." James Childress agrees that pragmatists concentrate too much energy on dismissing value theories, when they might be incorporated as prima facie normative claims within a broader pluralist or even monist framework; see Childress, "Response to Light and Norton."

44. Norton, *The Search for Sustainability*, 13–77, 88–103 (quoted at 58).

44. Norton, *The Search for Sustainability*, 58.

45. What Norton calls nature's "didactic value," in Norton, *The Search for Sustainability*, 38.

46. Norton, *Sustainability: A Philosophy*, 56–121.

47. Anthony Weston, "Beyond Intrinsic Value." Cf. Kelly Parker, "Pragmatism and Environmental Thought," 29–30.

48. Weston, "Beyond Intrinsic Value," 291–303. Cf. Katz, "Searching for Intrinsic Value," 314–15.

49. Rosenthal and Buchholz, "How Pragmatism *Is* an Environmental Ethic," 47.

50. See Kohak's organization of environmental ethics around types of experience, in "Varieties of Ecological Experience." Cristina Traina shows how to begin analysis of discrete strategies by the way they integrate pluralist dialogues into normative experience, in "Creating a Global Discourse in a Pluralist World: Strategies from Environmental Ethics."

51. Mary Midgley has argued that practical philosophy still needs to investigate its background "plumbing." This seems especially important for environmental issues, which seem to involve so much hidden or misunderstood conceptual plumbing. The project here is simply a different one, namely, to ask what makes for an adequately functional theory. See Midgley, *Utopias, Dolphins and Computers*, 1–14.

52. Goodpaster, "On Being Morally Considerable."

53. For one standard example, see Kelman, "Cost-Benefit Analysis: An Ethical Critique."

54. As in Robin Attfield's connection of intrinsic value theory and consequentialism; see Attfield, *Value, Obligation, and Meta-Ethics*. While environmental ethicists are often leery of consequentialist reasoning, especially with regard to cost-benefit analysis (CBA), there is nothing formally prohibitive to pursuing the strategy of nature's moral status within a consequentialist framework. See, for example, Adler, "Cost-Benefit Analysis, Static Efficiency, and the Goals of Environmental Law."

55. Callicott, "Non-Anthropocentric Value Theory and Environmental Ethics," 299. See also Callicott, *Beyond the Land Ethic*, chaps. 2–4. For a better account of an expanding moral circle along similarly Darwinian lines, see Jamieson, *Morality's Progress*.

56. Callicott lists "criteria which an adequate axiology must meet," including intrinsic value for ecosystems and individuals, differentially assigned according to wild and domestic, and sorted according to some evolutionary hierarchy. Callicott, "Non-Anthropocentric Value Theory and Environmental Ethics," 304.

57. Rolston, *Conserving Natural Value*, 168–80. See also Rolston, *Environmental Ethics: Duties to and Values in the Natural World*. Note the clarifications in Holmes Rolston, "Value in Nature and the Nature of Value."

58. While at first Callicott insisted that only his version of value could accomplish what a practical ethics requires, under pressure from pluralists he makes league with Rolston in order to hold that only a moral monism is practical for environmental ethics. See Callicott, "Rolston on Intrinsic Value: A Deconstruction," in *Beyond the Land Ethic*.

59. For a recent iteration of this claim, see Weston, "Multicentrism: A Manifesto."

60. Katz, "Searching for Intrinsic Value"; "Imperialism and Environmentalism"; and *Nature as Subject*.

61. Regan, *The Case for Animal Rights*. Cf. Taylor, *Respect for Nature: A Theory of Environmental Ethics*.

62. Singer, *Animal Liberation* and *Practical Ethics*. One of Singer's early essays on the subject appeared in an anthology edited by Kenneth Goodpaster, who had asked environmental ethicists to describe and defend the "considerability" of nature (see Goodpaster above); Singer, "Not For Humans Only."

63. Midgley, "Is a Dolphin a Person?"

64. See Regan, "The Nature and Possibility of an Environmental Ethic," and Agar, *Life's Intrinsic Value: Science, Ethics, and Nature*.

65. See Elliot, "Normative Ethics."

66. See O'Neill, "Varieties of Intrinsic Value"; Elliot, "Normative Ethics"; and O'Neill, "Meta-Ethics."

67. Rolston, *Environmental Ethics*, 1–44, 192–201.

68. Kohak's defense of a valued moral environment ties itself directly to the operation of practical reason, so that natural values and human moral reasoning presuppose each other; see Kohak, "The True and the Good: Reflections on the Primacy of Practical Reason."

69. See Shrader-Frechette, "Practical Ecology and Foundation for Environmental Ethics."

70. As he did during an October 2004 visit to the University of Virginia. See also Rolston, *Conserving Natural Value*, 161–63.

71. Plumwood, for example, thinks intrinsic value "fails to arouse the imagination or supply plausible narrative contexts"; Plumwood, *Environmental Culture*, 186.

72. O'Neill states that "while it is the case that natural entities have intrinsic value in the strongest sense of the term, i.e., in the sense of value that exists independently

of human valuation, such value does not as such entail any obligation on the part of human beings. The defender of nature's intrinsic value still needs to show that such value contributes to the well-being of human agents," in "Varieties of Intrinsic Value," 119. See also Musschenga, "Identity-Neutral and Identity-Constitutive Reasons for Preserving Nature."

73. Notably, Rolston's solution appeals to the motive power of environmental experience: "encounter . . . moves us." Notice the dramatic metaphors he uses to frame that encounter in "Caring for Nature: From Fact to Value, from Respect to Reverence."

74. See Elliot, "Intrinsic Value, Environmental Obligation and Naturalness."

75. Midgley, "Duties Concerning Islands."

76. O'Neill's own solution is the latter. See O'Neill, *Ecology, Policy, and Politics: Human Well-Being and the Natural World*.

77. See Jenkins, "Assessing Metaphors of Agency: Intervention, Perfection, and Care as Models of Environmental Practice."

78. Donovan, "Ecofeminist Literary Criticism: Reading the Orange." See also Morito, "Intrinsic Value: A Modern Albatross for the Ecological Approach."

79. So executed, says Birch, ethics becomes a "function of imperial power-mongering"; Birch, "Moral Considerability and Universal Consideration," 315.

80. See Evernden, *The Social Creation of Nature*.

81. See Waterton, "Performing the Classification of Nature."

82. Foucault, *The Order of Things*.

83. Thus the debate among theorists of nature's standing, about whether environmental ethics is concerned with animals of higher intelligence, sentient beings, endangered species, ecosystems, or the planetary balance has in part to do with whether the ethicist has been reading the primatology of Diane Fossey and Jane Goodall, or the physical zoology of Cleveland Hickman, or the conservation biology of E. O. Wilson, the evolutionary biology of Stephen J. Gould or Richard Dawkins, the ecology of Frederic Clements (usually mediated by Aldo Leopold), or the theoretical "Gaia" biology of James Lovelock. See Kirkman, *Skeptical Environmentalism: The Limits of Philosophy and Science*, and "The Problem of Knowledge in Environmental Ethics: A Counterchallenge."

84. See especially Worster, *Nature's Economy: A History of Ecological Ideas*; Bramwell, *Ecology in the Twentieth Century: A History*; Botkin, *Discordant Harmonies: A New Ecology for the 21st Century*; Nash, *The Rights of Nature: A History of Environmental Ethics*.

85. Simon Schama's meandering remembrance of European cultural landscapes intends, he says, to complexify contemporary discussion of nature, reminding Europeans that their cultural inheritance is shot through with the memory of many kinds of environmental experience. Schama, *Landscape and Memory*.

86. "All versions of revealed values in nature rely heavily upon particular human capacities and particular anthropocentric mediations . . . thus producing distinctively human discourses about intrinsic values. . . . If values reside in nature we have no scientific way of knowing what they are independently of the values implicit in the metaphors deployed. . . . We have loaded upon nature, often without knowing it, in our

science as in our poetry, much of the alternative desire for value to that implied by money." Harvey, *Justice, Nature, and the Geography of Difference*, 158, 162–3. Notice that Harvey recognizes that the discourse of intrinsic value represents a practical strategy for countering economic logics.

87. On delineating status: Callicott, *In Defense of the Land Ethic: Essays in Environmental Philosophy*; Katz, "Understanding Moral Limits in the Duality of Artifacts and Nature"; Haraway, *Modest-Witness@Second-Millennium.Femaleman-Meets-Oncomouse: Feminism and Technoscience*, and *Simians, Cyborgs, and Women: The Reinvention of Nature*.

88. King, "Environmental Ethics and the Built Environment" and "Toward an Ethics of the Domesticated Environment." See also Macauley, "Be-Wildering Order." Wendell Berry puts the same point somewhat differently: "Somewhere near the heart of the conservation movement as we have known it is the romantic assumption that, if we have become alienated from nature, we can become unalienated by making nature the subject of contemplation or art, ignoring the fact that we live necessarily in and from nature"; Berry, *Citizenship Papers*, 114.

89. See O'Neill, "Time, Narrative, and Environmental Politics."

90. Thompson, *The Spirit of the Soil*, 3–13; Fox, *Ethics and the Built Environment*.

91. For two other examples of potentially method-altering material environments see Light, "The Urban Blind Spot in Environmental Ethics," and Kirkman, "Reasons to Dwell on (If Not Necessarily in) the Suburbs." But Holmes Rolston argues that some new environments may simply call for deepening the conventional approach; see Rolston, "Environmental Ethics in Antarctica." And, in personal correspondence regarding his comments for this chapter, Rolston resisted the notion that troublesome or hybrid subject matter undoes an entire normative strategy.

92. Thus Andrew Light's prescription for including the "urban blind spot" rests in ethical attention to "restorative practices." See Light, "Restorative Relationships," and "The Urban Blind Spot in Environmental Ethics." Warwick Fox thinks the reframing necessitated by mixed environments goes further and broader, requiring a "general ethics," capable of integrating interhuman ethics, ethics of nature, and ethics of constructed environments. Fox proposes the concept of "responsive cohesion" for integrating the broader frame. Fox, *A Theory of General Ethics*.

93. One theorist writes a book distinguishing the natural from the artefactual because "the worrying thing about modern technology in the long run may not be that it threatens life on earth as we know it to be because of its polluting effects, but that it could ultimately humanize nature. Nature, as the 'Other,' would be eliminated." Lee, *The Natural and the Artefactual*, 4. See also Elliot, *Faking Nature: The Ethics of Environmental Restoration*, and Katz, "Understanding Moral Limits in the Duality of Artifacts and Nature."

94. Norton, *The Search for Sustainability*, 48; see also Light, "The Urban Blind Spot in Environmental Ethics."

95. For example, one constructivist anthology introduces its essays with this practical claim: "The crucial issue, therefore, is not that of policing boundaries

between 'nature' and 'culture' but rather, of taking responsibility for how our inevitable interventions in nature proceed." (It is odd, however, that the editors retain the "intervention" metaphor, which seems to refer to just that boundary.) Braun and Castree (eds.), *Remaking Reality: Nature at the Millennium*, 34.

96. Thus two critics lament that "a wave of relativistic anthropocentrism now sweeping the humanities and social sciences might have consequences for how policymakers and technocrats view and manage the remnants of biodiversity and remaining fragments of wilderness." Soulé and Lease (eds.), *Reinventing Nature? Responses to Postmodern Deconstruction*, 159. See also Kidner, "Fabricating Nature: A Critique of the Social Construction of Nature" and Rolston, "Nature for Real: Is Nature a Social Construct?"

97. Smith puts the same point differently: "We no longer need to rely on driving spurious ontological wedges between positions but can recognize that each position is, in a sense, a critique of the naturalness of the current status quo," and thus "indicative of differing analyses of social/natural relations." Smith, *An Ethics of Place*, 127.

98. J. Baird Callicott cautions against too easily correlating strategic differences with the boundaries of metaphysical commitments. Callicott's position deploys a form of subjectivism in the course of establishing intrinsic value for ecological entities. Whether or not his is an attractive proposal, Callicott's approach usefully disrupts the connection between metaethical commitments and what I have been calling normative strategies. For his position reminds us that while certain metaethical stances may characteristically fund certain strategies, they are not logically bound to do so. See O'Neill, "Varieties of Intrinsic Value," 121.

99. See the introduction to Oelschlaeger, *Postmodern Environmental Ethics*.

100. "Social construction" is itself a debated term, bearing a range of meanings with more and less intensive shades, more or less external causation; see Ian Hacking, *The Social Construction of What?* I refer to its use by the strategists of moral agency to argue that processes of human conditioning in reference of environmental concerns should be made the practical focus of environmental ethics.

101. Szerszynski, Heim, and Waterton (eds.), *Nature Performed: Environment, Culture and Performance*, 1. This book draws a distinction between "constructivist" and "performative" views, the latter bearing a more dialogical sense than the former.

102. "A renewed capacity to reread the production of historical-geographical difference is a crucial preliminary step towards emancipating the possibilities for future place construction. And liberating places . . . is an inevitable part of any progressive socioecological politics." Harvey, *Justice, Nature, and the Geography of Difference*, 326.

103. Ecofeminist critiques, to which we will soon come, have played a particularly strong role in highlighting the environmental relevance of broader cultural practices, and on the whole have been most concerned with the reconstructive task of reimagining the social relations that conduce toward greener social practices. Consider, for example, the association of critique and reconstruction in Warren, "The Power and Promise of Ecological Feminism."

104. Cronon, "The Trouble with Wilderness; or, Getting Back to the Wrong Nature," 79.

105. "Any way of looking at nature that encourages us to believe we are separate from nature—as wilderness tends to do—is likely to reinforce environmentally irresponsible behavior." Cronon, "The Trouble with Wilderness," 87.

106. Cronon reiterates these points stridently (even homiletically) in "Saving Nature in Time: The Past and Future of Environmentalism."

107. Consider the otherwise impudent assertion by Thomas Birch that wilderness areas function to suppress wildness, detaining it in the environmental equivalent of concentration camps. See Birch, "The Incarceration of Wilderness." Forcefully subverting the concept of wilderness through metaphors of incarceration, Birch's point is similar to Cronon's: insofar as they are associated with a complex of cultural attitudes and practices that cordon off nature into a narrow arena of both land and experience, wilderness areas are not only a cultural invention, but in fact devices for imperial control and capitalist discipline—geographical apologies for a hegemonic political order. (Since much of the deconstructive animus by critical environmental theorists was made possible by Foucault's work, how fitting that Birch invokes the lessons and metaphors from *Discipline and Punish* in order to criticize the most hallowed classification nature can receive.) Cronon and Birch do not want the United States to revoke the legal status of lands classed as wilderness (Cronon is on the board of The Wilderness Society); they rather want that status to function transformatively for a broader geographical set of social and political practices. In fact, these outspoken constructivists agree on some real presence to nature, resident in its "otherness," which exerts an ultimate normative force on environmental practices. Insofar as they appeal to that real presence they seem to have not quite shaken the strategy of nature's moral standing, even as they attempt to introduce a second strategy focusing on practices. See Jenkins, "Assessing Metaphors of Agency."

108. Vogel, *Against Nature: The Concept of Nature in Critical Theory*, 167, 172. The tension between the phrases "extent to which" and "always already" gestures toward the constructivist problem we are about to see: attempting to demonstrate nature's constitution without its total determination. Vogel tries to strike the balance elsewhere, notably in "Nature as Origin and Difference"; "Environmental Philosophy after the End of Nature"; and "The Nature of Artifacts."

109. Vogel, *Against Nature*, 168.

110. Vogel, *Against Nature*, 189. He is quoted approvingly by King, "Environmental Ethics and the Built Environment," 127.

111. See Smith, *Ethics of Place*, 116. On forms of justice in environmental ethics, see Schlosberg, "The Justice of Environmental Justice: Reconciling Equity, Recognition, and Participation in a Political Movement."

112. Buell, *The Environmental Imagination*, 2.

113. King, "Environmental Ethics and the Built Environment," 128.

114. The Park Service's new video for visitors, "Shenandoah, the Historic Wonderland," in fact makes a move toward this change from its previous version, "Shenandoah: The Gift."

115. See Whiteside, *Divided Natures: French Contributions to Political Ecology*.

116. Vogel, "Nature as Origin and Difference," 172.

117. This is the title of an essay in Langdon Winner, *The Whale and the Reactor: A Search for Limits in an Age of High Technology*. See also Salleh, "Working with Nature: Reciprocity or Control?"

118. Braun and Castree, *Remaking Reality*, 34.

119. Gottlieb, *Environmentalism Unbound*.

120. Bookchin, *The Ecology of Freedom*.

121. Luhmann, *Ecological Communication* and *Observations on Modernity*.

122. Preston, *Grounding Knowledge*, 40.

123. Smith, "Nature at the Millennium: Production and Re-Enchantment." See also Christopher Manes, "Nature and Silence."

124. This is precisely what worries Katz about conceding ground in the ecological restoration debates. Katz, "Understanding Moral Limits in the Duality of Artifacts and Nature."

125. David Kidner writes that "in a manner reminiscent of the way a New Zealand flatworm reduces its earthworm prey to a sort of amorphous jelly before ingesting it, so industrialism's colonization of the world operates by denying and dissolving any structure which is inconsistent with it." Kidner, "Fabricating Nature: A Critique of the Social Construction of Nature," 347. Callicott says about critical theory that "a far more likely option for a Realpolitik of difference in a shattered and fragmented world is naked power—backed either by bullets or bucks"; Callicott, "The Case against Moral Pluralism," 120. See also Kidner, "Industrialism and the Fragmentation of Temporal Structure."

126. For example, the last two pages of Neil Evernden's critique of nature lauds those writers who are able to convey the elusive wildness that environmentalism seeks. So also the last three pages of Whiteside, and the last page of Cronon's "The Trouble with Wilderness" asks for practices of respect and gratitude. Evernden, *The Social Creation of Nature*; Whiteside, *Divided Natures*; Cronon, "The Trouble with Wilderness." See Jenkins, "Assessing Metaphors of Agency," 139–40. Some of the following paragraphs are adapted from the latter article.

127. See the commentary by Freyfogle, *Bounded People, Boundless Land*, 121–25. Cf. Thompson, *The Spirit of the Soil*, 72–93. For his own commentary, see especially Berry, *What Are People For?*

128. Berry's stories function differently than Jim Cheney's awkward description of bioregional voices, precisely because Berry unites place and expression within the creativity of his characters. See Cheney, "Postmodern Environmental Ethics: Ethics as Bioregional Narrative." Berry seems closer to Mick Smith's revision of Cheney's attractive image. See Smith, "Cheney and the Myth of Postmodernism."

129. Berry, *Jayber Crow*.

130. King, "Narrative, Imagination, and the Search for Intelligibility in Environmental Ethics," 27. Cf. Ebenreck, "Opening Pandora's Box: Imagination's Role in Environmental Ethics." For one attempt to understand environmental writers as "lay ethicists," see Satterfield and Slovic (eds.), *What's Nature Worth?* 2.

131. See Preston, "Conversing with Nature in a Postmodern Epistemological Framework"; and Welchman, "The Virtues of Stewardship," 412–14, 423.

132. Barry Lopez, *Arctic Dreams*, 404–5.

133. Reimagination may, for some writers, especially with regard to the American continent, mean reclaiming lost forms of ecological personhood, perhaps reaching back before the deracination of native cultures. For just two examples among many, consider Camuto, *Another Country*, and Lopez, *The Rediscovery of North America*.

134. See, for example, Hill, "Ideals of Human Excellence and Preserving Natural Environments"; Frasz, "Environmental Virtue Ethics: A New Direction for Environmental Ethics"; O'Neill, *Ecology, Policy, and Politics*; and Welchman, "The Virtues of Stewardship."

135. See Raglon and Scholtmeijer, "Shifting Ground: Metanarratives, Epistemology, and the Stories of Nature."

136. Smith, *Ethics of Place*, 212. Stone realized early on that recognizing standing might have radically reformulative anthropological implications; see Stone, *Should Trees Have Standing?* 33–43.

137. See the very helpful discriminations in Mathews, "Deep Ecology."

138. Naess, "The Shallow and the Deep, Long-Range Ecology Movements." See also the interview with Naess reprinted in Devall and Sessions, *Deep Ecology*, 74.

139. Naess, "Intuition, Intrinsic Value and Deep Ecology" and "Self-Realization: An Ecological Approach to Being in the World"; Naess and Sessions, "Platform Principles of the Deep Ecology Movement," 49–53; Naess and Rothenberg, *Ecology, Community, and Lifestyle*.

140. See the summary discussion in Devall and Sessions, *Deep Ecology*, 65–68. Again the non/anthropocentric continuum fails us, for the crucial role for experience probably better accounts for the importance of wilderness in deep ecology than an extrinsically principled commitment to nature's status. Critics debate whether deep ecology is nonanthropocentric or anthropocentric, when it seems more adequate to say it is both and neither. Katz, "Against the Inevitability of Anthropocentrism"; Nelson, "An Amalgamation of Wilderness Preservation Arguments"; and Talbot, "The Wilderness Narrative and the Cultural Logic of Capitalism."

141. For example: "The person–planetary paradigm shift enables us to look at the world through the eyes of ecological processes and relationships," in Drengson, "Shifting Paradigms: From Technocrat to Planetary Person," 94. See also Gare, "The Postmodernism of Deep Ecology, the Deep Ecology of Postmodernism, and Grand Narratives," 209–10.

142. Examples, respectively: Ross, *Plenishment in the Earth*; Murdy, "Anthropocentrism: A Modern Version"; Peterson, *Being Human*; Preston, *Grounding Knowledge*; Rowlands, *The Environmental Crisis*.

143. For example, Pearce, Moran, and the Biodiversity Conservation Strategy Programme, *The Economic Value of Biodiversity*; Pearce, *Economic Values and the Natural World*.

144. Daly and Cobb, *For the Common Good*, 159. See also pages 7–21, 85–9, 160–74. Holmes Rolston agrees: "Call this [market valuing of nature] enlightened self-interest if you wish, but if the self has thousands of interconnections, we might just as well call it an entwined self, or a communal self. This is an ecological view of the self." Rolston, *Conserving Natural Value*, 156.

145. Matthew Adler demonstrates this connection by arguing that environmental economics must account for objective welfare interests of rational humans, which he qualifies by appealing to environmental justice concerns, as a way of indicating objective environmental dimensions to human dignity; Adler, "Cost-Benefit Analysis." Julian Agyeman argues that the discourse of "sustainable communities" can bring together environmental justice and sustainable economics; Agyeman, *Sustainable Communities*, 1–6, 57–87. Vandana Shiva might agree, as she equates resisting the globalizing market to resisting the "monoculture of the mind" that supposes human dignity can be reduced to a supply of a few commodities, calling instead for "living economies" that sustain the ecological conditions for diverse kinds of human dignity; *Earth Democracy*, 112.

146. One could argue that environmental justice accounts often belong in the second strategy because of their insistence on social practices of justice and participatory democracy. See, for example, Farber (ed.), *The Struggle for Ecological Democracy* and Bullard, *Dumping in Dixie*. However, because those practices intend to restore human dignity in part by restoring integrity to their environments, they gesture toward an ecological anthropology. See Buell, *Writing for an Endangered World*, 30–54. David Schlosberg would object to categorizing environmental justice within any one strategy, arguing that its irreducible pluralism escapes from any frame; Schlosberg, *Environmental Justice and the New Pluralism*, 110–13.

147. See, for example: Anderson and Boyle (eds.), *Human Rights Approaches to Environmental Protection*; Nickel, "The Human Right to a Safe Environment: Philosophical Perspectives on Its Scope and Justification."

148. Zarsky (ed.), *Human Rights and the Environment*; Thorme, "Establishing Environment as a Human Right," 319.

149. See Wilson and Kellert (eds.), *The Biophilia Hypothesis*; Kellert, *Kinship to Mastery*.

150. Kanner (ed.), *Ecopsychology*; Roszak, *The Voice of the Earth*; Shepard, *Nature and Madness*.

151. Macy, "The Ecological Self: Postmodern Ground for Right Action."

152. Quoted in Nash, *The Rights of Nature*, 196. On ecological personhood and anthropocentrism, see Katz, "Against the Inevitability of Anthropocentrism"; Manes, "Philosophy and the Environmental Task," 79; Mathews, *The Ecological Self*; Smith, *An Ethics of Place*, 212–16.

153. See Smith, *An Ethics of Place*, 165–67.

154. See Warren, "The Power and Promise of Ecological Feminism."

155. Plumwood, "Nature, Self, and Gender: Feminism, Environmental Philosophy, and the Critique of Rationalism," 162, 172. See also Zimmerman, "Rethinking the Heidegger–Deep Ecology Relationship"; Merchant, *Earthcare*, 185–215.

156. See Warren, "The Power and Promise of Ecological Feminism."

157. "To obtain a more adequate account than that offered by mainstream ethics and deep ecology, it seems that we must move toward the sort of ethics feminist theory has suggested, which can allow for both continuity and difference and for ties to nature which are expressive of the rich, caring relationships of kinship and friendship

rather than increasing abstraction and detachment from relationship"; Plumwood, "Nature, Self, and Gender," 164. See also Curtin, "Toward an Ecological Ethic of Care," and King, "Caring about Nature: Feminist Ethics and the Environment."

158. Michael Zimmerman describes how some thinkers have been attracted to ecofeminist and eco-phenomenological thought in order to address some of the difficulties within deep ecology; see Zimmerman, "What Can Continental Philosophy Contribute to Environmentalism," and *Contesting Earth's Future*.

159. Phenomenology "can account for our tendency to conceive of nature in these two perennial categories, indicate the limits of these ways of thinking, and provide an account . . . of that resistance nature offers us . . . that makes us unwilling to reduce it to a category of our collective creation or fabrication." Ted Toadvine, "Naturalizing Phenomenology," 125. See also Brown and Toadvine (eds.), *Eco-Phenomenology*; and Seamon (ed.), *Dwelling, Seeing, and Designing*.

160. See the importance of *poiesis* in the closing pages of Foltz, *Inhabiting the Earth*.

161. Abram, *The Spell of the Sensuous*. Cf. Kohak, *The Embers and the Stars*, 22, 46; and Oelschlaeger, *The Idea of Wilderness*, 321.

162. I recognize the strange absence from this chapter of Aldo Leopold, whose *Sand County Almanac* is claimed by theorists from each of the major strategies I have surveyed, and who may be the only environmental ethicist (if that is indeed what he was) ever recognized as a competent authority by a state Supreme Court. (See Goldstein, "Environmental Ethics and Positive Law," 8; and Lazarus, *The Making of Environmental Law*, 215–20.) Norton, Callicott, Wenze, Gaare, Minteer, and Sessions each claim Leopold for their own versions of environmental ethics. I have not assigned Leopold to any one strategy, not wishing to enter the literature of Leopold scholasticism. Leopold could lend support to any or all of the three strategies, and I might have argued that he models a way of integrating all three. But that interpretive claim, in which I am not invested, would have distracted from the survey's argument, attracting proxy criticism. Instead, I will occasionally return to key phrases and concepts from his *Almanac* in subsequent chapters as a way of recalling attention to the ethical scene he still shapes.

163. "If natural things have value, we cannot conceivably learn without experiences by which we are let in on them. With every such sharing there comes a caring . . . an advanced kind of experiencing . . . . Value must be lived through, experienced, so as to discern the character of the surroundings one is living through." Rolston, *Conserving Natural Value*, 161–62. See also Rolston, *Environmental Ethics*, 341–46.

164. Rolston, *Environmental Ethics*, 198–225.

165. All three strategies come together with particular normative urgency in Rolston, "Caring for Nature: From Fact to Value, from Respect to Reverence."

166. Plumwood, *Environmental Culture*, 237.

167. Plumwood, *Environmental Culture*, 218–34. Compare three elements of environmental reason in Guattari, *Three Ecologies*.

168. Smith, *An Ethics of Place*, 192, 204.

169. Smith, *An Ethics of Place*, 190–220.

170. Cf. David Sack on the unique adequacy of place ethics: "the very fact that place combines the unconstructed physical space in conjunction with social rules and meaning . . . enables places to draw together the three realms, and makes place constitutive of ourselves as agents." Quoted in Preston, *Grounding Knowledge*, 99.

171. Deane Curtin's *Environmental Ethics in a Postcolonial World* offers a good example of an approach clear about its own strategy from the beginning. Curtin opens by recognizing that any method must implicitly decide the identity of environmental ethics, presents his own criteria for practical success in the field, and then proceeds to develop an integrative place ethics responsive to the main vulnerabilities of each strategy.

Chapter 3

1. Johnson, "Losing and Finding Creation in the Christian Tradition," 18. See also Rasmussen, *Earth Community, Earth Ethics*, 181–94.

2. Michael Moody reports that the term "ecojustice" was coined (or at least made its public debut) in a 1972 strategic planning group of the American Baptist Churches; Moody, "Caring for Creation: Environmental Advocacy by Mainline Protestant Organizations," 239.

3. Although they sometimes describe ecojustice differently than I do, for more background see Smyth, *A Way of Transformation*; Bakken, Gibb Engel, and Engel, *Ecology, Justice, and Christian Faith*, 1–39; Gibson, "Introduction to the Journey"; Hessel, "Where Were/Are the U.S. Churches in the Environmental Movement?" and "The Church's Eco-Justice Journey."

4. It may also reflect growing suspicion of the rhetoric of sustainability, and continued preference for a human right to the environment finally abandoned by the United Nations Commission on Human Rights in the mid 1990s. See Cobb, *Sustainability: Economics, Ecology, and Justice*, 84.

5. Smyth, *Way of Transformation*, 1–39. See an account of ecojustice emerging with the Roman Catholic Church in Hart, *What Are They Saying About Environmental Theology?* 1–6, 100–107. Hart observes a decline in stewardship theologies within the Catholic Church, and a recent shift toward what I describe as the strategy of ecological spirituality.

6. Moody, "Caring for Creation: Environmental Advocacy by Mainline Protestant Organizations," 240.

7. As put by the spokesperson for the Ecojustice Working Group of the National Council of Churches. See Somplatsky-Jarman, Grazer, and LeQuire, "Partnership for the Environment among U.S. Christians: Report from the National Partnership for the Environment," 574. Compare Bakken, Gibb Engel, and Engel, *Ecology, Justice, and Christian Faith*, 5.

8. Hessel, "Eco-Justice Theology after Nature's Revolt," 9. See also Cobb, *Sustainability*, 20–21; Gibson, "Eco-Justice: What Is It?"

9. For evidence of this inclusivity, see the topics collected in Gibson (ed.), *Eco-Justice: The Unfinished Journey*.

10. National Council of Churches, "God's Earth Is Sacred: An Open Letter to Church and Society in the United States."

11. Gustafson, *Ethics from a Theocentric Perspective: Theology and Ethics*, vol. 1. Notice his different formulation later, adjusted for the technological power and prerogative of humanity: "We are to relate all things *to each other* in ways that concur with their relations to God." In Gustafson, *A Sense of the Divine*, 148 (my emphasis).

12. Johnston, "Economics, Eco-Justice, and the Doctrine of God"; Sun Ai Lee-Park, "The Forbidden Tree and the Year of the Lord."

13. McDaniel, *Of God and Pelicans*; Birch, "Christian Obligation for the Liberation of Nature," 61–63.

14. Jacobsen, "Biblical Bases for Ecojustice Ethics," 46–52.

15. Spencer, *Gay and Gaia: Ethics, Ecology, and the Erotic*, 115–26, 341–45; McFague, *The Body of God*.

16. Kehm, "The New Story: Redemption as Fulfillment of Creation," 105–6.

17. The Earth Bible Team, "Guiding Ecojustice Principles," 46–48.

18. Nash, *Loving Nature*, 95; cf. 166–78.

19. Nash, *Loving Nature*, 140–59. Northcott states that "Nash argues that the intrinsic value of the creation is established by its original and ongoing relationality to the creator God who loves the objects of the creation. . . . Christian ecological responsibility may then be most appropriately described in terms of the generosity and grace of divine love, which characterizes all God's relations with the earth, and of which all human acts of loving are a reflection." Northcott, *The Environment and Christian Ethics*, 143.

20. Rasmussen, *Earth Community, Earth Ethics*, 345–47, 99, 106, 270. Cf. Rasmussen, "Returning to Our Senses: The Theology of the Cross as a Theology for Eco-Justice."

21. Timothy Gorringe's proposal for building communities according to the designs of both nature and God, made possible by God's trinitarian indwelling of creation, demonstrates one avenue of pursuing what Rasmussen means here. See Gorringe, *A Theology of the Built Environment*.

22. Rasmussen, *Earth Community, Earth Ethics*, 90–93. Cf. Jung, *We Are Home*.

23. Rasmussen, *Earth Community, Earth Ethics*, 345.

24. This is Aldo Leopold's famous phrase. Leopold, *A Sand County Almanac*, 132.

25. The criteria of Leopold's famous maxim: "A thing is right when it tends to preserve the integrity, stability, and beauty of the biotic community." Leopold, *A Sand County Almanac*, 224–25.

26. See for example: Hallman, "Climate Change: Ethics, Justice, and Sustainable Community"; Martin-Schramm, "Population Growth, Poverty, and Environmental Degradation"; Martin-Schramm, *Population Perils and the Churches' Response*; Maguire and Rasmussen, *Ethics for a Small Planet*; Cobb, *Sustainability*, 21–33.

27. Rasmussen, *Earth Community, Earth Ethics*, 304.

28. On natural law and Christian ecological virtues, see Nash, "Seeking Moral Norms in Nature: Natural Law and Ecological Responsibility"; Van Wensveen, *Dirty*

Virtues; Bouma-Prediger, "Response to Louke Van Wensveen: A Constructive Proposal"; Bergant, *The Earth Is the Lord's*; Northcott, *The Environment and Christian Ethics*, 232–56, 314–17.

29. See, for example, Rolston, "Feeding People Versus Saving Nature?"

30. Rasmussen, *Earth Community, Earth Ethics*, 272. This is why ecojustice is more than simply a strategy for moral status, as appears in Daniel Cowdin's otherwise similar claim that the question for Christian environmental ethics is simply "how to theologize Aldo Leopold." See Cowdin, "The Moral Status of Otherkind in Christian Ethics," 261.

31. Koyama, "Cosmology and Justice in Ecumenical Perspective"; Hessel, "Ecojustice Theology after Nature's Revolt," 15; Martin-Schramm and Stivers, *Christian Environmental Ethics*, 34–37.

32. Moltmann insists on this point, against the christologies of Teilhard de Chardin and Karl Rahner. See Moltmann, *The Way of Jesus Christ*, 292–306.

33. Rasmussen, *Earth Community, Earth Ethics*, 292.

34. Rasmussen, *Earth Community, Earth Ethics*, 292.

35. Santmire, "Healing the Protestant Mind: Beyond the Theology of Human Dominion," 72–77.

36. A "covenant, in which humanity as the people of God and nature as the Promised Land are both represented as members of the covenant community" associates itself with the membership concepts of Aldo Leopold. Northcott, *The Environment and Christian Ethics*, 130.

37. Granberg-Michaelson, "Covenant and Creation," 31.

38. In the next chapter we will see how stewardship ethics approach covenant thinking, but from a focus on moral agency rather than creation's integrity.

39. Northcott, *The Environment and Christian Ethics*, 256; cf. 130, 164–77, 180–83.

40. See Brueggemann, *The Land*, 43–65. Churches in the Reformed traditions may find covenantal ecojustice especially appealing, both for its use of a biblical trope especially important for their tradition, and for its ability to incorporate specific biblical practices of discipleship and obedience under the aspect of stewardship. The books and essays of Wesley Granberg-Michaelson, General Secretary of the Reformed Church in America, display this hybrid strategy. See Granberg-Michaelson, "Covenant and Creation" and *A Worldly Spirituality*. While it makes less explicit use of covenantal language, Norman Wirzba's *Paradise of God* accomplishes an analogous integration of stewardship practices and law-guarded integrity of creation. Wirzba especially attends to agriculture as a test case for a decent ecological theology, further deepening the covenantal resonances of land and grace.

41. Northcott, *The Environment and Christian Ethics*, 164, 314.

42. Bernard Anderson, quoted by Kehm, "The New Story: Redemption as Fulfillment of Creation," 93.

43. Cf. Murray, *Cosmic Covenant: Biblical Themes of Justice, Peace, and the Integrity of Creation*, 162–75. Stephen Clark thinks that a biblical covenant asks humans to see themselves as neighbors of their fellow creatures, who also exist for their own sake before God, so that "awakening to realize the real beings of the creatures amongst

whom we live, we have the opportunity to forge new images, new ways of living, that accommodate the interests of all." Clark, *Biology and Christian Ethics*, 283–86, 297–99 (quote at 297).

44. Meditation on creation's integrity within monastic practices give further evidence that creation must form Christian life somehow. See Schaefer, "Grateful Cooperation: Cistercian Inspiration for Ecological Ethics" and Kardong, "Ecological Resources in the Benedictine Rule."

45. See the essays in Drees (ed.), *Is Nature Ever Evil?*

46. Rasmussen, *Earth Community, Earth Ethics*, 345–52.

47. Northcott, *The Environment and Christian Ethics*, 196–203, 231–33.

48. Gustafson, *Ethics from a Theocentric Perspective: Ethics and Theology*, vol. 2, 4–22.

49. Sideris, *Environmental Ethics, Ecological Theology, and Natural Selection.*

50. Holmes Rolston, campaigning for a Christian ecojustice ethic, points out the dissonance between the practical environmental prudence of a land ethic and the biblical ecological metaphors. See Rolston, "Environmental Ethics: Some Challenges for Christians."

51. Webb, *On God and Dogs*, 51–54, 181–84. See also Webb, "Ecology vs. the Peaceable Kingdom: Toward a Better Theology of Nature." For more support of this view, see Wennberg, *God, Humans, and Animals*, 46–51, 327–28.

52. Wes Jackson points out that the legacy of St. Francis is ambiguous here. While Lynn White proposes St. Francis as "patron saint for ecology" because of his communion with nature as sacred (initial evidence for loving the wild), Jackson reminds us that by befriending the animals St. Francis domesticates them. St. Francis famously pacifies the wolf of Gubbio, calling him to repentance and a reformed life living on handouts from town. Jackson, *Becoming Native to This Place*, 61–69.

53. Moltmann, *The Way of Jesus Christ*, 307–8.

54. Moltmann, *The Source of Life*, 121.

55. Moltmann, *The Spirit of Life*, 171–72.

56. Moltmann, *The Spirit of Life*, 10. On the simultaneous eclipse of creation and the Holy Spirit, see Bouma-Prediger, *The Greening of Theology*, 106–7.

57. Moltmann, *The Spirit of Life*, 177.

58. Moltmann, *God in Creation*, 58–64.

59. Moltmann, *The Spirit of Life*, 195–96, 212–13.

60. Moltmann, *God in Creation*, 21, 39, 59, 100, 169–70, 213–17; Moltmann, *Science and Wisdom*, 26–29, 44–47. Cf. Bouma-Prediger, *The Greening of Theology*, 230–40.

61. Moltmann, *Science and Wisdom*, 26–27.

62. Moltmann, *The Spirit of Life*, 200–205.

63. Baker, "Theology and the Crisis in Darwinism," 205.

64. See Bouma-Prediger, *The Greening of Theology*, 234–52.

65. Such was Moltmann's own response at the Spring Institute on Lived Theology, Charlottesville, Virginia, April 28, 2005.

66. Baker, "Theology and the Crisis in Darwinism," 206, and quoting Gerard Loughlin, 209.

67. Baker, "Theology and the Crisis in Darwinism."

CHAPTER 4

1. Bakken, "Stewardship."

2. I use the contested term "evangelical" to refer to those theologies that place special emphasis on the theological and moral primacy of biblical narrative, on Jesus Christ's redemptive action, and on individual conversion and discipleship. This chapter does not necessarily address or describe the religious views of contemporary American sects claiming the name "evangelical," except insofar as it describes a theological strategy used by some organizations to reach these populations.

3. John Passmore traces a notion of human stewardship over nature to the Chief Justice Matthew Hale in the American seventeenth century; Passmore, *Man's Responsibility for Nature*, 30. Lawrence Osborne traces Protestant theological pedigree for stewardship back to Calvin's gloss on Genesis 2:15; Osborne, *Guardians of Creation*, 141–42. Robin Attfield and Peter Bakken name both sources; see Attfield, *The Ethics of Environmental Concern*, 37–45; and Bakken, "Stewardship." See also Jenkins, "Stewardship," in *The Westminster Dictionary of Christian Ethics*.

4. Ball, "Evangelicals, Population, and the Ecological Crisis," 238.

5. Schaeffer, *Pollution and the Death of Man*; Santmire, *Brother Earth*. This call for environmental stewardship was taken up by *Christianity Today*, which, in a series of articles in the early 1970s, cautiously embraced Christian approaches to environmental problems. Grizzle, "Evangelicals and Environmentalism," 16.

6. Passmore, *Man's Responsibility for Nature*, 171–85.

7. Sider, *Rich Christians in an Age of Hunger*. John Henry Reumann notes that sustained practical theological reflections on stewardship "are very much a North American contribution to church practice and thought." See Reumann, *Stewardship and the Economy of God*, 52.

8. Mary Evelyn Jegen and Bruno Manno (eds.), *The Earth Is the Lord's*.

9. See www.ausable.org, and the EEN at www.creationcare.org.

10. In the same year, Wesley Granberg-Michaelson published his study of stewardship and then founded the New Creation Institute, which later merged into the Au Sable Institute. Granberg-Michaelson, *Ecology and Life*.

11. The 1988 NACCE conference released a statement that called on Christians to join in an ongoing social movement. Eight years later they deployed much different rhetoric, inviting Christians into their unique vocation to care for the good gifts of God. See Regenstein, *Replenish the Earth*, 160–63.

12. Quoted from an interview by Streiffert, "The Earth Groans and Christians Are Listening," 38–40. DeWitt (mistakenly) said this was the first time on the continent that Christians had gathered to approach justice, peace, and the integrity of creation as inseparable concerns; see Frame, "Planetary Justice," 74–75. While ignoring quite a bit of Christian environmental concern prior to 1988, that comment may indicate

DeWitt's sense that Christian environmentalism was poised to develop in unique theological directions.

13. See "An Open Letter to the Religious Community," http://www.nrpe.org/ statements/interfaith_statmts_ao1.htm.

14. See the "Declaration" and responses in Berry (ed.), *The Care of Creation*.

15. The EEN quoted by Kearns, "Noah's Ark Goes to Washington," 349. Michael Moody reports: "So there developed at the time somewhat unusual scenes of members of Congress asking aides to bring them their Bibles so they could have a theological debate with evangelical religious leaders over a scientifically based environmental law." See Moody, "Caring for Creation: Environmental Advocacy by Mainline Protestant Organizations," 249.

16. Pope, *Sierra*. Pope has since reported that his improved relations with the church increased his political influence; see Motavelli, "Stewards of the Earth." In the years since the Sierra Club has co-sponsored theologically-framed environmental campaigns, such as the "What Would Jesus Drive?" advertisements.

17. Measuring an evangelical blind spot by the percentage of textual attention in major Protestant theology textbooks, John Davis argues that evangelical reluctance to engage environmental problems can be traced to underdeveloped connections between the doctrine of creation and the doctrine of atonement, and recent initiatives to renewed biblical attention to the cosmic dimensions of Christ's atonement. John Davis, "Ecological 'Blind Spots' in the Structure and Content of Recent Evangelical Systematic Theologies."

18. Reichenbach and Anderson, *On Behalf of God*.

19. Passmore, *Man's Responsibility for Nature*, 28.

20. For a trenchant summary of complaints against stewardship, see Palmer, "Stewardship: A Case Study in Environmental Ethics." The essay was originally published in 1993 and has since provoked significant response from stewardship theologians.

21. A 1994 EEN publication, "Let the Earth Be Glad," quoted in Shibley and Wiggins, "The Greening of Mainline American Religion: A Sociological Analysis of the Environmental Ethics of the National Religious Partnership for the Environment," 341.

22. See Luke 16:1–13, Luke 19:10–27, Ephesians 1:10, and Ephesians 3:2.

23. See Swartley, "Biblical Sources of Stewardship," and Sider, "Biblical Foundations for Creation Care."

24. Hall, *Imaging God*, 192.

25. See, for example, Emmerich, "The Declaration in Practice: Missionary Earthkeeping."

26. Bouma-Prediger continues: "The phenomenology of grace and gratitude, whether between humans or between humans and God, suggests that the experience of gracious provision readily and rightly evokes a response of gratitude and care. . . . Grace begets gratitude and gratitude care." Bouma-Prediger, *For the Beauty of the Earth*, 178–79.

27. Hillyer, "Stewardship," 661.

28. Jegen and Manno (eds.), *The Earth Is the Lord's*. On risk and trust in God's way of owning, see Reichenbach and Anderson, "Tension in the Stewardship Paradigm."

29. DeWitt, *Caring for Creation*, 52; see also Swartley, "Biblical Sources of Stewardship," 23.

30. See Reumann, *Stewardship and the Economy of God.*

31. Hall, *Imaging God*, 200.

32. Zerbe, "The Kingdom of God," 82–87.

33. Cf. Murray, *Cosmic Covenant*, 84–88, 168–71.

34. Au Sable Institute, "Au Sable Institute Forum Statement," 126.

35. Kapur, "Let There Be Life," 174.

36. See Osborn, *Guardians of Creation*, 130–31. A stewardship theologian might then agree with Gordon Kaufman on the dangerously plural uses of nature by Christian theology, but rather than reconceiving grace to fit multiple uses, would likely reclaim grace to shift theological focus elsewhere. See Kaufman, "The Concept of Nature: A Problem for Theology."

37. Passmore, *Man's Responsibility for Nature*, 29.

38. Osborn, *Guardians of Creation*, 133; Nicholls, "Responding Biblically to Creation: A Creator-Centered Response to the Earth," 215–17. Cf. Granberg-Michaelson, "Covenant and Creation," 27–28; Au Sable, "Message to Individuals and Churches from the Participants," 131. Sider, "Biblical Foundations for Creation Care," 43–44.

39. See, for example, Barkey, *Environmental Stewardship in the Judeo-Christian Tradition*; Beisner, *Where Garden Meets Wilderness*; Derr, *Environmental Ethics and Christian Humanism.*

40. See Grant, "Religion and the Left: The Prospects of a Green Coalition."

41. Barron, "For God So Loved the Cosmos: The Good News, Ecology and Christian Ethics," 82.

42. Cf. Young, *Healing the Earth*, 214–16.

43. See, for example, DeWitt, "God's Love for the World and Creation's Environmental Challenge to Christianity," 140. Cf. Paterson, "Conceptualizing Stewardship in Agriculture within the Christian Tradition," 55.

44. For the two-books defense, see Dewitt, "Stewardship: Responding Dynamically to the Consequences of Human Action in the World." For a defense of biocentric aspects to stewardship, see Attfield, "Environmental Sensitivity and Critiques of Stewardship."

45. Reichenbach and Anderson, "Tensions in the Stewardship Paradigm," 118. For an argument that Benedictine monks model active stewardship practices akin to Aldo Leopold's land care, see Dubos, *A God Within.*

46. DeWitt argues that there is no dilemma because biblical environmental ethics and contemporary science are complementary. See DeWitt, "Spiritual and Religious Perspectives of Creation and Scientific Understandings of Nature."

47. Dewitt, "Stewardship," 151.

48. For mixed reviews on stewardship before natural limits, see Ball, "Evangelicals, Population, and the Ecological Crisis." On stewardship in regard to wilderness, see Braden, "On Saving the Wilderness: Why Christian Stewardship Is Not Sufficient."

49. See, for example, how Murray Rae responds to criticisms of the stewardship model by insistently reuniting it with God's redemptive purposes: Rae, "To Render Praise: Humanity in God's World," in *Environmental Stewardship: Critical Perspectives*.

50. Osborn, *Guardians of Creation*, 137.

51. "A failure of nerve in speaking of that highest work of God's creation, that supreme object of the divine compassion, that elect partner of God's divinity in the person of Christ suggests a failure of nerve about the meaning of the incarnation itself." O'Donovan, "Where Were You . . . ?" 93.

52. In answer to some criticism that Jesus is too often absent from Christian environmentalism, see Guelke, "Looking for Jesus in Environmental Ethics."

53. Manahan, "Christ as the Second Adam," 46.

54. See for example, the essays in DeWitt, *The Environment and the Christian*.

55. See Wilkinson (ed.), *Earthkeeping in the Nineties*, 275–77.

56. Van Leeuwen, "Christ's Resurrection and the Creation's Vindication," 65.

57. Wilson, "Evangelicals and the Environment: A Theological Concern," 302–4.

58. DeWitt, "Creation's Environmental Challenge to Evangelical Theology," 67.

59. Emmerich, "The Declaration in Practice: Missionary Earthkeeping," 154.

60. See Van Dyke et al., *Redeeming Creation: The Biblical Basis for Environmental Stewardship*, 62–65; and Harris, "Environmental Concern Calls for Repentance and Holiness."

61. Zerbe, "The Kingdom of God and the Stewardship of Creation," 82.

62. Cassel, "Stewardship: Experiencing and Expressing God's Nurturing Love," 28.

63. In reference to Philippians 2:5–8, see DeWitt, *Caring for Creation*, 40–41; Wirzba, *The Paradise of God*, 123–37; Murphy, *The Cosmos in the Light of the Cross*, 167–71.

64. Wilkinson (ed.), *Earthkeeping in the Nineties*, 294.

65. Hall, *The Steward*; Wilkinson (ed.), *Earthkeeping in the Nineties: Stewardship of Creation*, 317–19.

66. See for example, Van Dyke, *Redeeming Creation*, 98; and Young, *Healing the Earth*, 170–80. Hall explicitly address this sacrificial element in *Imaging God*, 195–98. Casell's interpretation may be the most helpful, implying self-sacrifice within appropriate limits: we should "accept undeserved limitations of personal power and privilege for the sake of others." See Cassel, "Stewardship: Experiencing and Expressing God's Nurturing Love," 33. See also Bratton and Nash, "Loving Nature: Eros or Agape?"

67. See the forthcoming book by Joseph Franke on these two martyrs. A synopsis is Franke, "Faith and Martyrdom in the Forest."

68. Wright, *Biology through the Eyes of Faith*, 179–80, 261.

69. Osborn, *Guardians of Creation*, 141–45.

70. Wright, *Biology through the Eyes of Faith*, 176.

71. O'Donovan, *Resurrection and Moral Order*, 183.

72. O'Donovan, *Resurrection and Moral Order*, 25.

73. See Ball, "The Use of Ecology in the Evangelical Protestant Response to the Ecological Crisis."

74. Oddly, stewardship theologies generally neglect reflection on farming, though we will soon come to an anabaptist exception. Another exception is Sider, "Biblical Sources of Stewardship." Compare the mixed review of stewardship and agriculture in Thompson, *The Spirit of the Soil*, 72–91, 147–49.

75. Kirschenmann and Kirschenmann, "A Transcendent Vision."

76. Thompson and Thompson, "Get Along But Don't Go Along," 58.

77. Berry, "The Gift of Good Land," 297, 303. For more on Berry's agricultural theology, see Wirzba, *The Paradise of God*.

78. Olson and Olson, "Showing Faith by Caring for the Land," 54.

79. Byron, "The Ethics of Stewardship," 45. See also Mark Graham's attempt to restore Christian reflections on agriculture to theological gift-giving: Graham, *Sustainable Agriculture*.

80. Wendell Berry's indictment remains classic; see Berry, *The Unsettling of America*.

81. The phrase "love's knowledge" comes from Martha Nussbaum's book of the same title. Many of the virtues she describes from moral reflections within narrative apply to the sort of stewardship practices the farmer-theologians discuss. See Nussbaum, *The Fragility of Goodness*.

82. Berry, *What Are People For?* 100.

83. Bratton and Nash, "Loving Nature: Eros or Agape?" 20, 24. See also Barron, "For God So Loved the Cosmos: The Good News, Ecology and Christian Ethics," 79–81.

84. Clifford "From Ecological Lament to a Sustainable *Oikos*," 251.

85. Wise, "A Review of Environmental Stewardship Literature and the New Testament," 117–34. Cf. Reid, "Enfleshing the Human: An Earth-Revealing, Earth-Healing Christology."

86. Manahan, "Christ as the Second Adam," 53.

87. Testerman, "Missionary Earthkeeping: Glimpses of the Past, Visions of the Future," 38; Jegen, "The Church's Role in Healing the Earth."

88. Dyrness, "Stewardship of the Earth in the Old Testament," 64.

89. Zerbe, "The Kingdom of God and the Stewardship of Creation," 83–90. See also Nicholls, "Responding Biblically to Creation: A Creator-Centered Response to the Earth."

90. Cf. Rolston, "Does Nature Need to Be Redeemed?"

91. Beisner, *Where Garden Meets Wilderness*, 15–25.

92. Quoted by Scott, "The Technological Factor: Redemption, Nature, and the Image of God," 375–76. See also Cole-Turner, "Toward a Theology for the Age of Biotechnology" and *The New Genesis*; as well as Brooke, "Improvable Nature?"

93. As for Van Leeuwen, quoting O. H. Steck, see Van Leeuwen, "Christ's Resurrection and the Creation's Vindication," 69.

94. As in Van Dyke et al., *Redeeming Creation*, 98–99.

95. Wilkinson (ed.), *Earthkeeping in the Nineties*, 298, 304–7. Osborn also appropriates Eastern Orthodox notions of stewardship; see Osborn, *Guardians of Creation*, 145–47.

96. This is also implied in Richard Bauckham's observation that stewardship often assumes, without theological justification, that human agency will improve nature; see Bauckham, "Stewardship and Relationship," 101.

97. Northcott, "The Spirit of Environmentalism," 168–71; Moltmann, "God's Covenant and Our Responsibility," 109–12.

98. O'Donovan, "Where Were You . . . ?" 90–91. Similarly, R. J. Berry writes that "stewardship means active management, not merely conscientious preservation"; Berry, "One Lord, One World: The Evangelism of Environmental Care," 22.

99. For bucolic description of what that looks like, see Kline, *Great Possessions.*

100. Weaver, "The New Testament and the Environment: Toward a Christology for the Cosmos," 123.

101. Redekop, "The Environmental Challenge before Us," 210.

102. Bean, "Toward an Anabaptist/Mennonite Environmental Ethic," 199.

103. Finger, "An Anabaptist/Mennonite Theology of Creation," 156.

104. Cf. Weaver, "The New Testament and the Environment: Toward a Christology for the Cosmos," 124–30.

105. See Wendell Berry's approving observations in Berry, *The Unsettling of America,* 21–27. Cf. Yoder, "Mennonites, Economics, and the Care of Creation."

106. Redekop, "Toward a Mennonite Theology and Ethic of Creation," 395; cf. Bean, "Toward an Anabaptist/Mennonite Environmental Ethic," 191–92.

107. Redekop, "Toward a Mennonite Theology and Ethic of Creation," 395. See also Redekop, "Mennonites, Creation, and Work."

108. Bean, "Toward an Anabaptist/Mennonite Environmental Ethic," 192.

CHAPTER 5

1. Peterson, "In and of the World? Christian Theological Anthropology and Environmental Ethics," 242.

2. Daly, "Ecofeminism, Reverence for Life, and Feminist Theological Ethics."

3. Kearns, "Saving the Creation: Religious Environmentalism."

4. Larry Rasmussen notes a connection between broadly Orthodox theological themes and the theological stances of ecofeminist and environmental justice thought; Rasmussen, *Earth Community, Earth Ethics,* 238–42.

5. Townes, *In a Blaze of Glory,* 55.

6. United Church of Christ, *Toxic Wastes in the United States.* For commentary on its impact, see Gottlieb, *Environmentalism Unbound,* 57–58; Miller-Travis, "Social Transformation through Environmental Justice"; Bullard, *Dumping in Dixie,* 113–14; Moody, "Caring for Creation: Environmental Advocacy by Mainline Protestant Organizations"; Marable, "Environmental Justice: The Power of Making Connection." A recent update to the report has just been released.

7. For example, see Bakken, Gibb Engel, and Engel, *Ecology, Justice, and Christian Faith,* 22.

8. See Riley, "Ecology Is a Sistah's Issue Too: The Politics of an Emergent Afrocentric Ecowomanism."

9. Hoyt, "Environmental Justice and Black Theology," 171.

10. Baker-Fletcher, *Sisters of Dust, Sisters of Spirit*, 57.

11. Tinker, "Ecojustice and Justice: An American Indian Perspective," 180, 185.

12. Townes, *In A Blaze of Glory*, 60, 66.

13. "If one cares about vulnerable human beings worldwide then sustainable development, with its simultaneous emphasis on environmental health as the basis of the economy, becomes an explicitly Christian concern. . . . Matthew 25.35–40 provides, in my opinion, one of the strongest bridges between simultaneously caring for the poor and for the environment. . . . Feeding the poor requires utmost attention to their fragile life support system." Guelke, "Looking for Jesus in Environmental Ethics," 130–31.

14. An example at once inspiring and cautionary is Martinus Daneel's *African Earthkeepers*. Daneel glories in the dual character of a religious mission that at once reclaims indigenous spirituality and replants indigenous species—a mission he presents as a theological extension of Zimbabwe's war for independence. The "war of the trees" redeems both land and inhabitants from colonial rule, reestablishing the communion of people and land. The cautionary question is: What distinguishes this from eco-fascism? Bellicose metaphors can be dangerous, especially given the way Zimbabwe's own Robert Mugabe has pillaged the rhetoric of African liberation for his own land repossessions.

15. Mark Wallace has also observed a strategic similarity between what he terms "anti-toxics" campaigners and deep ecologists: both groups have a "shared connectional worldview [that] is holistic in its vision of all life as codependent and interconnected." See Wallace, *Finding God in the Singing River*, 66–80 (quoted at 76). See also his "Environmental Justice, Neopreservationism, and Sustainable Spirituality."

16. Read part of the story in the January–February 1988 edition of *Mother Earth News*. See also Krueger, "The History of the NACCE."

17. For more of the story of 1987 and after, see Kearns, "Saving the Creation: Religious Environmentalism"; Lucas, "Eleventh Commandment Fellowship"; Muratore, "The New 'Teilhard' at the NACCE: Thomas Berry, the 'New Story' at the Battle for the Christian Mind."

18. See the NACCE website: http://nacce.org/index.html.

19. Kearns sees creation spirituality splitting from stewardship theologians, but she misses the subsequent dissolution of ecojustice from stewardship, and so allows a conservative-revisionist typology to dictate her interpretation.

20. For the rest of this chapter, the capitalized appearance of "Eastern" or "Orthodox" will refer to Eastern Orthodoxy.

21. For a Syriac exception, see Robert Murray on stewardship in Ephrem: "The Ephremic Tradition and the Theology of the Environment."

22. Contributing to the ambiguity within the Eastern Orthodox response may have been the strange status of one self-identifying Orthodox group with uncertain relationship to ecclesiastical communion: the Eleventh Commandment Fellowship from the Holy Order of MANS. See Lucas, "Eleventh Commandment Fellowship."

23. Fox, *Creation Spirituality*, xi. Ecofeminist connections of environmental justice and ecological spirituality lend some credence to Fox's claim, and further attest

to their shared strategy. The connections are evident in Karen Baker-Fletcher, *Sisters of Spirit, Sisters of Dust*. Recently, Sarah McFarland Taylor has made them richly clear in her description of the legacies of Thomas Berry and feminist thought in the emergence of environmentally activist Catholic religious women; *Green Sisters*, esp. 23–43. See chapter 12 for further comment on the significance of ecofeminist and womanist thought for environmental theology. Leonard Boff, by contrast, pursues a creation spirituality approach from the conventional liberation theology commitment to think from the cry of the "third-world" oppressed, thus implying that creation spirituality commitments may address alienations shared beyond privilege and power. See Boff, *Cry of the Earth, Cry of the Poor*; and *Ecology and Justice*, especially 104–14. Compare with an ecofeminist theology also from Brazil; Ivone Gebara, *Longing for Running Water*.

24. Berry, *The Dream of the Earth*, 130. See also Berry et al., *Befriending the Earth*.

25. Rohr, "Christianity and the Creation," 153.

26. Fox, *The Coming of the Cosmic Christ*, 133.

27. Fox, *Creation Spirituality*, 13.

28. Berry, *The Dream of the Earth*, 130–31.

29. Fox, *Coming of the Cosmic Christ*, 202. See also Fox, *Creativity: Where the Divine and Human Meet*.

30. Fox, *Original Blessing*, 299.

31. See Boff, *Cry of the Earth, Cry of the Poor*, 135–39.

32. Fox, *Creation Spirituality*, 10, 13 (my emphasis).

33. Fox, *Original Blessing*, 299

34. See Northcott, *The Environment and Christian Ethics*, 154–65; McFague, *The Body of God*, 69–73.

35. Not all sacramental approaches to environmental theology fit the strategy of ecological spirituality. For example, John Hart's *Sacramental Commons* draws on the theological resources of sacrament to elaborate conditions for creation's integrity, thus fitting his Christian environmental ethics into an ecojustice strategy.

36. Irwin, "The Sacramentality of Creation and the Role of Creation in Liturgy and Sacraments," 69–71, 87–89 (quoted at 69).

37. Toolan, *At Home in the Cosmos*, 32–40, 210–19; Mick, *Liturgy and Ecology in Dialogue*.

38. Lathrop, *Holy Ground*, 89, 70.

39. Habgood, "A Sacramental Approach to Environmental Issues," 47.

40. Habgood, "A Sacramental Approach to Environmental Issues," 51; Cf. Ruether, *Gaia and God*, 229–53; and Hill, *Christian Faith and the Environment*, 123–54.

41. Grey, *Sacred Longings*, 86.

42. It is here that Simon Oliver's otherwise fertile suggestions for sacramental creativity leave us uncertain; see Oliver, "The Eucharist before Nature and Culture."

43. Grey, *Sacred Longings*, 95.

44. Habgood, "A Sacramental Approach to Environmental Issues," 50–51. See also Habgood, *The Concept of Nature*, 154–57.

45. Murphy, *At Home on Earth*, 16, 82–83, 92–97.

46. Several ecofeminist theologians, whose works are especially attentive to the danger of despotic false orders, suggest that proper pictures of nature emerge through creative practices that critique the relation between environmental and female exploitations. See, for example, Eaton, "Ecological-Feminist Theology: Contributions and Challenges"; Primavesi, "Ecology and Christian Hierarchy."

47. Lathrop, *Holy Ground*, 17–20, 217–18.

48. Pugh, *Entertaining the Triune Mystery*. For Pugh, that means genetic engineering might be permitted as an appropriate performance of the human role of "created co-creator," but regulated by theological virtues of neighbor-love and prophetic justice (see 149–68).

49. Haught, *The Promise of Nature*, 7.

50. Hefner, *The Human Factor*.

51. See Haught, *The Promise of Nature*, 32–42, 65; Pugh, *Entertaining the Triune Mystery*, 67–69, 149–60; Hefner, *The Human Factor*, 27–43.

52. Ruether, *Gaia and God*, 229.

53. Kaufman, "The Theological Structure of Christian Faith and the Feasibility of a Global Christian Ethic," 157. Cf. Bracken, *The Divine Matrix*, 1–5.

54. Ruether, *New Woman, New Earth*, 83.

55. Keller, *Face of the Deep*, 7.

56. Keller, *Face of the Deep*, esp. 168–217.

57. Primavesi, *Sacred Gaia*, 60–61, 114–20, 143.

58. Her logic here recalls gift-exchange, perhaps explaining her turn to gift in a subsequent book—and hinting how that book's proposals might be made still better. Primavesi, *Gaia's Gift*, 112–35.

59. Ruether, *New Woman, New Earth*, 83.

60. Haught, *The Promise of Nature*, 102, 106. Haught says that human creativity can be "a self-disclosure of the cosmos" (53).

61. Hefner, "Nature, God's Great Project," 340.

62. Gebara, *Longing for Running Water*, 67.

63. Pugh, *Entertaining the Triune Mystery*, 173.

64. Cf. Horne, "Divine and Human Creativity," 138.

65. Ruether, *New Woman, New Earth*, 194–95.

66. Bratton, "Ecofeminism and the Problem of Divine Immanence/Transcendence," 31.

67. Gebara, *Longing for Running Water*, 183.

68. See Donald Worster on the paradox of the human in Gaia theory; Worster, *Nature's Economy*, 379–86.

69. This is Bill McKibben's worry in *The Comforting Whirlwind* and *The End of Nature*.

70. Henning engages process thought with environmental ethics in order to produce considered answers to these questions. For him a "kalogenic" cosmos produces a "kalocentric" ethic with obligations toward protecting and intensifying beauty, harmony and experience, as generators of good. See Henning, *The Ethics of Creativity*.

71. Teilhard, *The Phenomenon of Man*, 31, 236, 238.

72. Teilhard, *The Phenomenon of Man*, 237.

73. Teilhard, *Le Phenomene Humain*, 278 (my translation).

74. In du Lubac's summary; see du Lubac, *Teilhard De Chardin*, 48.

75. Teilhard, quoted by du Lubac, *Teilhard de Chardin*, 123.

76. Teilhard, quoted by du Lubac, *Teilhard de Chardin*, 153.

77. Teilhard, *Christianity and Evolution*, 31.

78. Polkinghorne, "Kenotic Action and Divine Action."

79. Peacocke, "The Cost of New Life."

80. Barbour, *Nature, Human Nature, and God*, 104–17, 126.

81. Keller, *Face of the Deep*, esp. 117. However, as Sarah Coakley shows, the kenotic alternative for describing God's activity within creation often assumes an agonistic view of freedom, in which God's presence restricts or constrains creatures. If creatures really are dependent on God, she argues, God's activity should increase creaturely freedom, not threaten it. See Coakley, "Kenosis," 3–39.

82. Palmer, *Environmental Ethics and Process Thinking*, 212–23.

83. Northcott, *The Environment and Christian Ethics*, 125–26. Teilhard wrote that to choose against realizing the promise of technology for redirecting evolution would be to act against nature itself. See Teilhard de Chardin, *The Phenomenon of Man*, 252–53.

84. French, "Subject-Centered and Creation-Centered Paradigms in Recent Catholic Thought," 59.

85. Du Lubac, *Teilhard De Chardin*, 31–42.

86. See Coakley, "Kenosis."

87. Scott, *A Political Theology of Nature*, 204–26.

88. Edwards, *A Theology of the Creator Spirit*, 34–46, 107–12.

89. Moltmann, *The Spirit of Life*, 95, 157, 176–79. Moltmann's metaphor of Spirit as *Lebensraum* is particularly felicitous, for it draws together the usual German term for wildlife habitat with life-granting moments of the Holy Spirit. For more suggestions on the association of Spirit and habitat, see Rogers, *After the Spirit*, esp. 149.

90. Other ecological meditations on the Spirit include Wallace, *Fragments of the Spirit*; Limouris, *Come, Holy Spirit, Renew the Whole Creation*; Johnson, *Women, Earth, and Creator Spirit*; Barbour, *Nature, Human Nature, and God*, 36, 125–26; Pannenberg, "The Doctrine of the Spirit and the Task of a Theology of Nature."

91. Edwards, *A Theology of the Creator Spirit*, 179.

92. See, for example, Gebara, *Longing for Running Water*, 50; Primavesi, "Ecology and Christian Hierarchy."

93. Although John Milbank dismisses her proposals as a "morass" of "American Green leisure theology," Milbank's own theological poietics lends itself toward a similar strategy of ecological spirituality. See his chapter, "Out of the Greenhouse," in Milbank, *The Word Made Strange*, 263. Cf. McFague, *Super, Natural Christians*, 118–75; McDaniel, *With Roots and Wings*, 215.

94. Cf. Moltmann, *God for a Secular Society*, 97; and Moltmann, *The Spirit of Life*, 7–10.

95. On connection of the Holy Spirit to ecological creativity, see Primavesi, *Sacred Gaia*, 60.

96. Wilkinson (ed.), *Earthkeeping in the Nineties*, 304–5.

97. Pugh, *Entertaining the Triune Mystery*, 173.

98. Du Lubac, *Teilhard de Chardin*, 49.

99. Fox, *Coming of the Cosmic Christ*, 102–3, 173, 210–12.

100. See, for example, how Elizabeth Theokritoff carefully repositions the Orthodox approach to environmental issues in Theokritoff, "Orthodoxy and the Environment."

101. Laurel Kearns fails to notice this missed opportunity because she too sees the Orthodox as simply conservative, aligned with the Evangelicals. That the Orthodox did not subsequently join the Evangelical Environmental Network suggests significant differences between the two. Kearns, "Saving the Creation: Religious Environmentalism." See the criticisms rehearsed in environmental context in Grdzelidze, "Creation and Ecology: How Does the Orthodox Church Respond to Ecological Problems?"

102. Tataryn writes: "In the Eastern tradition, the salvation of the cosmos is intrinsic to the saving work of Christ for the human race. Consequently, the Eastern Churches have a significant contribution to make in today's concern with environmental issues." See Tataryn, "The Eastern Tradition and the Cosmos," 41. This view is extensively described in Keselopoulos, *Man and the Environment*.

103. Oleksa shows how the doctrine of deification supports cultural and environmental support for the native ways of Alaskan peoples. See Oleksa, *Orthodox Alaska*.

104. For example, Sigurd Bergmann develops a liberatory approach to creation through Eastern pneumatology, while John Chryssavgis meditates on environmental issues under the aspect of icons. See: Bergmann, *Geist, Der Natur Befreit*; Chryssavgis, "The World of the Icon and Creation" and *Beyond the Shattered Image*, esp. 5–12.

105. His environmental sermons and papers are collected in Chryssavgis (ed.), *Cosmic Grace & Humble Prayer: The Ecological Vision of the Green Patriarch Bartholomew I.*

106. Sherrard, *The Rape of Man and Nature*, 25.

107. Patriarch Ignatius IV of Antioch, "Three Sermons on the Environment: Creation, Spirituality, Responsibility," 1.

108. Patriarch Ignatius IV, "Three Sermons on the Environment: Creation, Spirituality, Responsibility," 5, 14.

109. See Zizioulas, "Man the Priest of Creation: A Response to the Ecological Problem"; Zizioulas, "Preserving God's Creation: Three Lectures on Theology and Ecology"; Gregorios, *The Human Presence*, 70–71; Ware, "Who Is Man?"

110. Zizioulas, *Being as Communion*, esp. 62–64; Cf. Nesteruk, *Light from the East*, 119–22.

111. Guroian, *Ethics after Christendom*, 166.

112. Zizioulas, "Ecological Asceticism: A Cultural Revolution," 25; Cf. Chryssavgis, "The Beatitudes and the Beauty of the World" and "The World of the Icon and Creation."

113. Even, and perhaps especially, by simple gardening; see Guroian *The Fragrance of God*, 84.

114. Ruether, *Integrating Ecofeminism, Globalization, and World Religions*, 125; Ruether, "Ecofeminism: The Challenge to Theology," 107–8; Peacocke, *Paths from Science toward God*, 154; Moltmann, *Science and Wisdom*, 148–53; Fox, *Coming of the Cosmic Christ*, 21–22, 83–85.

115. Primavesi, "The Recovery of Wisdom: Gaia Theory and Environmental Policy"; Sherrard, *Human Image, World Image*, 175–78; also Sherrard, *Christianity: Lineaments of a Sacred Tradition*, 230–31; Deane-Drummond, *Creation through Wisdom*; Deane-Drummond, "The Feminine Face of God as a Metaphor for Ecotheology"; Deane-Drummond, *The Ethics of Nature*.

116. Deane-Drummond, *The Ethics of Nature*, 21, 214–32.

117. Edwards, *Jesus the Wisdom of God*, 69; Cf. Deane-Drummond, *Creation through Wisdom*, 233–48.

118. Considering biblical Wisdom in light of Deep Ecology, see Dell, "Green Ideas in the Wisdom Tradition."

119. Deane-Drummond, *The Ethics of Nature*, 22.

120. Gunton also suggests that Wisdom can help heal the disjuncture between createdness and redemption (which we saw diagnosed by Oliver Davies in chap. 1). See Gunton, "Christ, the Wisdom of God: A Study in Divine and Human Action."

121. Keller, *Face of the Deep*, 219. Wisdom also appears on the last page of Keller's "Postmodern 'Nature,' Feminism and Community."

122. Keller, *Face of the Deep*, 231.

123. Keller, *Face of the Deep*, 56.

124. Merton, *Witness to Freedom*, 4–6.

125. Deane-Drummond, *Creation through Wisdom*, 238–39.

CHAPTER 6

1. Ten years ago, a bibliographic survey found only three works explicitly utilizing Thomas, and there have been only a handful since; see Bakken, Gibb Engel, and Engel, *Ecology, Justice, and Christian Faith*. Among them, we will encounter Matthew Fox's interpretation along the way. William French uses Thomas to support a Catholic ecojustice ethic, with approval for Leopold's land ethic; see French, "Catholicism and the Common Good of the Biosphere." Recently Celia Deane-Drummond has developed her Wisdom-focused theological virtue ethic through Thomas; see Deane-Drummond, *The Ethics of Nature*. Louke Van Wensveen, in *Dirty Virtues*, develops a Thomist-inspired environmental virtue ethic, and shows how Thomas Berry uses and revises Thomist thought. See also Northcott, *Environment and Christian Ethics*, 226–58, 265–75; and Schaefer, "Thomas Aquinas." Not yet published at the time of writing, Robert L. Grant's *A Case Study in Thomistic Environmental Ethics* promises a "eudaimonistic ecoregionalism" developed in relation to a specific place, the Loess Hills of Iowa.

2. Santmire seems briefly intrigued by possibilities in Aquinas, but then turns away because of those two sins. See Santmire, *The Travail of Nature*, 85–95.

3. Sections of these two chapters are adapted from Jenkins, "Biodiversity and Salvation: Thomistic Roots for Environmental Ethics." However, the argument here and in the next chapter proceeds by a different tack than first appeared in that article. For a robust complaint about my article see Benzoni, "Thomas Aquinas and Environmental Ethics."

4. See Kerr, "'Real Knowledge' or 'Enlightened Ignorance': Eric Mascall on the Apophatic Thomisms of Victor Preller and Victor White." See also Kerr, *After Aquinas*, 35–52.

5. *Summa Contra Gentiles* [*SCG*] II.2; *Summa Theologiae* [*ST*] I.12.13 *ad* 1. A note on citations and translations of Thomas Aquinas: Citations from the *SCG* and other books will refer to book and chapter (II.2). Citations from the *ST* will be in the form: part, question, article, and sometimes paragraph (hence a reference to Part 1, Question 12, Article 13, in the response to objection 1 appears as I.12.13 *ad* 1). Quotations follow the English translations cited in the bibliography (most available from the InteLex Past Masters database), except where I note that I have made my own translation from the Latin texts cited in the bibliography, all of which are available from the *Corpus Thomisticum* database, www.corpusthomisticum.org.

6. Milbank and Pickstock, *Truth in Aquinas*, 34.

7. "Precisely if a science is the more Aristotelian the more it attends to its real and propositional first principles, sacred doctrine is the more Aristotelian the more it attends to revelation—both as propositional and as real." Rogers, *Thomas Aquinas and Karl Barth*, 17–31, 53–57 (quoted at 55).

8. Rogers, *Thomas Aquinas and Karl Barth*, 30.

9. See *De Doctrina Christiana* for his classical explanation.

10. Davies does not argue this point specifically, but I have been influenced here by his semiotic investigations; see Davies, "The Sign Redeemed: A Study in Christian Fundamental Semiotics." Cf. Aertsen, *Nature and Creature*, 230, 249–51.

11. Pieper, *Guide to Thomas Aquinas*, 44–46.

12. See Rogers, *Thomas Aquinas and Karl Barth*, 21–70.

13. Kerr, *After Aquinas*, 30.

14. Kerr, *After Aquinas*, 31.

15. For its role in grounding natural theology, Barth (in)famously called the Thomist *analogia entis* "antichrist" in the preface to *Church Dogmatics* I.1.

16. *ST* II-II.83.10 *ad* 3

17. See, e.g., Plumwood, "Nature, Self, and Gender: Feminism, Environmental Philosophy, and the Critique of Rationalism," 155–57.

18. Regenstein, *Replenish the Earth*, 72–74.

19. Marshall, *Christology in Conflict*, 176–89.

20. In reference to Wittgenstein's quip, "If a lion could speak, we would not be able to understand it," in *Philosophical Investigations* sec. 561. Cf. Bowlin, "Nature's Grace: Aquinas and Wittgenstein on Natural Law and Moral Knowledge," 164–66.

21. "Creation in the creature is nothing but a certain relation to the Creator [*creatio in creatura non sit nisi relatio quaedam ad creatorem*] as to the principle of its being." *ST* I.45.3 (my translation).

22. See Aertsen, *Nature and Creature*, 358–60.

23. Burrell, "Analogy, Creation, and Theological Language," 86.

24. *ST* I-II.109.3 (my translation).

25. Wippel argues that Thomas occasionally does explain the metaphysics of creatureliness without presuming prior knowledge of the existence of God. See Wippell, *The Metaphysical Thought of Thomas Aquinas*.

26. "In the coming of creatures from the first principle, there is a circling or gyration [*circulatio vel regiratio*], as it were, since all things return as to their to that from which they came as from their principle." *In. Sent.* 14.2.2 (my translation). On the *exitus–reditus* movement in the *Summa Theologiae*, see Chenu, *Toward Understanding Saint Thomas*, 311–14. Pieper sees the *Summa* repeating the circular, gyrative movement of creation and return; see Pieper, *Guide to Thomas Aquinas*, 101–2.

27. *ST* I.59.1

28. *ST* I.22.4. See also *SCG* III.69–70. Elsewhere, Aquinas writes: "For the first cause lends from the eminence of its goodness not only that other things are, but also that they are causes," *De Veritate* 11.1, quoted in Baldner and Carroll, *Aquinas on Creation*, 53.

29. I can only note here the importance of this noncompetitive double causality for explaining free, contingent creaturely action. The logic supports the intelligibility of salvation and arguably western science too. A few helpful commentators here include Burrell, *Knowing the Unknowable God*; Torrance, *Divine and Contingent Order*; Dupre, *Passage to Modernity*; Tanner, *God and Creation in Christian Theology*; Aertsen, *Nature and Creature*; Carroll, "Aquinas and the Metaphysical Foundations of Science."

30. In the case of rivers, the genus "life-practice" extends itself metaphorically, yet Thomas gives us reason to believe that so long as our speech includes reference to "healthy" or "wild" rivers, we retain a sense of what rivers properly "do." So too probably for such as oceans, plate tectonics, and climate systems.

31. *ST* III.2.1

32. Bowlin, "Nature's Grace: Aquinas and Wittgenstein on Natural Law and Moral Knowledge," 157.

33. *ST* I.44.4 *ad* 3 (my translation).

34. See Blanchette, *The Perfection of the Universe according to Aquinas*, 95.

35. *ST* I.44.4 (my translation). In his *Compendium of Theology*, Thomas says, "All movements and operations of every being are seen to tend to what is perfect . . . the perfection of anything is its goodness. Hence every movement and action of anything whatever tend toward good. . . . Therefore the movement and action of all things tend toward assimilation with the divine goodness" (I.1.103).

36. Williams, *The Ground of Union*, 65. Thomas, in *On the Divine Names* [*DDN*], in Matthew Fox's limpid translation:

> God, who is the cause of all, on account of an excess of the goodness that is God's own, loves all things. And from love God makes all things, giving them being. And perfects all things by filling them individually with their own perfections. . . . And God converts all things, that is, God orders them

toward Godself as toward an end. . . . For out of the love of God's own goodness . . . God wished to pour forth and share the divine goodness with others, as far as was possible, namely, through the mode of likeness, with the result that the divine goodness not only remained in God, but also flowed out to other things. (Quoted in Fox, *Sheer Joy: Conversations with Thomas Aquinas on Creation Spirituality*, 108)

37. *ST* 1.44.1. My strained translation tries to indicate how Thomas uses perfection language.

38. Williams, *The Ground of Union*, 49.

39. Aertsen, *Nature and Creature*, 128–31, 363–64.

40. Milbank and Pickstock, *Truth in Aquinas*, 9–10 (original italics).

41. *ST* I.103.2

42. Baldner and Carroll, *Aquinas on Creation*, 26, 48–53.

43. *Comp. Theol.* I.103.

44. "Things which are in themselves different may be considered as one, according as they are ordained to one common thing," *ST* 1-II.93.1.

45. *ST* I.47.1 (my translation). "Since the divine goodness could not be adequately represented by one creature alone, on account of the distance that separates each creature from God, it had to be represented by many creatures, so that what is lacking to one might be supplied by another" (*Comp. Theol.* 1.102). See also *ST* II-II.83.2.

46. *SCG*, II.35 (my translation). Blanchette, *The Perfection of the Universe*, 91–93.

47. "It [integrity] presupposes not only a plurality of parts but also a certain diversity among them, as in a well-articulated, or integral, organism." Blanchette, *The Perfection of the Universe*, 107. See *ST* I-II.93.1.

48. Bowlin, "Nature's Grace: Aquinas and Wittgenstein on Natural Law and Moral Knowledge," 158.

49. *SCG* III.94

50. See Blanchette, *The Perfection of the Universe*, 118–22.

51. Blanchette, *The Perfection of the Universe*, 125.

52. In I *Sentences*, 44.1.2 *ad* 6 (quoted in Blanchette, *Perfection of the Universe*, 126–27).

53. Blanchette, *The Perfection of the Universe*, 125.

54. *SCG* II.44 (quoted in Blanchette, *The Perfection of the Universe*, 125).

55. *ST* II-II.26.3

56. This discipline, says Michel Bastit, lets theology rediscover the "consistency of nature and the specificity of each being in its proper act" that is salvation's subject and patient. See Bastit, "Le thomisme est-il un aristotelisme?" 116 (my translation).

57. Rogers, *Thomas Aquinas and Karl Barth*, 48–49. Cf. Jordan, *The Alleged Aristotelianism of Thomas Aquinas*.

58. French, "Beast-Machines and the Technocratic Reduction of Life," 37. French goes on: "The same metaphysical model Thomas uses to stress hierarchical gradations of value linked to the scale of being also, at other points, leads Thomas to highlight continuities and linkages throughout a conjoined cosmos pulsing with life and sustained by God's energy and love."

59. As we will soon see, even Karl Barth's pessimism affirmed this much, though he remained polemically chary of allowing it much normative implication.

60. See *ST* I.12.1. Also:

> The end of the intellectual creature, to be achieved by its activity, is the complete actuation of its intellect by all the intelligibles for which it has a potency. In this respect it will become most like to God. For many things are quite beyond the reach of the senses. We can have but a slight knowledge of such things through information based on sense experience. We may get to know that they exist, but we cannot know what they are, for the natures of immaterial substances belong to a different genus from the natures of sensible things and excel them, we may say, beyond all proportion. . . . Accordingly we reach our last end when our intellect is actualized by some higher agent than an agent connatural to us, that is, by an agent capable of gratifying our natural, inborn craving for knowledge. So great is the desire for knowledge within us that, once we apprehend an effect, we wish to know its cause . . . our natural desire for knowledge cannot come to rest within us until we know the first cause, and that not in any way, but in its very essence. (*Comp. Theol.* 1.103–5)

61. *ST* I.12.2

62. On the contested career of that phrase, see du Lubac's groundbreaking *Surnaturel*, published in two books: *Augustinianisme et Theologie Moderne* and *Le Mystere du Surnaturel*.

63. *ST* I.1.1

64. *ST* III.9.3

65. The way of putting things in this paragraph and the following relies on Henri du Lubac and Eugene Rogers.

66. *ST* I.1.8 *ad* 2

67. Rogers, "Faith and Reason Follow Glory," 244.

68. *ST* I.12.1–2

69. *ST* 1.1.9: "It is natural to man to attain to intellectual truths through sensible objects, because all our knowledge originates from sense. Hence in Holy Writ spiritual truths are fittingly taught under the likeness of material things." On the distinction from angels: *ST* I.50.1–2; I.54–59.

70. *SCG* IV.55 (my translation).

71. See Burrell, "Analogy, Creation, and Theological Language," 77–80.

72. *ST* I.13.3; cf *ST* I.4.2. See Burrell, *Knowing the Unknowable God* , 51–61.

73. Ralph M. McInerny warns against "a confusion of the logical and the ontological," allowing simplistic analogies of being based on some steady proportion between God and creation. We can heed that warning through the asymmetrical yet nonarbitrary analogical vocabulary of excess and goodness worked out in the previous section on creation's integrity. See McInerny, *Aquinas and Analogy*, 160–63. Wippel points us to *1 Sent.* 35.14, arguing that were the relationship arbitrary, it would upset God's knowledge of creatures through God's self-knowledge; see Wippell, *The Metaphysical Thought of Thomas Aquinas*, 517–18, 551.

74. *ST* I.13.1

75. *ST* I.13.2

76. Rogers, "Faith and Reason Follow Glory," 445.

77. *ST* I.12.4: "the knowledge of every knower is ruled according to its own nature."

78. *ST* I.12.13 *ad* 1 (my translation).

79. Burrell, "Analogy, Creation, and Theological Language." For Burrell, this excessive possibility to analogical attribution presupposes its formation by ecclesial practices; see also Burrell, "Religious Life and Understanding: Grammar Exercised in Practice," 125–31. Cf. Hauerwas, "Connections Created and Contingent: Aquinas, Preller, Wittgenstein, and Hopkins," 87–89.

80. *ST* I.1.1. See Wippell, *The Metaphysical Thought of Thomas Aquinas*, 512–13.

81. Since "the knowledge of God is the cause of all things," then "natural things are midway between the knowledge of God and our knowledge. . . . Hence, as natural objects of knowledge are prior to our knowledge, and are its measure, so, the knowledge of God is prior to natural things, and is the measure of them" (*ST* I.14.8).

82. Fergus Kerr maintains that "reading the fourth gospel in tandem with the works of Aristotle, it seems . . . that he wanted the relatively down to earth 'empiricist' epistemology in place precisely to highlight the extraordinary nature of the consummation of the human mind in the eschatological gift of 'deiforming' nature." Kerr, "Aquinas after Marion," quoted in Nichols, *Discovering Aquinas*, xx.

83. *ST* I.12.3–5. "Accordingly if God is to be known as He is, in His essence, God Himself must become the forms of the intellect knowing Him" (*Comp. Theol.* I.105).

84. Knowing things by God's vision may be found in *ST* I.12.13 *ad* 3.

85. *Per hoc enim lumen fit creatura rationalis deiformis* (I.12.5 *ad* 3). See Williams, *The Ground of Union*, 42–47.

86. I find "deiform" appearing in only one other article in the *Summa*: III.36.1. See I-II.110.3 and III.1.2 for similar language about participating in the divine nature.

87. *De Virt.* 2.13, n. 64. For summary and commentary of recent writing on Thomist epistemology, see Miner, "Recent Work on Thomas in North America: Language, Anthropology, Christology."

88. *ST* I.16.1

89. Rogers, "Faith and Reason Follow Glory," 447. I borrow the term "courteously" from Rogers, who takes it from Julian of Norwich to translate Thomas's phrase *et disponit omnia suaviter*.

90. *ST* I.13.2

91. Milbank and Pickstock, *Truth in Aquinas*, 12.

92. *ST* I.1.3

93. Milbank and Pickstock, *Truth in Aquinas*, 12. Milbank and Pickstock describe how the hermeneutic circularity of creation repeats within the moment of sanctifying grace the movement of the *exitus–reditus* cosmology: "[Creaturely] goods can only be understood as good in their pointing away from themselves to the perfection they hint at. . . . That which clinches his exposition of the divine attributes is neither the ascent from affect to first cause nor the *a priori* grasp of the latter, but rather the (Dionysian) reading of the divine signs and symbols as disclosed in the hierarchies of participating

creatures. Such an hermeneutic space is . . . highly elusive and unstable, since it is grounded neither in firm *a posteriori* evidences, nor in solid *a priori* necessities" (30). Says Thomas: "And, just as creatures would be imperfect if they proceeded from God and were not ordained to return to God, so, too, their procession from God would be imperfect unless the return to God were equal to the procession. . . . Thus, it is necessary for the most excellent created intellects to know God, so that their knowledge be equal to the procession of creatures from God" (*Disputed Questions on Truth*, II.20.4).

94. Wonder at created things may attract our inquiring desire toward their cause, which we can only know finally in union with God; see *ST* I-II.3.8.

95. Kerr, *After Aquinas*, 31.

96. Fox, *Sheer Joy*, 139.

97. Williams, "Argument to Bliss: The Epistemology of the *Summa Theologiae*," 506. Williams reads the anthropology of *ST* I.84–86 in close association with *ST* I-II.109, on the necessity of grace.

98. *ST* III.23.1 *ad* 2

99. Williams, "Argument to Bliss: The Epistemology of the *Summa Theologiae*," 506.

100. On inflaming, see *SCG* II.2; on intoxication see Fox, *Sheer Joy*, 157.

101. "If creation is to proclaim God's praise and worship the Creator. . . . We can ask concerning anything that we are going to do that will affect the environment, 'Will this enhance or diminish the praise of God?' A thoughtful response to that question might be called a 'doxological impact statement.'" Murphy, *The Cosmos in the Light of the Cross*, 198.

102. In reference to Jean-Luc Marion, *Dieu sans l'etre: Hors-texte* (Paris: Librarie Artheme Fayard, 1982).

103. *SCG* III.112 (my translation, which renders *procuratae* as "governed" rather than "ruled.") Benzoni quotes this passage intending to upset my thesis, and lists other apparently anthropocentric lines from Thomas to reduce Thomas's ecological value to something like prudent exploitation; Benzoni, "Thomas Aquinas and Environmental Ethics."

104. This against Benzoni's complaint that "where Jenkins finds continuity, Thomas insists on discontinuity." I argue that Thomas divides in order to unite; and we know the theological significance of those differences from the perspective of unity. See Benzoni, "Thomas Aquinas and Environmental Ethics," 447.

105. Burrell, *Knowing the Unknowable God*, 9.

106. *SCG* III.112. Benzoni quotes this against my thesis; "Thomas Aquinas and Environmental Ethics," 454.

107. "The first perfection is found when a thing is perfect in its substance; and this perfection is the form of the whole, which arises from the integrity of the parts. . . . But the ultimate perfection, which is the end of the whole universe, is the perfect happiness of the saints. . . . The first perfection, however, which consists in the integrity of the universe, was in the first institution of things" (*ST* I.73.1; as translated by Blanchette, *The Perfection of the Universe*, 155).

108. Rowan Williams, *On Christian Theology*, 74 (here he is referring to Jacques Pohier on Thomas).

CHAPTER 7

1. Bowlin, *Contingency and Fortune in Aquinas's Ethics*, 22.

2. See chap. 3 above. "Overwrites" is Baker's own metaphor, pursuant to "a real logos of the bios" that opens the natural world to deification (personal correspondence, April 2005.) Baker's work on perfection and theurgy offers important resources for understanding how over-writing should be thought within a form of benign grace. See *Making Perfection*.

3. For a critical account of ancient and modern virtues that fortify agents against finitude, see Nussbaum, *The Fragility of Goodness*. For two contemporary accounts of virtue that show how agents claim ecological opportunities for flourishing, see Foot, *Virtues and Vices and Other Essays in Moral Philosophy*; and MacIntyre, *Dependent Rational Animals*.

4. *ST* I.96.1 *ad* 3 (my translation). The original is *Quod significatum est per hoc, quod Deus ad eum animalia adduxit, ut eis nomina imponeret, quae eorum naturas designant*. I render *experimentalem* as "empirical" in order to avoid the resonances with animal experimentation which Thomas probably did not mean.

5. *In Psalmos*, super 8. Elsewhere, again interpreting the dominion mandate of Psalm 8:5 in light of Romans 1:20, Thomas says that the higher use of creation, represented by the superfluous menagerie, continues eschatologically, so that although humans no longer need creatures, they will exist, perfected in goodness, so that our eyes may be comforted (*ST Suppl.* 91.1).

6. The phrase *naturaliter subiecta* appears in *ST* I.96.1 *resp.*

7. The *naturale desiderium* of *ST* I.12–13, discussed in chap. 6.

8. *ST* I.102.3 (my translation).

9. Referring to Thomas's reformation of virtue by charity, Milbank says that "there is also an Aristotelian gain here, over against Christian Platonism: the relationship to the divine itself is practical and rhetorical as well as theoretical, and God first has to 'teach' us, just as ethics must first be learnt from the virtuous." Milbank, *Theology and Social Theory*, 362.

10. *ST* III.60.4 (my translation).

11. *ST* II-II.81.7 (my translation).

12. See Preller, *Divine Science and the Science of God*, 268–69.

13. Preller, *Divine Science and the Science of God*, 251

14. Nichols, *Discovering Aquinas*, 158. See also Northcott, *Environment and Christian Ethics*, 227–28.

15. Schaefer, "The Virtuous Cooperator."

16. Porter, *Nature as Reason*, 54–55. Elsewhere she notes that Thomas offers resources for expanding our moral consideration to relations with the natural world, as in Porter, *The Recovery of Virtue*, 178.

17. Bowlin, *Contingency and Fortune in Aquinas's Ethics*, 17–18.

18. Porter worries that Bowlin's concept of virtue sells short the exercise of virtue for its own sake; see Porter, *Nature as Reason*, 165–66. Cf. Bowlin, *Contingency and Fortune in Aquinas's Ethics*, 136–37.

19. Nussbaum observes how for Aristotle in some cases "excellence . . . diminishes self-sufficiency and increases vulnerability." See Nussbaum, *The Fragility of Goodness*, 336. She means vulnerability to tragic luck, risk before the world, but she uses vulnerability and the phrase "fragility of the good" to argue that Aristotle exposed virtue to the world in order to regain (from Plato's Socratic legacy) certain goods available only from the world of transient natural experience. These are "relational goods," over which our flourishing does not gain absolute control yet on which it depends (343–72). We are in that way, she says, importantly akin to plants (1–8).

20. Pope, "Neither Enemy nor Friend: Nature as Creation in the Theology of Saint Thomas Aquinas." Cf. Hefner, "Can Nature Truly Be Our Friend?" and "Nature Good and Evil: A Theological Palette."

21. Contemplating creatures is "useful for building up our faith," because it "inflames the souls of humans with the love of divine goodness" (*SCG* II.2, my translation).

22. Habits are "possessed relations" internal to an agent (*ST* I.49.1–3); virtues are well-formed habits (*ST* I.55.1–2).

23. Milbank, *Theology and Social Theory*, chap. 11. Cf. Burrell and Malits, *Original Peace*.

24. Milbank, *Theology and Social Theory*, 333.

25. *ST* I.21.4 (my translation).

26. *ST* II-II.23.8

27. Milbank, *Theology and Social Theory*, 372. See also Hauerwas, *The Hauerwas Reader*, 116–41, 221–53. Hauerwas suggests that we do not read Thomas this way in part because his treatises on virtues are often abstracted from their theological context (see 40–43). Jean Porter, however, thinks that Hauerwas (and MacIntyre) undermine the unity of the virtues with socially arbitrary narratives; see Porter, *The Recovery of Virtue*, 121–26. I suggest that we agree with her demurral while clearly excluding finally heroic virtues. See Wadell, *Friends of God*.

28. Discussing Plato, Milbank says: "Without the idea of participation, a response 'appropriate to the circumstances' threatens to become something that must die with the circumstances, something dictated by the circumstances, rather than a good which the circumstances gave us occasion to realize, so revealing a new facet of the Good itself." However, the disconnection of participation and response, or contemplation and phronesis, bears defoliatory consequences; for the disruption "extended in the west to nature, and making become more and more emancipated as an autonomous realm of 'technology.'" Milbank, *Theology and Social Theory*, 354.

29. See Nussbaum, *Love's Knowledge*, 158–67, 261–85.

30. As in Milbank, *Theology and Social Theory*, 362–64.

31. *On Charity*, A.3

32. See *On Charity*, A.1–2

33. Porter, *Recovery of Virtue*, 171.

34. See *ST* I.49.3 *ad* 5.

35. Theologians therefore must be careful when loudly insisting on divine impassibility in close proximity to recoveries of Christian virtue, lest they

unintentionally recall the security-seeking of modernist virtue, restoring pagan magnanimity in Christian cloak. This may happen when description of divine participation jeopardizes the difference between human vulnerability and divine risk.

36. Hart, *The Doors of the Sea*, 101.

37. *ST* II-II.25.3. See also Schaefer, "Ethical Implication of Applying Aquinas's Notion of the Unity and Diversity of Creation to Human Functioning in Ecosystems," 226–27.

38. See Boff, *Cry of the Earth, Cry of the Poor*; de Gruchy, *Christianity, Art, and Transformation*; Gorringe, *A Theology of the Built Environment*.

39. Justice here denotes the rarer, more general sense; not interpersonal regulations among agents, but cosmic order. Justice "in this sense, is architectonic with respect to the other virtues," writes Porter (in "The Virtue of Justice," 273). If so, that means all these virtues are governed by a general frame that situates right action within an external order more comprehensive than human personhood. This justice refers to a relation of right order between part and whole, between the universe and God, amidst each creature (274).

40. *On Charity*, A.7; See Blanchette, *The Perfection of the Universe according to Aquinas*, 317–18.

41. Nichols, *Discovering Aquinas*, 101.

42. See Thomas's commentary on John's prologue; *Super Evangelium S. Ioaanis*, Prooemium. Cf. *SCG* IV.55.

43. *ST* I.93.2 *ad* 3. See Blanchette, *The Perfection of the Universe according to Aquinas*, 270–75, 295–00.

44. Blanchette, *The Perfection of the Universe according to Aquinas*, 282.

45. Blanchette, *The Perfection of the Universe according to Aquinas*, 299.

46. *ST* I.44.4 *ad* 3. Aertsen, in *Nature and Creature*, writes: "Because in man the gifts God gives to creatures come together and because man is the ultimate act of generation to which matter tends, in the union of human nature with the first Principle the entire creation comes, through a circulation, to its end." (361).

47. *ST* I.65.2

48. *ST* I-II.109.3 (my translation).

49. *De Veritate* I.2 *ad* 4; *De Verit.* II.2 *ad* 2. The soul becoming "all things" Thomas happily finds in both Aristotle (*De Anima*) and Augustine. See Fox, *Sheer Joy*, 137–39; Fox finds texts to support humanity's *capax universi*.

50. *Compendium Theologiae*, 1.1.148 (my translation).

51. Williams, "Argument to Bliss: The Epistemology of the *Summa Theologiae*," 519.

52. Milbank and Pickstock, *Truth in Aquinas*, 9.

53. See LeBlanc, "Eco-Thomism"; refer to *ST* II-II.76.4 *ad* 1.

54. See *ST* II-II.162–64.

55. See Ovitt, *The Restoration of Perfection*, 130–35, 162–63, 199–204.

56. *ST* I-II.2.1

57. *In Psalmos* 8. Note that both biblical paragraphs immediately give way to perverted uses of nature, ones that refuse to let nature be elevated by charity.

58. *ST* I-II.2.8

59. The issue of natural evils comes to us framed by evolutionary thinking; for Thomas of course it could not have been, though arguments might be made that his scientific outlook could accommodate the natural sciences after Darwin.

60. *ST* I.65.1 *ad* 2

61. *SCG* II.41

62. See *Super De Divinus Nominibus*; and commentary in Fox, *Sheer Joy*, 166–69.

63. *ST* I-II.21.1

64. *ST* II-II.25.4

65. Trying to explain natural human death, Thomas offers his *sed contra* in triplicate followed by an unusually long answer employing multiple distinctions (*ST* I-II.85.6).

66. "God neither wills evil to be done, nor wills it not to be done; but will to permit evil to be done; and this is a good" (*ST* I.19.9 *ad* 3). Cf. Carroll, "Creation, Evolution, and Thomas Aquinas," 327–30.

67. *ST* I-II.85.6; cf. Blanchette, *The Perfection of the Universe according to Aquinas*, 126–27.

68. *ST* I.49.1–2; cf *ST* I.19.9.

69. Usually discussed from the question of murder; *ST* II-II.64.7.

70. See Northcott, *The Environment and Christian Ethics*, 231.

71. See Wennberg, *God, Humans, and Animals*, 331.

72. *ST* I.22.2

73. See *ST* I.19.9. In turn human souls cannot be conformed to violence for "evil has no formal cause, rather it is a privation of form" (*ST* I.49.1).

74. "For a natural agent intends not privation or corruption, but the form to which is annexed the privation of some other form, and the generation of one thing, which implies the corruption of another" (*ST* I.19.9).

75. *ST* II-II.164.2

76. *ST* I.96.1; II-II.164.2

77. *ST* I.96.1 *ad* 2 (my translation).

78. *ST* I.104.2; see Van Nieuwehnhove, "'Bearing the Marks of Christ's Passion': Thomas' Soteriology," 281–82.

79. See Nichols, *Discovering Aquinas*, 79.

80. "Grace and virtue imitate the order of nature" (*ST* II-II.31.3).

81. Celia Deane-Drummond develops an environmental virtue ethic from Thomas, similarly drawing attention to the importance for human formation of knowing nature well. That importance derives from creation's relation to God in Wisdom, she argues, and focuses specifically on the operation of prudence. See Deane-Drummond, *The Ethics of Nature*, particularly chaps. 1, 2, and 9. For other accounts of environmental virtues and Thomas, see Van Wensveen, *Dirty Virtues*; Schaefer, "The Virtuous Cooperator"; LeBlanc, "Eco-Thomism."

82. *ST* I.103.4

83. *SCG* III.73 (my translation).

84. Francisco Benzoni disagrees with me especially here, on human concern for nonhuman goods; see "Thomas Aquinas and Environmental Ethics: A Reconsideration of Providence and Salvation," 473–76.

85. *ST* I.96.1–2

86. *ST* I.104.1–2

87. *ST* I.96.1 *ad* 3; cf. Halligan, "The Environmental Policy of Saint Thomas Aquinas," 790.

88. Blanchette, *The Perfection of the Universe according to Aquinas*, 141.

89. Note again that the rule operates this way in relation to natural evils; it would function differently for moral evils, likely ruling out the tyrannical hunting of humans for the promotion of heroism (as in Thomas's example of martyrs).

90. Gustafson, *Ethics from a Theocentric Perspective*, 45.

91. Gustafson, *Ethics from a Theocentric Perspective*, 46.

92. Cf. Gustafson, *Ethics from a Theocentric Perspective*, 53–57.

93. Blanchette, *The Perfection of the Universe according to Aquinas*, 319 (her final line, my italics).

94. *ST* I.96.2

95. See Pugh, *Entertaining the Triune Mystery*, 171; Powell, *Participating in God*, 48–50; Aertsen, *Nature and Creature*, 168–70. Aertsen and Powell both think the problem stems from insufficient trinitarian development in Thomas.

Chapter 8

1. A note on citations and translations: Quotations from Barth's *Church Dogmatics* will usually follow the English editions. They will be cited by volume/book, page number (e.g., II/2, 54). I have often modified the translations, since Barth has enough gender problems on his own without following the translators' "man" for "Mensch." Throughout I have attempted to render quotations with the more appropriate "humanity" or "humans," along with accompanying change in pronouns, and have occasionally substituted "God" for male pronouns referring to God. Where I have translated passages at any further variance from the English editions, I preface the citation with *KD* (e.g., *KD*, II/2, 54), referring to Barth, *Die Kirchliche Dogmatik*.

2. Santmire, *The Travail of Nature*, 149.

3. Gustafson, *Christ and the Moral Life*, 28–29.

4. Kehm, "The New Story: Redemption as Fulfillment of Creation," 93; Santmire, "Toward a Christology of Nature: Claiming the Legacy of Joseph Sittler and Karl Barth," 274.

5. Rolston, *Environmental Ethics*, 332. See also Kehm, "The New Story: Redemption as Fulfillment of Creation," 94–105; Santmire, *The Travail of Nature*, 152; Rasmussen, *Earth Community, Earth Ethics*, 190; and Mahan, Van Dyke, Sheldon and Brand, *Redeeming Creation*, 85–86.

6. Indinopulos, "The Critical Weakness of Creation in Barth's Theology."

7. Brueggemann, "The Loss and Recovery of Creation in Old Testament Theology"; McFague, *The Body of God*, 233 n. 6.

8. Keller, *Face of the Deep*, 84–97.

9. Moltmann, "Schöpfung, Bund und Herrlichkeit"; Welker, *Creation and Reality*.

10. III/4, 352; Busch, *Karl Barth*, 163, 187. On gender disorders in Barth, see further comment below.

11. See Santmire, *The Travail of Nature*, 155. Barth's peculiar certainty that defense of Switzerland was a definite Christian responsibility had to do with the character of its political witness, not because of its geographical character, its unique lands blessed by forms of inhabitation bearing their own sort of witness. Brueggeman's critique (below) may help explain this. Barth does say that mountains are a "supreme manifestation of earth" (III/1, 151) and Busch reports that a mountain in New Zealand has been named for Barth (see Busch, *Karl Barth*, 277).

12. For the famous exchange see, Barth and Brunner, *Natural Theology*. On the horseback rides, see Busch, *Karl Barth*, 293.

13. Fern agrees that the complaints reduce to a common concern about the effects on creation of Barth's insistence on the infinite difference of God from the world. See Fern, *Nature, God, and Humanity*, 201–210.

14. As with Thomas Aquinas in the previous chapter, my reading of Barth shows itself only indirectly as it is tested by questions from environmental ethics. I mention these three aspects in order to establish a provisional association between Barth, stewardship theology, and the strategy of moral agency.

15. To Aquinas, Barth replies that if God's being is indeed in God's act, then theological science must follow God's aseity. He writes that "only with this proviso can we think and speak realistically in a theology of the Word of God—only under the presupposition that the act-character of the reality of God on which Thomas laid so much stress is brought into play in a way completely different from the way in which Thomas appeared to do . . . the *similitudo Dei* must be given to us in every moment as something new from heaven." (McCormack, *Karl Barth's Critically Realistic Dialectical Theology*, 387.) This is what George Hunsinger calls "objectivism," and it cuts right against the soteriological integrity to creation we explored with Thomas in the previous two chapters. See Hunsinger, *How to Read Karl Barth*, 35–36.

16. For clear exposition of this corollary, see Torrance, *Divine and Contingent Order*.

17. This combines what Hunsinger identifies as "particularism" and "actualism." See Hunsinger, *How to Read Karl Barth*, 30–33, 67–90.

18. See Biggar, *The Hastening That Waits*, 7–15, 84–90.

19. On the importance of correspondence and parable, see Gorringe, *Karl Barth*, 168. See also Biggar, *The Hastening That Waits*, 76–78; and Webster, *Barth's Ethics of Reconciliation*, 185–98.

20. See II/2, §36.

21. Hunsinger (ed.), *Karl Barth and Radical Politics*, 201–4.

22. Which is to say that, for Barth, God's subjectivity grounds a kind of "biblical realism" or "christological realism."

23. See the critiques of the strategy of moral agency in chap. 2.

24. II/2, 546.

25. III/4, 4.

26. II/2, 546.

27. III/4, 4.

28. III/4, 27. Note that Barth's careful specification of the continuous material field for the ethical event appears just after an excursus on Bonhoeffer, and that III/4 begins in immediate praise for Bonhoeffer's *Ethics* (see III/4, 4, 19–23). Bonhoeffer worried early on that Barth's encounter could appear so vertically constituted that social (and ecological) dimensions of the arena disappeared. In *Sanctorum Communio*, Bonhoeffer proposed how to discover the social within the form of God's self-revelation, a project continued in *Act and Being* and later in *Ethics*. On Bonhoeffer's revision of revelational aseity in Barth, see Marsh, *Reclaiming Dietrich Bonhoeffer*, 1–33.

29. See III/2, 3–6.

30. *KD* III/4, 28 (*CD* III/4, 27).

31. "Saga" translates *die Sage*. Barth says he uses saga "in the sense of an intuitive and poetic picture of a pre-historical reality of history which is enacted once and for all within the confines of time and space" (*KD* III/1, 81, 88).

32. The second subsection title of III/1 §41.

33. "Everything that precedes only prefigures this decision and prepares for it. By its very nature it is preliminary. It points beyond itself to God's further decisions in His dealings in this theatre" (III/1, 182).

34. III/1, 181–82.

35. III/1, 144.

36. See III/1, 157.

37. *KD* III/1, 203 (*CD* III/1, 181–82).

38. *KD* III/1, 233 (*CD* III/1, 207).

39. After the peace is broken, says Barth, a new order is established, reflective of that brokenness and its suffering (III/1, 208–9).

40. III/1, 207–8, 143–44.

41. III/1, 214.

42. *KD*, III/1, 252–53 (*CD*, III/1, 221–24).

43. "Gnädenreich kein Fremdkörper"; *KD* III/1, 254 (*CD* III/1, 225).

44. III/1, 187.

45. In the command of God to bring forth provisioning vegetation, says Barth, "earth now becomes and is an active subject . . . an archetype of the capacity for obedience" (III/1, 153).

46. III/1, 288.

47. III/1, 200–205 (at 205). Barth does say that the dominion given humanity is fitting according to the divine likeness of humanity in its male–female relatedness. That, however, is no autonomous claim to dominion but the natural feature God claims in granting and commanding dominion (206). See further discussion below on problems with making sexual difference the characteristic correspondent to dominion.

48. III/1, 225.

49. Lowe, *Theology and Difference*, 143. Catherine Keller objects to Lowe's "odd affinity between a tehomic multidimensionality and Barth's anti-tehomic polemic"; Keller, *Face of the Deep*, 85.

50. In their environment, humans have all around them a "spectacle of submission to this Word" (III/1, 177). Barth suggests that ecological dependency reminds humanity of their own obedience (III/1, 207).

51. Barth says that dominion cannot legitimate an absolute human control, "with the view that such things as the tunnelling and levelling of mountains, or the drying up or diversion of rivers, cannot be described as blasphemous assault." Perhaps they are not, the Old Testament does not clearly tell us, says Barth; but dominion provides no justificatory appeal in their favor (III/1, 205–6).

52. III/1, 152.

53. III/1, 107–9, 153–68, 172–73.

54. Keller, *Face of the Deep*, 96.

55. Barth:

> The earth now becomes and is an active subject, bringing forth plants and trees as commanded. But it does not do this in its own creative power, nor as an agent side by side with the divine Word and work but because it was made worthy to hear God's fiat, and receiving it as such was enabled to do what is certainly could not have done of and by itself. It may be said that we have here an archetype of the capacity for obedience (*potentia oboedentialis*) on the part of the creature. . . . *Deshe,* vegetation is now the epitome of all that the earth was to bring forth . . . and did bring forth . . . in this capacity for obedience and act of obedience. (III/1, 153)

Throughout his exegesis of both sagas, vegetation consistently appears as a trope for the earth's freedom and God's creativity.

56. *KD* III/1, 158.

57. *Wohnsitz* is Barth's usual name for the arena of humanity's living-space, but Barth lets a gradual shift from vocabularies of *Raum* to those of *Ort* slowly redevelop the resonances of "dwelling-place."

58. III/1, 109. Barth goes on to make clear that the rejected mythical world does not judge primeval forces, but the cosmic consequences of human sin. As such, God's judgment does not lie on nature spirits, but on the disfigurement and perversion of God's good creation. It lies on human freedom, and so it lies on Christ's obedience. "And at this one point and in this one creation God is the One who is judged and suffers in the place and for the salvation and preservation of the rest of creation" (109). See also Gorringe's insistence that Barth "must be read as a tremendous affirmation of the goodness of the created order in the face of Auschwitz and the destruction of the war years" (Gorringe, *Karl Barth*, 12–13).

59. *KD* III/1, 287.

60. See III/1, 231–33, 267–69.

61. III/1, 206.

62. III/1, 228–29. See Whitehouse, "Karl Barth on the 'Work of Creation': A Reading of Church Dogmatics, III/1."

63. "Das Wesen, das um der Erde willen und um ihr zu dienen, geschaffen werden musste," *KD* III/I, 266 (*CD* III/1, 235).

64. III/1, 179.

65. III/1, 235.

66. III/1, 235.

67. *KD*, III/1, 268.

68. III/1, 237.

69. III/1, 238.

70. III/1, 237.

71. III/1, 249, 253.

72. III/I, 255. Later Barth says the imagery of water carries both senses, comparing the destruction held back by God to a catena of biblical passages in which water appears blessed, welcome, and necessary (III/1, 279–81). When he comes to baptism, however, Barth restrains his aquatics, saying "there is no theology of water as such." See, IV/4: *Baptism*, 45.

73. III/1, 280.

74. III/1, 254.

75. Compare *KD* III/1, 252–53 with *KD* III/1, 283–87.

76. III/1, 251. For contemporary place ethics, perhaps Barth suggests that authentic places participate in the paradigmatic placeness of Eden. But for the ideological dangers of Edenic environmental ethics, see Merchant, *Reinventing Eden*.

77. *KD* III/1, 284 (*CD* III/1, 251).

78. On *Lebensodem*: *odem* is archaic German for "breath," used, for example, to translate Psalm 150 in Luther's Bible. Barth's *Lebensodem* makes for a significant parallel with *Lebensraum*; see *KD* III/1, 282–83.

79. *KD*, III/1, 275 (*CD* III/1, 242).

80. III/1, 249–50.

81. III/1, 250, 60.

82. Eden is a particular locale from which we know the whole cosmos: "es wird auch hier in diesem Teil das Ganze betrachtet" (*KD* III/1, 284).

83. *KD*, III/1, 285–86. (*CD*, III/1, 250–51). "Die Aufgabe des Menschen an diesem Ort besteht darin, ihn zu bebauen und zu bewahren— wörtlich: ihn zu bedienen and zu bewachen" (*KD*, III/1, 288).

84. Barth seems particularly taken with trees of Eden, repeating their mention at every turn. When he comes to the fall, Barth implies that God removes Adam and Eve in order to protect the trees, the destruction of which would also have been the destruction of humanity (III/1, 257, 154–55).

85. *KD*, III/1, 288–89.

86. III/1, 237; see also III/1, 254.

87. III/1, 255.

88. III/4, §53–55.

89. III/4, 336. Humans receive their lives "as a divine act of trust that [they] may live . . . remembering that [they] must finally given an account of [their] stewardship and use" (III/4, 336).

90. See III/4, 324–26.

91. III/4, 337.

92. "The command of God creates respect for it" (III/4, 339).

93. III/4, 348–49.

94. III/4, 349–50.

95. *KD*, III/4, 399.

96. Er is nicht zum Herrn über die Erde, aber als Herr auf der so ausgesttaten Erde eingesetzt (*KD*, III/4, 398).

97. III/4, 351.

98. III/4, 351–52. "A really good horseman cannot really be without God [*wirklich Gottloser*]." *KD* III/4, 400 (*CD* III/4, 352).

99. III/4, 353–55 (quoted at 354).

> The slaying of animals is really possible only as an appeal to God's reconcil-
> ing grace, as its representation and proclamation . . . making use of the
> offering of an alien and innocent victim and claiming its life for ours. . . . The
> killing of animals in obedience is only possible as a deeply reverential act of
> repentance, gratitude, and praise on the part of the forgiven sinner in face of
> the One who is the Creator and Lord of man and beast. The killing of
> animals, when performed with the permission of God and by His command,
> is a priestly act of eschatological character. (III/4, 354–55)

See also III/1, 178, 209–10. For commentary see Linzey, *Animal Theology*, 54–56, 129–31.

100. III/4, 355. Vegetarianism and other forms of abstention from animal killing or suffering have their rightful place as a sign of creation's coming liberation and peace, as a protest against sinful violence. See III/4, 355–56; and Linzey, *Animal Theology*, 131.

101. III/1, 206.

CHAPTER 9

1. II/2, 509.

2. Justification, sanctification, and vocation are the titles for the three moments in which Barth treats good human action under the aspect of reconciliation; IV/1, §61; IV/2, §66; and IV/3, §71.

3. See also Webster, *Barth's Moral Theology*, 9–10, 43–48. This is the implication of what Hunsinger calls Barth's particularism, objectivism, and realism; see Hunsinger, *How to Read Karl Barth*. Bonhoeffer wanted Barth to locate the church within the form of God's self-revelation), and Barth may have eventually taken the suggestion to heart, for by volume IV the church and the Holy Spirit appear where we might have expected individual responsibility.

4. Justification, sanctification, and vocation are treated uniquely, but Barth makes clear that they are inseparable moments of God's act in Christ, not a successive series of possibilities (IV/3, 510–11).

5. III/4, 19–23. That relational setting of command within reconciliation, says David Haddorff, is the main difference from the divine command in Brunner and Bonhoeffer, for whom it appears within the doctrine of creation: "the divine command

in Barth emerges within an ongoing covenantal history between God and the moral subject structured by spheres of divine action in the creation, reconciliation, and redemption of humanity." Haddorff, "The Postmodern Realism of Barth's Ethics," 276.

6. See IV/2, 409. Notice how volume IV repeats the opening frames of III/4 (esp. 19–37).

7. Barth, *Church Dogmatics* IV/ 4, 9–12.

8. III/3, 92.

9. Barth: "Und neben seinem Wirken ist Raum für das seines Geschöpfes" (*KD* III/3, 104).

10. III/3, 76–81.

11. III/2, 166.

12. III/2, 172. "As we must say of humanity that it is what it is only in gratitude towards God, we shall have to say the same of all other creatures. They too exist as they are preserved by God's Word of grace spoken in their midst, and as they accept the validity of His promise given to them also. They too are threatened, and they too held by the Word of God . . . their being can only exist in thankfulness. They share this characteristic with us" (III/2, 172–73). III/2, 149: For the Word "has certainly been spoken to all creatures as a true and valid promise."

13. For more on the "rules" of Barth's noncompetitive doctrine of creation, see Tanner, *God and Creation in Christian Theology*; Torrance, *Divine and Contingent Order*.

14. III/3, 92, 165. Cf. Torrance, *Divine and Contingent Order*, 26–38.

15. III/2, 173.

16. "To set up of itself any effective opposition, to offer any real resistance, the creature would have to repeat the divine act of creation, approving, dividing, and calling. . . . But the creature is not God, and therefore is in no position to do this" (III/3, 77).

17. III/2, 23–25, 89.

18. In fact, it may be that the values of other creatures outshine humans in ways we are not even able to perceive. We have no way of judging those values, says Barth, and so no way of measuring ourselves against them. See III/2, 79–90.

19. See III/2, 191–92 (quote at 188).

20. III/3, 65 (*KD*, III/3, 74). Just before that statement Barth says that God preserves human creatures by preserving their context or interrelation (*Zussamenghang*) with all creatures. God uses the ecological habitat of creatures for the sake of the covenant of grace; but humans do not acquire the prerogative of that use. "It is a purely spiritual relationship in which God himself acts directly, and the creature can only point other creatures to that divine work and testify concerning it, but cannot in any way advance or mediate that work. . . . And the spiritual relationship of the creature in the covenant of grace is the dominant pattern or type of what God does when God preserves creation" (III/3, 65).

21. III/2, 188–90.

22. IV/2, 30.

23. Barth's treatment of the human creature in III/2 precisely repeats his organization in §41 and §42 of III/1 on creation and covenant: God's *creatio ex nihilo* of the real human is the "external basis" of the covenant, whose actual form is determined by the "internal form" of the covenant: the relations of God acting ad extra.

24. III/3, 217.

25. III/2, 143.

26. IV/1, 26–28. Barth notes that Christ's election perfects the work of Noah's ark (III/1, 180).

27. III/4, 654–59.

28. Cf. III/2, 224.

29. Webster, *Barth's Ethics of Reconciliation*, 80.

30. IV/1, 48.

31. The pattern is Barth's adoption of Hegelian *Aufhebung*, which by now obviously underlies Barth's successive exegetical association of divine act and created place.

32. *KD* II/2, 220 (*CD* II/2, 199).

33. *KD* IV/3, 43 (*CD* IV/3, 41), where Barth also uses neighborhood (*Nachbarschaft*), and sphere (*Bereich*).

34. *KD*, IV/2, 173 (*CD*, IV/2, 155).

35. Eugene Rogers writes: "In the election account in II/2 and all the way through the four and a half mammoth volumes of IV, God becomes human precisely in order to become vulnerable, woundable, penetrable, the object for human prying open" (private correspondence).

36. IV/1, 180–99.

37. IV/1, 206–9.

38. IV/1, 50; cf. II/2, 81–90.

39. IV/2, 398.

40. IV/1, 37.

41. III/1, 109–10.

42. Hunsinger (ed.), *Karl Barth and Radical Politics*, 187: "parabolic witness rather than direct realization."

43. Gorringe, *Karl Barth*, 171. "Build it up" of course lends stewardship a Pauline valence, analogous to the interpersonal ecclesial fellowship.

44. See how life in the Spirit allows humans to mimic Christ's dominion in IV/2, 320–67.

45. Jesus Christ is shown as Lord through his going into the place of alienation (*erweist sich in seinem Weg in die Fremde*) (*KD*, IV/1, 171).

46. IV/3, 43. See also IV/4, 15: God's ruling "is a definitely shaped and qualified action. . . . His powerful action is the great and active Yes of his free and gracious address to the world created by him, and to [humanity] who is at the heart of it."

47. IV/1, 432. See IV/1 §60 and IV/2 §65.

48. IV/4, 228.

49. See Ruether, *New Woman, New Earth*; Merchant, *Reinventing Eden*; White, "The Historical Roots of our Ecological Crisis."

50. Moltmann, "Schöpfung, Bund und Herrlichkeit"; Welker, *Creation and Reality*.

51. III/3, 48.

52. "Like every other creature [humans were] created for the glory of God and only in that way for their own salvation," (IV/1, 420).

53. IV/1, 433–35.

54. IV/3, 697; see IV/1, 409–10.

55. IV/3, 699. Cf. Bonhoeffer, *Creation and Fall*, 42–43.

56. IV/4, 228 (modified for gender).

57. IV/4, 15.

58. Cf. IV/4, 237.

59. Bonhoeffer, *Creation and Fall*, 43.

60. III/4, 22.

61. On the anarchic sociopolitical trajectories in Barth, see Hunsinger (ed.), *Karl Barth and Radical Politics*, 180–90.

62. III/1, 200–206; III/2, 291–316.

63. III/1, 184–88.

64. Cf. Gorringe, *Built Environment*, 205–10.

65. Keller, *Face of the Deep*.

66. III/4, 170–72.

67. Moltmann, "Schöpfung und Bund" and *God in Creation*, 161–62, 252–55. Female pronouns might in fact be more appropriate for Barth's image and role of humanity as servant. At least, the human response seems typologically female in Barth's gendered order. The implications for Christology can be easily exploited: Christ's journey into a far country is not only descent into creatureliness, into sin and mortality, it is a kind of transsexual crossing, from maleness to femaleness. Barth invites all sorts of similar gleeful explorations by his unfortunate insistence on a gender-coded order; despite all his protests that divine order and created order are disanalogous (e.g., IV/3, 151), he nonetheless holds the subordination of female to male in correspondence to that of humanity to God, church to Christ, and Son to Father (see III/2, 284–86).

68. Moltmann, "Schöpfung und Bund," 122 (my translation).

69. Keller helped me to see the importance of the distinction (private correspondence).

70. Scandalous in two senses: the darkening is shameful to human sin, and it renders nature a *skandalon*, a spiritual stumbling block.

71. IV/4, 123.

72. III/2, 17–19; IV/3, 149–50; IV/4, 117, 120–24.

73. IV/3, 151–52.

74. See IV/3, 47–48, 163–64. The coming of the Word puts "the knowledge of creation in indissoluble connection with the covenant" (III/2, 11).

75. IV/3, 137–38, 163–64.

76. IV/3, 164 (my emphasis).

77. Stoevesandt (ed.), *A Late Friendship*, 42. Quoted in Rogers, *Thomas Aquinas and Karl Barth*, 206.

78. Barth, *A Shorter Commentary on Romans*, 28. Thanks to Eugene Rogers for pointing me to this passage.

79. Biggar, *The Hastening That Waits*, 155; see also 52–55 for how Barth christologically determined debate over the orders of creation.

80. Tanner, "Creation and Providence," 119.

81. III/3, 41.

82. IV/1, 410.

83. III/3, 49. Cf. Moltmann, *God in Creation*, 61–63. In the view of Thomas Torrance, that christocentric frame includes the necessary conditions for *establishing* natural science, namely contingent independence and open dependence:

> The interrelation between the incarnation of the Logos and the creation of the all things visible and invisible out of nothing by that same Logos. . . . far from reducing the being and rationality of the contingent world to unreality and insignificance, establishes their reality and secures their significance. . . . That is to say, the incarnation has the constant effect of affirming the contingent intelligibility of the creation, reinforcing the requirement to accept it as the specific kind of rationality proper to the physical world, and as the only kind capable of providing evidential grounds for knowledge of the universe in its own natural processes. (Torrance, *Divine and Contingent Order*, 33–34)

Cf. Pannenberg, *Toward a Theology of Nature*, 32–33, 113.

84. Barth says that Augustine, Anselm, Luther, and Calvin could all say this: within the event of Jesus Christ, creation must be seen as grace, its secret ordination for God revealed (III/1, 29–31).

85. See IV/3, 153.

86. IV/3, 141–47.

87. IV/3, 159. The passage goes on, "when God speaks God's one and total Word concerning the covenant which is the internal basis of creation, this symphony is in fact evoked, and even the self-witness of creation in all the diversity of its voices can and will give its unanimous applause" (IV/3, 159–60; see also III/3, 45–52). Elsewhere Barth comments on the psalms of creation's praise, saying God summons nature to add its voices to Israel's praise (IV/3, 692). The particularist election of Israel elicits universal and polyphonous response. In fact. when human witness fails, says Barth. Some creaturely (especially animal) witnesses "will often speak more forcefully and impressively than all human witnesses" (III/1, 178).

88. IV/3, 147.

89. See IV/3, 592–601.

90. IV/3, 147.

91. IV/3, 148.

92. III/2, 3.

93. III/2, 12.

94. III/2, 78–79, 136–38, 147.

95. III/2, 15.

96. See Johnson, *The Mystery of God*, 71.

97. See Rogers, *Thomas Aquinas and Karl Barth,* on christocentric *scientia* in both.

98. III/2, 11.

99. III/2, 17.

100. III/2, 78.

101. II/2, 88: "Is it not necessary that we should first show who and what God is in His dealing with His creation, who and what the God is whose dealing corresponds to what does actually take place and is made known at this centre?"

102. "There is no doubt that in Jn. 1.3 (and 1.10) a cosmogenic function is ascribed to the Logos. But there is also no doubt that the Evangelist did not adopt the concept for the sake of this interpretation of it. . . . [but rather] he recalls this interpretation in order to emphasize and elucidate what he has said in vv. 1 and 2" (II/2, 97). On the connection of the Johannine prologue with the cosmological Pauline prologues, Barth again sees assurances of the priority of Christ's self-revelation (II/2, 99). Barth makes Christ's connection with "all things" serve the strength of Barth's doctrine of election. See I/1, 458–60, 506–8; III/1, 51–56; III/2, 136–37, 147; IV/1, 44–47; IV/4, 13–21.

103. For example, IV/4, 21. See also Barth's reluctance to name humans "microcosm"; III/1, 150, 208; III/2, 15, 368; III/4, 573.

104. Von Balthasar, *The Theology of Karl Barth*; McCormack, *Karl Barth's Critically Realistic Dialectical Theology*.

105. It would be interesting to read Barth's indirect way through the salvation-time of revelation into place against Martin Heidegger's late arrival to place, indirectly arrived through the timed character of Dasein. Edward Casey's chapter, "Proceeding to Place by Indirection: Heidegger," would be the place to start that comparative reading; Casey, *The Fate of Place*, 243–84.

106. Gorringe, *A Theology of the Built Environment*, 4–5.

107. Gorringe, *A Theology of the Built Environment*, 13–14, 250.

108. Scott, *A Political Theology of Nature*, 222.

109. Scott, *A Political Theology of Nature*, 233–58.

110. Brueggemann, "The Loss and Recovery of Creation in Old Testament Theology."

111. For example, Sallie McFague complains that "perhaps as far back as Luther's retreat to the self as the locus of contact between God and the world, the natural world has been considered irrelevant to theology. Only history, and only human history, has been seen as the place where God touches our reality. . . . This tradition continued into our own century with Karl Barth's insistence that the reality of creation is known in the person of Jesus Christ (creation is enclosed within redemption)"; McFague, *The Body of God*, 233 n.6. Brueggeman agrees with McFague and implicitly blames Barth for the unnecessary awkwardness of McFague's reinstatement of embodied place.

112. Santmire, *Nature Reborn*, 117.

113. See Busch, *Karl Barth*, 312.

114. De Gruchy, *Reconciliation*, 48; also 69–71.

115. IV/1, 99–101 (modified with "she").

CHAPTER 10

1. Staniloae, *The Experience of God*, vol. 1, 1.

2. Lossky, *The Mystical Theology of the Eastern Church*, 100–110; quoted at 101.

3. Schmemann, *For the Life of the World*, 11–18.

4. In this chapter and the next, all capitalized appearances of "Eastern" or "Orthodox" will refer to the Eastern Orthodox Church or its theological tradition.

5. Russell points out that deification appears athematically in the Greek fathers until the sixth century, when *theosis* is first given formal definition by

Pseudo-Dionysius: "Theosis is the attaining of likeness to God and union with him so far as is possible." Only with Maximus in the seventh century does deification become a theological topic in its own right. See Russell, *The Doctrine of Deification in the Greek Patristic Tradition*, 1.

6. *Qu.1 in Gen.*, quoted in Jules Gross, *The Divinization of the Christian according to the Greek Fathers*, 207.

7. See Russell, *The Doctrine of Deification*, 14, 262.

8. See von Balthasar, *Cosmic Liturgy*, 210–40.

9. Von Balthasar says that the dyophysite christology embodies "Maximus' conception of the world, a mystery that holds within itself the solution of all the world's riddles: the unification of God and the world, the eternal and the temporal, the infinite and the finite, in the hypostatization of a single being"; von Balthasar, *Cosmic Liturgy*, 235.

10. For evidence of how much contemporary Orthodox environmental thought takes its leave from Maximus, especially his "*logoi* in the Logos" formula, see Theokritoff, "Embodied Word and New Creation: Some Modern Orthodox Insights concerning the Material World."

11. Von Balthasar, *Cosmic Liturgy*, 235.

12. *Ambiguum 7*, in Blowers and Wilken (eds.), *On the Cosmic Mystery of Jesus Christ*, 54. Citations from Maximus will usually follow available English translations; in cases where I have done my own translation I then cite the *Patrologia Graeca* (*PG*) or *Corpus Christianorum* (*CC*).

13. Maximus quotes Ephesians 1:10 and recalls Ireneaus with the use of *anakephalaiosis*. (Note how closely recapitulation sits with Paul's use of *oikonomia*, foreshadowing the liturgical economy of Maximus's mystagogy.) *Amb. 7*, in Blowers and Wilken, 55; see also *Ad Thalassium 60*, in Blowers and Wilken, 124.

14. Thunberg, *Microcosm and Mediator*, 75–77.

15. *Amb. 41*, in Migne (ed.), *PG*, 1310a..

16. See Thunberg, *Man and the Cosmos*, 79. It also, as David Yeago points out, helps to explain how the biblical Christ is the immanent Logos in a movement of cosmic redemption: "He who apprehends the mystery of the cross and the burial apprehends the inward principles (logoi) of created things; while he who is initiated into the inexpressible power of the resurrection apprehends the purpose for which God first established everything." (Yeago, "Jesus of Nazareth and Cosmic Redemption," 163–65.)

17. "When we call the visible species and external forms of created things garments and interpret the logoi according to which they were created as flesh, we likewise [as with scripture] conceal him with the former and reveal him with the latter"—just as a body makes one present by simultaneously concealing and revealing (*Amb. 10*, quoted in Yeago, "Jesus of Nazareth and Cosmic Redemption," 183).

18. In *Amb. 10* the transfiguration of Christ illuminates the garments he wears, revealing scripture and creation as the clothing of Christ.

19. See von Balthasar, *Cosmic Liturgy*, 71–73, 146–48, 164. For a proto-Thomist interpretation of Maximus, see Garrigues, *Maxime Le Confesseur*.

20. Lossky, *Mystical Theology*, 94–99. Further: "Each being is in effect the sensible expression of a divine idea and divine intention," in Dalmais, "La theorie des 'logoi' des creatures chez Saint Maxime le Confesseur," 246 (my translation).

21. See von Balthasar, *Cosmic Liturgy*, 213–15. There are sometimes significant theological distinctions between *physis* and *ousia*; they are often used as synonyms but are sometimes used in ancient Christian thought to distinguish the individual natures subsistent in a person from a shared "substance," respectively. So too for *hypostasis* and *prosopon*; they are often used as synonyms but are sometimes used to distinguish a capacity for subjectivity from an actual person, respectively. To focus on how Maximus and then Bulgakov develop a theological relationship between the two pairs of concepts, I will use them as synonyms. But that invites controversy immediately; see note 22.

22. *Ad Thalass.* 60, PG, 209c. One might object that "*tō tēs hupostaseōs logō*" should be translated, "through the principle of the Person," interpreting hypostasis to here refer to the specific person of Christ, or more accurately, "by the structure of Christ's hypostasis," to maintain the distinction from "prosopon" (see note 21). "Logic of personhood" suggests a general anthropomorphic concept that regulates thought about the incarnation, and operates beyond it to shape theological anthropology and cosmology. In that objection lies the sort of criticism that Lossky directs at Bulgakov, indicating a "neo-patristic" suspicion of kataphatic tendencies in the philosophical theology of modern Orthodoxy. I translate the passage as I do to follow how Bulgakov interprets Maximus. "Logic of hypostaticity" or "principle of hypostasia" might be more accurate, and would come closer to what Bulgakov's sophiology engages, but I keep to the more readable "personhood" here to keep these introductory remarks on Maximus relatively clear. Thanks to Christopher Beeley for discussing the translation. Cf. the same passage in Blowers and Wilken (eds.), *On the Cosmic Mystery*, 123.

23. Quoted by von Balthasar, *Cosmic Liturgy*, 226–27; cf., 118.

24. See Thunberg, *Man and the Cosmos*, 71–74, 51.

25. *Amb.* 41 in Louth, *Maximus the Confessor*, 157–58.

26. *Amb.* 41, PG, 1308b.

27. In 1952 Dalmais stated that a study of the *logos/tropos* couple, which "becomes in the work of Maximus a universal instrument," deserves its own monograph. I believe we still await that study. Dalmais, "La theorie des 'logoi,'" 247 (my translation).

28. Cf. Yeago, "Jesus of Nazareth and Cosmic Redemption." 173–75.

29. Dalmais, "La theorie des 'logoi,'" 246.

30. See von Balthasar, *Cosmic Liturgy*, 219, 70.

31. "The result of the Fall is not that natures are distorted in themselves, but rather that natures are misused: the Fall exists at the level not of *logos*, but of *tropos*"; Louth, *Maximus the Confessor*, 57.

32. See Larchet, *La divinisation de l'homme selon Saint Maxime le Confesseur*, 141–51; Sherwood, *The Earlier Ambigua of Saint Maximus the Confessor and His Refutation of Origenism*, 164–66, 177–80.

33. *Amb.* 71, PG, 1409B. With interesting implications for Bulgakov's turn to divine kenosis and creaturely creativity in the next chapter, Maximus associates these

Wisdom texts with the Pauline theme of divine foolishness, which Maximus calls an overabundant phronesis (*hyperballousan phronēsin*).

34. *Amb.* 71 in Louth, *Maximus the Confessor*, 166.

35. *Amb.* 71; See also his *Chapters on Knowledge* in Berthold (ed.), *Maximus Confessor*, 140, 148–49. Adam Cooper writes: "The impermanence of this universe drives us on to discern the proper purpose and goal of things determined by their *logoi* whose diversity converges metaphysically and teleologically in the unity of the Logos himself." Just as a human body initially draws one's neighbor in attraction, properly onward to the fullness of one's personhood, so too the fragility of creation invites us into the mystery of the cosmos. (Cooper, *The Body in St. Maximus the Confessor*, 100.)

36. This connection of change and divinization explains why Thunberg says that Teilhard appropriates Maximian views; see Thunberg, *Man and the Cosmos*, 137.

37. Larchet, *La Divinization*, 105–7.

38. Von Balthasar, *Cosmic Liturgy*, 227.

39. Maximus speculates that perhaps the evasiveness of nature to our mastering endeavors, its facility for frustrating the efforts of our will, is more evidence of the Logos at play in creation, delighting in reminding us of our contingency and the gift-character of creation (*Amb.* 71).

40. *Ad Thalass.* 60, in Blowers and Wilken (eds.), *On the Cosmic Mystery*, 123–24.

41. See von Balthasar, *Cosmic Liturgy*, 227–29. "The relationship of the ideas to God is that of supremely free production, not that of a necessity of nature" (119).

42. Von Balthasar's exultant summary:

> His ecstatic vision of a holy universe, flowing forth, wave upon wave, from the unfathomable depths of God, whose center lies always beyond the creatures' reach; his vision of a creation that realizes itself in ever more distant echoes, until it finally ebbs away at the borders of nothingness, yet which is held together, unified, and "brought home" . . . through the ascending unities of an awestruck love; his vision of a creation dancing in the festal celebration of liturgical adoration, a single organism made up of inviolable ranks of heavenly spirits and ecclesial offices, all circling round the brilliant darkness of the central mystery. (*Cosmic Liturgy*, 58)

43. *The Church's Mystagogy*, in Berthold (ed.), *Maximus Confessor*, 86. On world as a human, see Berthold (ed.), *Maximus Confessor*, 196–97. For the garments of the transfiguration, see *Amb.* 10.

44. Evdokimov, "Nature," 12.

45. *Amb.* 41, *PG*, 1313b.

46. In their commentary, Blowers and Wilken (eds.), *On the Cosmic Mystery*, 38.

47. See Williams, "The Myths We Live By."

48. Ware, in the foreword to Staniloae, *Experience of God*, vol. 1, xxi.

49. Louth, "Recent Research on St. Maximus the Confessor: A Survey," 84. See also Miller, *The Gift of the World*, esp. chaps. 2 and 4.

50. Staniloae, *The Experience of God*, vol. 2, 1.

51. Volume 1, 1: "the two revelations are not divorced from one another." Volume 2, 1: "Eastern Christianity . . . has never conceived them separately from one another."

52. Staniloae is clear: "by 'world' both nature and humanity are understood; or when the word 'world' is used to indicate one of these realities, the other is always implied as well"; Staniloae, *Experience of God*, vol. 2, 1.

53. Bartos, *Deification in Eastern Orthodox Theology*, 131.

54. Staniloae, "Commentaires," 487. All translations from "Commentaires" are my own, from the French translation of Père Aurel Grigoras.

55. Staniloae, *Experience of God*, vol. 2, 2.

56. Staniloae, *Experience of God*, vol. 2, 2; Staniloae, "Commentaires," 328.

57. Staniloae, *Experience of God*, vol. 1, 3.

58. Staniloae, *Experience of God*, vol. 2, 55–56.

59. Staniloae, *Experience of God*, vol. 2, 55–56.

60. Staniloae, *Experience of God*, vol. 2, 60–62.

61. Staniloae, *Theology and the Church*, 201–2; Staniloae, *Experience of God*, vol. 1, 3–6, 26–36.

62. Staniloae, *Theology and the Church*, 191.

63. "The world is called to be humanized entirely . . . in a way that the human being is not called to become . . . a 'cosmicized' man. The destiny of the cosmos is found in man, not man's destiny in the cosmos." Staniloae, *Experience of God*, vol. 1, 5.

64. Staniloae, "Commentaires," 488.

65. Staniloae, "Commentaires," 375.

66. Staniloae, *Experience of God*, vol. 1, 1–13.

67. Staniloae, "Commentaires," 488.

68. Staniloae, "Commentaires," 14, 18–19 (my emphasis).

69. Staniloae, *Experience of God*, vol. 1, 4. Further: "It is not the human who is ensconced as some one of the components of creation and adapted to it; but all the components of creation are ensconced in the human and adapted to him" (Staniloae, "Commentaires," 328).

70. Staniloae, *Experience of God*, vol. 1, 4. It should be pointed out that "bearing the stamp" is a Maximian image, from *Ambiguum* 7.

71. Staniloae, *Orthodoxe Dogmatik*, 319. All translations from this volume are my own, from the German.

72. Staniloae, *Experience of God*, vol. 2, 59.

73. Staniloae, *Experience of God*, vol. 1, 5.

74. Staniloae, *Experience of God*, vol. 2, 48. Compare the way Alexei Nesteruk uses the Maximian tradition to conceptualize scientific understanding as the form of hypostatization, in Nesteruk, *Light from the East*, 208–45.

75. Staniloae, *Experience of God*, vol. 1, 5–6, 23, 98–99; Staniloae, *Experience of God*, vol. 2, 53; Staniloae, "Commentaires," 338.

76. Staniloae, *Experience of God*, vol. 1, 25 (my emphasis).

77. Staniloae affirms negatively that transcendence does not violate nature (*Experience of God*, vol. 1, 4, 27–28), and that the Logos is always already the immanent

goal of creatures (*Experience of God,* vol. 1, 35–36); but in the few places that would seem to require theological language for nonhuman creatures' own agency, Staniloae adopts rhetoric in which God speaks through nature (*Experience of God,* vol. 1, 21, 98–99).

78. One reader observed that Staniloae's dogmatics could be read as a brief for Monsanto, so glorious does humanizing transformation appear (Eugene Rogers, seminar conversation).

79. One of the few places: Staniloae, *Experience of God,* vol. 1, 212–15.

80. Staniloae, *Experience of God,* vol. 2, 45.

81. Staniloae, *Experience of God,* vol. 2, 46. Interestingly, Staniloae holds that misuse of creation does not make nature more plastic, but more opaque, more resistant to humanization; see *Experience of God,* vol. 2, 173.

82. Staniloae, *Experience of God,* vol. 2, 4–5.

83. Staniloae, *Experience of God,* vol. 2, 13, 21–23; Staniloae, *Experience of God,* vol. 1, 165–68; Staniloae, "The World as Gift and Sacrament of God's Love."

84. Staniloae, *Orthodoxe Dogmatik,* 320.

85. Staniloae, *Orthodoxe Dogmatik,* 290–91.

86. *Unfading Light,* as quoted in Bamford's foreword to Bulgakov, *Sophia,* viii–x.

87. See the end of chap. 5. In contrast, remember how little attention Staniloae pays to Wisdom.

88. Bulgakov, "Hagia Sophia," 13. Louth observes that Bulgakov narrates the experience in Sophia to show that "this conversion to nature is also a conversion to himself" (Louth, "Father Sergii Bulgakov on the Mother of God," 149).

89. In a November 2005 American Academy of Religion conference presentation, John Milbank called this dogmatic project "the most significant theology of the two preceding centuries," for the way it "recover[s] the sense that there is no great gulf between creation and deification" (Milbank, "Sophiology and Theurgy: The New Theological Horizon").

90. Bulgakov, "Autobiographical Notes," quoted in Bamford's foreword to Bulgakov, *Sophia,* xiv.

91. Cf. Hopko, "Receiving Father Bulgakov," 380–82.

92. Nichols, "Bulgakov and Sophiology," 23.

93. Cf. Nichols, "Wisdom from Above? The Sophiology of Father Sergius Bulgakov," 606.

94. Newman, "Sergius Bulgakov and the Theology of Divine Wisdom," 42. Staniloae thus appears kataphatic on the side of hypostasis while apophatic about natures. Making short shrift of a complex controversy, we might say Lossky's solution requires a rigorous apophasis while Bulgakov's embraced a more thorough kataphasis. Norman Russell points out that the possibility for this move was already displayed in Pseudo-Dionysius; see Russell, *The Doctrine of Deification,* 252.

95. Bulgakov, "Summary of Sophiology," 43. Cf. Bulgakov, *Sophia,* 31–35: "God has, or possesses, or is characterized by, Glory and Wisdom, which cannot be separated from him since they represent his dynamic self-revelation in creative action, and also in his own life" (at 31).

96. Arjakovsky, "The Sophiology of Father Sergius Bulgakov and Contemporary Western Theology," 210. Says Bulgakov, "the very conception of Ousia itself is but that of Sophia, less fully developed" (Bulgakov, *Sophia*, 36).

97. See Chryssavgis, "Sophia, the Wisdom of God: Sophiology, Theology, and Ecology."

98. Bulgakov, *Sophia*, 95.

99. Bulgakov, *The Bride of the Lamb*, 45.

100. See Newman, "Sergius Bulgakov and the Theology of Divine Wisdom," 52.

101. Bulgakov, *The Bride of the Lamb*, 7.

102. Bulgakov, "Summary of Sophiology," 44.

103. Bulgakov, "The Lamb of God: On the Divine Humanity," 190.

104. Bulgakov, "Summary of Sophiology," 43.

105. Bulgakov, *The Bride of the Lamb*, 45.

106. Bulgakov, *The Bride of the Lamb*, 7.

107. Bulgakov, *The Comforter*, 198.

108. Bulgakov, *The Bride of the Lamb*, 44.

109. As Barbara Newman explains, "the sophianic foundation of the world can be seen, not only in its present order and beauty, but also in its evolution toward a predestined end" (Newman, "Sergius Bulgakov and the Theology of Divine Wisdom," 53).

110. "With reference to the divine foundation of being, creation is a divine world, whereas in its aseity and self-centredness it is a natural world, i.e., a world striving to become but not yet having become the full revelation of Sophia" (Bulgakov, *The Comforter*, 211).

111. Miroslaw Tataryn says this means that "Bulgakov's understanding of creation is of particular value to those Christians who are searching for a contemporary eco-theology" (Tataryn, "Sergius Bulgakov," 321).

112. Nichols, "Bulgakov and Sophiology," 25.

113. See Williams, "The Theology of Vladimir Nikolaievich Lossky: An Exposition and Critique," 53–63. See also Valliere, *Modern Russian Theology*, 388–89. This danger may be the reason Staniloae so enthusiastically emphasizes the personal in his version of cosmic deification. In his own statement of "the Orthodox view of salvation," Staniloae praises "the Russian theologians" for helping the church reclaim the cosmic dimensions of salvation resident in the Greek fathers, and then goes on to rigorously maintain the primacy of the personal. See Staniloae, *Theology and the Church*, 187.

114. See for example, Deane-Drummond, *Creation through Wisdom*, 84–99.

115. Bulgakov, "Hypostasis and Hypostaticity: Scholia to the *Unfading Light*." See the commentary by Rowan Williams (ed.), *Sergii Bulgakov*, 165.

116. Bulgakov, *Karl Marx as a Religious Type*, esp. 54–58, 85–90; Bulgakov, "Heroism and Asceticism: Reflections on the Religious Nature of the Russian Intelligentsia." Cf. Meerson, "Sergei Bulgakov's Philosophy of Personality."

117. Bulgakov, *Karl Marx as a Religious Type*, 112–13.

118. Bulgakov, *Karl Marx as a Religious Type*, 90.

119. Bulgakov, "Social Teaching in Modern Russian Orthodox Theology," 10–11. He goes on to say that the promise of cosmic transfiguration shows that Christian

action "includes not only personal ascetic and spiritual life, but also creativity in the world and in human society" (15).

120. Bulgakov, quoted in Nicolas Zernov, *The Russian Religious Renaissance of the Twentieth Century*, 231.

121. As we will see in the next chapter, Bulgakov maintains the historical significance of creativity against Origen's *apocatastasis*. Perfection and transfiguration cannot mean a "return" to a certain state, unqualified by the actions of the "intervening" life. See Bulgakov, *Apocatastasis and Transfiguration*; see also Bulgakov, *Sophia*, 147–48. Otherwise John O'Donnell's worry that Bulgakov's cosmic view offends creaturely freedom would have some purchase; that is precisely why Bulgakov consistently denies the Origenist view. See O'Donnell, "The Trinitarian Panentheism of Sergei Bulgakov," 43.

122. Bulgakov, *The Bride of the Lamb*, 56.

123. Bulgakov, *Philosophy of Economy*, 135.

124. Deane-Drummond affirms that Bulgakov's attention to Sophia offers "a way of greening Christology so that wider issues such as the environment come into view in the scope of salvation history" (*Creation through Wisdom*, 237).

CHAPTER II

1. Von Balthasar, *Cosmic Liturgy*, 190. See a similar view, comparing Origen and Russian theology in Meyendorff, "Creation in the History of Orthodox Theology."

2. Von Balthasar, *Cosmic Liturgy*, 192.

3. The resonance deepens further if von Balthasar is correct that Dostoevsky's model for Aloysha was Bulgakov's teacher, Vladimir Soloviev. See von Balthasar, *The Glory of the Lord*, 295.

4. "Someone visited my soul at that hour," says Aloysha of his nighttime rapture beneath cathedral towers and starry skies, in Dostoevsky, *The Brothers Karamazov*, 333–34. "In that evening my soul was stirred" says Bulgakov of his encounter with Sophia beneath mountainous towers and sunset skies. (Quotation from *Unfading Light*, quoted in Bamford's foreword to *Sophia*.)

5. See Masing-Delic, *Abolishing Death*.

6. From *Unfading Light*, quoted in Evtuhof, *The Cross and the Sickle*, 134.

7. From a letter to Rachinskii, quoted in Evtuhof, *The Cross and the Sickle*, 135.

8. Evtuhof, *The Cross and the Sickle*, 135.

9. Rasmussen opens his book *Earth Community, Earth Ethics* with Aloysha's prostrate embrace of the earth (6–7). And when asked what his ecojustice theology means practically, he has been known to simply read the passage out loud (as he did for example at the October 1998 Ecumenical Earth Conference at Union and Auburn Seminaries, New York City).

10. "The hero now shares with the Earth the deep longing for the face of Christ, for the 'beauty that will save the world.'" Wiseman, "The Sophian Element in the Novels of Fyodor Dostoevsky," 166.

11. Wendy Wiseman points out that Aloysha's despair drives him to the female vixen Grushenka, and he is restored to integrity by witnessing her coquettish visage broken by word of Father Zossima's death (Wiseman, "The Sophian Element in the Novels of Fyodor Dostoevsky," 175–82). See also Solovyov, *Lectures on Divine Humanity*, especially lectures 9–12; and Epstein, "Daniil Andreev and the Russian Mysticism of Femininity."

12. Cf. Masing-Delic, *Abolishing Death*, 107–10; Deane-Drummond, *Creation through Wisdom*, 82–83.

13. When defending his sophiology, he carefully distances himself from Soloviev and Dostoevsky while still claiming Sophia as Russian Orthodoxy's special proclamation to the western world. See Bulgakov, *Sophia*, 2–11.

14. Wiseman, "The Sophian Element in the Novels of Fyodor Dostoevsky," 181.

15. Tataryn, "History Matters: Bulgakov's Sophianic Key," 206. This means that Bulgakov also breaks with the gender typologies of Soloviev. See Meehan, "Wisdom/ Sophia, Russian Identity, and Western Feminist Theology"; see also David, "The Influence of Jacob Boehme on Russian Religious Thought."

16. Bulgakov devotes more text to defending himself against pantheism than gnosticism; see especially the opening section of Bulgakov, *The Bride of the Lamb*.

17. Miner, *Truth in the Making*. Miner is much more worried about the loss of the supernatural, and focused in particular on the role of creativity in epistemology, but his argument suggests a wider scope.

18. Consider, for example, the associative relation between Bulgakov's *sobornost* ecclesiology and Florensky's critique of monadic logic: both attempt to restore relationality to our sense of fundamental reality. Compare Bulgakov, *The Orthodox Church*, 14–33, 77–85; and Florensky, *The Ground and Pillar of the Truth*, 20–52.

19. Evtuhof, *The Cross and the Sickle*, 5–8; Figes, *Natasha's Dance*, 65–66, 300–302.

20. Figes, *Natasha's Dance*, 194; Cf. Rosenthal, "The Search for a Russian Orthodox Work Ethic."

21. See Evtuhof, *The Cross and the Sickle*, 28–34. Angry at his betrayal, Trotsky dismissed Bulgakov's disavowal of Marxism a classist embrace of bourgeois capitalism; see Trotsky, *Their Morals and Ours*, 19. But Bulgakov is no more amenable to technophilic markets of capitalism. He is repulsed by the mechanized violence of both "barbarian means of violating the virgin soil," wanting instead, as we will see, the organic economy reflecting the village household (Evtuhof, *The Cross and the Sickle*, 35).

22. Valliere sees a related contextual debate: the contest between modernity and dogma. See Valliere, "Sophiology as the Dialogue of Orthodoxy with Modern Civilization," and Behr, "Faithfulness and Creativity." Cf. Bulgakov, "Dogma and Dogmatic Theology."

23. Evtuhof, *The Cross and the Sickle*, 139.

24. Bulgakov in "Priroda v filosofii V. Solovieva" in *O. Vladimire Solovieve*; quoted by Evtuhof, *The Cross and the Sickle*, 138.

25. Milbank, "Sophiology and Theurgy: The New Theological Horizon," 19. Cf. Solovyov, *Lectures on Divine Humanity*, lectures 11 and 12.

26. Bulgakov, *The Bride of the Lamb*, 149, 139, 315; cf. Bulgakov, *The Comforter*, 201–10.

27. The gloss of Rowan Williams, in his commentary; see Williams (ed.), *Sergii Bulgakov*, 169.

28. Comparing Teilhard and Bulgakov, see Deane-Drummond, *Creation through Wisdom*, 91–99, 238–39.

29. Russell observes that Maximus could talk about the a divine–human symbiosis; Bulgakov extends the model to include a third relation, of humanity (and of the divine–human dyadic symbiosis) with creation (for a triadic symbiosis, more properly trinitarian). Russell, *The Doctrine of Deification in the Greek Patristic Tradition*, 270.

30. Williams, "Creation, Creativity and Creatureliness: The Wisdom of Finite Existence," 11.

31. Valliere, "Sophiology as the Dialogue of Orthodoxy with Modern Civilization," 182.

32. Thus "grounding the world as the revelation of God." Bulgakov, "Hypostasis and Hypostaticity: Scholia to the *Unfading Light*," 25.

33. In his commentary, Williams (ed.), *Sergii Bulgakov*, 165.

34. Gallaher and Kukota, "Protopresbyter Sergii Bulgakov: Hypostasis and Hypostaticity: Scholia to the *Unfading Light*," 15.

35. Bulgakov, *Sophia*, 26–30, 50–52. "Sophia is not a hypostasis, although, belonging to the hypostases, she is hypostatized from all eternity" (Bulgakov, *The Comforter*, 191).

36. Bulgakov, *The Comforter*, 195.

37. See Gallaher and Kukota, "Protopresbyter Sergii Bulgakov." The complexifying of causative associations is one way Bulgakov helps bend the gender typologies (which nonetheless he retains); see Meehan, "Wisdom/Sophia, Russian Identity, and Western Feminist Theology."

38. See commentary of Williams (ed.), *Sergii Bulgakov*, 165. Bulgakov writes that "inasmuch as the energy of God is not allegory or abstraction, neither is Sophia" (Bulgakov, "Hypostasis and Hypostaticity: Scholia to the *Unfading Light*," 25). Milbank suggests that this inversion of Palamas amounts to a subtle rejection of the distinction, confirmed in the way Bulgakov aligns the kenotic act of God with the divine essence; see Milbank, "Sophiology and Theurgy: The New Theological Horizon."

39. Palamas quoting Maximus, in Meyendorff (ed.), *Gregory Palamas*, 84.

40. Or "transfiguration without catastrophe." Rosenthal, "The Nature and Function of Sophia in Sergei Bulgakov's Prerevolutionary Thought," 172.

41. Bulgakov, *The Bride of the Lamb*, 102–3.

42. Bulgakov, *The Bride of the Lamb*, 149.

43. Bulgakov, *The Holy Grail and the Eucharist*, 34.

44. Bulgakov's sophiology lets divinization unite two biblical images: creation praising God and the church personalized, says Arjakovsky, in "The Sophiology of Father Sergius Bulgakov and Contemporary Western Theology," 228–29.

45. Cf. von Balthasar, *Cosmic Liturgy*, 227, 245–46, 262–63.

46. Commenting on Bulgakov, Eugene F. Rogers, *After the Spirit*, 41.

47. Rogers, *After the Spirit*, 40–41. Rogers in fact first made the comment about Monsanto in connection with Staniloae and later saw Bulgakov's vulnerability to the same charge.

48. Bulgakov, *Philosophy of Economy*, 153.

49. Masing-Delic, *Abolishing Death*, 76–122.

50. In contrast to later Soviet uses of this tradition for industrialized subjugation; see Evtuhof, *The Cross and the Sickle*, 70–72.

51. Bulgakov, *The Bride of the Lamb*, 332.

52. Bulgakov, *Philosophy of Economy*, 122.

53. Bulgakov, *The Holy Grail and the Eucharist*, 51–57.

54. Bulgakov, *The Comforter*, 201.

55. Bulgakov, *The Bride of the Lamb*, 332; cf. 150.

56. Hughes, "Bulgakov's Move from a Marxist to a Sophic Science," 43. Cf. Horne, "Divine and Human Creativity."

57. Recall the "habitus" of place-expression from Mick Smith, mentioned in chap. 2.

58. Bulgakov, *The Comforter*, 209.

59. Bulgakov, *Sophia*, 72.

60. Deane-Drummond, *Creation through Wisdom*, 87

61. Bulgakov, *The Comforter*, 211. Bulgakov, with uncertain implication for debates in religion and science, adds: "Theology (and sophiology in particular) encounters natural science here, whose task it is to become the theology of nature."

62. Bulgakov, *The Holy Grail and the Eucharist*, 59.

63. Bulgakov, *The Comforter*, 213. Bulgakov's student Paul Evdokimov was chary of sophiology, but his interpretation of icons shows the mark of his teacher. Evdokimov explains that icons impose their own principles of vision, letting images of transfigured nature conform the beholder to the glory of deification. Bulgakov intends precisely that paideutic: glory teaching human perception through nature. See Evdokimov, *The Art of the Icon*, 220–25, 350–53.

64. Bulgakov, "Hypostasis and Hypostaticity: Scholia to the *Unfading Light*," 37.

65. Bulgakov, *Philosophy of Economy*, 40.

66. Bulgakov, *The Bride of the Lamb*, 332.

67. "The real basis of the union of the two natures in Christ seems to lie in the mutual relationship as two variant forms of divine and created wisdom." Bulgakov, *Sophia*, 88.

68. These two witnesses also appear in the figures of Mary, the Queen of Creation who surrenders herself to be filled with glory, and of John the Baptist, the one who cries out for God, striving with the wilderness. See Bulgakov, *The Friend of the Bridegroom*; and "The Burning Bush."

69. Bulgakov, "The Lamb of God: On the Divine Humanity," 194.

70. "The internally emanated Son and Spirit are already the Creation as gift and response, expression and interpretation." Milbank, "Sophiology and Theurgy: The New Theological Horizon," 15.

71. "It is possible to say, with Bulgakov, that the Father's self-utterance in the generation of the Son is an initial kenosis within the Godhead that underpins all subsequent kenosis"; von Balthasar, *Theo-Drama*, 322. Thanks to Anthony Baker for drawing my attention to this passage, cited in Baker, "The Kenosis Problem in von Balthasar's Reading of Bulgakov." Baker's pithy summary of the way divine kenosis underlies cosmic deification: "There is finally only a single drama, and that is the one that involves the infinite distance of the Father and Son, and their equally infinite bond in the Spirit. *This* drama provides the opening for the various levels of creation, and the deification of creation as strata dependent on, and in a constant state of return to, the perichoresis" (Baker, "Making Perfection, 225).

72. Which is why Bulgakov can say in a homily: "At the creation of the world the seed of trees for the Cross was planted in it—the cedar, the oak, the cypress; on the day when the earth was bidden to bring forth every kind of plant, the trees for the Cross sprang up." Bulgakov, "The Power of the Cross," 170.

73. So says Milbank, "Sophiology and Theurgy: The New Theological Horizon," 21–22.

74. "It is not only animate and rational creation which receives the powers of resurrection, rather the whole of creation rises in Christ's Body, crying out exultantly with the joy of Easter." Bulgakov, "Meditations on the Joy of the Resurrection," 301–3.

75. Bulgakov, "Social Teaching in Modern Russian Orthodox Theology," 15–16; and Bulgakov, "Lamb of God," 193. Because the perichoretic love issues in a kenotic act of creation, one can even say that "God Himself has included in creation the self-creative activity of creatures, this activity is new even before the face of God Himself as the Creator, although not in His eternity" (Bulgakov, *The Comforter*, 218). Anthony Baker thinks von Balthasar quailed before Bulgakov's affirmation of that newness, thus missing both the fullness of creation's theurgical *theopoiesis* and Bulgakov's vindication of Maximian christology. See Baker, "The Kenosis Problem in von Balthasar's Reading of Bulgakov," 229.

76. Bulgakov, *The Comforter*, 193. Indeed "it is by this force that plants grow, animals live, minerals have their slumbering being, and human life is sustained" (*The Comforter*, 201).

77. Rogers, *After the Spirit*, 148–49. Two pages later, Rogers uses Bulgakov for his example of how theologians might show the narrative role for nature in the work of the Spirit.

78. "God's kenosis in relation to creation consists in the fact that God posits, along with His absolute, supramundane being, the becoming being of the creaturely world, and in this becoming being the presence of creaturely freedom, corresponding with his self-determination and correlated with his 'will'" (Bulgakov, *The Bride of the Lamb*, 142).

79. When Bulgakov refers to "a chaos that has been conquered, tamed, and illuminated from within," the key point is *from within* (Bulgakov, *Philosophy of Economy*, 13). Chaos is the interval in which creaturely sophia manifests herself. Cf. Deane-Drummond, *Creation through Wisdom*, 223–29, 245–46.

80. Paul Gavrilyuk, however, interprets Bulgakov's kenosis in line with a competitive view subjective freedoms found in some process thought, apparently the conclusion of reading Bulgakov after Hegel, rather than after Maximus. See Gavrilyuk, "The Kenotic Theology of Sergius Bulgakov."

81. See Bulgakov, *The Comforter*, 185–200.

82. Rogers, *After the Spirit*, 152. Note how that connects nature's deification to biblical stories of covenant inclusion, of the Jews and Gentiles—and thus to the paradigmatic tropes of salvation. Rogers turns to Bulgakov when he wants to show how reclaiming the Spirit affirms the way nature participates in biblical narrative, with "changes of an almost human character." For more on how Rogers presents nature as a character in a liturgically enacted narrative of communion with God, see Rogers, "Nature with Water and the Spirit."

83. The worry of Bulgakov's contemporary, Vasily Vasilyevich Rozanov. See Rozanov, "Sweet Jesus and the Sour Fruits of the World."

84. Bulgakov, *Sophia*, 17.

85. Bulgakov, *The Comforter*, 305.

86. Florensky, *The Ground and Pillar of the Truth*, 216, 230.

87. Bulgakov, "Hypostasis and Hypostaticity: Scholia to the *Unfading Light*," 38. Gallaher and Kukota say this refers to Spinoza and Goethe ("Protopresbyter Sergii Bulgakov," 38 n. 71), but it also clearly recalls Maximus describing creatures as Christ's garments in *Ambiguum* 10.

88. Bulgakov thus retains the universal scope of the transforming vocation found in Fyodorov's vision, but does so by theologically appropriating for all creation Berdyaev's insistence on freedom. See Bulgakov, "Social Teaching in Modern Russian Orthodox Theology," 17–20; Cf. Berdyaev, "The Ethics of Creativity," 245–60.

89. Bulgakov, *Sophia*, 20.

90. See Bulgakov, "Social Teaching in Modern Russian Orthodox Theology," 17–18.

91. Bulgakov, "The Unfading Light," 150.

92. Bulgakov, "Heroism and Asceticism," 32.

93. Bulgakov, "Heroism and Asceticism," 31–39. There remains, however, the possibility of a "demonic asceticism," which opens itself authentically to the world but presents only its darkness and corruption. See Bulgakov's somewhat disturbing commentary on Picasso, "The Corpse of Beauty."

94. See Theokritoff on "ecological asceticism" in Bulgakov and contemporary Orthodox figures, in "Embodied Word and New Creation: Some Modern Orthodox Insights Concerning the Material World," 234–36.

95. Again this recalls the figures of Mary and of John the Baptist, who together Bulgakov says are the very figure of creatureliness. See Bulgakov, *The Friend of the Bridegroom*, 137–38. Passive and active, consummated and yearning, Mary and John the Baptist together sum up the microcosmos. In Mary's perfect christological participation the world is glorified and in her the divine Sophia revealed. She is "the sunlit summit of the world," the transfigured mountain in whom Christ's glory is manifest (Bulgakov, "The Burning Bush," 90–95). John the Baptist represents the

earth's call toward the heavens, "the dry earth thirsting to receive the rain of heaven." In his wilderness striving, John renounces himself in anticipation of creation's glory (Bulgakov, *The Friend of the Bridegroom*, 9–15).

96. Williams, "Creation, Creativity, and Creatureliness," 4–7.

97. Cf. Foster, *Marx's Ecology*, 68–88.

98. Bulgakov, *The Bride of the Lamb*, 322–23.

99. Bulgakov, *The Orthodox Church*, 170–72.

100. See Williams, "Creation, Creativity, and Creatureliness."

101. Bulgakov, *Philosophy of Economy*, 102. "Flesh" refers to a line of theological inquiry in Pavel Florensky, connecting the glory of creation with the salvific covenants in Genesis and Luke. One might consider theological associations with projects like that of David Abram, who evokes a phenomenology of ecological relationality by drawing on the concepts of "flesh" in Merleau-Ponty. See Abram, *The Spell of the Sensuous*.

102. Bulgakov, "Social Teaching in Modern Russian Orthodox Theology," 20.

103. See Williams's commentary in Williams (ed.), *Sergii Bulgakov*, 129–31.

104. Bulgakov, *Philosophy of Economy*, 134; Cf. Bulgakov, "Lamb of God," 215.

105. Evtuhof, *The Cross and the Sickle*, 155.

106. Evtuhof's brings out the *oikos* resonances by adding a subtitle to her translation of *Filosofiia khoziaistva:* "The Household of God." In her introduction to *Philosophy of Economy*, Evtuhof suggests that as Marxism finally failed the Soviet project in late twentieth century, Bulgakov's sophic economy provides material for reevaluating the identity and character of a Russian economy (30–31).

107. So says Arjakovsky, "The Sophiology of Father Sergius Bulgakov and Contemporary Western Theology," 232. Rogers observes that while Bulgakov's economy "is in effect a pneumatology from below," Schmemann attempts to avoid the metabolic overtones by articulating the divine economy of the world "from above." See Rogers, *After the Spirit*, 41–45; Cf. Hopko, "Receiving Father Bulgakov," 374.

108. Bulgakov, "The Unfading Light," 151.

109. Bulgakov, *Philosophy of Economy*, 149; Bulgakov, *The Bride of the Lamb*, 79–83.

110. Bulgakov, *The Comforter*, 209.

111. See Bulgakov, *Apocatastasis and Transfiguration*, 11–12; and Bulgakov, *Sophia*, 144–45.

112. From *Unfading Light*, quoted in Crum, "Sergius N. Bulgakov: From Marxism to Sophiology," 22. Cf. Maximus, *Ambiguum* 42 and commentary in Dalmais, "La theorie des 'logoi' des creatures chez Saint Maxime le Confesseur," 246–47.

113. Bulgakov, "Meditations on the Joy of the Resurrection," 303.

114. Bulgakov, *Apocatastasis and Transfiguration*, 24.

115. Bulgakov, "Meditations on the Joy of the Resurrection," 301.

116. Notice the association with Hans Urs von Balthasar, for whom the crucified Christ is the form of the world and of God's self-revelation.

117. Maximus associates the play of the Logos with the foolishness of God; see *Ambiguum* 71. Cf. Deane-Drummond, *Creation through Wisdom*, 236.

118. Bulgakov, "Religion and Art," 191.

119. All quotations are from Bulgakov, "The Exceeding Glory," 189–91.

CHAPTER 12

1. I borrow the sentence from Barry Lopez, who penned it for a story that names feelings of unease between the power of landscape beauty and an almost unseen world of human destructions. Barry Lopez, *About This Life*, 117.

2. These description rely on Jeff Alexander, *The Muskegon*.

3. See, for example, Robert Elliot, "Faking Nature," Eric Katz, "The Big Lie," and Katz, "Understanding Moral Limits." See also the discussion in chap. 2.

4. I developed similar covenantal and bioregional themes in a sermon for Rhinebeck Reformed Church's "Sustainability Sunday," Rhinebeck, N.Y., April 2007. The phrase "cast your lines for the heart-skipping tug of grace" I may have unconsciously borrowed from David Lee Duncan's, *The River Why*.

5. For examples of environmental reflection from this tradition, see Wes Granberg-Michaelson, "Covenant and Creation"; Susan Schreiner, *The Theater of God's Glory*. Oliver O'Donovan's normative privilege for resurrected order seems to belong here as well; O'Donovan, *Resurrection and Moral Order*.

6. Larry Rasmussen's *Earth Community, Earth Ethics* may still be the best model here, as he seamlessly integrates biblical, theological, cultural, scientific, and literary commentary.

7. For a start in womanist soteriology, see the essays in Townes, *Embracing the Spirit*.

8. Williams, "Straight Talk, Plain Talk: Womanist Words about Salvation," 118–19.

9. Baker-Fletcher, *Sisters of Spirit, Sisters of Dust*, 16, 115–26.

10. Stephen Bouma-Prediger, *The Greening of Theology*, 105–6.

11. Eugene Rogers and Robert Jenson have been particularly concerned for the disappearance of the Spirit; Eugene Rogers, "The Mystery of the Spirit in Three Traditions"; Eugene Rogers, "Eclipse of the Spirit in Karl Barth"; Robert Jenson, "You Wonder Where the Spirit Went"; Robert Jenson, *Systematic Theology*, vol. 2, chap. 9 ("The Pneumatological Problem").

12. This is precisely the argument in Agustinus Dermawan, "The Spirit in Creation and Environmental Stewardship: A Preliminary Pentecostal Response."

13. See books in the bibliography by Denis Edwards, Elizabeth Johnson, Jürgen Moltmann, and Mark Wallace.

14. By following three traditions and three strategies, this book lends itself to trinitarian speculations. The three strategies outline three theological tasks for environmental theology: we need better understanding of creation's internal relation to God, of how God's saving work modulates human habitation, and of how creaturely creativity participates in God's creativity. Those tasks map onto theological domains typologically assigned to the Father, the Son, and the Holy Spirit, respectively. The practical strategies of Christian environmental ethics might move us toward revisiting and reconsidering theologies of the trinity.

15. See Conradie, "Towards an Ecological Reformulation of the Christian Doctrine of Sin."

16. Mary Evelyn Tucker pointed out to me that a "socially embodied, sustainable ecology of grace" sounds very near to a "cosmology," which I began the book by criticizing. So I must finally admit the nearness of cosmology and soteriology. This book began by supposing that patterns of grace generate the patterns of cosmology, yet here in the conclusion anticipates cosmological reformulations of the grammars of grace. The relations look reciprocal and the distinctions unstable. My priority for soteriology intends to preserve that reflexivity.

17. For the Ugandan communities, those social dimensions have recently involved joining a network of small groups offering their tree-planting as a carbon offset service. Assisted by an NGO promoting a prototype of carbon-credit trading, the groups offer multinational companies (or any eBay customer wishing to offset her personal carbon emissions) credits against the carbon sinks their trees create. See www.tist.org. Whatever the political justice or ecological efficacy of planting trees to trade carbon offsets, the remarkable thing here is how rural church groups in the global South have entered global climate change initiatives on their own theological terms.

18. See http://www.goldmanprize.org/recipients/recipients.html. In December 2006 two activists working with Father Tamayo's environmental justice organization, Heraldo Zuniga and Roger Ivan Murillo Cartagena, were assassinated.

Works Cited

Abram, David. *The Spell of the Sensuous*. New York: Random House, 1996.

Adler, Matthew D. "Cost-Benefit Analysis, Static Efficiency, and the Goals of Environmental Law." *Boston College Environmental Affairs Law Review* 31 (2004): 591–605.

Aertsen, Jan. *Nature and Creature: Thomas Aquinas's Way of Thought*. New York: E. J. Brill, 1988.

Agar, Nicholas. *Life's Intrinsic Value: Science, Ethics, and Nature*. New York: Columbia University Press, 2001.

Agyeman, Julian. *Sustainable Communities and the Challenge of Environmental Justice*. New York: New York University Press, 2005.

Alexander, Jeff. *The Muskegon: The Majesty and Tragedy of Michigan's Rarest River*. East Lansing: Michigan State University Press, 2006.

Anderson, Michael, and Alan Boyle, eds. *Human Rights Approaches to Environmental Protection*. Oxford: Clarendon Press, 1996.

Arjakovsky, Antoine. "The Sophiology of Father Sergius Bulgakov and Contemporary Western Theology." *St. Vladimir's Theological Quarterly* 49, nos. 1–2 (2005): 219–35.

Attfield, Robin. "Environmental Sensitivity and Critiques of Stewardship." In Berry, *Environmental Stewardship: Critical Perspectives*.

———. *The Ethics of Environmental Concern*. New York: Columbia University Press, 1983.

———. *Value, Obligation, and Meta-Ethics*. Atlanta: Value Inquiry Book Series, 1995.

Attfield, Robin, and Andrew Belsey, eds. *Philosophy and the Natural Environment*. Cambridge: Cambridge University Press, 1994.

Au Sable Institute. "Au Sable Institute Forum Statement." *Evangelical Review of Theology* 17, no. 2 (1993): 122–33.

———. "Message to Individuals and Churches from the Participants." Paper presented at the "Living Your Life as Vocation" conference, Mancelona, Michigan, 1990.

Augustine of Hippo. *On Christian Doctrine*. Translated by D. W. Robertson. Upper Saddle River, N.J.: Prentice Hall, 1958.

Baker, Anthony. "The Kenosis Problem in von Balthasar's Reading of Bulgakov." Paper presented at the Annual Conference of the American Academy of Religion, Atlanta 2003.

———. "Making Perfection: An Experiment in Theological Ontology." Dissertation, University of Virginia, 2004.

———. "Theology and the Crisis in Darwinism." *Modern Theology* 18, no. 2 (2002): 183–215.

Baker-Fletcher, Karen. *Sisters of Spirit, Sisters of Dust: Womanist Wordings on God and Creation*. Minneapolis: Fortress, 1998.

Bakken, Peter. "Stewardship." In *The Encyclopedia of Religion and Nature*, ed. Bron Taylor. New York: Thoemmes Continuum, 2005.

Bakken, Peter W., Joan Gibb Engel, and Ronald J. Engel. *Ecology, Justice, and Christian Faith: A Critical Guide to the Literature*. Westport, Conn.: Greenwood Press, 1995.

Baldner, Steven E., and William E. Carroll. *Aquinas on Creation: Writings on the 'Sentences' of Peter Lombard*. Toronto: Pontifical Institute of Mediaeval Studies, 1997.

Ball, Jim. "Evangelicals, Population, and the Ecological Crisis." *Christian Scholar's Review* 28, no. 2 (1998): 226–53.

———. "The Use of Ecology in the Evangelical Protestant Response to the Ecological Crisis." *Perspectives on Science and Christian Faith* 50 (1998): 32–38.

von Balthasar, Hans Urs. *Cosmic Liturgy: The Universe according to Maximus the Confessor*. Translated by Brian E. Daley. San Francisco: Ignatius Press, 2003.

———. *The Glory of the Lord: A Theological Aesthetics*. Vol. 3: *Studies in Theological Style: Lay Styles*. Translated by Andrew Louth, John Saward, Martin Simon, and Rowan Williams. San Francisco: Ignatius Press, 1986.

———. *Theo-Drama: Theological Dramatic Theory*. Vol. 4: *The Action*. Translated by Graham Harrison. San Francisco: Ignatius Press, 1994.

———. *The Theology of Karl Barth*. New York: Doubleday, 1972.

Barbour, Ian. *Nature, Human Nature, and God*. Minneapolis: Fortress Press, 2002.

Barkey, Michael B. *Environmental Stewardship in the Judeo-Christian Tradition: Jewish, Catholic and Protestant Wisdom on the Environment*. Washington, D.C.: Acton Institute for the Study of Religion and Liberty, 2000.

Barron, Duane. "For God So Loved the Cosmos: The Good News, Ecology and Christian Ethics." *Restoration Quarterly* 47, no. 2 (2005): 69–82.

Barth, Karl. *Church Dogmatics*. Translated by Geoffrey William Bromiley and Thomas Forsyth Torrance. Edinburgh: T. & T. Clark, 1956–1975.

———. *Church Dogmatics IV/4: The Christian Life: Lecture Fragments*. Grand Rapids, Mich.: W. B. Eerdmans, 1981.

———. *Church Dogmatics IV/4: Baptism: Lecture Fragment*. New York: T. & T. Clark, 1969.

———. *Die Kirchliche Dogmatik*. Zurich: Evangelischer Verlag Ag., 1947.

———. *A Shorter Commentary on Romans*. Richmond, Va.: John Knox, 1959.

Barth, Karl, and Emil Brunner. *Natural Theology: Comprising 'Nature and Grace' by Professor Dr. Emil Brunner and the Reply 'No!' by Dr. Karl Barth*. Translated by Peter Fraenkel. Eugene, Ore.: Wipf and Stock, 2002.

Bartos, Emil. *Deification in Eastern Orthodox Theology: An Evaluation and Critique of the Theology Dumitru Staniloae*. Carlisle: Paternoster Press, 1999.

Bastit, Michel. "Le thomisme est-il un aristotelisme?" *Revue Thomiste* 101, no. 1 (2001): 101–16.

Bauckham, Richard. "Stewardship and Relationship." In Berry, *The Care of Creation*.

Bean, Heather Ann Ackley. "Toward an Anabaptist/Mennonite Environmental Ethic." In Redekop, *Creation and the Environment: An Anabaptist Perspective on a Sustainable World*.

Behr, John. "Faithfulness and Creativity." In Behr, Louth, and Conomos, *Abba: The Tradition of Orthodoxy in the West*.

Behr, John, Andrew Louth, and Dimitri Conomos, eds. *Abba: The Tradition of Orthodoxy in the West*. Crestwood, N.Y.: St. Vladimir's Seminary Press, 2003.

Beisner, E. Calvin. *Where Garden Meets Wilderness: Evangelical Entry into the Environmental Debate*. Grand Rapids, Mich.: Acton Institute for the Study of Religion and Liberty, 1997.

Benzoni, Francisco. "Thomas Aquinas and Environmental Ethics." *The Journal of Religion* 85, no. 3 (2005): 446–76.

Berdyaev, Nicolai. "The Ethics of Creativity." In Schmemann, *Ultimate Questions*.

Bergant, Dianne. *The Earth Is the Lord's: The Bible, Ecology, and Worship*. Collegeville, Minn.: Liturgical Press, 1998.

Bergmann, Sigurd. *Geist, der Natur Befreit: Die Trinitarische Kosmologie Gregors von Nazianz im Horizont Einter Okologischen Theologie der Befreiung*. Mainz: Matthias-Grunewald-Verlag, 1995.

Berry, R. J., ed. *The Care of Creation*. Downers Grove, Ill.: Inter-Varsity Press, 2000.

———, ed. *Environmental Stewardship: Critical Perspectives*. New York: T. & T. Clark, 2006.

———. "One Lord, One World: The Evangelism of Environmental Care." In Brandt, *God's Stewards: The Role of Christians in Creation Care*.

Berry, Thomas. *The Dream of the Earth*. San Francisco: Sierra Club Books, 1988.

Berry, Thomas, Thomas E. Clarke, Stephen C. P. Dunn, and Anne Lonergan. *Befriending the Earth: A Theology of Reconciliation between Humans and the Earth*. Mystic, Conn.: Twenty-Third Publications, 1991.

Berry, Wendell. *Citizenship Papers: Essays by Wendell Berry*. Washington, D.C.: Shoemaker and Hoard, 2003.

———. "The Gift of Good Land." In *The Art of the Commonplace*, ed. Norman Wirzba. Washington, D.C.: Shoemaker & Hoard, 2002.

———. *Jayber Crow*. New York: Counterpoint Press, 2001.

Berry, Wendell. *The Unsettling of America.* San Francisco: Sierra Club Books, 1977.

_____ . *What Are People For?* New York: North Point Press, 1990.

Buell, Lawrence. *Writing for an Endangered World: Literature, Culture, and Environment in the U.S. and Beyond.* Cambridge, Mass.: Belknap Press of Harvard University Press, 2001.

Biggar, Nigel. *The Hastening That Waits: Karl Barth's Ethics.* Oxford Studies in Theological Ethics. New York: Oxford University Press, 1993.

Birch, Charles. "Christian Obligation for the Liberation of Nature." In Birch, Eakin, and McDaniel, *Liberating Life: Contemporary Approaches to Ecological Theology.*

Birch, Charles, William Eakin, and Jay B. McDaniel, eds. *Liberating Life: Contemporary Approaches to Ecological Theology.* Maryknoll, N.Y.: Orbis, 1990.

Birch, Thomas H. "The Incarceration of Wilderness." In Oelschlaeger, *Postmodern Environmental Ethics.*

_____ . "Moral Considerability and Universal Consideration." *Environmental Ethics* 15, no. 4 (1993): 313–32.

Blanchette, Olivia. *The Perfection of the Universe according to Aquinas: A Teleological Cosmology.* University Park: The Pennsylvania State University Press, 1992.

Blowers, Paul, and Robert Louis Wilken, eds. *On the Cosmic Mystery of Jesus Christ: Selected Writings from St. Maximus the Confessor.* Crestwood, N.Y.: St. Vladimir's Seminary Press, 2003.

Boff, Leonardo. *Cry of the Earth, Cry of the Poor.* Maryknoll, N.Y.: Orbis Books, 1997.

_____ . *Ecology and Justice.* Maryknoll, N.Y.: Orbis Books, 1995.

Bonhoeffer, Dietrich. *Act and Being.* New York: Octagon Books, 1983.

_____ . *Creation and Fall: Two Biblical Studies.* Translated by John Fletcher. New York: Touchstone, 1997.

_____ . *Ethics.* Edited by Eberhard Bethge, translated by Neville Horton Smith. New York: MacMillan, 1962.

_____ . *Sanctorum Communio: A Theological Study of the Sociology of the Church.* Translated by Nancy Lukens. Minneapolis: Fortress Press, 1998.

Bookchin, Murray. *The Ecology of Freedom: The Emergence and Dissolution of Hierarchy.* Cheektowaga, N.Y.: Black Rose Books, 1991.

Bosch, David. *Transforming Mission: Paradigm Shifts in Theology of Mission.* Maryknoll, N.Y.: Orbis, 1991.

Botkin, Daniel. *Discordant Harmonies: A New Ecology for the 21st Century.* New York: Oxford University Press, 1990.

Bouma-Prediger, Steven. *For the Beauty of the Earth.* Grand Rapids, Mich.: Baker Academic Press, 2001.

_____ . *The Greening of Theology: The Ecological Models of Rosemary Radford Ruether, Joseph Sittler, and Jürgen Moltmann.* Atlanta: Scholars Press, 1995.

_____ . "Response to Louke Van Wensveen: A Constructive Proposal." In Hessel and Reuther, *Christianity and Ecology.*

Bowlin, John. *Contingency and Fortune in Aquinas's Ethics.* New York: Cambridge University Press, 1999.

_____. "Nature's Grace: Aquinas and Wittgenstein on Natural Law and Moral Knowledge." In Stout and MacSwain, *Grammar and Grace: Reformulations of Aquinas and Wittgenstein.*

Bracken, Joseph. *The Divine Matrix: Creativity as Link between East and West.* Maryknoll, N.Y.: Orbis, 1995.

Braden, Kathleen. "On Saving the Wilderness: Why Christian Stewardship Is Not Sufficient." *Christian Scholar's Review* 28, no. 2 (1998): 254–69.

Bramwell, Anna. *Ecology in the Twentieth Century: A History.* New Haven: Yale University Press, 1989.

Brandt, Don, ed. *God's Stewards: The Role of Christians in Creation Car.* Monrovia, Calif.: Worldvision International, 2002.

Bratton, Susan Power. *Christianity, Wilderness, and Wildlife: The Original Desert Solitaire.* Scranton, Pa.: University of Scranton Press, 1993.

_____. "Ecofeminism and the Problem of Divine Immanence/Transcendence." *Christianity and Scientific Belief* 6, no. 1 (1994): 21–40.

_____. "The New Christian Ecology." In *Earth Ethics*, ed. James Sterba. Upper Saddle River, N.J.: Prentice-Hall, Inc., 1995.

_____. "The Undoing of the Environment: Assessing the European Religious Worldview." In *Earth at Risk: An Environmental Dialogue between Religion and Science*, ed. Donald Conroy and Rodney Peterson, 213–38. Amherst, N.Y.: Humanity Books, 2000.

Bratton, Susan, and James Nash. "Loving Nature: Eros or Agape?" *Environmental Ethics* 14, no. 1 (1992): 3–25.

Braun, Bruce, and Noel Castree, eds. *Remaking Reality: Nature at the Millennium.* New York: Routledge, 1998.

Brennan, Andrew. "Moral Pluralism and the Environment." *Environmental Values* 1, no. 1 (1992): 15–33.

Brown, Charles S., and Ted Toadvine, eds. *Eco-Phenomenology: Back to the Earth Itself.* Albany: State University of New York Press, 2003.

Brooke, John Hedley. "Improvable Nature?" In Drees, *Is Nature Ever Evil?*

Brueggemann, Walter. *The Land: Place as Gift, Promise, and Challenge in Biblical Faith.* Minneapolis: Fortress Press, 2002.

_____. "The Loss and Recovery of Creation in Old Testament Theology." *Theology Today* 53, no. 2 (1996): 177–90.

Buell, Lawrence. *The Environmental Imagination.* Cambridge, Mass.: Harvard University Press, 1995.

_____. *Writing for an Endangered World: Literature, Culture, and Environment in the U.S. and Beyond.* Cambridge, Mass.: Belknap Press of Harvard University Press, 2001.

Bulgakov, Sergei. *Apocatastasis and Transfiguration.* Translated by Boris Jakim. New Haven: The Variable Press, 1995.

_____. *The Bride of the Lamb.* Translated by Boris Jakim. Grand Rapids, Mich.: Eerdmans, 2002.

_____. "The Burning Bush." In Pain and Zernov, *A Bulgakov Anthology.*

Bulgakov, Sergei. *The Comforter*. Translated by Boris Jakim. Grand Rapids, Mich.: Eerdmans, 2004.

———. "The Corpse of Beauty." In Pain and Zernov, *A Bulgakov Anthology*.

———. "Dogma and Dogmatic Theology." In *Tradition Alive*, ed. Michael Plekon. Lanham, Md.: Rowman and Littlefield, 2003.

———. "The Exceeding Glory." In Pain and Zernov, *A Bulgakov Anthology*.

———. *The Friend of the Bridegroom: On the Orthodox Veneration of the Forerunner*. Translated by Boris Jakim. Grand Rapids, Mich.: Eerdmans, 2003.

———. "Hagia Sophia." In Pain and Zernov, *A Bulgakov Anthology*.

———. "Heroism and Asceticism: Reflections on the Religious Nature of the Russian Intelligentsia." In *Vekhi: A Collection of Articles About the Russian Intelligentsia*, ed. Marshall S. Shatz and Judith E. Zimmerman. London: M. E. Sharpe, 1994.

———. *The Holy Grail and the Eucharist*. Translated by Boris Jakim. Hudson, N.Y.: Lindisfarne, 1997.

———. "Hypostasis and Hypostaticity: Scholia to the *Unfading Light*." *St. Vladimir's Theological Quarterly* 49, no. 1–2 (2005): 17–46.

———. *Karl Marx as a Religious Type: His Relation to the Religion of Anthropotheism of Ludwig Feuerbach*. Translated by Luba Barna. Belmont, Mass.: Nordland Publishers, 1979.

———. "The Lamb of God: On the Divine Humanity." In Williams, *Sergii Bulgakov: Towards a Russian Political Theology*.

———. "Meditations on the Joy of the Resurrection." In Schmemann, *Ultimate Questions*.

———. *The Orthodox Church*. Translated by Lydia Kesich. Crestwood, N.Y.: St. Vladimir's Seminary Press, 1988.

———. *Philosophy of Economy: The World as Household*. Translated by Catherine Evtuhof. New Haven: Yale University Press, 2000.

———. "The Power of the Cross." In Pain and Zernov, *A Bulgakov Anthology*, 169–74.

———. "Religion and Art." In *The Church of God: An Anglo-Russian Symposium*, ed. E. L. Mascall. London: SPCK, 1934.

———. "Social Teaching in Modern Russian Orthodox Theology." In *The Twentieth Annual Hale Memorial Sermon*. Evanston, Ill.: Seabury-Western Theological Seminary, 1934.

———. *Sophia: The Wisdom of God*. Hudson, N.Y.: Lindisfarne Press, 1993.

———. "A Summary of Sophiology." *St. Vladimir's Theological Quarterly* (2005): 43–46.

———. "The Unfading Light." In Williams, *Sergii Bulgakov: Towards a Russian Political Theology*.

Bullard, Robert. *Dumping in Dixie: Race, Class, and Environmental Quality*. Boulder, Colo.: Westview Press, 1990.

Burrell, David. "Analogy, Creation, and Theological Language." In Van Nieuwenhove and Wawrykow, *The Theology of Thomas Aquinas*.

———. *Knowing the Unknowable God*. South Bend, Ind.: University of Notre Dame Press, 1986.

_____. "Religious Life and Understanding: Grammar Exercised in Practice." In Stout and MacSwain, *Grammar and Grace: Reformulations of Aquinas and Wittgenstein*.

Burrell, David B., and Elena Malits. *Original Peace: Restoring God's Creation*. New York: Paulist Press, 1997.

Busch, Eberhard. *Karl Barth: His Life from Letters and Autobiographical Texts*. Philadelphia: Fortress Press, 1976.

Byron, William J. "The Ethics of Stewardship." In Jegen and Manno, *The Earth Is the Lord's: Essays on Stewardship*.

Callicott, J. Baird. "Animal Liberation: A Triangular Affair." *Environmental Ethics* 2 (1980): 311–28.

_____. *Beyond the Land Ethic: More Essays in Environmental Philosophy*. SUNY Series in Philosophy and Biology. Albany: State University of New York Press, 1999.

_____. "The Case against Moral Pluralism." *Environmental Ethics* 12 (1990): 99–124.

_____. *In Defense of the Land Ethic: Essays in Environmental Philosophy*. SUNY Series in Philosophy and Biology. Albany: State University of New York Press, 1989.

_____. "Non-Anthropocentric Value Theory and Environmental Ethics." *American Philosophical Quarterly* 21, no. 4 (1984): 299–309.

Callicott, J. Baird, and Michael P. Nelson, eds. *The Great New Wilderness Debate*. Athens: University of Georgia Press, 1998.

Camuto, Christopher. *Another Country: Journeying toward the Cherokee Mountains*. Athens: University of Georgia Press, 1997.

Carroll, William E. "Aquinas and the Metaphysical Foundations of Science." *Sapientia* 54, no. 1 (1999): 69–91.

_____. "Creation, Evolution, and Thomas Aquinas." *Revue des Questions Scientifiques* 171, no. 4 (2000): 319–47.

Carson, Rachel. *The Sense of Wonder*. New York: HarperCollins, 1998.

Cassel, J. David. "Stewardship: Experiencing and Expressing God's Nurturing Love." *American Baptist Quarterly* 17, no. 1 (1998): 26–40.

Casey, Edward S. *The Fate of Place: A Philosophical History*. Berkeley: University of California Press, 1997.

Cheney, Jim. "Postmodern Environmental Ethics: Ethics as Bioregional Narrative." *Environmental Ethics* 11, no. 2 (1989).

Chenu, Marie-Dominique. *Toward Understanding Saint Thomas*. Translated by A. M. Landry and D. Hughes. Chicago: Regnery Publishing, 1964.

Childress, James. "Response to Light and Norton." Paper presented at the "Environmental Letters/Environmental Law" conference, University of Virginia, 2005.

Chryssavgis, John. "The Beatitudes and the Beauty of the World." *Sophia* 8, no. 1 (2002): 23–42.

_____. *Beyond the Shattered Image*. Minneapolis: Light and Life Publishing, 1999.

_____. "Sophia, the Wisdom of God: Sophiology, Theology, and Ecology." *Diakonia*, 34, no. 1 (2001): 5–19.

_____. "The World of the Icon and Creation." In Hessel and Reuther, *Christianity and Ecology*.

Chryssavgis, John., ed. *Cosmic Grace & Humble Prayer: The Ecological Vision of the Green Patriarch Bartholomew I*. Grand Rapids, Mich.: Eerdmans, 2003.

Clark, Stephen R. L. *Biology and Christian Ethics*. Cambridge: Cambridge University Press, 2000.

Clifford, Anne. "From Ecological Lament to a Sustainable *Oikos*." In Berry, *Environmental Stewardship: Critical Perspectives*.

Coakley, Sarah. "Kenosis: Theological Meanings and Gender Connotations." In Polkinghorne, *The Act of Love: Creation as Kenosis*.

———. *Powers and Submissions: Spirituality, Philosophy, and Gender*. Oxford: Blackwell, 2002.

Cobb, John B. *Sustainability: Economics, Ecology, Justice*. Maryknoll, N.Y.: Orbis Books, 1992.

———. *Sustaining the Common Good: A Christian Perspective on the Global Economy*. Cleveland: The Pilgrim Press, 1994.

Cohen, R. S., and A. I. Tauber, eds. *Philosophies of Nature: The Human Dimension*. Boston: Kluwer Academic Publishers, 1998.

Cole-Turner, Ronald. *The New Genesis: Theology and the Genetic Revolution*. Louisville, Ky.: Westminster John Knox, 1993.

———. "Toward a Theology for the Age of Biotechnology." In *Beyond Cloning: Religion and the Remaking of Humanity*, ed. Ronald Cole-Turner. Harrisburg, Pa.: Trinity Press International, 2001.

Conradie, Ernst. *Hope for the Earth: Vistas on a New Century*. Bellville, South Africa: University of Western Cape, 2000.

———. "Towards an Ecological Reformulation of the Christian Doctrine of Sin." *Journal of Theology for Southern Africa* 122, no. 1 (2005): 4–22.

Cooper, Adam G. *The Body in St. Maximus the Confessor: Holy Flesh, Wholly Deified*. Oxford: Oxford University Press, 2005.

Cowdin, Daniel. "The Moral Status of Otherkind in Christian Ethics." In Hessel and Reuther, *Christianity and Ecology*.

Cronon, William. "Saving Nature in Time: The Past and Future of Environmentalism." Paper presented at the "Environmental Letters/Environmental Law" conference, University of Virginia, 2005.

———. "The Trouble with Wilderness; or, Getting Back to the Wrong Nature." In *Uncommon Ground: Rethinking the Human Place in Nature*, ed. William Cronon. New York: W. W. Norton, 1996.

Crosby, Donald A. "Experience as Reality: The Ecological Metaphysics of William James." In *Religious Experience and Ecological Responsibility*, eds. Donald A. Crosby and Charley D. Hardwick. New York: Peter Lang, 1996.

Crum, Winston F. "Sergius N. Bulgakov: From Marxism to Sophiology." *St. Vladimir's Theological Quarterly* 27, no. 1 (1983): 3–25.

Curtin, Deane. *Environmental Ethics for a Postcolonial World*. Lanham, MD: Rowman & Littlefield, 2005.

———. "Toward an Ecological Ethic of Care." In Warren, *Ecological Feminist Philosophies*.

Dalmais, Irenee-Henri. "La théorie des 'logoi' des créatures chez Saint Maxime le Confesseur." *Revue des sciences philosophiques et théologiques* 36, no. 2 (1952): 244–49.

Daly, Herman and Cobb, John. *For the Common Good: Redirecting the Economy Toward Community, the Environment, and a Sustainable Future.* Boston: Beacon Press, 1994.

Daly, Lois K. "Ecofeminism, Reverence for Life, and Feminist Theological Ethics." In *Feminist Theological Ethics*, ed. Lois K. Daly. Louisville, Ky.: Westminster John Knox, 1994.

Daneel, Marthinus. *African Earthkeepers.* Maryknoll, N.Y.: Orbis, 2001.

David, Zdenek. "The Influence of Jacob Boehme on Russian Religious Thought." *Slavic Review* 21, no. 1 (1962): 43–64.

Davies, Oliver. *The Creativity of God: World, Eucharist, Reason.* New York: Cambridge University Press, 2004.

_____. "The Sign Redeemed: A Study in Christian Fundamental Semiotics." *Modern Theology* 19, no. 2 (2003): 219–42.

Davis, John Jefferson. "Ecological 'Blind Spots' in the Structure and Content of Recent Systematic Theologies." *Journal of the Evangelical Theological Society,* 43, no. 2 (2000): 273–86.

Davison, Aidan. *Technology and the Contested Meanings of Sustainability.* Albany: State University of New York Press, 2001.

Deane-Drummond, Celia. *Creation through Wisdom: Theology and the New Biology.* Edinburgh: T. & T. Clark, 2000.

_____. *The Ethics of Nature.* Oxford: Blackwell, 2004.

_____. "The Feminine Face of God as a Metaphor for Ecotheology." *Feminist Theology* 16 (1997): 11–31.

_____. "Wisdom with Justice." *Ethics in Science and Environmental Politics.* 2002: 65–74.

Dell, Katherine. "Green Ideas in the Wisdom Tradition." *Scottish Journal of Theology* 47, no. 4 (1994): 423–51.

Dermawan, Agustinus. "The Spirit in Creation and Environmental Stewardship: A Preliminary Pentecostal Response toward Ecological Theology." *Asian Journal of Pentecostal Studies,* 6, no. 2 (2003): 199–217.

Derr, Thomas Sieger. *Environmental Ethics and Christian Humanism.* Nashville: Abingdon Press, 1996.

_____. "Religious Models for Environmentalism: Rediscovery or Retrofitting?" *Princeton Seminary Bulletin* 24, no. 1 (2003): 94–103.

Devall, Bill, and George Sessions. *Deep Ecology: Living as If Nature Mattered.* Layton, Utah: Gibbs Smith, 1985.

DeWitt, Calvin B. *Caring for Creation: Responsible Stewardship of God's Handiwork.* Grand Rapids, Mich.: Baker Publishing Group, 1998.

_____. "Creation's Environmental Challenge to Evangelical Theology." In Berry, *The Care of Creation.*

_____, ed. *The Environment and the Christian: What Does the New Testament Say About the Environment?* Grand Rapids, Mich.: Baker Publishing Group, 1991.

DeWitt, Calvin B. "God's Love for the World and Creation's Environmental Challenge to Christianity." *Evangelical Review of Theology* 17, no. 2 (1993): 134–49.

_____. "Spiritual and Religious Perspectives of Creation and Scientific Understandings of Nature." In Kellert and Farnham, *The Good in Nature and Humanity.*

_____. "Stewardship: Responding Dynamically to the Consequences of Human Action in the World." In Berry, *Environmental Stewardship: Critical Perspectives.*

Donovan, Josephine. "Ecofeminist Literary Criticism: Reading the Orange." *Hypatia* 11, no. 2 (1996): 161.

Dostoevsky, Fyodor. *The Brothers Karamazov.* Translated by Constance Garnett. New York: Signet Classics, 1957.

Drees, William B., ed. *Is Nature Ever Evil? Religion, Science and Value.* New York: Routledge, 2003.

Drengson, Alan. "Shifting Paradigms: From Technocrat to Planetary Person." In Drengson and Inoue, *The Deep Ecology Movement: An Introductory Anthology.*

Drengson, Alan, and Yuichi Inoue, eds. *The Deep Ecology Movement: An Introductory Anthology.* Berkeley: North Atlantic Books, 1995.

Dubos, Rene. *A God Within.* London: Angus & Robertson, 1973.

Duncan, David James. *The River Why.* San Francisco: Sierra Club Books, 1983.

Dunlap, Thomas. *Faith in Nature: Environmentalism as Religious Quest.* Seattle: University of Washington Press, 2004.

Dupre, Louis. *Passage to Modernity.* New Haven: Yale University Press, 1993.

Dyrness, William. "Stewardship of the Earth in the Old Testament." In Granberg-Michaelson, *Tending the Garden: Essays on the Gospel and the Earth.*

Earth Bible Team, The. "Guiding Ecojustice Principles." In *Readings from the Perspective of Earth*, ed. Norman C. Habel. Cleveland: Pilgrim Press, 2000.

Eaton, Heather. "Ecological-Feminist Theology: Contributions and Challenges." In Hessel, *Theology for Earth Community: A Field Guide.*

Ebenreck, Sara. "Opening Pandora's Box: Imagination's Role in Environmental Ethics." *Environmental Ethics* 18, no. 1 (1996): 3–18.

Edwards, Denis. *Jesus the Wisdom of God: An Ecological Theology.* Maryknoll, N.Y.: Orbis Books, 1995.

_____. *A Theology of the Creator Spirit.* Maryknoll, N.Y.: Orbis Books, 2004.

Elliot, Robert, ed. *Environmental Ethics.* Oxford Readings in Philosophy. New York: Oxford University Press, 1995.

_____. *Faking Nature: The Ethics of Environmental Restoration.* Environmental Philosophies Series. New York: Routledge, 1997.

_____. "Intrinsic Value, Environmental Obligation and Naturalness." *Monist* 75 (1992): 138–60.

_____. "Normative Ethics." In Jamieson, *A Companion to Environmental Philosophy.*

Emmerich, Susan Drake. "The Declaration in Practice: Missionary Earthkeeping." In Berry, *The Care of Creation.*

Epstein, Mikhail. "Daniil Andreev and the Russian Mysticism of Femininity." In *The Occult in Russian and Soviet Culture*, ed. Bernice Glatzer Rosenthal, 325–55. Ithaca, N.Y.: Cornell University Press, 1997.

Evdokimov, Paul. *The Art of the Icon: A Theology of Beauty*. Translated by Stephen Bigham. Redondo Beach, Calif.: Oakwood Publications, 1990.

———. "Nature." *Scottish Journal of Theology* 18, no. 1 (1965): 1–22.

Evernden, Neil. *The Social Creation of Nature*. Baltimore: John Hopkins University Press, 1992.

Evtuhof, Catherine. *The Cross and the Sickle: Sergei Bulgakov and the Fate of Russian Religious Philosophy*. Ithaca, N. Y.: Cornell University Press, 1997.

Farber, Daniel. *Eco-Pragmatism: Making Sensible Environmental Decisions in an Uncertain World*. Chicago: University of Chicago Press, 1999.

———, ed. *The Struggle for Ecological Democracy: Environmental Justice Movements in the United States*. New York: The Guilford Press, 1998.

Farley, Margaret. "Religious Meanings for Nature and Humanity." In Kellert and Farnham, *The Good in Nature and Humanity*.

Fern, Richard *Nature, God, and Humanity*. Cambridge: Cambridge University Press, 2002.

Figes, Orlando. *Natasha's Dance: A Cultural History of Russia*. New York: Picador, 2002.

Finger, Thomas. "An Anabaptist/Mennonite Theology of Creation." In Redekop, *Creation and the Environment: An Anabaptist Perspective on a Sustainable World*.

Florensky, Pavel. *The Ground and Pillar of the Truth*. Translated by Boris Jakim. Princeton: Princeton University Press, 1997.

Foltz, Bruce V. *Inhabiting the Earth: Heidegger, Environmental Ethics, and the Metaphysics of Nature*. Atlantic Highlands, N.J.: Humanities Press, 1993.

Foot, Philippa. *Virtues and Vices and Other Essays in Moral Philosophy*. Berkeley: University of California Press, 1978.

Foster, John Bellamy. *Marx's Ecology*. New York: Monthly Review Press, 2000.

Foucault, Michel. *The Order of Things*. New York: Random House, 1970.

Fox, Matthew. *The Coming of the Cosmic Christ: The Healing of Mother Earth and the Birth of a Global Renaissance*. San Francisco: Harper & Row, 1988.

———. *Creation Spirituality: Liberating Gifts for the Peoples of the Earth*. San Francisco: HarperSanFrancisco, 1991.

———. *Creativity: Where the Divine and Human Meet*. New York: Jeremy Tarcher, 2004.

———. *Original Blessing: A Primer in Creation Spirituality Presented in Four Paths, Twenty-Six Themes, and Two Questions*. Santa Fe: Bear, 1983.

———. *Sheer Joy: Conversations with Thomas Aquinas on Creation Spirituality*. San Francisco: HarperSanFrancisco, 1992.

Fox, Warwick, ed. *Ethics and the Built Environment*. New York: Routledge, 2000.

———. *A Theory of General Ethics: Human Relationships, Nature, and the Built Environment* Cambridge, Mass.: MIT Press, 2006.

Frame, Randy. "Planetary Justice." *Christianity Today* 32, no. 17 (1988).

Franke, Joseph. "Faith and Martyrdom in the Forest." *The Witness Magazine*, March 9, 2005.

Frasz, Geoffrey B. "Environmental Virtue Ethics: A New Direction for Environmental Ethics." *Environmental Ethics* 15, no. 3 (1993): 259–74.

French, William C. "Beast-Machines and the Technocratic Reduction of Life." In *Good News for Animals?*, ed. Charles Pinches and Jay B. McDaniel. Maryknoll, N.Y.: Orbis Books, 1993.

———. "Catholicism and the Common Good of the Biosphere." In *An Ecology of the Spirit: Religious Reflection and Environmental Consciousness*, ed. Michael Barnes. Lanham, Md.: University Press of America, 1994.

———. "Subject-Centered and Creation-Centered Paradigms in Recent Catholic Thought." *Journal of Religion* 70 (1990): 48–72.

Freyfogle, Eric T. *Bounded People, Boundless Land: Envisioning a New Land Ethic.* Washington, D.C.: Island Press, 1998.

Fuller, Robert C. "American Pragmatism Reconsidered: William James' Ecological Ethic." *Environmental Ethics* 14 (1992): 159–76.

Gallaher, Anastassy Brandon, and Irina Kukota. "Protopresbyter Sergii Bulgakov: Hypostasis and Hypostaticity: Scholia to the *Unfading Light*." *St. Vladimir's Theological Quarterly* 49, no. 1–2 (2005): 5–16.

Gare, Arran. "The Postmodernism of Deep Ecology, the Deep Ecology of Postmodernism, and Grand Narratives." In Katz, Light, and Rothenberg, *Beneath the Surface: Critical Essays in the Philosophy of Deep Ecology.*

Gardner, Gary T. *Inspiring Progress: Religions' Contributions to Sustainable Development.* New York: W. W. Norton, 2006.

Garrigues, Juan Miguel. *Maxime le Confesseur: La charite, avenir divin de l'homme.* Paris: Editions Beauchesne, 1976.

Gavrilyuk, Paul L. "The Kenotic Theology of Sergius Bulgakov." *Scottish Journal of Theology* 58, no. 3 (2005): 251–69.

Gebara, Ivone. *Longing for Running Water: Ecofeminism and Liberation.* Minneapolis: Fortress Press, 1999.

Gessner, David. *The Prophet of Dry Hill.* Boston: Beacon Press, 2005.

———. *Sick of Nature.* Lebanon, N.H.: Dartmouth Press, 2005.

Gibson, William E. "Eco-Justice: What Is It?" *The Egg* 2, no 4 (1982).

———, ed. *Eco-Justice: The Unfinished Journey.* Albany: State University of New York Press, 2004.

———. "Introduction to the Journey." In Gibson, *Eco-Justice: The Unfinished Journey.*

Goldstein, Robert J. "Environmental Ethics and Positive Law." In *Environmental Ethics and Law*, ed. Robert J. Goldstein. London: Ashgate, 2004.

Goodpaster, Kenneth E. "On Being Morally Considerable." *The Journal of Philosophy* 75, no. 6 (1978): 308–25.

Gorringe, Timothy. *Karl Barth: Against Hegemony.* Christian Theology in Context. New York: Oxford University Press, 1999.

———. *A Theology of the Built Environment.* Cambridge: Cambridge University Press, 2002.

Gottlieb, Roger, ed. *The Ecological Community: Environmental Challenges for Philosophy, Politics, and Morality.* New York: Routledge, 1997.

———. *Environmentalism Unbound: Exploring New Pathways for Change.* Cambridge, Mass.: MIT Press, 2001.

_____. *A Greener Faith: Religious Environmentalism and Our Planet's Future*. New York: Oxford University Press, 2006.

_____, ed. *The Oxford Handbook of Religion and Ecology*. New York: Oxford University Press, 2006.

Graham, Mark E. *Sustainable Agriculture: A Christian Ethic of Gratitude*. Cleveland: Pilgrim Press, 2005.

Granberg-Michaelson, Wesley. "Covenant and Creation." In Birch, Eakin, and McDaniel, *Liberating Life: Contemporary Approaches to Ecological Theology*.

_____. *Ecology and Life: Accepting Our Environmental Responsibility*. Waco, Tex.: World Publishing Group, 1988.

_____, ed. *Tending the Garden: Essays on the Gospel and the Earth*. Grand Rapids, Mich.: Eerdmans, 1987.

_____. *A Worldly Spirituality: The Call to Redeem Life on Earth*. New York: Harper & Row, 1984.

Grant, Don Sherman. "Religion and the Left: The Prospects of a Green Coalition." *Environmental Ethics* 19, no. 2 (1997): 115–34.

Grant, Robert L. *A Case Study in Environmental Ethics: The Ecological Crisis in the Loess Hills of Iowa*. Lewiston, N.Y.: The Edwin Mellen Press, 2007.

Grdzelidze, Tamara. "Creation and Ecology: How Does the Orthodox Church Respond to Ecological Problems?" *The Ecumenical Review* 54, no. 3 (July 2002): 211–18.

Gregorios, Paulos Mar. *The Human Presence: Ecological Spirituality and the Age of the Spirit*. Warwick, N.Y.: Amity House, 1978.

Grey, Mary C. *Sacred Longings: The Ecological Spirit and Global Culture*. Minneapolis: Fortress Press, 2004.

Grizzle, Raymond. "Evangelicals and Environmentalism." *Trinity Journal* 19 (1998): 3–27.

Grizzle, Raymond, and Christopher Barret. "The One Body of Christian Environmentalism." *Zygon* 33, no. 2 (1998): 233–53.

Gross, Jules. *The Divinization of the Christian according to the Greek Fathers*. Translated by Paul A. Onica. Anaheim, Calif.: A & C Press, 2002.

de Gruchy, John. *Christianity, Art, and Transformation: Theological Aesthetics in the Struggle for Justice*. Cambridge: Cambridge University Press, 2001.

_____. *Reconciliation: Restoring Justice*. Minneapolis: Augsburg Fortress, 2003.

Guattari, Felix. *The Three Ecologies*. Translated by Ian Pindar and Paul Sutton. New Brunswick, N.J.: Athlone Press, 2000.

Guelke, Jean Kay. "Looking for Jesus in Environmental Ethics." *Environmental Ethics* 26, no. 2 (2004): 115–34.

Gunton, Colin E. "Christ, the Wisdom of God: A Study in Divine and Human Action." In *Where Shall Wisdom Be Found?*, ed. Stephen C. Barton. Edinburgh: T. & T. Clark, 1999.

_____, ed. *The Doctrine of Creation*. Edinburgh: T. & T. Clark, 1997.

Guroian, Vigen. *Ethics after Christendom*. Grand Rapids, Mich.: Eerdmans, 1994.

_____. *The Fragrance of God*. Grand Rapids, Mich.: Eerdmans, 2006.

Gustafson, James. *Ethics from a Theocentric Perspective*. 2 vols. Chicago: University of Chicago Press, 1981–1984.

———. *Christ and the Moral Life*. New York: Harper & Row, 1968.

———. *A Sense of the Divine: The Natural Environment from a Theocentric Perspective*. Cleveland: Pilgrim Press, 1994.

Habgood, John. *The Concept of Nature*. London: Darton, Longman, and Todd, 2002.

———. "A Sacramental Approach to Environmental Issues." In Birch, Eakin, and McDaniel, *Liberating Life: Contemporary Approaches to Ecological Theology*.

Hacking, Ian. *The Social Construction of What?* Cambridge, Mass.: Harvard University Press, 1999.

Haddorff, David W. "The Postmodern Realism of Barth's Ethics." *Scottish Journal of Theology* 57, no. 3 (2004): 269–86.

Hall, Douglass John. *Imaging God: Dominion as Stewardship*. Grand Rapids, Mich.: Eerdmans, 1986.

———. *The Steward: A Biblical Symbol Come of Age*. Grand Rapids, Mich.: Eerdmans, 1990.

Halligan, Patrick. "The Environmental Policy of Saint Thomas Aquinas." *Environmental Law* 19 (1989): 767–806.

Hallman, David G. "Climate Change: Ethics, Justice, and Sustainable Community." In Hessel and Reuther, *Christianity and Ecology*.

Haraway, Donna Jeanne. *Modest-Witness@Second-Millennium.Femaleman-Meets-Oncomouse: Feminism and Technoscience*. New York: Routledge, 1997.

———. *Simians, Cyborgs, and Women: The Reinvention of Nature*. New York: Routledge, 1991.

Harris, Peter. "Environmental Concern Calls for Repentance and Holiness." In Brandt, *God's Stewards: The Role of Christians in Creation Care*.

Hart, David Bentley. *The Doors of the Sea*. Grand Rapids, Mich.: Eerdmans, 2005.

Hart, John. *Sacramental Commons: Christian Ecological Ethics*. Lanham, Md.: Rowman & Littlefield, 2006.

———. *What Are They Saying about Environmental Theology?* New York: Paulist Press, 2004.

Harvey, David. *Justice, Nature, and the Geography of Difference*. Oxford: Blackwell, 1996.

Hauerwas, Stanley. "Connections Created and Contingent: Aquinas, Preller, Wittgenstein, and Hopkins." In Stout and MacSwain, *Grammar and Grace: Reformulations of Aquinas and Wittgenstein*.

———. *The Hauerwas Reader*. Durham, N.C.: Duke University Press, 2001.

Haught, John F. *The Promise of Nature*. Mahwah, N.J.: Paulist Press, 1993.

Hefner, Philip. "Can Nature Truly Be Our Friend?" *Zygon* 29 (1994): 507–28.

———. *The Human Factor: Evolution, Culture, and Religion*. Minneapolis: Fortress Press, 1993.

———. "Nature Good and Evil: A Theological Palette." In Drees, *Is Nature Ever Evil?*

———. "Nature, God's Great Project." *Zygon* 27, no. 3 (1992): 327–41.

Henning, Brian. *The Ethics of Creativity: Beauty, Morality, and Nature in a Processive Cosmos*. Pittsburgh: University of Pittsburgh Press, 2005.

Hessel, Dieter, ed. *After Nature's Revolt: Eco-Justice and Theology.* Minneapolis: Fortress Press, 1992.

———. "The Church's Eco-Justice Journey." In Gibson, *Eco-Justice: The Unfinished Journey.*

———. "Eco-Justice Theology after Nature's Revolt." In Hessel, *After Nature's Revolt: Eco-Justice and Theology.*

———, ed. *Theology for Earth Community: A Field Guide, Ecology and Justice.* Maryknoll, N.Y.: Orbis Books, 1996.

———. "Where Were/Are the U.S. Churches in the Environmental Movement?" In Hessel, *Theology for Earth Community: A Field Guide.*

Hessel, Dieter T., and Rosemary Radford Ruether, eds. *Christianity and Ecology: Seeking the Well-Being of Earth and Humans, Religions of the World and Ecology.* Cambridge, Mass.: Harvard University Press, 2000.

Hill, Brennan. *Christian Faith and the Environment: Making Vital Connections.* Maryknoll, N.Y.: Orbis, 1998.

Hill, Thomas E. "Ideals of Human Excellence and Preserving Natural Environments." *Environmental Ethics* 5 (1983): 211–24.

Hillyer, P. N. "Stewardship." In *New Dictionary of Theology,* ed. Sinclair Ferguson and David Wright. Downers Grove, Ill.: InterVarsity Press, 1988.

Hopko, Thomas. "Receiving Father Bulgakov." *St. Vladimir's Theological Quarterly* 42, no. 3–4 (1998): 373–83.

Horne, Brian. "Divine and Human Creativity." In Gunton, *The Doctrine of Creation.*

Hoyt, Thomas. "Environmental Justice and Black Theology." In Hessel, *Theology for Earth Community: A Field Guide.*

Hughes, John. "Bulgakov's Move from a Marxist to a Sophic Science." *Sobornost* 24, no. 2 (2002): 29–47.

Hunsinger, George. *How to Read Karl Barth: The Shape of His Theology.* New York: Oxford University Press, 1991.

———, ed. *Karl Barth and Radical Politics.* Philadelphia: Westminster Press, 1976.

Ignatius IV of Antioch. "Three Sermons on the Environment: Creation, Spirituality, Responsibility." *Sourozh* 38 (1989): 1–14.

Indinopulos, Thomas A. "The Critical Weakness of Creation in Barth's Theology." *Encounter* 33 (1972): 159–69.

Irwin, Kevin W. "The Sacramentality of Creation and the Role of Creation in Liturgy and Sacraments." In *Preserving the Creation: Environmental Theology and Ethics,* ed. Kevin W. Irwin and Edmund D. Pellegrino. Washington, D.C.: Georgetown University Press, 1994.

Jackson, Wes. *Becoming Native to This Place.* New York: Counterpoint, 1994.

Jacobsen, Diane. "Biblical Bases for Eco-Justice Ethics." In Hessel, *Theology for Earth Community: A Field Guide.*

Jamieson, Dale, ed. *A Companion to Environmental Philosophy.* Malden, Mass.: Blackwell, 2003.

———. *Morality's Progress: Essays on Humans, Other Animals, and the Rest of Nature.* Oxford: Oxford University Press, 2002.

Jegen, Mary Evelyn. "The Church's Role in Healing the Earth." In Granberg-Michaelson, *Tending the Garden: Essays on the Gospel and the Earth.*

Jegen, Mary Evelyn, and Bruno Manno, eds. *The Earth Is the Lord's: Essays on Stewardship.* New York: Paulist Press, 1978.

Jenkins, Willis. "Assessing Metaphors of Agency: Intervention, Perfection, and Care as Models of Environmental Practice." *Environmental Ethics* 27, no. 2 (2005): 135–54.

———. "Biodiversity and Salvation: Thomistic Roots for Environmental Ethics." *Journal of Religion* 83, no. 3 (2003): 401–20.

———. "Islamic Law and Environmental Ethics: How Jurisprudence (*usul al-fiqh*) Mobilizes Practical Reform." *Worldviews: Environment, Culture, Religion* 9, no. 3 (Fall 2005): 338–64.

———. "A New Earth Day: Emerging Anglican Environmentalisms." *The Witness,* April 20, 2005.

———. "Stewardship." In *The Westminster Dictionary of Christian Ethics,* ed. James Childress. Louisville, Ky.: Westminster John Knox, forthcoming.

———. "Stewardship after the End of Nature: Karl Barth and Environmental Ethics." *Scottish Journal of Theology,* forthcoming.

Jenson, Robert. *Systematic Theology.* Vol. 2. Oxford: Oxford University Press, 1997.

———. "You Wonder Where the Spirit Went." *Pro Ecclesia* 2, no. 3 (1993): 296–304.

Johnson, Elizabeth. "Losing and Finding Creation in the Christian Tradition." In Hessel and Reuther, *Christianity and Ecology.*

———. *Women, Earth, and Creator Spirit.* New York: Paulist Press, 1993.

Johnson, Luke Timothy. "Caring for the Earth: Why Environmentalism Needs Theology." *Commonweal* 132, no. 13 (2005): 16–20.

Johnson, William Stacy. *The Mystery of God: Karl Barth and the Postmodern Foundations of Theology.* Louisville, Ky.: Westminster John Knox, 1997.

Johnston, Carol. "Economics, Eco-Justice, and the Doctrine of God." In Hessel, *After Nature's Revolt: Eco-Justice and Theology.*

Jones, Serene. *Feminist Theory and Christian Theology: Cartographies of Grace.* Minneapolis: Fortress Press, 2000.

Jordan, Mark. *The Alleged Aristotelianism of Thomas Aquinas.* Rome: Pontifical Institute of Mediaeval Studies, 1992.

Jung, L. Shannon. *We Are Home: A Spirituality of the Environment.* Mahwah, N.J.: Paulist Press, 1993.

Kanner, Allen D., ed. *Ecopsychology: Restoring the Earth, Healing the Mind.* San Francisco: Sierra Club Books, 1995.

Kapur, Praveen. "Let There Be Life." *Evangelical Review of Theology* 17, no. 2 (1993): 168–75.

Kardong, Terence. "Ecological Resources in the Benedictine Rule." In LaChance and Carrol, *Embracing Earth.*

Katz, Eric. "Against the Inevitability of Anthropocentrism." In Katz, Light, and Rothenberg, *Beneath the Surface: Critical Essays in the Philosophy of Deep Ecology.*

———. "The Big Lie: Human Restoration of Nature." *Research in Philosophy and Technology,* 12 (1992): 231–41.

_____. "Imperialism and Environmentalism." In Gottlieb, *The Ecological Community*.

_____. *Nature as Subject*. Lanham, Md.: Rowman and Littlefield, 1997.

_____. "A Pragmatic Reconsideration of Anthropocentrism." *Environmental Ethics* 21 (1999): 377–90.

_____. "Searching for Intrinsic Value: Pragmatism and Despair in Environmental Ethics." In Light and Katz, *Environmental Pragmatism*.

_____. "Understanding Moral Limits in the Duality of Artifacts and Nature." *Ethics and the Environment* 7, no. 1 (2002): 138–46.

Katz, Eric, Andrew Light, and David Rothenberg, eds. *Beneath the Surface: Critical Essays in the Philosophy of Deep Ecology*. Cambridge, Mass.: MIT Press, 2000.

Kaufman, Gordon. "A Problem for Theology: The Concept of Nature." *Harvard Theological Review* 65, no. 3 (1972): 337–66.

_____. "The Theological Structure of Christian Faith and the Feasibility of a Global Christian Ethic." *Zygon* 38, no. 1 (2003): 147–61.

Kearns, Laurel. "The Context of Eco-Theology." In *The Blackwell Companion to Modern Theology*, ed. Gareth Jones. Malden, Mass.: Blackwell, 2004.

_____. "Noah's Ark Goes to Washington: A Profile of Evangelical Environmentalism." *Social Compass* 44, no. 3 (1997): 349–66.

_____. "Saving the Creation: Christian Environmentalism in the United States." *Sociology of Religion* 57, no. 1 (1996): 55–70.

_____. "Saving the Creation: Religious Environmentalism." Dissertation, Emory University, 1994.

Kehm, George H. "The New Story: Redemption as Fulfillment of Creation." In *After Nature's Revolt: Eco-Justice and Theology*, ed. Dieter Hessel. Minneapolis: Augsburg Fortress Press, 1992.

Keller, Catherine. *Face of the Deep: A Theology of Becoming*. New York: Routledge, 2003.

_____. "Postmodern 'Nature,' Feminism and Community." In Hessel, *Theology for Earth Community: A Field Guide*.

Kellert, Stephen R. *Kinship to Mastery: Biophilia in Human Evolution and Development*. Washington, D.C.: Island Press, 1997.

Kellert, Stephen R., and Timothy J. Farnham, eds. *The Good in Nature and Humanity*. Washington, D.C.: Island Press, 2002.

Kelman, Stephen. "Cost-Benefit Analysis: An Ethical Critique." *Regulation* 33 (1981): 33–40.

Kenel, Sally. "Nature and Grace: An Ecological Metaphor." In *An Ecology of the Spirit: Religious Reflection and Environmental Consciousness*, ed. Michael Barnes. Lanham, Md.: University Press of America, 1994.

Kerr, Fergus. *After Aquinas: Versions of Thomism*. Malden, Mass.: Blackwell, 2002.

_____. "Aquinas after Marion." *New Blackfriars* 76 (1995): 354–64.

_____. "'Real Knowledge' or 'Enlightened Ignorance': Eric Mascall on the Apophatic Thomisms of Victor Preller and Victor White." In Stout and MacSwain, *Grammar and Grace: Reformulations of Aquinas and Wittgenstein*.

Keselopoulos, Anestis G. *Man and the Environment: A Study of St. Symeon the New Theologian*. Crestwood, N.Y.: St. Vladimir's Press, 2001.

Kidner, David W. "Fabricating Nature: A Critique of the Social Construction of Nature." *Environmental Ethics* 22, no. 4 (2000): 339–57.

―――. "Industrialism and the Fragmentation of Temporal Structure." *Environmental Ethics* 26 (2003): 135–54.

King, Roger J. H. "Caring About Nature: Feminist Ethics and the Environment." In Warren, *Ecological Feminist Philosophies*.

―――. "Environmental Ethics and the Built Environment." *Environmental Ethics* 22 (2000): 115–31.

―――. "Narrative, Imagination, and the Search for Intelligibility in Environmental Ethics." *Ethics and the Environment* 4, no. 1 (1999): 23–38.

―――. "Toward an Ethics of the Domesticated Environment." *Philosophy and Geography* 6.1 (2003): 3–14.

Kirkman, Robert. "The Problem of Knowledge in Environmental Ethics: A Counter challenge." In Gottlieb, *The Ecological Community*.

―――. "Reasons to Dwell on (If Not Necessarily in) the Suburbs." *Environmental Ethics* 26, no. 1 (2004): 77–96.

―――. *Skeptical Environmentalism: The Limits of Philosophy and Science*. Bloomington: Indiana University Press, 2002.

Kirschenmann, Fred, and Janet Kirschenmann. "A Transcendent Vision." In Slattery, *Caretakers of Creation: Farmers Reflect on Their Life and Work*.

Kline, David. *Great Possessions: An Amish Farmer's Journal*. Berkeley: North Point Press, 1990.

Kohak, Erazim. "The Ecological Dilemma: Ethical Categories in a Biocentric World." In Cohen and Tauber, *Philosophies of Nature: The Human Dimension*.

―――. *The Embers and the Stars*. Chicago: University of Chicago Press, 1984.

―――. *The Green Halo*. Chicago: Open Court, 2000.

―――. "The True and the Good: Reflections on the Primacy of Practical Reason." In Cohen and Tauber, *Philosophies of Nature: The Human Dimension*.

―――. "Varieties of Ecological Experience." *Environmental Ethics* 19, no. 2 (1997): 153–71.

Kornblatt, Judith Deutsch, and Richard F. Gustafson, eds. *Russian Religious Thought*. Madison: University of Wisconsin Press, 1996.

Koyama, Kosuke. "Cosmology and Justice in Ecumenical Perspective." In Hessel, *Theology for Earth Community: A Field Guide*.

Krueger, F. W. "The History of the NACCE." In *Christian Ecology: Building an Environmental Ethic for the Twenty-First Century*, ed. F. W. Krueger. San Francisco: The North American Conference on Christianity and Ecology, 1987.

LaChance, Albert, and John E. Carrol, eds. *Embracing Earth*. Maryknoll, N.Y.: Orbis Books, 1994.

Lambert, Darwin. *The Undying Past of the Shenandoah National Park*. Boulder, Colo.: Roberts Rinehart Publishers, 1989.

Larchet, Jeane-Claude. *La divinisation de l'homme selon Saint Maxime le Confesseur*. Paris: Les Editions du Cerf, 1996.

Lathrop, Gordon. *Holy Ground: A Liturgical Cosmology*. Minneapolis: Fortress Press, 2003.

Lazarus, Richard J. *The Making of Environmental Law*. Chicago: University of Chicago Press, 2004.

LeBlanc, Jill. "Eco-Thomism." *Environmental Ethics* 21, no. 3 (1999): 293–306.

Lee, Keekok. *The Natural and the Artefactual*. Lanham, Md.: Lexington Books, 1999.

Lee-Park, Sun Ai. "The Forbidden Tree and the Year of the Lord." In Ruether, *Women Healing Earth: Third World Women on Ecology, Feminism, and Religion*.

Leopold, Aldo. *A Sand County Almanac*. Oxford: Oxford University Press, 1949.

Light, Andrew. "Callicott and Naess on Pluralism." In Katz, Light, and Rothenberg, *Beneath the Surface: Critical Essays in the Philosophy of Deep Ecology*.

———. "Compatibilism in Political Ecology." In Light and Katz, *Environmental Pragmatism*.

———. "Has Environmental Ethics Rested on a Mistake?" Paper presented at the "Environmental Letters/Environmental Law" conference, University of Virginia, 2005.

———. "Environmental Pragmatism as Philosophy or Metaphilosophy?" In Light and Katz, *Environmental Pragmatism*.

———. "Materialists, Ontologists, and Environmental Pragmatists." In Gottlieb, *The Ecological Community*.

———. "Restorative Relationships." In *Healing Nature, Repairing Relationships: Landscape Architecture and the Restoration of Ecological Spaces*, ed. R. France. Cambridge, Mass.: MIT Press, 2004.

———. "The Urban Blind Spot in Environmental Ethics." *Environmental Politics* 10, no. 1 (2001): 7–35.

Light, Andrew, and Avner De-Shalit. *Moral and Political Reasoning in Environmental Practice*. Cambridge, Mass.: MIT Press, 2003.

Light, Andrew, and Eric Katz, eds. *Environmental Pragmatism*. Environmental Philosophies. New York: Routledge, 1995.

Limouris, Gennadios. *Come, Holy Spirit, Renew the Whole Creation: An Orthodox Approach for the Seventh Assembly of the World Council of Churches*. Brookline, Mass.: Holy Cross Orthodox Press, 1990.

Lindbeck, George. *The Nature of Doctrine: Religion and Theology in a Postliberal Age*. Philadelphia: Westminster Press, 1984.

Linzey, Andrew. *Animal Theology*. Springfield: University of Illinois Press, 1995.

Lopez, Barry. *About This Life*. New York: Vintage Books, 1998.

———. *Arctic Dreams*. New York: Vintage Books, 1986.

———. "Introduction." In *The Best American Spiritual Writing 2005*, ed. Philip Zaleski. New York: Houghton Mifflin, 2005.

———. *The Rediscovery of North America*. New York: Vintage Books, 1992.

———. *Resistance*. New York: Alfred A. Knopf, 2004.

Lossky, Vladimir. *The Mystical Theology of the Eastern Church*. London: James Clarke, 1957.

Louth, Andrew. "Father Sergii Bulgakov on the Mother of God." *St. Vladimir's Theological Quarterly* 49, no. 1–2 (2005): 145–64.

———. *Maximus the Confessor*. London: Routledge, 1996.

Louth, Andrew. "Recent Research on St. Maximus the Confessor: A Survey." *St. Vladimir's Theological Quarterly* 42, no. 1 (1998): 67–84.

Lowe, Walter James. *Theology and Difference: The Wound of Reason.* Bloomington: Indiana University Press, 1993.

du Lubac, Henri. *Augustinianisme et théologie moderne.* Paris: Editions Montaigne, 1965.

_____. *Le mystère du surnaturel.* Paris: Editions Montaigne, 1965.

_____. *Teilhard de Chardin: The Man and His Meaning.* New York: Hawthorne Books, 1965.

Lucas, Peter. "Environmental Ethics: Between Inconsequential Philosophy and Unphilosophical Consequentialism." *Environmental Ethics* 24, no. 4 (2002): 353–70.

Lucas, Philip C. "Eleventh Commandment Fellowship." In *The Encylopedia of Religion and Nature,* ed. Bron Taylor. New York: Thoemmes Continuum, 2005.

Luhmann, Niklas. *Ecological Communication.* Chicago: Polity Press, 1989.

_____. *Observations on Modernity.* Stanford: Stanford University Press, 1998.

Luke, Brian. "Solidarity across Diversity: A Pluralistic Rapprochement of Environmentalism and Animal Liberation." In Gottlieb, *The Ecological Community.*

Macauley, David. "Be-Wildering Order." In Gottlieb, *The Ecological Community.*

MacIntyre, Alasdair C. *Dependent Rational Animals: Why Human Beings Need the Virtues.* Chicago: Open Court, 1999.

MacKinnon, Mary Heather, and Moni McIntyre, eds. *Readings in Ecology and Feminist Theology.* Kansas City: Sheed & Ward, 1995.

Macy, Joanna. "The Ecological Self: Postmodern Ground for Right Action." In Mackinnon and McIntyre, *Readings in Ecology and Feminist Theology.*

Maguire, Daniel C., and Larry L. Rasmussen. *Ethics for a Small Planet: New Horizons on Population, Consumption, and Ecology.* SUNY Series in Religious Studies. Albany: State University of New York Press, 1998.

Manahan, Ronald. "Christ as the Second Adam." In DeWitt, *The Environment and the Christian.*

Manes, Christopher. "Nature and Silence." In Oelschlaeger, *Postmodern Environmental Ethics.*

_____. "Philosophy and the Environmental Task." *Environmental Ethics* 10, no. 1 (1988): 75–82.

Marable, Manning. "Environmental Justice: The Power of Making Connection." In Hessel, *Theology for Earth Community: A Field Guide.*

Marietta, Don, and Lester Embree, eds. *Environmental Philosophy and Environmental Activism.* Lanham, Md.: Rowman & Littlefield, 1995.

Marion, Jean-Luc. *Dieu sans l'être: Hors-texte.* Paris: Librarie Artheme Fayard, 1982.

Marsh, Charles. *God's Long Summer: Stories of Faith and Civil Rights.* Princeton: Princeton University Press, 1997.

_____. *Reclaiming Dietrich Bonhoeffer.* New York: Oxford University Press, 1994.

Marshall, Bruce. *Christology in Conflict: The Identity of a Saviour in Rahner and Barth.* Oxford: Blackwell, 1987.

Martin-Schramm, James B. "Population Growth, Poverty, and Environmental Degradation." *Theology and Public Policy* 4, no. 2 (1992): 26–38.

———. *Population Perils and the Churches' Response*. Geneva: World Council of Churches Publications, 1997.

Martin-Schramm, James B., and Robert L. Stivers. *Christian Environmental Ethics: A Case Method Approach*. Maryknoll, N.Y.: Orbis Books, 2003.

Masing-Delic, Irene. *Abolishing Death: A Salvation Myth of Russian Twentieth-Century Literature*. Stanford: Stanford University Press, 1992.

Mathews, Freya. "Deep Ecology." In Jamieson, *A Companion to Environmental Philosophy*.

———. *The Ecological Self*. Savage, Md.: Barnes & Noble Books, 1991.

Maximus Confessor. *Maximus Confessor: Selected Writings and Notes*. Translated by George C. Bertheld. Classics of Western Spirituality. New York: Paulist Press, 1985.

McCormack, Bruce L. *Karl Barth's Critically Realistic Dialectical Theology: Its Genesis and Development, 1909–1936*. Oxford: Clarendon, 1997.

McDaniel, Jay. *Of God and Pelicans: A Theology of Reverence for Life*. Louisville, Ky.: Westminster John Knox, 1989.

———. *With Roots and Wings: Christianity in an Age of Ecology and Dialogue*. Maryknoll, N.Y.: Orbis Books, 1995.

McFague, Sallie. *The Body of God*. Minneapolis: Fortress Press, 1993.

———. "An Earthly Theological Agenda." In MacKinnon and McIntyre, *Readings in Ecology and Feminist Theology*.

———. *Super, Natural Christians*. Minneapolis: Fortress, 1997.

McGrath, Alister. *The Reenchantment of Nature*. New York: Random House, 2002.

McInerny, Ralph M. *Aquinas and Analogy*. Washington, D.C.: Catholic University of America Press, 1996.

McKibben, Bill. *The Comforting Whirlwind: God, Job, and the Scale of Creation*. Grand Rapids, Mich.: Eerdmans, 1994.

———. *The End of Nature*. New York: Random House, 1989.

Meehan, Brenda. "Wisdom/Sophia, Russian Identity, and Western Feminist Theology." *Cross Currents* 46, no. 2 (1996): 149–68.

Meerson, Michael A. "Sergei Bulgakov's Philosophy of Personality." In Kornblatt and Gustafson, *Russian Religious Thought*.

Merchant, Carolyn. *Earthcare: Women and the Environment*. New York: Routledge, 1996.

———. *Reinventing Eden*. New York: Routledge, 2003.

Merton, Thomas. *Witness to Freedom: Letters in Times of Crisis,* ed. William H. Shannon. New York: Harcourt Brace & Company, 1994.

Meyendorff, John. "Creation in the History of Orthodox Theology." *St. Vladimir's Theological Quarterly* 27, no. 1 (1983): 27–37.

———, ed. *Gregory Palamas: The Triads*. Mahwah, N.J.: Paulist Press, 1983.

Michael, Mark A. "What's In a Name? Pragmatism, Essentialism, and Environmental Ethics." *Environmental Values* 12, no. 3 (2003): 361–79.

Mick, Lawrence E. *Liturgy and Ecology in Dialogue.* Collegeville, Minn.: The Liturgical Press, 1997.

Midgley, Mary. "Duties Concerning Islands." In Elliot, *Environmental Ethics.*

_____. "The End of Anthropocentrism." In Attfield and Belsey, *Philosophy and the Natural Environment.*

_____. "Is a Dolphin a Person?" In *The Animal Ethics Reader,* ed. Susan Armstrong and Richard Botzler. New York: Routledge, 2003.

_____. *Utopias, Dolphins and Computers.* New York: Routledge, 1996.

Migne, J. P., ed. *Patrologia Graeca.* Vols. 90–91. Paris, 1865.

Milbank, John. "Sophiology and Theurgy: The New Theological Horizon." American Academy of Religion Annual Conference, Philadelphia, November, 2005.

_____. *Theology and Social Theory: Beyond Secular Reason.* Oxford: Blackwell, 1990.

_____. *The Word Made Strange.* Oxford: Blackwell, 1997.

Milbank, John, and Catherine Pickstock. *Truth in Aquinas.* London: Routledge, 2001.

Miller, Charles. *The Gift of the World: An Introduction to the Theology of Dumitru Staniloae.* Edinburgh: T. & T. Clark, 2000.

Miller-Travis, Vernice. "Social Transformation through Environmental Justice." In Hessel and Reuther, *Christianity and Ecology.*

Miner, Robert. *Truth in the Making: Creative Knowledge in Theology and Philosophy.* New York: Routledge, 2004.

_____. "Recent Work on Thomas in North America: Language, Anthropology, Christology." In *Contemplating Aquinas: On the Varieties of Interpretation,* ed. Fergus Kerr. London: SCM Press, 2003.

Minteer, Ben. "Intrinsic Value for Pragmatists?" *Environmental Ethics* 23, no. 1 (2001): 57–76.

_____. *The Landscape of Reform: Civic Pragmatism and Environmental Thought in America.* Cambridge, Mass.: MIT Press, 2006.

Minteer, Ben A., and Robert E. Manning. "An Appraisal of the Critique of Anthropocentrism and Three Lesser Known Themes in Lynn White's 'The Historical Roots of Our Ecologic Crisis.'" *Organization and Environment* 18, no. 2 (June 2005): 163–76.

Moltmann, Jürgen. *God for a Secular Society.* Minneapolis: Fortress Press, 1999.

_____. "God's Covenant and Our Responsibility." In Berry, *The Care of Creation.*

_____. *God in Creation: A New Theology of Creation and the Spirit of God.* San Francisco: Harper & Row, 1985.

_____. *Science and Wisdom.* Translated by Margaret Kohl. London: SCM Press, 2003.

_____. "Schöpfung, Bund und Herrlichkeit." *Evangelische Theologie* 48, no. 2 (1988): 108–27.

_____. *The Source of Life: The Holy Spirit and the Theology of Life.* Minneapolis: Fortress Press, 1997.

_____. *The Spirit of Life: A Universal Affirmation.* Translated by Margaret Kohl. Minneapolis: Fortress Press, 1992.

_____. *The Way of Jesus Christ: Christology in Messianic Dimensions.* Translated by Margaret Kohl. Minneapolis: Fortress Press, 1993.

Moody, Michael. "Caring for Creation: Environmental Advocacy by Mainline Protestant Organizations." In *The Quiet Hand of God*, ed. Robert Wuthnow and John Evans. Berkeley: University of California Press, 2002.

Morito, Bruce. "Intrinsic Value: A Modern Albatross for the Ecological Approach." *Environmental Values* 12 (2003): 317–36.

Motavelli, Jim. "Stewards of the Earth." *E Magazine* 13, no. 6 (Nov/Dec 2002).

Muir, John. *Nature Writings*. New York: Library of America, 1997.

Muratore, S. "The New 'Teilhard' at the NACCE: Thomas Berry, the 'New Story' at the Battle for the Christian Mind." *Epiphany* 8, no. 2 (1988): 6–14.

Murdy, William H. "Anthropocentrism: A Modern Version." In *Environmental Ethics: Divergence & Convergence*, ed. Susan Armstrong and Richard Botzler. Boston: McGraw-Hill, 2004.

Murphy, Charles. *At Home on Earth: Foundations for a Catholic Ethic of the Environment*. New York: Crossroad, 1989.

Murphy, George L. *The Cosmos in the Light of the Cross*. New York: Trinity Press International, 2003.

Murray, Robert. *Cosmic Covenant: Biblical Themes of Justice, Peace, and the Integrity of Creation*. London: Sheed & Ward, 1992.

———. "The Ephremic Tradition and the Theology of the Environment." *Hugoye: Journal of Syriac Studies* 2, no. 1 (1999). Accessed online at: http://syrcom.cua.edu/Hugoye/Vol2No1/HV2N1Murray.html

Musschenga, Albert W. "Identity-Neutral and Identity-Constitutive Reasons for Preserving Nature." *Journal of Applied Philosophy* 21, no. 1 (2004): 77–88.

Naess, Arne. "Intuition, Intrinsic Value and Deep Ecology." *The Ecologist* 14, no. 5–6 (1984): 201–4.

———. "Self-Realization: An Ecological Approach to Being in the World." In Drengson and Inoue, *The Deep Ecology Movement: An Introductory Anthology*.

———. "The Shallow and the Deep, Long-Range Ecology Movements." *Inquiry* 16 (1973): 95–100.

Naess, Arne and David Rothenberg. *Ecology, Community, and Lifestyle: Outline of an Ecosophy*. Cambridge: Cambridge University Press, 1988.

Neass, Arne, and George Sessions. "Platform Principles of the Deep Ecology Movement." In Drengson and Inoue, *The Deep Ecology Movement: An Introductory Anthology*.

Nash, James. *Loving Nature: Ecological Integrity and Christian Responsibility*. Cleveland: Pilgrim Press, 1991.

———. "Seeking Moral Norms in Nature: Natural Law and Ecological Responsibility." In Hessel and Reuther, *Christianity and Ecology*.

Nash, Roderick. *The Rights of Nature: A History of Environmental Ethics, History of American Thought and Culture*. Madison: University of Wisconsin Press, 1989.

National Council of Churches. "God's Earth Is Sacred: An Open Letter to Church and Society in the United States." Washington, D.C.: National Council of Churches, 2004.

Nelson, Michael P. "An Amalgamation of Wilderness Preservation Arguments." In Callicott and Nelson, *The Great New Wilderness Debate*.

Nelson, Robert. "Environmental Religion: A Theological Critique." *Case Western Reserve Law Review* 55.1 (2004): 51–80.

Nesteruk, Alexei V. *Light from the East: Theology, Science, and the Eastern Orthodox Tradition*. Minneapolis: Fortress Press, 2003.

Newman, B. "Sergius Bulgakov and the Theology of Divine Wisdom." *St. Vladimir's Theological Quarterly* 22 (1978): 39–73.

Nicholls, Bruce J. "Responding Biblically to Creation: A Creator-Centered Response to the Earth." *Evangelical Review of Theology* 17, no. 2 (1993): 209–22.

Nichols, Aidan. "Bulgakov and Sophiology." *Sobornost* 13, no. 2 (1992): 17–31.

———. *Discovering Aquinas: An Introduction to His Life, Work, and Influence*. Grand Rapids, Mich.: Eerdmans, 2002.

———. "Wisdom from Above? The Sophiology of Father Sergius Bulgakov." *New Blackfriar's* 85, no. 1000 (2004): 598–613.

Nickel, James. "The Human Right to a Safe Environment: Philosophical Perspectives on Its Scope and Justification." *Yale Journal of International Law* 18, no. 1 (1993): 281–95.

Northcott, Michael. *The Environment and Christian Ethics*. Cambridge: Cambridge University Press, 1996.

———. "The Spirit of Environmentalism." In Berry, *The Care of Creation*.

Norton, Bryan G. "Applied Philosophy vs. Practical Philosophy: Toward Environmental Policy Integrated according to Scale." In *Environmental Philosophy and Environmental Activism*, ed. Don Marietta and Lester Embree. Lanham, Md.: Rowman & Littlefield, 1995.

———. "Environmental Ethics and Weak Anthropocentrism." *Environmental Ethics* 6 (1984): 131–48.

———. "Integration or Reduction: Two Approaches to Environmental Values." In Light and Katz, *Environmental Pragmatism*.

———. "The Re-Birth of Environmentalism as Pragmatic, Adaptive Management." Paper presented at the "Environmental Letters/Environmental Law" conference, University of Virginia, 2005.

———. *Searching for Sustainability: Interdisciplinary Essays in the Philosophy of Conservation Biology*. Cambridge: Cambridge University Press, 2003.

———. *Sustainability: A Philosophy of Adaptive Ecosystem Management*. Chicago: University of Chicago Press, 2005.

———. *Toward Unity among Environmentalists*. New York: Oxford University Press, 1991.

Nussbaum, Martha C. *The Fragility of Goodness: Luck and Ethics in Greek Tragedy and Philosophy*. Cambridge: Cambridge University Press, 1986.

———. *Love's Knowledge: Essays on Philosophy and Literature*. New York: Oxford University Press, 1990.

O'Donnell, John. "The Trinitarian Panentheism of Sergei Bulgakov." *Gregorianum* 76, no. 1 (1995): 31–45.

O'Donovan, Oliver. *Resurrection and Moral Order: An Outline for Evangelical Ethics.* Grand Rapids, Mich.: Eerdmans, 2001.

———. "Where Were You . . . ?" In Berry, *The Care of Creation.*

Oelschlaeger, Max. *Caring for Creation: An Ecumenical Approach to the Environmental Crisis.* New Haven: Yale University Press, 1994.

———. *The Idea of Wilderness.* New Haven: Yale University Press, 1991.

———. *Postmodern Environmental Ethics.* Albany: State University of New York Press, 1995.

Oleksa, Michael J. *Orthodox Alaska: A Theology of Mission.* Crestwood, N.Y.: St. Vladimir's Seminary Press, 1998.

Oliver, Simon. "The Eucharist before Nature and Culture." *Modern Theology* 15, no. 3 (1999).

Olson, Larry, and Carolyn Olson. "Showing Faith by Caring for the Land." In Slattery, *Caretakers of Creation: Farmers Reflect on Their Life and Work.*

O'Neill, John. *Ecology, Policy, and Politics: Human Well-Being and the Natural World.* London: Routledge, 1993.

———. "Meta-Ethics." In Jamieson, *A Companion to Environmental Philosophy.*

———. "Time, Narrative, and Environmental Politics." In Gottleib, *The Ecological Community.*

———. "Varieties of Intrinsic Value." *Monist* 75 (1992): 208–27.

Osborn, Lawrence. *Guardians of Creation.* London: Apollos, 1993.

Ovitt, George Jr. *The Restoration of Perfection: Labor and Technology in Medieval Culture.* New Brunswick, N.J.: Rutgers University Press, 1987.

Pain, James, and Nicolas Zernov, ed.s. *A Bulgakov Anthology.* London: SPCK, 1976.

Palmer, Clare. *Environmental Ethics and Process Thinking.* New York: Oxford University Press, 1998.

———. "Stewardship: A Case Study in Environmental Ethics." In Berry, *Environmental Stewardship: Critical Perspectives.*

Pannenberg, Wolfhart. "The Doctrine of the Spirit and the Task of a Theology of Nature." *Theology* 75 (1972): 8–21.

———. *Toward a Theology of Nature: Essays on Science and Faith.* Louisville, Ky.: Westminster John Knox Press, 1993.

Parker, Janet, and Roberta Richards. "Christian Ethics and the Environmental Challenge." In Hessel, *Theology for Earth Community: A Field Guide.*

Parker, Kelly. "Pragmatism and Environmental Thought." In Light and Katz, *Environmental Pragmatism.*

Passmore, John. *Man's Responsibility for Nature: Ecological Problems and Western Traditions.* New York: Charles Scribner's Sons, 1974.

Paterson, John L. "Conceptualizing Stewardship in Agriculture within the Christian Tradition." *Environmental Ethics* 25, no. 1 (2003): 43–58.

Peacocke, Arthur. "The Cost of New Life." In Polkinghorne, *The Act of Love: Creation as Kenosis.*

———. *Paths from Science toward God.* New York: One World Publications, 2001.

Pearce, David W. *Economic Values and the Natural World.* London: Earthscan, 1993.

Pearce, David W., Dominic Moran, and Biodiversity Conservation Strategy Programme. *The Economic Value of Biodiversity*. London: Earthscan, 1994.

Peterson, Anna. "In and of the World? Christian Theological Anthropology and Environmental Ethics." *Journal of Agricultural and Environmental Ethics* 12 (2000): 237–61.

Peterson, Anna Lisa. *Being Human: Ethics, Environment, and Our Place in the World*. Berkeley: University of California Press, 2001.

Pieper, Josef. *Guide to Thomas Aquinas*. Translated by Richard and Clara Winston. San Francisco: Ignatius, 1991.

Plumwood, Val. *Environmental Culture*. London: Routledge, 2002.

_____. "Nature, Self, and Gender: Feminism, Environmental Philosophy, and the Critique of Rationalism." In Warren, *Ecological Feminist Philosophies*.

Polkinghorne, John, ed. *The Act of Love: Creation as Kenosis*. Grand Rapids, Mich.: Eerdmans, 2001.

_____. "Kenotic Action and Divine Action." In Polkinghorne, *The Act of Love: Creation as Kenosis*.

Pope, Carl. *Sierra*, November/December 1998.

Pope, Stephen J. "Neither Enemy nor Friend: Nature as Creation in the Theology of Saint Thomas Aquinas." *Zygon* 32, no. 2 (1997): 219–31.

Porter, Jean. *Nature as Reason: A Thomistic Theory of the Natural Law*. Grand Rapids, Mich.: Eerdmans, 2005.

_____. *The Recovery of Virtue: The Relevance of Aquinas for Christian Ethics*. 1st ed. Louisville, Ky.: Westminster John Knox Press, 1990.

_____. "The Virtue of Justice." In *The Ethics of Aquinas*, ed. Stephen J. Pope. Washington, D.C.: Georgetown University Press, 2002.

Powell, Samuel M. *Participating in God: Creation and Trinity*. Minneapolis: Fortress Press, 2003.

Preller, Victor. *Divine Science and the Science of God: A Reformulation of Thomas Aquinas*. Princeton: Princeton University Press, 1967.

Preston, Christopher. "Conversing with Nature in a Postmodern Epistemological Framework." *Environmental Ethics* 22, no. 3 (2000): 227–40.

_____. *Grounding Knowledge*. Athens: University of Georgia Press, 2003.

Primavesi, Anne. "Ecology and Christian Hierarchy." In *Women as Sacred Custodians of the Earth? Women, Spirituality and the Environment*, ed. Alaine M. Low and Soraya Tremayne. New York: Bergahn Books, 2001.

_____. *Gaia's Gift*. London: Routledge, 2003.

_____. "The Recovery of Wisdom: Gaia Theory and Environmental Policy." In *Spirit of the Environment*, ed. David Edward Cooper and Joy A Palmer. London: Routledge, 1998.

_____. *Sacred Gaia*. London: Routledge, 2000.

Pugh, Jeffrey C. *Entertaining the Triune Mystery: God, Science, and the Space Between*. Harrisburg, Pa.: Trinity Press International, 2003.

Rae, Murray. "To Render Praise: Humanity in God's World." In Berry, *Environmental Stewardship: Critical Perspectives*.

Raglon, Rebecca, and Marian Scholtmeijer. "Shifting Ground: Metanarratives, Epistemology, and the Stories of Nature." *Environmental Ethics* 18, no. 1 (1996): 19–38.

Rasmussen, Larry L. "Cosmology and Ethics." In Tucker and Grim, *Worldviews and Ecology: Religion, Philosophy, and the Environment.*

———. *Earth Community, Earth Ethics.* Maryknoll, N.Y.: Orbis Books, 1996.

———. "Returning to Our Senses: The Theology of the Cross as a Theology for Eco-Justice." In Hessel, *After Nature's Revolt: Eco-Justice and Theology.*

Rawls, John. *Political Liberalism.* New York: Columbia University Press, 1993.

Redekop, Calvin, ed. *Creation and the Environment: An Anabaptist Perspective on a Sustainable World.* Baltimore: Johns Hopkins University Press, 2000.

———. "The Environmental Challenge before Us." In Redekop, *Creation and the Environment: An Anabaptist Perspective on a Sustainable World.*

———. "Mennonites, Creation, and Work." *Christian Scholar's Review* 22 (1993): 348–66.

———. "Toward a Mennonite Theology and Ethic of Creation." *Mennonite Quarterly Review* 60 (1986): 387–403.

Regan, Tom. *The Case for Animal Rights.* London: Routledge & Kegan Paul, 1983.

———. "The Nature and Possibility of an Environmental Ethic." *Environmental Ethics* 3, no. 1 (1983): 19–34.

Regenstein, Lewis G. *Replenish the Earth: A History of Organized Religion's Treatment of Animals and Nature—Including the Bible's Message of Conservation and Kindness toward Animals.* New York: Crossroad, 1991.

Reichel, Elizabeth. "Cosmology." In *The Encyclopedia of Religion and Nature*, ed. Bron Taylor. New York: Thoemmes Continuum, 2005.

Reichenbach, Bruce, and V. Elving Anderson. *On Behalf of God: A Christian Ethic for Biology.* Grand Rapids, Mich.: Eerdmans, 1995.

———. "Tension in the Stewardship Paradigm." In Berry, *Environmental Stewardship: Critical Perspectives.*

Reid, Duncan. "Enfleshing the Human: An Earth-Revealing, Earth-Healing Christology." In *Earth Revealing, Earth Healing: Ecology and Christian Theology*, ed. Denis Edwards. Collegeville, Minn.: The Liturgical Press, 2001.

Reumann, John Henry. *Stewardship and the Economy of God.* Grand Rapids, Mich.: Eerdmans, 1992.

Ruether, Rosemary Radford, ed. *Women Healing Earth: Third World Women on Ecology, Feminism, and Religion.* Maryknoll, N.Y.: Orbis Books, 1996.

Riley, Shamara Shantu. "Ecology Is a Sistah's Issue Too: The Politics of an Emergent Afrocentric Ecowomanism." In *Ecofeminism and the Sacred*, ed. Carol J. Adams, 191–203. New York: Continuum, 1992.

Rogers, Eugene F. *After the Spirit: A Constructive Pneumatology from Resources Outside the Modern West.* Grand Rapids, Mich.: Eerdmans, 2005.

———. "Eclipse of the Spirit in Karl Barth." In *Conversing with Barth*, ed. John C. McDowell and Mike Higton. Aldershot, Hampshire: Ashgate, 2004.

———. "Faith and Reason Follow Glory." In Van Nieuwenhove and Wawrykow, *The Theology of Thomas Aquinas.*

Rogers, Eugene F. "Nature with Water and the Spirit: a response to Rowan Williams." *Scottish Journal of Theology* 56, no.1 (2003): 89–100.

———. "The Mystery of the Spirit in Three Traditions: Calvin, Rahner, Florensky or, You Keep Wondering Where the Spirit Went," *Modern Theology* 19, no. 2 (2003): 243–60.

———. *Thomas Aquinas and Karl Barth: Sacred Doctrine and the Natural Knowledge of God.* South Bend, Ind.: University of Notre Dame Press, 1995.

Rohr, Richard. "Christianity and the Creation." In LaChance and Carrol, *Embracing Earth.*

Rolston III, Holmes. "Caring for Nature: From Fact to Value, from Respect to Reverence." *Zygon* 39, no. 2 (2004): 277–302.

———. *Conserving Natural Value.* New York: Columbia University Press, 1994.

———. "Environmental Ethics in Antarctica." *Environmental Ethics* 24, no. 2 (2002): 115–34.

———. "Does Nature Need to Be Redeemed?" *Zygon* 29, no. 2 (1994): 205–29.

———. *Environmental Ethics: Duties to and Values in the Natural World.* Ethics and Action. Philadelphia: Temple University Press, 1988.

———. "Environmental Ethics: Some Challenges for Christians." *The Annual of the Society of Christian Ethics* (1993): 163–68.

———. "Feeding People Versus Saving Nature?" In Gottlieb, *The Ecological Community.*

———. "Nature for Real: Is Nature a Social Construct?" In *The Philosophy of the Environment,* ed. T. D. J. Chappell. Edinburgh: University of Edinburgh Press, 1997.

———. "Value in Nature and the Nature of Value." In Attfield and Belsey, *Philosophy and the Natural Environment.*

Rosenthal, Bernice Glatzer. "The Nature and Function of Sophia in Sergei Bulgakov's Prerevolutionary Thought." In Kornblatt and Gustafson, *Russian Religious Thought.*

———. "The Search for a Russian Orthodox Work Ethic." In *Between Tsar and People: Educated Society and the Quest for Public Identity in Late Imperial Russia,* ed. E. W. Clowes, S. E. Kassow, and J. L. West. Princeton: Princeton University Press, 1991.

Rosenthal, Sandra B., and Rogene A. Buchholz. "How Pragmatism *Is* an Environmental Ethic." In Light and Katz, *Environmental Pragmatism.*

———. "Nature as Culture: John Dewey's Pragmatic Naturalism." In Light and Katz, *Environmental Pragmatism.*

Ross, Stephen David. *Plenishment in the Earth.* Albany: State University of New York Press, 1995.

Roszak, Theodore. *The Voice of the Earth: An Exploration of Ecopsychology.* New York: Simon & Schuster, 1992.

Routley, Richard. "Is There a Need for a New, an Environmental Ethic?" *Proceedings of the Fifteenth World Congress of Philosophy* 1 (1973): 205–10.

Rowlands, Mark. *The Environmental Crisis: Understanding the Value of Nature.* New York: St. Martin's Press, 2000.

Rozanov, Vasily Vasilyevich. "Sweet Jesus and the Sour Fruits of the World." In Schmemann, *Ultimate Questions*.

Ruether, Rosemary Radford. "Ecofeminism: The Challenge to Theology." In Hessel and Reuther, *Christianity and Ecology*.

———. *Gaia and God: An Ecofeminist Theology of Earth Healing*. New York: HarperCollins, 1992.

———. *Integrating Ecofeminism, Globalization, and World Religions: Nature's Meaning*. Lanham, Md.: Rowman & Littlefield, 2005.

———. *New Woman, New Earth*. Boston: Beacon Press, 1995.

———. *Sexism and God-talk: Toward a Feminist Theology*. London: SCM Press, 1983.

Rupp, George. "Religion, Modern Secular Culture, and Ecology." *Daedalus* 130, no. 4 (2001): 23–30.

Russell, Edmund. *War and Nature: Fighting Humans and Insects with Chemicals from World War I to Silent Spring*. Cambridge: Cambridge University Press, 2001.

Russell, Norman. *The Doctrine of Deification in the Greek Patristic Tradition*. Oxford: Oxford University Press, 2004.

Sagoff, Mark. *Price, Principle, and the Environment*. Cambridge: Cambridge University Press, 2004.

Salleh, Ariel. "Working with Nature: Reciprocity or Control?" In *Environmental Philosophy: From Animal Rights to Radical Ecology*, ed. Michael E. Zimmerman and J. Baird Callicott. Upper Saddle River, N.J.: Prentice-Hall, 1998.

Sanders, Scott Russell. *Hunting for Hope: A Father's Journeys*. Boston: Beacon Press, 1999.

Santmire, H. Paul. *Brother Earth: Nature, God, and Ecology in Time of Crisis*. New York: T. Nelson, 1970.

———. "Healing the Protestant Mind: Beyond the Theology of Human Dominion." In Hessel, *After Nature's Revolt: Eco-Justice and Theology*.

———. *Nature Reborn: The Ecological and Cosmic Promise of Christian Theology*, Theology and the Sciences. Minneapolis: Fortress Press, 2000.

———. "Toward a Christology of Nature: Claiming the Legacy of Joseph Sittler and Karl Barth." *Dialog* 34 (1995): 270–80.

———. *The Travail of Nature: The Ambiguous Ecological Promise of Christian Theology*. Philadelphia: Fortress Press, 1985.

Satterfield, Terre, and Scott Slovic, eds. *What's Nature Worth? Narrative Expressions of Environmental Values*. Salt Lake City: University of Utah Press, 2004.

Schaefer, Jame. "Ethical Implication of Applying Aquinas's Notion of the Unity and Diversity of Creation to Human Functioning in Ecosystems." Dissertation, Marquette University, 1994.

———. "Grateful Cooperation: Cistercian Inspiration for Ecological Ethics." *Cistercian Studies Quarterly* 37, no. 2 (2002): 187–203.

———. "The Virtuous Cooperator." *Worldviews: Environment, Culture, Religion* 7 (2003): 171–95.

———. "Thomas Aquinas." In *The Encyclopedia of Religion and Nature*, ed. Bron Taylor. New York: Thoemmes Continuum, 2005.

Schaeffer, Francis A. *Pollution and the Death of Man: The Christian View of Ecology*. Wheaton, Ill: Tyndale House Publishers, 1970.

Schama, Simon. *Landscape and Memory*. New York: Alfred A. Knopf, 1995.

Scharper, Stephen Bede. *Redeeming the Time*. New York: Continuum, 1997.

Schlosberg, David. "The Justice of Environmental Justice: Reconciling Equity, Recognition, and Participation in a Political Movement." In Light and de-Shalit, *Moral and Political Reasoning in Environmental Practice*.

Schmemann, Alexander. *For the Life of the World*. Crestwood, N.Y.: St. Vladimir's Seminary Press, 1998.

———, ed. *Ultimate Questions: An Anthology of Modern Russian Religious Thought*. New York: Holt, Rinehart and Winston, 1965.

Schreiner, Susan. *The Theater of God's Glory: Nature and the Natural Order in the Through of John Calvin*. Grand Rapids, Mich.: Baker Books, 1991.

Schweiker, William. *Theological Ethics and Global Dynamics: In the Time of Many Worlds*. Oxford: Blackwell, 2004.

Schwöbel, Christoph. "God, Creation and the Christian Community: The Dogmatic Basis of a Christian Ethic of Createdness." In Gunton, *The Doctrine of Creation*.

Scott, Peter. *A Political Theology of Nature*. Cambridge: Cambridge University Press, 2003.

———. "The Technological Factor: Redemption, Nature, and the Image of God." *Zygon* 35, no. 2 (2000): 371–84.

Seamon, David, ed. *Dwelling, Seeing, and Designing: Toward a Phenomenological Ecology*. Albany: State University of New York Press, 1993.

de-Shalit, Avner. *The Environment between Theory and Practice*. New York: Oxford University Press, 2000.

Schlosberg, David. *Environmental Justice and the New Pluralism: The Challenge of Difference for Environmentalism*. New York: Oxford University Press, 1999.

Sheldon, Joseph K. *Rediscovery of Creation: A Bibliographic Study of the Church's Relation to the Environmental Crisis*. American Theological Library Association Bibliography Series, no. 29. Meutchen, N.J.: Scarecrow Press, 1992.

Shellenberger, Michael, and Ted Nordhaus. "The Death of Environmentalism: Global Warming Politics in a Post-Environmental World." Paper presented at the Environmental Grantmakers Association meeting, Koloa, Hawaii, October, 2004.

Shepard, Paul. *Nature and Madness*. San Francisco: Sierra Club Books, 1982.

Sherrard, Philip. *Christianity: Lineaments of a Sacred Tradition*. Brookline, Mass.: Holy Cross Orthodox Press, 1998.

———. *Human Image, World Image: The Death and Resurrection of Sacred Cosmology*. Ipswich, Suffolk: Golgonooza Press, 1992.

———. *The Rape of Man and Nature*. Ipswich, Suffolk: Golgonooza Press, 1987.

Sherwood, Polycarp. *The Earlier Ambigua of Saint Maximus the Confessor and His Refutation of Origenism*. Rome: Orbis Catholicus, 1955.

Shibley, Mark A., and Jonathan L. Wiggins. "The Greening of Mainline American Religion: A Sociological Analysis of the Environmental Ethics of the National Religious Partnership for the Environment." *Social Compass* 44, no. 3 (1997): 333–48.

Shiva, Vandana. *Earth Democracy: Justice, Sustainability, and Peace*. Cambridge, M.A.: South End Press, 2005.

Shrader-Frechette, Kristin. "Environmental Ethics." In *The Oxford Handbook of Practical Ethics*, ed. Hugh LaFollette. New York: Oxford University Press, 2003.

————. "Practical Ecology and Foundations for Environmental Ethics." *The Journal of Philosophy* 92, no. 12 (1995): 621–35.

Sider, Ronald J. "Biblical Foundations for Creation Care." In Berry, *Care of Creation*.

————. "Biblical Sources of Stewardship." In Jegen and Manno, *The Earth Is the Lord's: Essays on Stewardship*.

————. *Rich Christians in an Age of Hunger: A Biblical Study*. Downers Grove, Ill.: InterVarsity Press, 1977.

Sideris, Lisa. *Environmental Ethics, Ecological Theology, and Natural Selection*. New York: Columbia University Press, 2003.

Singer, Peter. *Animal Liberation*. New York: Ecco, 2002.

————. "Not For Humans Only: The Place of Nonhumans in Environmental Issues." In *Ethics and Problems of the 21st Century*, ed. K. E. Goodpaster and K. M. Sayre. Notre Dame: Notre Dame University Press, 1979.

————. *Practical Ethics*. 2nd ed. Cambridge: Cambridge University Press, 1993.

Sittler, Joseph. "Ecological Commitment as Theological Responsibility." *Zygon* 5 (1970): 172–81.

————. *Essays on Nature and Grace*: Fortress Press, 1972.

Slattery, Patrick, ed. *Caretakers of Creation: Farmers Reflect on Their Life and Work*. Minneapolis: Augsburg Press, 1991.

Smith, Mick. "Cheney and the Myth of Postmodernism." *Environmental Ethics* 15, no. 3 (1993): 3–18.

————. *An Ethics of Place*. Albany: State University of New York Press, 2001.

Smith, Neil. "Nature at the Millenium: Production and Re-Enchantment." In Braun and Castree, *Remaking Reality: Nature at the Millenium*.

Smyth, Geraldine. *A Way of Transformation: A Theological Evaluation of the Conciliar Process of Mutual Commitment to Justice, Peace, and the Integrity of Creation, World Council of Churches, 1983–1991*. Berne: Peter Lang AG/European Academic Publishers, 1995.

Solovyov, Vladimir. *Lectures on Divine Humanity*. Translated by Peter Zouboff. Hudson, N.Y.: Lindisfarne, 1995.

Somplatsky-Jarman, William, E. Walter Grazer, and Stan L. LeQuire. "Partnership for the Environment among U.S. Christians: Report from the National Partnership for the Environment." In Hessel and Reuther, *Christianity and Ecology*.

Soulé, Michael E., and Gary Lease. *Reinventing Nature? Responses to Postmodern Deconstruction*. Washington, D.C.: Island Press, 1995.

Spencer, Daniel T. *Gay and Gaia: Ethics, Ecology, and the Erotic*. Cleveland: Pilgrim Press, 1996.

Staniloae, Dumitru. "Commentaires." In *Ambigua*, ed. Emmanuel Ponsoye, 375–540. Paris: Les Editions de l'Ancre, 1994.

Staniloae, Dumitru. *The Experience of God*. Translated by Ioan Ionita and Robert
    Barringer. 2 vols. Brookline, Mass.: Holy Cross Orthodox Press, 1994–2000.
_____. *Orthodoxe Dogmatik*. Translated by Hermann Pitters. Vol. 3 (Parts 5 and 6).
    Dusseldorf: Benziger Verlag, 1995.
_____. *Theology and the Church*. Translated by Robert Barringer. Crestwood, N.Y.: St.
    Vladimir's Seminary Press, 1980.
_____. "The World as Gift and Sacrament of God's Love." *Sobornost* 5, no. 9 (1969):
    662–73.
Stenmark, Mikael. "The Relevance of Environmental Ethical Theories for Policy
    Making." *Environmental Ethics* 24, no. 2 (2002): 135–48.
Sterba, James. "Reconciling Anthropocentric and Nonanthropocentric Ethics."
    Environmental Values 3 (1994): 229–44.
Stout, Jeffrey, and Robert MacSwain, eds. *Grammar and Grace: Reformulations of
    Aquinas and Wittgenstein*. London: SCM Press, 2004.
Streiffert, Kristin. "The Earth Groans and Christians Are Listening." *Christianity Today*
    33, no. 13 (1989): 38–40.
Stoevesandt, Hinrich, ed. *A Late Friendship: The Letters of Karl Barth and Carl
    Zuckmayer*. Grand Rapids, Mich.: Eerdmans, 1982.
Stone, Christopher. "Moral Pluralism and the Course of Environmental Ethics."
    Environmental Ethics 10, no. 2 (1988): 139–54.
_____. *Should Trees Have Standing? Toward Legal Rights for Natural Objects*. Los Altos,
    Calf.: William Kaufmann, 1974.
Sun Ai-Lee Park. "The Forbidden Tree and the Year of the Lord." In Ruether, *Women
    Healing Earth: Third World Women on Ecology, Feminism, and Religion*.
Swartley, William. "Biblical Sources of Stewardship." In Jegen and Manno, *The Earth
    Is the Lord's: Essays on Stewardship*.
Sylvan, Richard, and David Bennet. *The Greening of Ethics: From Anthropocentrism to
    Deep Green Theory*. Tucson: University of Arizona Press, 1994.
Szerszynski, Bronislaw. *Nature, Technology, and the Sacred*. Oxford: Blackwell
    Publishing, 2005.
Szerszynski, Bronislaw, Wallace Heim, and Claire Waterton. *Nature Performed:
    Environment, Culture and Performance*. Oxford: Blackwell, 2003.
Talbot, Carl. "The Wilderness Narrative and the Cultural Logic of Capitalism." In
    Callicott and Nelson, *The Great New Wilderness Debate*.
Tanner, Kathryn. "Creation and Providence." In *The Cambridge Companion to Karl
    Barth*, ed. John Webster. Cambridge: Cambridge University Press, 2000.
_____. *God and Creation in Christian Theology: Tyranny or Empowerment?* New York:
    Blackwell, 1988.
Tataryn, Myroslaw. "The Eastern Tradition and the Cosmos." *Sobornost* 11, no. 1–2
    (1989): 41–52.
_____. "History Matters: Bulgakov's Sophianic Key." *St. Vladimir's Theological
    Quarterly* 49, no. 1–2 (2005): 203–18.
_____. "Sergius Bulgakov (1871–1944): Time for a New Look." *St. Vladimir's
    Theological Quarterly* 42, no. 3–4 (1998): 315–38.

Taylor, Bron. "Introduction." In *The Encyclopedia of Religion and Nature*. Bron Taylor, ed. New York: Thoemmes Continuum, 2005.

_____. "Nature Religion." In *The Encyclopedia of Religion*, ed. Lindsay Jones. New York: Macmillan, 2005.

Taylor, Paul W. *Respect for Nature: A Theory of Environmental Ethics*. Princeton: Princeton University Press, 1986.

Taylor, Sarah McFarland. *Green Sisters: A Spiritual Ecology*. Cambridge, Mass.: Harvard University Press, 2007.

Teilhard de Chardin, Pierre. *Christianity and Evolution*. Translated by Rene Hague. New York: Harcourt Brace & Co, 1969.

_____. *Le phénomène humain*. Paris: Editions de Seuil, 1955.

_____. *The Phenomenon of Man*. Translated by Bernard Wall. New York: Harper & Row, 1959.

Testerman, Dennis E. "Missionary Earthkeeping: Glimpses of the Past, Visions of the Future." In *Missionary Earthkeeping*, ed. Calvin B. DeWitt and Gillean Phrance. Macon, Ga.: Mercer University Press, 1992.

Theokritoff, Elizabeth. "Embodied Word and New Creation: Some Modern Orthodox Insights Concerning the Material World." In Behr, Louth, and Conomos, *Abba: The Tradition of Orthodoxy in the West*.

_____. "Orthodoxy and the Environment." *Sourozh* 58 (1994): 13-.

Thomas Aquinas. *Sancti Thomae de Aquino Opera Omnia*, Leonine Edition. Vols. 4–12, 13–15, 22, 42. Rome, 1882.

_____. *In Librum B. Dionysii De Divinis Nominibus Expositio*. Parma Edition. Taurini Text, 1950.

_____. *In Psalmos Davidis Expositio*. Parma Edition, 1863.

_____. *Scriptum Super Sententiis*. Parma Edition, 1856.

_____. *Super Evangelium S. Ioannis Lectura*. Parma Edition, Taurini Text, 1952.

_____. *Commentary on the Gospel of St. John*. Translated by James Weisheipl and Fabian Larcher. Albany, N.Y.: Magi Books, 1980.

_____. *Compendium of Theology*. Translated by Cyril Vollert. St. Louis: B. Herder, 1952.

_____. *Disputed Questions on Truth*. Translated by Robert Mulligan. Chicago: Henry Regnery Co., 1952.

_____. *On Charity*. Translated by Lottie H. Kendzierski. Milwaukee: Marquette University Press, 1960.

_____. *Summa Contra Gentiles*. Translated by English Dominican Fathers. New York: Benziger Brothers, 1924.

_____. *Summa Theologica*. Translated by English Dominican Fathers. New York: Benziger Brothers, 1948.

Thompson, Paul B. "Pragmatism and Policy: The Case of Water." In Light and Katz, *Environmental Pragmatism*.

_____. *The Spirit of the Soil: Agriculture and Environmental Ethics*. Environmental Philosophies Series. New York: Routledge, 1995.

Thompson, Richard, and Sharon Thompson. "Get Along but Don't Go Along." In Slattery, *Caretakers of Creation: Farmers Reflect on Their Life and Work*.

Thoreau, Henry David. *Henry David Thoreau: Collected Essays and Poems*. New York: Library of America, 2001.

Thorme, M. "Establishing Environment as a Human Right." *Denver Journal of International Law and Policy* 19, no. 2 (1991): 301–42.

Thunberg, Lars. *Man and the Cosmos: The Vision of St. Maximus the Confessor*. Crestwood, N.Y.: St. Vladimir's Seminary Press, 1985.

_____. *Microcosm and Mediator: The Theological Anthropology of Maximus the Confessor*. Chicago: Open Court Publishing, 1995.

Tinker, George. "Ecojustice and Justice: An American Indian Perspective." In Hessel, *Theology for Earth Community: A Field Guide*.

Toadvine, Ted. "Naturalizing Phenomenology." *Philosophy Today* 43, SPEP Supplement (1999): 124–33.

Toolan, David. *At Home in the Cosmos*. Maryknoll, N.Y.: Orbis Books, 2001.

Torrance, Thomas Forsyth. *Divine and Contingent Order: Nihil Constat De Contingentia Nisi Ex Revelatione*. New York: Oxford University Press, 1981.

Townes, Emilie, ed. *Embracing the Spirit: Womanist Perspectives on Hope, Salvation, and Transformation*. Maryknoll, N.Y.: Orbis, 1997.

Townes, Emilie. *In a Blaze of Glory: Womanist Spirituality as Social Witness*. Nashville: Abingdon, 1995.

Traina, Cristina L. H. "Creating a Global Discourse in a Pluralist World: Strategies from Environmental Ethics." In *Christian Ethics: Problems and Perspectives*, ed. Lisa Sowle Cahill and James Childress. Cleveland: Pilgrim Press, 1996.

Trotsky, Leon. *Their Morals and Ours*. New York: Pathfinder Press, 1969.

Tucker, Mary Evelyn. "Religion and Ecology: The Interaction of Cosmology and Cultivation." In Kellert and Farnham, *The Good in Nature and Humanity*.

_____. "The Role of Religions in Forming an Environmental Ethics." In Hessel, *Theology for Earth Community: A Field Guide*.

_____. *Worldly Wonder: Religions Enter Their Ecological Phase*. Chicago: Open Court Publishing, 2003.

Tucker, Mary Evelyn, and John Grim. "Introduction: The Emerging Alliance of World Religions and Ecology." *Daedalus* 130, no. 4 (2001): 1–22.

_____. "Series foreword." In Hessel and Reuther, *Christianity and Ecology*.

_____, eds. *Worldviews and Ecology: Religion, Philosophy, and the Environment*. Maryknoll, N.Y.: Orbis Books, 1994.

United Church of Christ Commission for Racial Justice. *Toxic Wastes and Race in the United States: A National Report on the Racial and Socioeconomic Characteristics of Communities with Hazardous Waste Sites*. New York: United Church of Christ, 1987.

Vaillancourt, Jean-Guy, and Madeleine Cousineau. "Introduction." *Social Compass* 44, no. 3 (1997): 315–20.

Valliere, Paul. *Modern Russian Theology: Bukharev, Soloviev, Bulgakov*. Grand Rapids, Mich.: Eerdmans, 2000.

_____. "Sophiology as the Dialogue of Orthodoxy with Modern Civilization." In Kornblatt and Gustafson, *Russian Religious Thought*.

Van Dyke, Fred, David C. Mahan, Joseph K. Sheldon, and Raymond H. Brand. *Redeeming Creation: The Biblical Basis for Environmental Stewardship*. Downers Grove, Ill.: InterVarsity Press, 1996.

Van Leeuwen, Raymond C. "Christ's Resurrection and the Creation's Vindication." In DeWitt, *The Environment and the Christian*.

Van Nieuwehnhove, Rik. "'Bearing the Marks of Christ's Passion': Aquinas' Soteriology." In Van Nieuwehnhove and Wawrykow, *The Theology of Thomas Aquinas*.

Van Nieuwehnhove, Rik, and Joseph Wawrykow, eds. *The Theology of Thomas Aquinas*. South Bend, Ind.: University of Notre Dame Press, 2005.

Van Wensveen, Louke. *Dirty Virtues*. Atlantic Highlands, N.J.: Humanities Press, 1998.

Varner, Gary E. *In Nature's Interests? Interests, Animal Rights, and Environmental Ethics*. New York: Oxford University Press, 1998.

Vogel, Steven. *Against Nature: The Concept of Nature in Critical Theory*. Albany: State University of New York Press, 1996.

——. "Environmental Philosophy after the End of Nature." *Environmental Ethics* 24, no. 1 (2002): 23–39.

——. "Nature as Origin and Difference." *Philosophy Today* 42 (1998): 169–81.

——. "The Nature of Artifacts." *Environmental Ethics* 25, no. 3 (2003): 149–68.

Wadell, Paul. *Friends of God: Virtues and Gifts in Aquinas*. New York: Peter Lang, 1991.

Wallace, Mark I. "Environmental Justice, Neopreservationism, and Sustainable Spirituality." In Gottlieb, *The Ecological Community*.

——. *Finding God in the Singing River*. Minneapolis: Augsburg Fortress Press, 2005.

——. *Fragments of the Spirit: Nature, Violence, and the Renewal of Creation*. New York: Continuum, 1997.

Ware, Kallistos. "Who Is Man?" *Again Magazine* 20, no. 4 (1997/8): 27–31.

Warren, Karen J., ed. *Ecological Feminist Philosophies*. Indianapolis: Indiana University Press, 1996.

——. "The Power and Promise of Ecological Feminism." In Warren, *Ecological Feminist Philosophies*.

Waterton, Claire. "Performing the Classification of Nature." In Szerszynski, Heim, and Waterton, *Nature Performed: Environment, Culture and Performance*.

Weaver, Dorothy Joan. "The New Testament and the Environment: Toward a Christology for the Cosmos." In Redekop, *Creation and the Environment: An Anabaptist Perspective on a Sustainable World*.

Webb, Stephen H. "Ecology vs. the Peaceable Kingdom: Toward a Better Theology of Nature." *Soundings* 79 (1996): 239–52.

——. *On God and Dogs: A Christian Theology of Compassion for Animals*. New York: Oxford University Press, 1998.

Webster, John B. *Barth's Moral Theology: Human Action in Barth's Thought*. Edinburgh: T. & T. Clark, 1998.

——. *Barth's Ethics of Reconciliation*. New York: Cambridge University Press, 1995.

Welchman, Jennifer. "The Virtues of Stewardship." *Environmental Ethics* 19, no. 4 (1999): 411–23.

Welker, Michael. *Creation and Reality.* Minneapolis: Fortress, 1999.

Wennberg, Robert. *God, Humans, and Animals: An Invitation to Enlarge our Moral Universe.* Grand Rapids, Mich.: Eerdmans, 2003.

Wenz, Peter. "Minimal, Moderate, and Extreme Moral Pluralism." *Environmental Ethics* 15, no. 1 (1993): 61–74.

Weston, Anthony. "Before Environmental Ethics." *Environmental Ethics* 14, no. 4 (1992): 321–28.

———. "Beyond Intrinsic Value: Pragmatism in Environmental Ethics." *Environmental Ethics* 7, no. 1 (1985): 321–29.

———. "Multicentrism: A Manifesto." *Environmental Ethics* 26, no. 1 (2004): 25–40.

White, Lynn. "The Historical Roots of Our Ecologic Crisis." *Science* 155 (1967): 1203–7.

Whitehouse, W. A. "Karl Barth on the 'Work of Creation': A Reading of Church Dogmatics, III/1." In *Reckoning with Karl Barth,* ed. Nigel Biggar. Oxford: Mowbray and Co., 1988.

Whiteside, Kerry. *Divided Natures: French Contributions to Political Ecology.* Cambridge, Mass.: MIT Press, 2002.

Whitney, Elspeth. "Lynn White, Ecotheology, and History." *Environmental Ethics* 15, no. 2 (1993): 151–69.

Wilkinson, Loren, ed. *Earthkeeping in the Nineties: Stewardship of Creation.* Eugene, Ore.: Wipf and Stock, 2003.

Williams, A. N. "Argument to Bliss: The Epistemology of the *Summa Theologiae.*" *Modern Theology* 20, no. 4 (2004): 505–26.

———. *The Ground of Union: Deification in Aquinas and Palamas.* New York: Oxford University Press, 1999.

Williams, Dolores. "Straight Talk, Plain Talk: Womanist Words about Salvation in a Social Context." In Townes, *Embracing the Spirit: Womanist Perspectives on Hope, Salvation, and Transformation.*

Williams, Rowan. "Creation, Creativity and Creatureliness: The Wisdom of Finite Existence." Lecture at St. Theosevia Centre for Christian Spirituality, Oxford, April 2005.

———. "The Myths We Live By." Lecture at Lambeth Palace, July 2004.

———. *On Christian Theology.* Oxford: Blackwell, 2000.

———, ed. *Sergii Bulgakov: Towards a Russian Political Theology.* Edinburgh: T. & T. Clark, 1999.

———. "The Theology of Vladimir Nikolaievich Lossky: An Exposition and Critique." Ph.D. diss., Oxford University, 1975.

Williams, Terry Tempest. *Refuge: An Unnatural History of Family and Place.* New York: Random House, 1991.

Wilson, E. O. *The Creation: An Appeal to Save Life on Earth.* New York: W. W. Norton, 2006.

Wilson, E. O., and Stephen R. Kellert, eds. *The Biophilia Hypothesis.* Washington, D.C.: Island Press, 1993.

Wilson, Jonathan R. "Evangelicals and the Environment: A Theological Concern." *Christian Scholar's Review* 28, no. 2 (1998): 298–307.

Winner, Langdon. *The Whale and the Reactor: A Search for Limits in an Age of High Technology*. Chicago: University of Chicago Press, 1986.

Wippell, John F. *The Metaphysical Thought of Thomas Aquinas: From Finite Being to Uncreated Being*. Washington, D.C.: Catholic University of America Press, 2000.

Wirzba, Norman. *The Paradise of God: Renewing Religion in an Ecological Age*. New York: Oxford University Press, 2003.

Wise, David. "A Review of Environmental Stewardship Literature and the New Testament." In DeWitt, *The Environment and the Christian*.

Wiseman, Wendy. "The Sophian Element in the Novels of Fyodor Dostoevsky." *St. Vladimir's Theological Quarterly* 49, no. 1–2 (2005): 165–82.

Wittgenstein, Ludwig. *Philosophical Investigations*. Translated by William Brenner. Albany: State University of New York Press, 1999.

Worster, Donald. *Nature's Economy: A History of Ecological Ideas*. New York: Cambridge University Press, 1985.

_____. *Nature's Economy: A History of Ecological Ideas*. Cambridge: Cambridge University Press, 1994.

Wright, Richard T. *Biology through the Eyes of Faith*. San Francisco: Harper & Row, 1989.

Yeago, David. "Jesus of Nazareth and Cosmic Redemption: The Relevance of St. Maximus the Confessor." *Modern Theology* 12, no. 2 (1996): 163–93.

Yoder, Michael L. "Mennonites, Economics, and the Care of Creation." In Redekop, *Creation and the Environment: An Anabaptist Perspective on a Sustainable World*.

Young, Richard. *Healing the Earth: A Theocentric Perspective on Environmental Problems and Their Solutions*. Nashville: Broadman and Holman, 1994.

Zarsky, Lyuba, ed. *Human Rights and the Environment: Conflicts and Norms in a Globalizing World*. London: The Nautilus Institute, 2002.

Zerbe, Gordon. "The Kingdom of God and the Stewardship of Creation." In DeWitt, *The Environment and the Christian*.

Zernov, Nicolas. *The Russian Religious Renaissance of the Twentieth Century*. New York: Harper & Row, 1963.

Zimmerman, Michael E. *Contesting Earth's Future: Radical Ecology and Postmodernity*. Sacramento: University of California Press, 1997.

_____. "Rethinking the Heidegger–Deep Ecology Relationship." *Environmental Ethics* 15, no. 3 (1993): 195–224.

_____. "What Can Continental Philosophy Contribute to Environmentalism?" In *Rethinking Nature: Essays in Environmental Philosophy*, ed. Bruce V, Foltz and Robert Frodeman. Bloomington: Indiana University Press, 2004.

Zizioulas, Metropolitan John. *Being as Communion*. Crestwood, N.Y.: St. Vladimir's Seminary Press, 1985.

_____. "Ecological Asceticism: A Cultural Revolution." *Sourozh* 67 (1997): 22–25.

_____. "Man the Priest of Creation: A Response to the Ecological Problem." In *Living Orthodoxy in the Modern World*, ed. Andrew Walker and Costa Carras. Crestwood, N.Y.: St. Vladimir's Seminary Press, 2000.

_____. "Preserving God's Creation: Three Lectures on Theology and Ecology." *King's Theological Review* 12 (1989): 1–5.

Index